338

This book to be retur

CW00969087

3

The GI War against Japan

Also by Peter Schrijvers:
THE CRASH OF RUIN: American Combat Soldiers in Europe during World War II

The GI War against Japan

American Soldiers in Asia and the Pacific during World War II

Peter Schrijvers

palgrave
macmillan

First published 2002 by
PALGRAVE MACMILLAN
Houndmills, Basingstoke, Hampshire RG21 6XS and
175 Fifth Avenue, New York, N.Y. 10010
Companies and representatives throughout the world

PALGRAVE MACMILLAN is the global academic imprint of the Palgrave Macmillan division of St. Martin's Press, LLC and of Palgrave Macmillan Ltd. Macmillan® is a registered trademark in the United States, United Kingdom and other countries. Palgrave is a registered trademark in the European Union and other countries.

ISBN 0–333–771338

This book is printed on paper suitable for recycling and made from fully managed and sustained forest sources.

A catalogue record for this book is available from the British Library

A catalog record for this book is available from the Library of Congress

10   9   8   7   6   5   4   3   2   1
11   10   09   08   07   06   05   04   03   02

Printed and bound in Great Britain by
Antony Rowe Ltd, Chippenham and Eastbourne

To
Urbain Schrijvers
my father
and
Marie-Louise Dejardin
my mother

Contents

Preface

Many intense and fascinating years of research and writing it took me to get intimately acquainted with the American soldiers who fought in Europe during World War II and to bring to life their experiences in *The Crash of Ruin*. Meanwhile, curiosity had told me long before I finished my book on war in the Old World that my next project would be devoted to the other half of the intriguing story: the GI experience in Asia and the Pacific.

The very moment I started my mental trip to the other side of the world, however, I could not help being reminded of Ernie Pyle. Famous correspondent who made his name as the chronicler of the common American soldier in Europe, Pyle moved on to the Pacific at the end of the war. When in February 1945 he stopped in Hawaii on his way to the unfamiliar front, he felt somewhat insecure and out of place. "Covering this Pacific war was, for me, like learning to live in a new city," he wrote. "The methods of war, the attitude toward it, the homesickness, the distances, the climate – everything was different from what we had known in the European war. At first, I couldn't seem to get my mind around it, or my fingers on it. I suspected it would take months to get adjusted."[1]

The war refused to give Ernie Pyle more than weeks: a Japanese bullet on Ie Shima killed him on 18 April 1945. I, on the other hand, was fortunate enough to be granted several years to try and understand this horrific war. And I was doubly fortunate to be allowed to do so in the perfect peace and tranquility that reign on the shores of Lake Geneva, not far from where Mary Wollstonecraft Shelley once thought long and hard about *Frankenstein*, that other monster of human making.

Whereas *The Crash of Ruin* focuses on frontline ground troops for a number of reasons, this book takes a close look at all branches of the American military, including rear area troops. Infantry units played their most important role in the Southwest Pacific. Elsewhere in the Pacific, combat was mainly the business of naval, amphibious, and air forces. In sharp contrast with the Pacific, however, large numbers of GIs in the China–Burma–India theater belonged to supply and service troops. Moreover, the distinction between front and rear, so striking in the European war, makes less sense in Asia and the Pacific, where isolation and boredom haunted soldiers without exception, and rear bases were often as primitive and unhealthy as the battlefields themselves.[2]

African-American soldiers played vital roles in Asia and the Pacific, especially in the much-needed service and labor units. But in a war that was to a large extent racial in nature, the African–American experience, from Tonga to China, was inevitably quite distinct from that of white Americans. If in this book I have left out the story of African-American troops, it is only because I deemed it too different and important not to deserve special treatment in a separate study. It should, therefore, be understood that when in this book I talk of 'GIs' or 'American soldiers,' I am referring to white Americans, unless stated otherwise.

To be able to write this book, I immersed myself in thousands of pages of diaries, letters, and memoirs, many of them unpublished. They are the personal testimonies of servicemen and -women as diverse as Americans can be. From the Indiana poultry farmer to the Louisiana engineer. From the New York teacher to the Wyoming high-school kid. From the Texan airplane mechanic to the marine from Pennsylvania's steel-mill town. Each soldier fought his own private war with the opponent, the environment, and himself. A book like this cannot hope to capture the uniqueness of an individual experience and does not pretend to offer a reading of the war in which each single soldier might recognize himself fully. What this book does, instead, is point to patterns of perception, experience, and behavior – that is, thoughts and acts shared by enough American soldiers, no matter how diverse in personal background, to make them remarkable and significant.

The patterns that have thus emerged from a careful reading of the personal documents of countless GIs are organized in three large parts. The first part shows that, even in the midst of war, Americans could not help thinking of the lands across the Pacific as a continuation of their own continental Far West. This is the story of the war theater as frontier, triggering in GIs the reflexes of pioneers, romantics, missionaries, and imperialists. The second part details the frontier's tenacious resistance to control. It offers an account of the manifold American frustrations flowing from the region's oppressive wilderness, threatening demographics, and impenetrable mentality. The final part charts the ever-escalating fury to which American troops abandoned themselves in response to the region's stubborn refusal to submit. It is the part that evokes not only the murderous violence emanating from flesh and blood, but also the massive destruction wreaked by impersonal military-industrial tools when unleashed by infuriated humans.

This book is the account of more than one war. The GIs' story first and foremost is, of course, the story of America's resounding victory over Japan. A victory against a spectral enemy who ruled the night and sank beneath the surface by day. The defeat of a foe who appeared to defy hunger, time, and logic. The conquest of an earth so otherworldly it did not seem ready to accept people.

However, the GIs' tale at the same time is also the tale of the West's defeat in Asia. American soldiers were well aware that the price for victory in this region was extraordinarily high, whether in the form of casualties per acre or, ultimately, in the form of atomic power unleashed. Yet, while they were pushing back the enemy, they could see that they were also laying bare hotbed after hotbed of discontent with foreign involvement, whether

Japanese or Western. GIs were disquieted both by the unfathomable nature of the peoples in the region and by their resilience to the Western message. They were increasingly shocked by their pride, arrogance, and rebelliousness. To say, in the words of Christopher Thorne, that the "European powers were now essentially finished there, although there were a few death-throes to come," is hindsight. But GIs realized better than any other contemporaries that the revolutionary nationalist, democratic, and communist forces which they witnessed from up close, from John Frum in the New Hebrides to the Hukbalahaps in the Philippines, did not bode well for continued control of these coveted frontiers. To have opened Pandora's atomic box amidst these very forces made the future all the more uncertain.[3]

The vacuums left by the weakening of Europe's colonial overlords and the defeat of Japan allowed the US a great increase of power in the region. To say that its attempts to enforce its will on the far side of the Pacific in the wake of World War II represented, still in the words of Thorne, "no more than a coda" to an era of Western dominance that had stretched from the late Middle Ages to the middle of the twentieth century, is hindsight, too. But no Americans could have better understood the depths of frustration and despair experienced by their countrymen and -women in Korea and Vietnam than the veterans who had suffered in the war against Japan. As such, this book is also the story of disembodied victory in Asia. Of victory as specter. One of the many haunting the region.[4]

Acknowledgments

Books like *The Crash of Ruin* and this one owe everything to the magnificent repositories devoted to collecting and safeguarding the personal documents of US soldiers. Such repositories are tributes to America's war veterans more fitting perhaps than even the most impressive monuments. I returned with pleasure to the incredibly rich World War II collections of the US Army Military History Institute at Carlisle, Pennsylvania. I renewed with even more pleasure my acquaintance with Dr. Richard Sommers, Mr. David Keough, and Mrs. Pamela Cheney of the archives section and with Mr. John Slonaker of the library. My thanks go also to the many other people at the Institute who, as always, were helpful with anything from finding the right source to locating the best steak house. My first visit to the University of Tennessee at Knoxville was equally pleasant. Mr. William B. Eigelsbach and his staff were most forthcoming in retrieving documents from the World War II Collection, part of the James D. Hoskins Library's Special Collections. Meanwhile, Professor G. Kurt Piehler and Mr. Johnny Goins of the University of Tennessee's Center for the Study of War and Society provided intellectual stimulation, excellent dinners, and spacious quarters with a stunning view of a Blue Mountain straight from the novel.

Over the years my research has been much facilitated also by consultation of various materials at the Center for the study of War and Society and the Royal Library's Center for American Studies in Brussels and the Imperial War Museum in London. I also greatly benefited from a visit to the university libraries of the San Diego area in California.

I would not have been able to write this book without the intellectual and logistical support of the Institut Universitaire de Hautes Études Internationales in Geneva, Switzerland, where I lectured in US Foreign Relations History for four years. Thanks go to all my colleagues at the history section; the section's secretary, Mrs. Jeannine Charron; and the Institute's library staff, in particular Mrs. Martine Basset. I am also grateful in acknowledging substantial financial support for this research project from the Swiss National Science Foundation.

For their caring professionalism and good sense of humor, I would like to thank my editors: Mr. Cameron Laux and Mrs. Luciana O'Flaherty at Palgrave and Mrs. Jennifer Hammer at New York University Press. A word of thanks also to Palgrave's Mrs. Kate Schofield and Mrs. Patricia Wiltshire.

Special thanks go to Professor Allan R. Millett, whose interest in my career and whose encouragement have remained unflagging. It is good to know that a giant in the field is prepared to give one an occasional nudge.

Among the many graduate students who have taught me in Geneva, I would like to single out Xavier Guillaume, who was so kind to read the manuscript in his customary critical way, and Jérôme Élie. I am much indebted also to two guardians of the English language: Greg Resar, American friend, original mind, and Oslo's budding novelist, and Kathy Monnier-Wynne Willson, British friend, Geneva's mother of expatriates, and social lifeline. A separate word of thanks goes to Dominique Bouts, MD, for practicing medicine with a heart and without frontiers.

I would like to pay special tribute to my family. My father and mother for making their children believe from the very beginning that they could be whatever they wanted, without promising that it would come easy. My sisters Christel and Karin and brother Jan for proving my parents right when on occasion I doubted them. All of them for loving me for who I am.

Even in the midst of her own trek across America, my sister Karin has managed to have me benefit not only from her linguistic training and experience whenever I pleased, but also from her organizational knack, ranging from the selection of the right laptop to the choice of appropriate yoga techniques.

Hours spent outside the realm of history have been made most agreeable by a family-in-law as rich in variety as in kindness: Martin, Theo, Jan, Lillian, Willy, Christel, Jordy, and Roel.

Finally, my wife Elle has been indispensable as research assistant, bibliographer, and general manager of monkish patience. She has been irreplaceable as weatherer of storms, doldrums, and tantrums with sphinxlike demeanor. She has been admirable simply for wanting to put up with it all. Without her this book would not have come to life.

List of Abbreviations

ANGAU	Australian New Guinea Administrative Unit
AWOL	Absent without leave
CBI	China–Burma–India Theater
CIC	Counterintelligence Corps
DUKW	Amphibious truck
LST	Landing ship, tank
LVT	Landing vehicle, tracked
MP	Military policeman
NCO	Noncommissioned officer
NICA	Netherlands Indies Civil Administration
OSS	Office of Strategic Services
POW	Prisoner of war
SWPA	Southwest Pacific area
USNR	United States Naval Reserve
USS	United States Ship
VD	Venereal Disease
VE	Victory in Europe
WAC	Women's Auxiliary Corps

een stille kracht, een stille macht,
vijandig aan ons temperament, aan ons bloed, aan ons lichaam, aan onze ziel,
  aan onze beschaving,
aan al wat óns goeddunkt te doen en te zijn en te denken.

a hidden force, a hidden power,
hostile to our temperament, our blood, our bodies, our souls, our civilization,
to all that seems to us the right thing to do and be and think.

On the *fin-de-siècle* atmosphere in the
Dutch colony of Java.
Louis Couperus, *De Stille Kracht*, 1900.
Translation by Alexander Teixeira de Mattos

Part I
Frontier

1
Pioneers

Frontiersmen and immigrants: nearly every white GI boarding a ship bound for the Pacific could trace his origins as an American to such ancestors. It was, therefore, almost inevitable that the experience of strange vessels, endless seas, and daunting destinations should trigger flashbacks of both groups of predecessors among American soldiers.[1]

Most GIs were reluctant soldiers, thrust into a volatile odyssey by forces beyond their control. Their uprooted forefathers would have recognized this feeling with a pang. That is perhaps why in spirit they sailed with the GIs all the way to the distant war. "The rails were lined with we involuntary temporary immigrants," a GI noted when approaching Calcutta, India, on the Hooghly River in the spring of 1944, "eager for a first look at the unknown world we were entering." The immigrants of the past refused to let go of their soldier offspring even as the GIs descended the gangplanks. "We climbed out into the white sunlight," said a dive-bomber pilot who stepped onto Ulithi, one of the Caroline atolls, "and stood gawking and uncertain, like immigrants in a strange country."[2]

Yet the flashback of immigration was the weaker and less common one. It was America's frontier past that pervaded the memories of GIs as they sailed westward for war. The frontier was, after all, one of the oldest American myths, with roots going back to the colonial era. Moreover, the media of modern mass culture had made the frontier myth one of the most enduring ones. Dime novels and serials in cheap newspapers, for example, had kept the frontier alive long after it had been declared closed in 1890. When the US embarked on its overseas imperialist adventure in 1898, its soldiers spontaneously took the frontier legacy with them into the Pacific. Those in the military who now controlled Hawaii and the Philippines rather than the continental West, proudly identified themselves as 'homesteaders,' convinced as they were of their superiority to the American soldiers on the 'mainland.'[3]

After World War I, movies in particular ensured that the legacy of the frontier lived on in powerful images. In the three years immediately preceding the Japanese attack on Pearl Harbor in 1941, the Western movie genre suddenly underwent a remarkable revival as it became part of a larger effort to renew the patriotic optimism of Americans that had been dealt hard blows by the Great Depression. Its percentage of Hollywood's total movie production tripled in this short period, and most new Westerns were ambitious productions, many of them in vivid color.[4]

The American people had been bred on frontier heroes for centuries. It was no wonder then that, during World War II, the US military, too, harked back to that mythical past when communicating with its soldiers in the Pacific. In its series of popularized soldier guides to foreign countries, for example, the booklet on Australia built its attempt to generate goodwill towards the inhabitants Down Under almost entirely on the premise that Australians, like Americans, were first and foremost "a pioneer people." The guide's second chapter was completely devoted to Australia as "A Pioneer Land." It conceded, almost with a sense of envy, that the Aussies were "a generation closer to their pioneer ancestors than we are to ours." But the parallels it was able to draw between both countries nevertheless remained abundant and clear. Australia's vast continent, for instance, had gradually been explored by "a small group of inquisitive courageous men." "Men," the guide trumpeted with pride, "like our own Lewis and Clark who helped open the West." The booklet went on to say, in words reminiscent of the famous American frontier historian Frederick Jackson Turner, that as a result of this shared pioneer experience, both peoples had come to treasure similar values. Like Americans, the Australians had developed "a lively sense of independence and 'rugged individualism.'" They, too, believed "in personal freedom" and had created "one of the world's greatest democracies." And, of course, they loved sports.[5]

The war in the Pacific allowed GIs to relive the American pioneer experience in more ways than one. The Wild West might have been announced tamed around 1890, but to many GIs, America's continental West had retained the unmistakable air of frontier. Although some American soldiers left for the war in Asia from the east coast, traveling eastward over the Atlantic and Indian Oceans or westward via the Panama Canal, most soldiers sailed directly into the Pacific from ports on the west coast. To GIs native to the eastern parts of the US, this gradual trek to the American West, in a succession of training camps, was in itself quite an adventure. For a soldier from Rhode Island who had never been further west than Washington, DC, even the train ride to a military camp in Indiana could be the experience of a lifetime.

Soldiers from the Midwest in turn were easily awed by the arduous trip to the Far West. After he had arrived at Camp Stoneman, California, early in 1943, an officer and poultry farmer from Indiana wrote to his parents: "You never realize what a big country we have until you make a trip like this. The mountains, rocks and rivers are something to look at." And, as if to make sure that his family back east would fully grasp the spatial dimensions he was trying to convey, he sent them a haphazard litany of the territories he had covered: "The various states that we have passed through are as follows: Mississippi, Tennessee, Kansas, Colorado, Utah, Kentucky, Indiana, Illinois, Missouri, Nevada and California."[6]

Yet the real West was always like quicksilver: just when you thought you could touch it, it suddenly receded again. Thus, to a rancher from as far west as Wyoming, on his way to the Naval Training Station at San Diego, it was California that truly exuded a frontier spirit, with its "sweet almost primitive quality."[7]

In many a letter and diary entry, excited soldiers talked about America's mountains, rocks and rivers, but also of its swamps, salt flats and deserts. A pioneer reflex revealed itself almost as soon as the Mississippi was crossed, if not before. "The highlight of my trip west," admitted a WAC from Rochester, New York, in 1943, "was my first glimpse of the prairie in Nebraska, with scattered windmills and grazing white-faced cattle." The Western movie had clearly instructed novices in what to look for. A year later, when the Rochester cryptanalyst entered Nevada on her way to a camp in California, the final pieces of her own private Western fell into place upon detecting "the plaintive howl of a coyote somewhere in the distance." It gave her a thrill and goose bumps.[8]

If the American West appeared wild and California sweetly primitive to some GIs, the Pacific Ocean beyond presented itself as a frontier of unfathomable proportions to most American soldiers. "Great joy in camp we are in *view* of the *Ocian* . . . this great Pacific Octean which we been so long anxious to See." Those were the words George Rogers Clark scribbled in his journal in the early morning of 7 November 1805 – words that generations of overland explorers had hoped to be able to pen down. Faced by the same watery prairies almost a century and a half later, the GIs' pioneering nerve twitched even more than it had in view of the Great Plains and Rocky Mountains. This, a soldier blurted out when his train went around a bend in California and revealed the mighty ocean, was "the place of adventure and excitement, stretching out to the horizon and beyond, Hawaii, the Philippines, Indonesia, China, and Japan."[9]

Carried by the massive swells of the Pacific, the Far West would recede ever further, eventually melting into the Far East. But it was the ocean frontier rather than Asia that initially absorbed all of the American soldiers' attention. Many a GI from the numerous landlocked states had never laid eyes on any of the seas bordering the US. Their surprise at seeing the Pacific Ocean was, therefore, often no less than that expressed by explorers Lewis and Clark early in the nineteenth century. When two soldiers of the 37th 'Buckeye' Division arrived at Fort Ord, California, in the summer of 1944, the men from Ohio and Kentucky were instantly taken aback by the ocean. "Suddenly," one wrote, "both of us just sucked in our breath, staring in silent amazement. The bus had just topped a hill, and spread before us, stretching a straight blue line from northern to southern horizon, lay the Pacific Ocean. We had never seen anything larger than the Ohio River."[10]

Some GIs had never before so much as seen a sizeable boat, let alone an ocean. A female soldier from New York state, about to sail all the way across the Pacific from California to New Guinea, stared in disbelief at a prewar luxury ship of the Matson Line. "Our ship, the *Lurline*, loomed huge before us. I had never seen such a gigantic one." "In fact," she confessed, "the only boat I'd ever encountered was the ferry boat I once took across Lake Ontario." As the war dragged on, even the US Navy saw itself forced to accept ever more landlubbers. When the Fifth Fleet assembled in the Pacific in the summer of 1943 for the offensive against the Gilberts and Marshalls, for example, half its ships were brand-new. But even its veteran ships by that time were run over 75 percent by reserve officers, and manned almost 50 percent by bluejackets who had never been to sea.[11]

American popular culture had kept alive not only the memory of the pioneers of the land. After all, Americans had made the leap from the continental frontier to that of the Pacific Ocean as soon as they had established an independent republic. The *Empress of China*, the first American ship to trade with Asia, had arrived in Canton in 1784, barely a year after the end of the Revolutionary War. The US Navy had become active in the Pacific as early as 1813. By the late 1830s, it was diligently mapping the South Pacific; by the mid-1850s, it was charting the ocean's northern reaches.

Never, however, were American sailors more numerous in all of the Pacific than during the era of whaling. American whalers first poured into the Pacific in the 1790s. By the late 1830s, sailors from Nantucket and New Bedford dominated the trade, and they continued to do so until the end of the golden era of whaling in the late 1850s. American culture had begun to celebrate these manifold pioneers of the sea at least as early as Herman Melville's *Moby Dick*. The ranks of the Daniel Boones and Buffalo Bills had gradually been swelled by the Ahabs and Queequegs, stubborn seamen battling the seas and winds to earn a meager but honest living. Even a century later, some of the tiny Pacific islands the GIs passed were still carrying the names of a Starbuck, a Johnston, a Baker, and a Howland – all American whaling captains.[12]

Perhaps it was out of respect and awe for the courage and suffering of men like these, that American soldiers, almost without exception, joined in the ancient rituals of the deep-sea sailors, as they themselves now ventured far into the solitary Pacific. Traditionally, a man had become a seaman not only by learning the work and language of the waves, but by means of a ritual initiation or sailor's baptism. This initiation had first appeared among

English seamen in the late seventeenth century and had gradually spread to all seafaring nationalities. It was a classical rite of passage, practiced when newcomers – sailors, later also passengers – first crossed the equator, or what old salts called 'the line.' In the original initiation, the newcomer had a choice between paying a fine in the form of brandy and sugar or being plunged deep into the ocean from the main yard arm while attached to a rope. In the early eighteenth century, Neptune, the pagan god of the sea, was added to the ritual as a symbolic figure overseeing the ceremony.[13]

In the mid-twentieth century, American sailors and soldiers alike religiously adhered to this age-old maritime tradition while en route to the war in Asia. For them, too, sailing across the equator into that unknown southern part of the world and its mysterious ocean remained an important rite of passage, a test of stamina made worse by the prospect of battle. Rare, therefore, was the ship aboard which this event, this 'crossing of the line' as it was known among GIs, was not celebrated with a ceremony during World War II. On occasion, entire convoys took part in this custom. Early in October 1944, for example, the fleet carrying the assault troops of the XXIV Corps for the invasion of Leyte sailed from Eniwetok, atoll in the northwest Marshalls, to Manus, island of the Admiralties. In doing so, it crossed the equator, and since many of the men aboard had freshly arrived from Hawaii, they still had to be initiated. For that purpose, even in this battle-geared convoy, most captains allowed time to be taken out for the ancient ritual.[14]

The ritual differed only slightly from ship to ship during the war in the Pacific. It retained the essence of the original initiation, even though it did not escape certain changes. "Yes, we had a shellback party on the way over," a soldier comforted his nervous mother after having arrived in the Pacific from California in 1944, "but we never got thrown in the ocean." Indeed, plunging novices into the deep from the main yard arm had been abandoned. Less dangerous and cumbersome rituals had come to replace it. In order for the green soldiers – or 'polliwogs' – to become veterans of the sea – or 'shellbacks' – they had to climb onto platforms from which they were then pushed into large tanks filled with salt water. Sometimes they were simply drenched with seawater by means of fire hoses. Nurses, WACs, and other servicewomen underwent similar fates with few exceptions.[15]

King Neptune also remained an integral part of the ceremony, which on some ships could last up to four days. The polliwogs had disturbed the king's aquatic realm. They were therefore charged with trespassing and judged in a court overseen by Neptune himself. To this Royal Court, a variety of other characters were added in what often took on the appearance of an outrageous play. The leading roles were played by those who had crossed the equator before. Davy Jones, the personification of the bottom of the sea, served as ceremony master, and it was to him that the captain symbolically relinquished control of his ship for the time being. It could happen that

Davy Jones was respectfully moved about the ship seated on a make-shift throne, sometimes carried by African–American servicemen. Other servicemen dressed up as judges, bailiffs, and members of the jury. There was, of course, nearly always a Queen of the Realm, played by a soldier pretending to possess voluptuous breasts. Finally, there was a Royal Baby as well, often impersonated by the fattest seaman aboard. To this ragtag bunch, crews routinely added a riotous music band – playing anything from clarinets to pots and pans – as well as a mixture of pirates, peg legs, and devils. The latter more or less symbolically terrorized the polliwogs with swab handles, shillelaghs, and pitchforks – some of them electrically charged.

Most often, the proceedings were rather good-natured, amounting to nothing more than what one soldier described as "some strenuous naval horseplay." Polliwogs had to appear in court. There they were made to kneel, sing, swallow vile substances, and perform a host of other ludicrous tasks, the most common of which were drinking from the Royal Baby's milk bottle and kissing his grease-smeared belly.

From time to time, however, the ceremony, like other rites of passage, turned nasty, even violent. In November 1944, an enlisted sailor from Oklahoma described the just completed ritual aboard the destroyer USS *Howorth* in painstaking detail to his wife. It had been quite an ordeal for the polliwogs as things had apparently gotten somewhat out of hand. Men had been beaten until backs, buttocks, and legs turned black and blue. Others had been blasted from up close with high-pressure hoses until they were crying with pain. Insult had been added to injury by forcing the polliwogs to crawl through a huge upturned canvas that contained water mixed with all kinds of filth, including excreta. "I didn't mind the initiation. I enjoyed it throughout," the bruised yeoman complained, "except when they got cruel." At least one victim took revenge by roughing up his tormenter a few days later.[16]

Women were not spared from Neptune's wrath. But it seems the king was more lenient towards the other sex in mixed ceremonies. When the hospital ship USS *Refuge* crossed the equator on its long journey from Virginia to the Philippines in 1944, the shellbacks treated the nurses to a mock haircut; they shaved the heads of the male polliwogs to the scalp.[17]

There was a war on, of course, and in danger zones sea captains had no time for the frivolities of a Royal Court. Yet, even then, an effort could be made to provide American troops with a memento upon crossing 'the line' that for a long time would separate them from home and peace. Those aboard the USS *Sea Scamp*, for example, were given a small card fitting a billfold. It contained the name of the ship and passenger, as well as the date of the crossing. The card certified that its bearer had been "duly initiated as a trusted shellback." It went on to say that "the customary initiatory practices were dispensed with as this area was a war zone in which an attack at any time might occur."[18]

Although most Americans had already assumed a radically new identity by donning a uniform, it was Neptune's ritual on the open seas which seemed to make them shed their past entirely. By the time they 'crossed the line,' GIs had penetrated so far into the blue void that there remained nothing for them to do other than to look ahead. The transformation into shell-backs further sharpened the Americans' pioneer reflex. Once initiated, soldiers began to gaze in search of fresh lands with increased anticipation, their eyes straining to be among the first to sight new frontiers. "We are just like explorers," rejoiced a seaman from Massachusetts as his ship was navigating between the Philippine Islands on its way to Mindoro in December 1944, "we do not want to miss a thing."[19]

The craving for new frontiers had already gnawed at some while under-going training at home. A marine pilot, stationed at Miramar, Florida, had felt the itch each time he heard old hands talk about the faraway islands they had seen. "The tellers were like old explorers," he explained, "or like the sailor in that painting of the boyhood of Sir Walter Raleigh, and we were the listening boys." But now, freshly baptized into the Ancient Order of the Deep, GIs were no longer mere listeners. Some even began comparing themselves with the historic heroes of the sea. "One month ago we set sail, the same day of the month that Columbus discovered land," a soldier wrote to his wife on 12 June 1943. "I don't suppose there is any connection between the two." Still, the thought had crossed his mind. To American soldiers, Columbus was, of course, a favorite. Those sailing from the east coast in particular could not but be reminded of him when they made their way through the Caribbean. Yet Columbus was soon joined by equally illustrious heroes who had made their mark in the Pacific. "We were now in the south seas," exclaimed one proud new shellback, "explored by Cook, Tasman and Bligh."[20]

Like the eyes of Cook, Tasman, and Bligh, those of the GIs could strain for weeks without spotting as much as a speck of land. And as time passed, nervous anticipation continued to build. False sightings increased. When a ship, carrying troops to India via the Pacific in 1944, did at last pass Australia very early in the morning of the seventeenth day after it had left California, the GIs aboard had already heard so many rumors of land that many of them disregarded what this time was the real announcement and slept through the grand occasion.[21]

Those with sea legs, however, knew that birds were the most reliable messengers of land. Moreover, on some vessels the sighting of land was announced in true fashion. One sailor remembered that when the crew of his destroyer detected one of the Philippine Islands in the distance in early 1945, they actually sounded "the medieval 'Land Ho.'" In most cases that sufficed to turn decks into beehives. Soldiers would crazily run up and down the stairways, yelling and gesturing, and in no time everyone not absolutely needed below deck would be topside, anxiously scanning the horizon. "I was profoundly affected," a soldier wrote to his wife after his ship had at last dropped anchor at Eniwetok Island. "The crew was excited as birds, and lined the rail like crows to look at the scene."[22]

The actual sight of Pacific islands and Asian coasts brought back many more ancient memories of exploration. "It was on the morning of the 6th of April that we sighted Australia." The sentence is as solemn as if it was penned down by James Cook himself. But it was written in 1942 by an American Army engineer who had been underway from the east coast for six weeks. The GIs were made to feel solemn by many a scene that appeared to have jumped right out of their high-school history books. On approaching the coastline, local inhabitants received the Americans in ways reminiscent of centuries past. Steel war vessels were often greeted by inquisitive locals in small wooden craft. In some places they had never before seen Americans. In others they were irresistibly drawn to them because of their abundant supplies. When the USS *Montpelier* pulled into Leyte in the morning of 3 January 1945, a sailor described the Filipino reception in his diary as follows: "A lot of natives in boats pulled close to the ship. There were men, women and children in them. Guess they had the whole family. We threw cigarettes, food, and clothing to them. Their boats held about 4 people. It had a big piece of bamboo on each side so it would not tip over." It might as well have been a scene from the journal of Ferdinand Magellan.[23]

There were also grim reminders of the dangers that explorers of all times shared. A marine aboard a ship skirting Australia's Great Barrier Reef, on its way to New Caledonia, observed "several hulks of wooden ships stranded high and dry, apparently blown there years ago by some storm." They made him sink into quiet reflection. The trials and tribulations of exploration in the Pacific could make one almost forget that there was a war on.[24]

Much of Asia and the Pacific presented itself to the GIs as a virtually unexplored frontier simply because they themselves had never been there. In reality, of course, the greater part of the region had been subjected and mapped by an array of European nations in the centuries that had passed since the arrival of the first Portuguese and Spanish navigators. In fact, the US itself had become an important participant in these efforts in the course of the nineteenth century, as its flag was carried from Hawaii all the way to territories in sight of the Chinese coast. If it was the Portuguese navigator Magellan who had died exploring the Philippines for Spain, for example, it was the Stars and Stripes that had been flying over these islands for several decades when the Japanese took over in 1942. Yet, despite almost half a millennium of systematic exploration by Westerners, parts of the vast ocean and the lands beyond remained in effect untouched by and unknown to them. In those territories, more than anywhere else in Asia and the Pacific, the pioneer imagination of the GIs was allowed to run wild.

The US military itself did much to center attention on these gray areas in its GI guides to Asia and the Pacific, as if attempting to heighten the soldiers' interest in the war once again by playing on America's frontier memory. Distance was, thus, hammered into a badge of honor. "[I]t probably never occurred to you that you might some day soldier in Asia," the *Guide to Burma* surmised – quite correctly – then continued: "Burma is half way around the world from the United States. You are probably going farther from your own home and your family for the sake of your country than you have ever gone before." The American penetration of 'virgin' frontiers was also written up in adventurous words and tones exalting the imagination. A sample from the *Guide to India* illustrates this: "Some of the wildest and least explored country on the globe is to be found in the north. There are the blazing deserts of Sind and Baluchistan, the flat moist tracks of Bengal, and the wheat fields of the Punjab and the United Provinces. . . . In the hill districts of Assam, for instance, some tribes are almost untouched by modern civilization." The *Guide to New Guinea* conceded that hardy government officers and mineral prospectors from other Western countries had already covered "an amazing amount" of the inhospitable region. But it added that the large island, nevertheless, remained "one of the great empty frontiers of the earth," as if to point towards its vast potential for enterprising Americans.[25]

The soldiers gradually found out themselves that there remained much to be explored in Asia and the Pacific. Even in the Philippines, which had been under American rule for over 40 years, GIs had to fight their way across territory that the colonials before them had never clearly put on a map. The rugged Sierra Madre in mountainous northern Luzon turned out to be only partially explored. The trails the GIs did find appeared to have been made by wild pigs, not human beings. Sections of the Cordillera Central were trackless and unknown, too. During the conquest of eastern Mindanao as well, American soldiers ran into mountains and rivers that the maps said did not exist.[26]

Such pristine conditions triggered scientific curiosity in some soldiers. When John Gaitha Browning arrived in New Guinea with the 592nd Engineer Amphibian Regiment in October 1943, he responded as if President Thomas Jefferson had personally made him part of a brand-new Lewis and Clark expedition. "Every bug, bird, butterfly, tree, and weed is strange here, and will – no doubt – continue to be so," he wrote in his diary, "for there have been few, if any, books published on the wild things of this country where few white men came before the war."[27]

Browning, of course, was a painter who for years had observed the fauna and flora of Arizona and New Mexico, and now stubbornly continued to pursue his interests, ornithological guides in hand, while hacking his way through steamy jungles. But many more soldiers responded to their belated metamorphosis into pioneers with a measure of excitement and much disbelief. A stunned officer with the 43rd Division in Aitape, New Guinea, wrote to his fiancée: "Mountains to 16,000 feet and in the interior glaciers as yet unexplored by white men. In the mountains also, native tribes who have never seen white men, the last remnants of the stone age period using stone hatchets, knives and implements."[28]

To have this experience in New Guinea was one thing, to encounter people in China who appeared never to have seen "white men" was more incredible still. Yet in several of the Middle Kingdom's isolated rural areas that is exactly what happened to the Americans. GI pamphlets tried to prepare the soldiers for this massive culture shock. They warned that in some areas the Chinese could be afraid of Westerners, who appeared "queer" to them, among other things because they were "hairier," a physical peculiarity that was thought to reflect a lack of civilization. Some mothers might actually try to shield their children from GIs for fear that the foreigners might cast "an evil shadow."[29]

Conversely, GIs were told to expect being gazed at long and hard. One of the phrases in the Chinese section of their Asian language booklet implored: "Please ask these people staring at me to go away; I want privacy." The phrase proved futile. When a downed American airman, given shelter by the Chinese for several days, was asked to make an appearance in a nearby park to say goodbye to the locals before returning to his base, he was met by the mayor and what he claimed were no less than 15,000 curious peasants.[30]

The fascination of these people for the outlandish Americans knew no bounds. There were peasants who had not the least idea of where the US was situated. Some did not know there was an ocean between them; others thought America was just another remote part of China. A surgeon stationed in Kweilin in 1944 lamented: "They consider it no breach of etiquette whatever to crowd into your quarters and watch you complete your toilet, set up your cot, and make your bed, and within five minutes they probably know as much about the contents of your baggage as you do. Men, women, and children stand in open-mouthed, wide-eyed amazement at the many curious gadgets and strange customs exhibited by these fabulous [Americans]."[31]

GIs risked losing their bearings by being dropped in the middle of nowhere. They perused the simplified maps of their pocket guides to no avail, then begged family and friends at home to help track their travels and send them more detailed information. Orders in the US for National Geographic maps shot up 600 percent during the war.[32]

The military, too, became involved in a mad scramble for maps. But it soon realized that frontiers refuse to be charted easily. The American counteroffensive that was launched in the islands north and northeast of Australia catapulted troops into some of the least explored areas of the

world. The sophisticated maps on which modern militaries had come to
rely simply did not exist for the Solomon Islands and New Guinea. Good
maps were lacking throughout the campaign in Guadalcanal. Some of the
planning of the 1st Marine Division had to be based on a crude prewar
sketch put together by colonial officials. It aided in locating some trails and
buildings, but showed neither contour lines nor elevations. US commanders
learned that on Bougainville Island European colonials were still relying on
eighteenth-century surveys drawn up by the French explorer Louis-Antoine
de Bougainville himself.[33]
  Similar problems occurred throughout the Pacific. Americans preparing
the offensive against the British Gilbert Islands, for instance, found the
charts and tide tables recently provided by the US Navy Hydrographic
Office not much more accurate than the maps from the Wilkes expedition
of 1841.[34]
  Amazingly, the geographical knowledge of what had been American
possessions for almost half a century was sometimes not much better
either. On Guam, for example, unit commanders rarely knew exactly where
they were because of inadequate maps. The Philippine colony had been
America's jewel in the crown. But when US troops penetrated Leyte's central mountain range, they were seriously handicapped because the area had
not been properly charted. When the Corps of Engineers began to plan the
invasion of Luzon, they found much of it to be "unknown country," too,
because most of the American engineers with firsthand knowledge of its
terrain had been killed or made prisoners by the Japanese.[35]
  The Americans often fared no better on the Asian mainland. For the
campaign in Burma and the work on the Ledo Road, they had to make do
with maps of British and Chinese origin, many of which, they discovered,
were out of date and inaccurate. The language booklet for airmen downed
over the vast interior of China made sure to teach them how to ask, "Please
show me on any map you may have where I am." But it hastened to add:
"Unless there is a school around it is very difficult to find a map among the
Chinese."[36]
  Circumstances thus forced Americans to gain knowledge of the elusive
frontiers by a variety of means other than maps. In certain regions of
China, for example, American engineer units surveyed the terrain themselves. That procedure was, of course, impossible in the many areas already
occupied by the enemy, although submarines did conduct reconnaissance
of enemy beaches and coasts, and at times even landed patrols. The military also increasingly relied on aerial photography. Yet, despite rapid
progress, many technical limitations remained. Moreover, steamy Pacific
islands went through long periods of heavy fog, and dense jungle canopies
kept many terrain features hidden.[37]
  At wit's end, the military more than once turned to anyone who might
possess even minimal knowledge of the terrain in which they were about

to risk troops: colonial officials, naval officers, missionaries, travelers, traders – even schooner skippers. In 1942, for instance, scores of former Solomon residents were interviewed in New Zealand and Australia in preparation for the invasion of Guadalcanal. Some of them were actually offered commissions by the Australian military and attached to America's 1st Marine Division as guides, advisers, and pilots.[38]

These makeshift efforts did not, however, suffice to unlock the frontiers. Over and over again, the terrain confronted GIs with unexpected difficulties due to faulty mapping and a smarting lack of information. Inaccurate charts bungled the landings in the mangrove swamps of Biak Island off Dutch New Guinea. Faulty tidal information grounded assault boats on the jagged coral of Tarawa's lagoon reef. In New Georgia, hills were found where they should not have been. When US troops near Dutch New Guinea's Maffin Bay stormed Lone Tree Hill, named after the single tree depicted on their map, they were gobbled up by dense rain forest. Even for the Philippine island of Leyte, distance inaccuracies on maps could be as high as 50 percent. During the battle for Buna, Papua New Guinea, the only maps available were Australian sketches so rudimentary that they showed some rivers flowing up over mountains. Lewis and Clark would have felt at home. The Americans had become frontiersmen all over again.[39]

If GIs lacked physical maps in this utterly strange geographical environment, then they somewhat compensated for it by almost instinctive reference to an invaluable mental map, that of their own American West. That the GIs did so should not be surprising, as that frontier had been for so long what historian Richard Slotkin has called "one of the primary organizing principles" of American historical memory.[40]

It could happen that among the veterans of the prewar expeditions in Central America and the Caribbean one came across an occasional reference to the more recent Latin American 'frontier.' The 5th Marines, for instance, entered the Pacific War with a regimental flag that had attached to its top battle streamers dating back to both the Great War and what the men called 'the Banana Wars.' For expert appraisals of the war during the early Solomons campaign in 1942, war correspondents turned to these veterans of what Ira Wolfert described as "Central America bushfighting." "Looks like the Japs'll take to the hills," Richard Tregaskis quoted a marine on Guadalcanal. "Another Nicaragua. They'll be in here alive next month, fighting in the jungles."[41]

Still, the overwhelming majority of GIs would refer, time and again, not to Central America as a mental map of frontier, but to the much older American 'Wild West.' An awe-struck soldier of the 495th Port Battalion in New Guinea wrote home early in 1944 that he had just laid eyes on the – now motorized – 7th Cavalry Regiment. "This is the same organization," he wrote rapturously, "that went into the Little Big Horn under General Custer and came out without a man!" One might have thought he had just seen the regiment on horseback with his own eyes.[42]

The US military consciously cultivated the memory of this frontier. American ships went to war with the names of the *Chickasaw, Arapaho, Potawatomi, Molala, Tawasa,* and *Sioux*. Volunteer pilots en route to China in October 1941 fashioned themselves crew cuts and called each other Algonquin Indians. Soldiers in the Pacific front lines gave each other the hairdo of Mohawks.

After no more than a few days on Guadalcanal, war correspondent Ira Wolfert concluded for himself that the Pacific War was not a Banana War, but "a ruthless, tracking, potshotting, Indian kind of war." The soldiers agreed. A medic of the Americal Division on Guadalcanal told his diary that jungle warfare was "nothing more than Indian fighting using more powerful weapons."[43]

Servicemen scarcely went through a motion without triggering similar frontier recollections. When ships slid out of Leyte Gulf and into the Surigao Strait, they moved "Indian file, silent as Indians on the warpath." When a truck convoy entered the Philippine town of Cebu and formed a circle for a bivouac, they did so "like the old wagon trains did against the Indians." When marines on Okinawa sat together and broke out K rations, they "squatted Indian-fashion."[44]

What the Europeans had identified as the Far East, from an American point of view had always more logically appeared to be a 'Far West.' As early as the 1850s, for instance, this was exactly how popular American magazines were referring to the newly opened Chinese and Japanese empires across the Pacific. The American designation did more, however, than ensure geographical rectification. It also hinted at a potential process of continuity in US history. The Pacific and Asian 'far west' was at the same time a 'new west.' It contained, in other words, the promise of yet another boundless frontier. That became most obvious after the Spanish-American War of 1898, when the US molded the Pacific island groups of Hawaii, Samoa, and the Philippines into formal colonies. Touring the Philippines in 1902, Lieutenant General Nelson A. Miles made a point of visiting the 5th Infantry, the unit he had joined as commanding officer in 1869. There he nostalgically allowed himself to reminisce with his old comrades. "At that time the regiment was on the frontier," he fondly recalled, "has been on the frontier ever since, and I now find it . . . still on the frontier; on the frontier of our island possessions."[45]

To the American soldiers of the 1940s, the immense region of Asia and the Pacific often presented itself as a veritable physical continuation of their country's old continental frontier. Indeed, many were the circumstances in which GIs saw the Far East, as if in a kaleidoscope, change into their own Far West. The British settlement colonies of the South Pacific most easily invited comparisons with the American West. New Zealand's shores, for instance, reminded GIs of California's coastline, and its towns of Texan settlements. "The whole continent of Australia," the Chief of Staff of the United States Forces in Australia wrote in February 1942, "is as undeveloped as the central United States was before the Civil War, or even more so." Though this officer somewhat exaggerated the situation, many a GI reported that Australia bore an uncanny resemblance to the Old West. Hunting kangaroos from jeeps and playing poker into the night, a submarine crew on leave in western Australia claimed that both Perth and the much smaller town of Fremantle breathed "a certain frontier town atmosphere," which by that time had become "unfamiliar and strange to us Americans."[46]

Such frontier comparisons also extended across the Pacific and onto the Asian mainland. Few GIs could have expected the Hawaiian Islands to exude anything like an American frontier atmosphere. But in some regards they did just that. Besides the more obvious cultivation of sugar and pineapple, cattle-raising had become an important industry in Hawaii, and with its Parker Ranch the island group boasted one of the largest cattle ranches in the world. Flabbergasted GIs on Maui talked of cowboys riding along dusty roads and through towns with wooden sidewalks. It gave some of the settlements on this island, acknowledged a marine replacement who had just arrived from San Diego, California, "a touch of the Old West."[47]

A similar touch could occasionally be noted in the Philippines. In February 1945, MPs on the island of Luzon found the bullet-riddled body of a soldier of the 244th Port Company. He had allegedly been killed by an African-American soldier close to a house of prostitution somewhere in the swamps near Dagupan. His fellow soldiers were aggrieved, but not surprised. "That combination of gun, liquor and women has already made for several deaths," one comrade noted in his diary. "Here frontier conditions exist; it is a place for a man to stay sober."[48]

Nowhere, however, did American soldiers find conditions more reminiscent of those of the American frontier than in the mountain ranges and rolling plains of mainland Asia. The Flying Tigers' *Guide to Shangai* contrasted the cosmopolitan city with the vast interior, which it readily dubbed "the 'Wild West' of China." Another booklet for troops stationed in the Chinese theater expressed fear that some GIs might be tempted to compare Kunming, one of the great American hubs of activity near the Burmese border, unfavorably with, say, Brooklyn. It therefore urged them to keep in mind that "when Kunming was laid out originally it was pretty good for its purpose – a great frontier garrison post."[49]

Americans stationed in the China–Burma–India theater did not think such analogies far-fetched. A Flying Tiger, slowly making his way from Burma into China in the days following the Japanese attack on Pearl Harbor, could not but admit that this region reminded him "somewhat of the American West." At Maymyo, a hill-resort for English colonials, the hustle and bustle, the horses and oxcarts, and the main street dominated by the Foster Hotel, swiftly transported the airman back to his own country's past. Even the ancient Burmese city of Lashio was steeped in the activity and atmosphere that could easily have belonged to what he called "an early Western American boom town."[50]

Americans experienced similar sensations in the Chinese interior. An officer who was part of an American truck convoy, traveling the long way from Kunming to Sian to establish a new OSS basis, compared the land to "the prairies of America," and asserted that its people had retained "a kind of primitive vigor which reminds an American of pioneer country." When the sun began to set on the first day of the long trip, the Americans abruptly took appropriate action, almost unthinkingly, as if in a pioneer reflex: "We arranged our vehicles in a circle, each one pointing out like the spokes of a wheel. In the middle, we built a bonfire and had supper."[51]

Superimposing the old American West on Asia and the Pacific was further facilitated by the fact that the inhabitants of the region inevitably reminded GIs of Native Americans. Some of the tribal customs found on Pacific islands, for example, were not unlike those of the American Indians. Soldier and artist John Gaitha Browning witnessed dance ceremonies in New Guinea which he described as "surprisingly similar to some Apache dances."[52]

Most striking, however, was the physical resemblance of many of the Asian peoples to American Indians. That the American Indians originated among "the Tartar tribes in northern Asia" had been orthodox opinion even among the Puritans of the seventeenth century. The Asian trek across the Bering Strait had been common knowledge in American schoolbooks at least as early as the 1830s. Still, the fierceness of the parallels in Asia – the pronounced cheek-bones, the straight black hair, the terracotta-like skin – formed an almost eerie reminder of the racial connection with the long-subjected American Indian.[53]

It did much to sharpen flashbacks of the frontier. American soldiers had already experienced a strong resonance of the Wild West while putting down the Filipino rebellion in the first years of the twentieth century. On Samar, for instance, the Pulahanes with their uncut hair, magic rituals, and belief in the reincarnation of warriors who died in battle, might as well have been Sioux continuing their Ghost Dance uprising. Half a century later, Asia was still pregnant with such resonance for American soldiers. One GI noted that the Igorots who joined them as guides in the mountains of northern Luzon were "like wild Indians" who "would rather fight than eat." The Kachins of northern Burma behaved like Indians in their own way, regularly relocating their villages and rebuilding them almost overnight. American OSS forces operating near the Chinese-Tibetan border observed that the Lisu tribe lived in dwellings that were in effect "built like American teepees."[54]

In the frontier environment of the Pacific War, American soldiers put a premium on whatever pioneer skills had managed to survive the tooth of time. On Guadalcanal, during that first encounter with jungle and Japanese, soldiers were all too happy to fall back on comrades deemed more experienced for no other reason than that they had grown up far from the urbanized east. Men from the 1st Marine Division, for instance, lauded the raccoon, coyote, and wolf hunters in their unit for their relentless patrolling, their stalking skills, and their crucial roles as camp protectors and trail clearers. When, somewhat later, a National Guard unit arrived on the island as reinforcement, the marines felt rather uneasy about these green troops. But the commanding officer of the unit, the 164th Infantry from the Dakotas, promptly assured them that he had with him "a bunch of rugged farm boys" who could "handle the Japs." That was pedigree enough to lay the marines' doubts to rest.[55]

At sea as on land, the pioneer quality of comrades-in-arms had a reassuring effect on Americans. An officer aboard the USS *Tern*, a tug operating from Hawaii, wrote to his wife about the skipper of a similar vessel near him: "It's a pleasure to watch him. He reminds me of some of the raw-boned type of farmer-woodsmen one meets in the hills back home. A typical pioneer type who loves to do battle with the wind, rain, ocean or any form of nature. You have the feeling he would go out in the woods with an axe and build a wagon or most anything."[56]

Still, the pioneer skills of America were never equal to the task in a war fought in a singularly baffling and treacherous new environment. And so, like the European pioneers in America who had on occasion turned to the Indians for assistance, American soldiers now solicited the help of the indigenes of Asia and the Pacific to increase their chances of survival. Military guides, particularly those published in the early stages of the war, urged the Americans to do so. "I wish to emphasize the fact," concluded the author of one of them, "that the most effective way of preparing yourselves for the South Sea wilds is to contact natives at the earliest opportunity." The early campaigns, after all, were to be decided in some of the most unexplored and inhospitable regions of the world. It was a time, too, when American logistical support was still weak, and supply lines were easily cut off. Soldiers on their way to the Solomons and New Guinea, for example, received crash courses from their pocket guides on how to live off the land. The booklets frantically taught them how to drain water from lianas, how to make fish spears and traps, how to find crocodile eggs, and how to appreciate the culinary delights of anything from flying foxes to lizards.[57]

The sons and daughters of America's pioneers soon discovered, however, that even in so seemingly simple a matter as determining which fish were edible, which would cause skin irritation, and which would kill, they could not do without the expertise of locals. That expertise proved vital, too, in many other unforeseen matters. Engineers building bridges in a race against time in the Buna perimeter in 1942, for instance, received invaluable assistance from the Papuans, who not only pointed out the right trees to cut, but demonstrated how to sink poles into river beds by hand, and how to lash timbers together with nothing but bark.[58]

It was the expertise of scouting, however, that proved to be one of the most important indigenous contributions to the American war effort. The 1st Marine Division had barely landed on Guadalcanal in 1942, for instance, when General Vandegrift found himself eagerly accepting into his lines some 60 native scouts who had been heartily recommended by a British colonial officer. Throughout the Southwest Pacific, the 'coast watchers' in particular played a crucial role. Their network stretched from New Caledonia all the way up to the Dutch East Indies across the New Hebrides, the Solomons, and New Guinea. Small groups of white colonials, armed with radio stations, relayed to Allied headquarters the movements of enemy ships, planes, and ground forces. They also helped bring downed airmen and shipwrecked sailors to safety. Yet they could never have accomplished these tasks without the help of thousands of natives who guarded trails and posts, gathered intelligence, spied in Japanese camps, and retrieved soldiers from jungle labyrinths and choppy seas.[59]

Like the explorers and pioneers of that earlier frontier, Americans were quick to enlist natives whenever they landed on yet another hostile coast or trekked into yet another forbidding jungle. Each time, their familiarity with local terrain and enemy troop deployments proved to be of inestimable value. From Papua New Guinea to Burma, legions of natives thus served as indispensable scouts, rangers, and guides – like so many Sacagaweas.

To build and hold the goodwill of indigenous allies, American troops resorted to an elaborate trinket trade, not unlike that developed by the European and American explorers of yore. When Meriwether Lewis spent the winter of 1807 with Thomas Jefferson after his heralded expedition in the Pacific Northwest, he told the president that future explorers should make sure to take with them as trade goods "blue beads," as he had learned that the Indians attached great value to them. Almost a century and a half later, Americans in the Pacific were relearning the value of cheap jewelry and other trifles. "Can you pick me up some ten cent store beads?" a soldier on Guadalcanal implored his parents in California. "Preferably yellow or red. Anyhow the brightest you can find. Also the cheapest. Better send along maybe a dozen rings from Woolworth's." He explained that the natives did not want money, but that bright jewelry purchased expert guides and loyal carriers. John Gaitha Browning, the GI who had lived as a painter among the Indians of the American Southwest, had had the forethought of hoarding needles to trade in the Southwest Pacific. His comrades in New Guinea were soon begging him to part with at least some of them. But Browning was unmoved: "I said 'No!' and meant it. I had cornered the market and didn't intend to let the opportunity be lost to someone who didn't think of the fact that natives like needles, fishhooks, and plug tobacco."[60]

The Lewis and Clark expedition had carried not only beads, but trade articles as varied as cloth, medallions of the president, and medicines. American troops put together elaborate and rather unorthodox trade lines, too. One of the pamphlets on New Guinea, for example, advised GIs to carry matches, razor-blades, handkerchiefs, and red and black "paint" powder as well as knives, calico, files, mouth organs, and mirrors. It pointed out that salt was much sought after in the mountains, whereas stick tobacco served as "a kind of secondary currency" across the entire island. To this trade list, a US Army report on the Saidor operation of early 1944 added blankets, spoons, cooking utensils, biscuits, sugar, rice, and "tomahawks." In the interior of New Guinea, tribes appeared to value mother-of-pearl and rare shells as much as colored beads. It prompted the US Army Services of Supply to purchase some 2,000 gold-lip shells with which to pay native workers.[61]

On the Asian mainland, similar forms of compensation sprang up. In the hills on the border between India and Burma, loyal Naga tribesmen took salt and blankets as pay. American airmen operating over mountainous country in southwest China carried a booklet in which Generalissimo Chiang Kai-shek urged the Lolo tribesmen in their own language to escort downed soldiers back to Sichang, where they could count on receiving "silver, salt, cloth and flag of honor in the way of rewards." During the campaign in northern Burma, the OSS organized hundreds of warriors from the Kachin tribe into a ranger unit. The Americans paid the Kachin Ranger – who reminded them, according to the official history of the campaign, "of the American Indian in his greatest days" – with silver rupees, cloth, needles and thread, raw opium, and medicines.[62]

Whereas GIs habitually paid natives trifles for their services, they were fully aware that the lands these people lived on might one day offer Americans tremendous natural riches. Like their forefathers on the North American continent, GIs in Asia and the Pacific were continually tantalized by the valuable resources that seemed to be there for the taking.

As Richard Slotkin has shown, the mystique of the American frontier sprang not only from its boundless "virgin land," but from lodes of seemingly inexhaustible raw materials. The American West was not just a frontier; it was a "resource frontier." If that was true of the Old West, however, it was even more true of that most distant 'West,' stretching into and beyond the Pacific Ocean. America's appearance on European maps had, after all, been merely the byproduct of an enterprise geared towards finding a passage to India and its fabled wealth of "ivory, apes, and peacocks."[63]

That purpose had remained alive among the colonists of North America's eastern seaboard. In the seventeenth century, for instance, Virginia organized several expeditions "to find out the East India Sea." In revolutionary America, too, there was little informed opinion about Asia. If people knew about it at all, it was as a wellspring of luxuries. President Jefferson hoped that Lewis and Clark would find rivers in the Northwest that could serve as a highway to the Pacific and offer the young republic a shortcut to the dazzling China trade. In the nineteenth century, with Americans poised on the Pacific seaboard, trade with China grew head over heels. It was a trade not in necessities, but in luxuries – tea, spices, silks, and porcelain, which served only to strengthen the vision of Asia as an inexhaustible treasurehouse. Meanwhile, Americans roamed the Pacific seas and islands for additional luxuries. Whalers filled holds with baleen, spermaceti oil, and ambergris; traders gathered sandalwood, tortoise shell, *beche de mer*, oysters, and pearl. So strong was the lure of the Pacific Basin, historian Arrell Morgan Gibson has noted, that after more than a hundred years of American exploration and exploitation "it still seemed newborn."[64]

Indeed, around the turn of the century, a series of world fairs and expositions in the US were still showcasing Asia mainly as a region of unimaginable riches. Beginning with the Centennial Exposition, for example, the Japanese entered the American imagination as an artistic people that seemed particularly gifted in shaping precious materials. In Philadelphia, and at several subsequent exhibitions, millions of Americans strolled through Japanese exhibits overflowing with priceless lacquered ware, porcelains, bronzes, silks, and embroideries.[65]

In 1771, Philip Morin Freneau and Hugh Henry Brackenridge wrote a poem for the commencement exercises at Princeton entitled "The Rising Glory of America." In it, they foresaw a future in which

> fleets shall then convey rich Persia's silks,
> Arabia's perfumes, and spices rare
> Of Philippine, Coelebe and Marian isles,
> Or from the Acapulco coast our India then,
> Laden with pearl and burning gems of gold.

The letters and diaries of GIs who fought in the Pacific War of the 1940s sounded neither so grandiose nor so eloquent. But the observations and ideas expressed in them nevertheless reflected a similar tradition of looking at Asia as a resource frontier and treasure-house, with much of its potential still dormant and begging to be tapped. "This is a typical South Sea Island country," a sergeant from Ohio informed his mother in a letter on the Philippines, "undeveloped, brimming with natural resources and unsurpassed in beauty." His was merely a quick superficial survey of the opportunities in the Pacific

Basin. But a closer look at the soldiers' appraisals of the region reveals the full extent to which they resembled the visions of the American pioneers who had preceded them on older frontiers.[66]

The agents of expansion in the American West – trappers, miners, oil prospectors, and traders – all gladly joined the ranks of the GIs in the Pacific. In November 1943, a ship that had taken on a batch of American troops in California several weeks earlier, was hugging the Australian coast on its way to New Guinea. It lacked good washing facilities and as it drew closer to the equator the men aboard were hot, dirty, and unshaven. The vessel was called the USS *John Jacob Astor*, in honor of the New York merchant who had once owned an empire built on the mountains of furs caught in the Pacific Northwest by Indians and trappers. Hunters and trappers had been among the first agents of expansion in the Far West. But America's animal resources, from beaver to buffalo, had dwindled dramatically. The breathtaking game paradise that Lewis and Clark had encountered from the Ohio to the Columbia Rivers had all but vanished by the time the *John Jacob Astor* anchored off New Guinea. In New Guinea, however, it still existed. Pigeons, parakeets, parrots, hornbills, and cockatoos wrestled for space with countless other birds in the lush foliage, while tree kangaroos, cassowaries, wallabies, cuscus, and bandicoots made Americans think that God had started creation all over again. From New Guinea to Burma, GIs in their journals and letters took careful stock of the immense gaming opportunities that the region had to offer, sharing their enthusiasm with the urbanized folk they had left behind in the east. Guides to New Guinea taught GIs the art of snares, of spring traps, of noose and trigger devices, and of tubular fish traps. From the Flying Tigers who organized hunts among the massive flocks dotting the Yunnan swamps to the soldiers constructing bamboo traps to catch jackals in India, Americans came alive again as trappers from an era long thought lost.[67]

Those other hardy pioneers, the miners and oil prospectors, followed close on the heels of the trappers. The numerous military guides to Asia and the Pacific made sure to wet the GIs' appetites for the region's tremendously rich industrial minerals. India's resources in high-grade iron ore were described as "the largest in the world." Melanesia, with its copper, coal, iron, and zinc, was identified as "one of the important mineral zones of the earth." The island of New Caledonia was touted as "a solid block of metal" that "acre for acre, mile for mile" held some of the world's richest deposits of nickel, chromite, cobalt, and iron. It was here, one pamphlet pointed out, that nickel was mined in huge open pits "in much the same way that we mine copper in Utah, New Mexico, and Arizona." America's Far West kept on duplicating itself.[68]

Oil was given special attention. What made the Dutch East Indies "the treasure house of Asia," remarked one military guide, was without a doubt the islands' rich oil deposits. And so much more of the black gold could be hidden elsewhere in the unexplored region. "The greatest puzzle today is," said a GI pamphlet on the riches of New Guinea, "whether this region will become a major source of petroleum." It was enough to make some Americans dream of viscous El Dorados. As the USS *Montpelier* skirted the southeastern coasts of mysterious Borneo in June 1945, wild stories spread among its crew about a place called Balikpapan. One sailor in his journal claimed that it was "loaded with oil and it is rolling down the hills like water." "You could even drown in some places," he gasped without ever having seen it, "it is so deep."[69]

Still, it was the thought of the legendary precious stones of 'the Orient' and of its precious metals that could excite American soldiers like nothing else. "For centuries," one GI booklet commenced its fairytale, "India's gold and diamonds and precious stones have enabled native princes to decorate themselves in glittering splendor unequaled anywhere." The fairy tale never seemed to have come to an end, not even in an Asia at war. According to one GI, in Ceylon even the servants in the American mess hall wore small rubies in their pierced ears. In the Philippines, civilians advised American soldiers to scrutinize captured Japanese swords because the hollow hilts were thought to hide diamonds, rubies, and emeralds. When a soldier of a portable surgical hospital in Burma learned that the caves in the surrounding Kamaing Hills were not Japanese dug-outs, but jade mines, the dismayed American jotted in his diary: "I had been skipping some green stones across the river in Kamaing. Now I knew that these pieces of green rock that I threw away were raw Jade." Before long, GIs were enthusiastically mining the entire region for precious and semi-precious stones, going on buying sprees with handfuls of dollars that they did not know what else to spend on. Opal, turquoise, and amethyst in Australia. Sapphires in India and Ceylon. Jade in Singapore, Burma, and China. So feverish was the American hunt for precious stones on the cheap that Indian merchants managed to sell GIs rubies carved out of taillight lenses.[70]

And then there was, of course, gold. The mineral that had made pioneers come rushing to California in the 1840s made the hearts of Americans in the Pacific Basin beat faster again in the 1940s. In the fall of 1944, soldiers of the 5th Replacement Depot in New Guinea were swimming in a crystalline stream when one of them noticed bright yellow specks flash in the sandbars below. The find caused tremendous commotion. This was Oro Bay, and for quite a while now American soldiers had been hearing rumors of Japanese and Australians deserters who were said to be working abandoned gold mines in the surrounding mountains. Incredulous GIs grabbed whatever treasures they could from the stream bed, stuffing pockets and socks with nuggets. Some considered marking the spot to return to after the war; others contemplated staking an official claim with Australian authorities. "We recognized," admitted one soldier, "the signs of gold fever."

The frenzy subsided only when the GIs learned from a reliable source that what they had discovered was nothing more than pyrite or "fool's gold." Still, the real thing appeared to be everywhere in the Pacific Basin. GI brochures talked about the Australian "Golden Mile" that had attracted miners from all over the world, including California. They mentioned the gold mines of Fiji and the Solomons. They described the tantalizing Morobe gold fields of New Guinea, the island the Spanish had once called *Isla del Oro*. Even while carrying heavy US equipment in the mountains of Luzon, the Igorots wore "solid gold bracelets," twisted around their wrists and arms. It was no wonder then that GIs, in their time off, could be seen panning for gold in the Pacific until the very end of the war.[71]

If GIs in the Pacific were reborn as trappers and miners, they also came alive as traders reminiscent of the American pioneers who had stepped from the *Empress of China* in Canton in 1784. "American interest in China," one pamphlet reminded the GIs, "has been strong ever since the New England merchant captains began to tap the Chinese market." It was not long before the letters and diaries of American soldiers across the region were reading like the inventories of the New England merchant ships of old. When the USS *Mount Olympus* anchored off Vogelkop, Dutch New Guinea, several GIs decided to paddle ashore with the help of some natives. Within hours, they returned with armloads of rare orchids. They had them appraised by a soldier who happened to have been a florist in civilian life and estimated their exotic treasure "at $600, current Chicago prices." GIs in India snapped up silver jewelry and leather goods as fast as they could, meanwhile scouring towns and cities for the much valued cashmere. In the summer of 1945, a nurse warned her parents in Iowa to be on the lookout for a package from India containing a carved wooden box, brass candlesticks, silver bracelets, a lamp made of shell, a sandalwood fan, and carved ivory elephants.[72]

GI guides to China proffered advice on "what and how much to pay for native Chinese products, such as silk, bronze, porcelain, jade, and curios in general." They included tips on how to recognize cracked porcelain and how to spot glass imitations of jade. Among other things, they heartily recommended buying silver water-cooled pipes in Chengtu, Foochow lacquer rice bowls in Kweilin, and brocaded and embroidered Mandarin coats. Even the guide to Okinawa allowed space for purchasing tips regarding the famous lacquer ware of the Japanese Ryukyu chain, while GIs searched the wartorn island not only for lacquer cups, bowls, and boxes, but also for hand-embroidered kimonos and other fine silk clothing.[73]

Americans who had been led to believe that across the Pacific loomed inexhaustible resource frontiers and treasure-houses were far from disappointed. On Wednesday evening, 16 May 1945, chaplain Charles Dayton,

USNR, was to hold a talk in Honolulu on Korea, Japan, China, and India. It was open to all service personnel, and the announcement in the weekly magazine for Americans stationed on Oahu encouraged soldiers to attend with the promise of colored slides taken by the chaplain himself, who had lived in Asia for many years. GIs also received assurances that the presentation would "not be political or economic," but would instead "deal primarily with the home life of these peoples." Then, in a final attempt to ensure a captive audience, the announcement built in the ultimate teaser. "Business men," it reminded, "see fortunes in the rebuilding of Manila, and the China trade with its teak, tea, silks, furs, rugs, and jades is ever exciting." And it spoke the mind of many when it noted: "As the war progresses in the Far East, Americans are thinking of this hitherto almost forbidden territory as a new frontier."[74]

2
Romantics

Frontiers, by their very nature of being unexplored and unknown, are lands ruled by the imagination. As Richard Slotkin has pointed out, as late as the end of the nineteenth century, the American West itself was still "a space defined less by maps and surveys than by myths and illusions, projective fantasies, wild anticipations, extravagant expectations." How then could that much more distant frontier to the west be anything but a world of dreams and illusions? Indeed, only the existence of such fantasies regarding the Pacific and Asia can help us explain the touristy mood that enveloped Americans even as they made the trek across the ocean as soldiers bound for war.[1]

The trip to the Pacific seaboard sufficed to awaken in the soldier not only something of the pioneer, but also of the tourist. Late in 1941, a soldier from Nebraska, who had been ordered to Hawaii, packed his bags to travel to the Californian port of embarkation. He did not travel alone. "To get there," he recalled, "my parents, sister, brother-in-law . . . and I took an auto trip through the scenic Northwest and down the coast to San Francisco." California had enough to offer to satisfy even the most spoiled traveler. "[M]iles of vineyards and orange groves," gaped a soldier from Kentucky who had never been away from home before he went off to Fort Ord, California, in the summer of 1944, and "bunches of the largest grapes I had ever seen." Even in "those strenuous first days" at the Naval Training Station in San Diego, a would-be sailor, fresh from high school in Wyoming, sensed an unmistakable "holiday air."[2]

An atmosphere of vacationing became even more palpable as soldiers boarded the ships that would carry them across the ocean. Before the war, overseas travel had been something only the happy few could afford – "a rich man's game," as one soldier called it. If travel to Europe had been the preserve of an elite, then Pacific cruises had been meant only for the very rich and exotic, those who could afford the shameful luxury of endless drifting without purpose. Many of the "enthusiastic tourists" whom the GI *Guide to Hawaii* mentioned, for instance, had been movie stars and other celebrities. The travelers who had cruised to China, another military pamphlet reminded the soldiers, had paid no less than "a small fortune" for the privilege. And here now were GIs of all walks of life, gazing up to the Titanics of the Pacific Ocean: the *President Polk*, the *Mount Vernon*, the *Lurline*, the *Monterey*; all luxury liners, some belonging to the famous Matson Navigation Company that for decades had steamed wealthy tourists to their island resorts. In January 1944, a Kansan doctor of the 407th Collecting Company was ordered aboard the *Mount Vernon*. "I was the advance party and chose a luxurious bunk bed in the 3-room cabin assigned me." "I had," he relished, "a private fresh air tube and bed light. It showed me how the rich had once traveled on this luxury liner."[3]

Granted, the ocean liners had not managed to escape the scars of war. They had been renamed, painted gray, blacked out. The huge swimming pool of the *New Amsterdam* had been converted into a mess hall for enlisted men. Granted, many soldiers never got to see the inside of a luxury liner. Instead, they crossed the ocean on anything from carriers and destroyers to banana boats and old tubs. Some 35 percent of those traveling aboard troopships claimed that the conditions were poor, citing meager meals, severe crowding, and lack of ventilation. Yet, despite all this, on many a ship plying the bright Pacific, an almost festive mood could be found that would have been hard to detect on vessels sailing the gray Atlantic to the Old World of dashed hopes.[4]

The weather had much to do with this. On 13 December 1942, the USS *Montpelier* left Philadelphia. It was snowing, and the winds gusting across the ocean were so icy that sailors on watch had to protect their faces with thick masks. But all that abruptly changed when the ship nosed into the Pacific via the Panama Canal. "After the cold, rough Atlantic," exhaled one sailor, "it was like going to Paradise." Like obedient tourists, soldiers took to sunbathing with a vengeance in the Pacific, where the radiant sun combined with mellow winds to paint bronze, salt-air tans. A delighted soldier, whose ship had only recently entered the Pacific, told his parents in Tennessee that every day he left work at four in the afternoon, jumped in his shorts, and then rushed to the flight deck to take a sun bath. Apparently, he was not the only one. "Some of the boys," he added, "have been burned to a crisp and have really suffered." Despite such casualties, the sun worshiping continued in the best holiday tradition until the end of the war. "Proceeding south to avoid typhoon reported heading this way," a pilot aboard the carrier *Cowpens* jotted in his diary as they were readying to strike Japan early in August 1945. Then he added, without comment: "A sunbather was washed over side but was rescued by destroyer."[5]

The voyages across the Pacific were, of course, exceedingly long, leaving soldiers with too many empty hours on their hands. Troops therefore tried to kill time in many an unsoldierly fashion. Sunbathing, like the drawn-out ritual of King Neptune, was only one of the ways. In fact, GIs had a preference for recreating the scenes they imagined to have taken place among rich tourists while their cruise ships plied the Pacific in peacetime. Aboard the *Monterey*, troops heading for New Guinea in the autumn of 1944 decided to organize auditions and improvise an orchestra. Before long, they were holding regular dances in the afternoons. "I sat there blowing my saxophone," recalled one soldier, "wondering what it must have been like to have played for the swanky tourists on this great Matson Liner during its expensive cruises into the South Seas before the war." The *Monterey* matinees were by no means an exception. Troops aboard the USS *West Point*, for example, steaming towards New Caledonia in 1944, attended dances on the promenade decks during the day and went to see movies in the evening. Or take the *Tjisadane*, a Dutch East Indies transport en route to Guadalcanal in 1942. During the afternoons, soldiers could be found singing "the lilting, lusty songs men like to sing." In the evenings, on the other hand, they were soothed by "Strauss waltzes and a few light classics" aired by the ship's loudspeakers. The 843rd Anti-Aircraft Artillery Battalion, on its way to India in 1944, put together a jazz combo for the entertainment of all of the ship's passengers. And the band played on, all the way to the war.[6]

Seen from sun-drenched California and the azure ocean, war could not but appear unreal. "The whole thing," observed correspondent Ira Wolfert while preparing to leave Hawaii for Guadalcanal in 1942, "with that blue Hawaiian sky over it and the thick yellow sunlight coloring it, didn't look like going up to the front line at all, but like something in a magazine." Even a marine aboard a ship sailing into Pearl Harbor some time after the Japanese attack could note that when somebody on the deck at last recognized Diamond Head, "for a moment the mood was that of a cruise ship," a "holiday mood." To him, as to many other soldiers, Hawaii remained, he admitted, "the edge of a world," part of a "romantic mythology." War had, of course, battered its way into the placid Pacific, and the soldiers could unmistakably see the blackened wreckage of the ships sunk on the day of infamy. Still, the marine had to admit that he "couldn't put the two together into one place."[7]

A romantic reflex more than once made it hard for American soldiers to imagine war and the Pacific going hand in hand. Their automatic response to the region was romantic in the first place because it was not based on facts. That did not mean, however, that GIs were allowed to pour fantasies into the region at random. For, indeed, this distant western frontier of the imagination had already been colonized, and as the soldiers encroached upon it, they were all but forced to resort to prefabricated illusions. These illusions were the product of a variety of mass media and, above all, the brainchild of mass entertainment.

American soldiers traveled to their overseas destinations with an astonishing lack of reliable information grounded in the realities of the region. That was especially true in the early days of the war. "On August 6th, we were called to formation on the deck," a marine remembered of his trip to the Solomons aboard the USS *Zielan* in 1942. "An officer on the deck read a few pages written by a famous man and wife team, who were known worldwide for exploring and photographing wild game. I believe they were called 'the Johnsons.'" The marines dutifully listened to excerpts on the islands that described their natural beauty, the picture-postcard coconut groves of Guadalcanal, and the golf courses on Tulagi. However preposterous this information might have sounded in the context of war, it was still more than most American soldiers could expect to get their hands on at a time when the conflict was still young. Early in 1942, for instance, the 101st Quartermaster Regiment was made part of Task Force 6814 and sent to the South Pacific to guard the route to Australia. The unit found itself on its way without a scrap of information on local conditions. Upon arrival at the first destination, its officers hurriedly stocked up on even the most obscure booklets they could find dealing with the islands of New Caledonia, the Solomons, and the New Hebrides. Some turned out to be reprints of outdated anthropological material published in Australia and New Zealand. Others were clumsy translations of the observations of old-time French residents. Before long, the unit's cadre was briefing soldiers with the help of dubious information gleaned from booklets titled *Discoveries by d'Entrecasteaux* and *Strange Stories from the South Seas*, and from chapters named "Tubuai, First Hide-Out of the *Bounty* Mutineers." One of the covers showed natives with large rings through their noses climbing trees.[8]

As the war progressed, America's armed forces gradually began producing a series of guides, booklets, and pamphlets aimed at familiarizing soldiers at least somewhat with the bewildering spectrum of foreign cultures before disembarking them. But how much could GIs really learn about the complex tribes of New Guinea and the sophisticated cultures of the Asian mainland from pocket-sized booklets containing some scant forty pages, illustrative drawings included? Moreover, as these publications tried to target the 'average' soldier, they almost inevitably resorted to colorful vignettes and facile generalizations, leaving many blank spaces for the reader to fill in. Yet as a US War Department survey showed, these were the very booklets on which the overwhelming majority of troops relied for a better understanding of the foreign countries and peoples they were about to encounter. Aboard a ship on its way to India in 1944, a soldier in less than an evening browsed through three military booklets that covered most of the Asian mainland. When he put them down, the enlightened GI wrote in his diary: "I'm off to dreamland with my mind full of those Indian and Chinese religions, customs, and dress. What a night this is going to be."[9]

The void of reliable information surrounding Asia and the Pacific was all too easily filled with the images and illusions that had been created, and continued to be tirelessly polished, by media as varied as cartoons, comic strips, magazines, pulp fiction, literature, plays, and movies. Of all these sources, American soldiers identified novels and movies as by far the most important. They had shaped the Pacific Basin, particularly Hawaii and the South Pacific – or 'South Seas' – into the ultimate terrestrial paradise. So much so, that GIs were using 'South Seas' as a generic name for all of the Pacific, as if this paradise stretched endlessly from pole to pole.

Military pocket guides tried to warn the soldiers. "Some things you won't find," said the booklet on New Guinea, "for they never really existed at all outside the imagination of novelists and movie directors." The warnings fell on deaf ears. After all, how could a terse service manual in a few minutes undo the paradise conjured up by a weighty literary tradition of centuries? That tradition had first been set in motion by European explorers and writers, from Magellan's journals to Cook's best-selling volumes and Robert Louis Stevenson's *In the South Seas*. Though most GIs were not steeped in Europe's literary canon, almost all did at least know – however vaguely – Daniel Defoe's *Robinson Crusoe* and the Edenic island he was associated with (most were unaware that Crusoe's island was, in fact, situated in the Atlantic, off the coast of Brazil).

Moreover, America had been adding to the Old World tradition as soon as its sailors, merchants, and whalers began navigating the Pacific. Early in the nineteenth century already, stories of beachcombers – abandoned sailors or deserters living charmed lives on Pacific islands – had entered American folklore through the oral tradition. The first American novelist chronicling paradise in the South Seas was Herman Melville in the 1840s. Melville, though, seems to have been a favorite with neither soldiers nor sailors on US warships, perhaps because he had created also one of the most notorious sea monsters of the Pacific. But the American literary tradition encompassed many more famous novels on the Pacific, from Stoddard's *South Sea Idylls* of the 1870s to Hall and Nordhoff's *Bounty Trilogy* of the 1930s. Such lively novels informed infinitely more soldiers about the Pacific than did accurate but ponderous historical and geographical volumes.[10]

"I finished the book I was reading today," a soldier wrote from New Guinea to his mother in October 1944. "Parts of it were about these South Sea Islands and was very interesting to me especially the part about the natives. Jack London is a good writer of adventure." Indeed, this Californian author, whose novels had done much to stimulate tourism in Hawaii between the wars, seems to have been a literary favorite among the military readership in the Pacific. *Yank* correspondent Mack Morriss, for instance, described a town on the island of Efate to the soldiers as "strictly from Jack London's *South Sea Tales*." In 1942, intelligence officers of the 1st Marine Division actually turned to analyzing London's short story "The Red One" to learn whatever they could about the landing areas at Guadalcanal and Tulagi.[11]

London was certainly not the only novelist who had helped prefabricate illusions about the Pacific among GIs. When, for a moment in October 1944, it flashed through the mind of a WAC on her way west by train that she might be sent to Alaska rather than overseas, she became quite upset. "It had to be the Pacific," she insisted. "I was all set for palm trees and tropic isles, a dream ever since I'd read Frederick O'Brien's *White Shadows in the South Seas*." This was a soldier whose mirage had flowed from the pen of a New York journalist who owed a best-selling book to the idealized villages and women of the Marquesas Islands.[12]

Many soldiers had never possessed much of a taste for reading. Yet even they were familiar with quite a few authors, or at least their creations, thanks to the still more powerful medium of film. The first encounter with Pacific atolls more than once reminded soldiers, for instance, of the story of the priest who was shipwrecked with a prostitute and found himself fighting temptation on a sensual island. GIs had perhaps not read Somerset Maugham, but they had seen *Rain*, the movie based on the Englishman's novel, starring Walter Huston and Joan Crawford. Similarly, soldiers who had never heard of Edgar Rice Burroughs were undoubtedly familiar with his brainchild, *Tarzan of the Apes*. Some twelve immensely popular movies with Johnny Weismuller in the 1930s and early 1940s had made Tarzan – the embodiment of uninhibited life in the tropics – more than lord of the African jungle. GIs caught his fleeting shadow throughout the Pacific, where islands with lianas strong as cable inevitably looked like "regular Tarzan country" and any gifted swimmer was instantly hailed by his comrades as "a movie Tarzan."[13]

Whether adapted from books or based on original screenplays, GIs mentioned film after film as their frame of reference in the Pacific. In New Guinea, they recalled *Trader Horn*; in the Marianas, *South of Pago Pago*; in the South Pacific, pirate movies starring Errol Flynn. When naval engineers were told to draw up plans for bases on Christmas atoll as quickly as possible and could not find reliable geographical surveys, they watched *Tabu*, a movie shot on the islands before the war, to get an idea of the terrain. Meanwhile, whiffs of movie songs drifted with the ocean currents: *Down Where the Trade Winds Blow, Moon of Manakoora, South Sea Islands Magic*.[14]

No movies shaped Pacific perceptions more, however, than those featuring Dorothy Lamour – or Dottie Lamour as the soldiers lovingly called her. This sensual actress from sultry New Orleans starred in a number of Paramount movies that were among the top money earners in the late 1930s and 1940s. In most of them, tropical islands were the location, with Lamour uncomplicatedly playing a beautiful woman wrapped in a sarong. The titles of her movies readily gave away Hollywood's interpretation of the Pacific: *The Jungle Princess, Beyond the Blue Horizon, Rainbow Island, Her Jungle Love*. So popular did the 'sarong queen' become, that GI guide after

GI guide saw itself obliged to warn soldiers in the Pacific that if they were looking for her world, it would be in vain.[15]

Although Dorothy Lamour, for example, also starred in *Moon over Burma*, the sarong queens and hula girls of the movies abruptly abandoned most of the Americans who went as far as the Asian mainland. Here, however, soldiers immediately hooked up with a bunch of new writers and directors to guide them through the unknown. When an American volunteer arrived in Rangoon in November 1941 to join the Flying Tigers in China, the thought immediately occurred to him that this was "probably the city in which most writers stayed while working on their books about Burma." "Probably those writers stayed at the Grand Hotel, which is really quite modern," he continued to muse, "and it could have been there that they turned out their mysteries." Likewise, visits to secluded Tibet by soldiers stationed in China could not but bring to mind the vivid images of best-selling books. "Until this war few Americans had ever traveled within its boundaries," an artillery officer wrote to his wife in Virginia. "You'll recall that Shangrila in James Hilton's 'The Lost Horizon' is supposedly located among the Mts. of the Moon in Tibet." John Gussak's preparations for his daunting task as provost marshal for all of northern Burma and the Indian state of Assam were at least partly based on novels. "Stayed indoors all afternoon reading Eve Curies book 'Among the Warriors,'" he noted in his diary while sailing from Australia to India in June 1944. "Very interesting. She covers China & India besides other places and I read everything I can get hold of about these places."[16]

Still, the most preferred literary source among American troops assigned to Burma and India was the British poet and novelist Rudyard Kipling. Kipling had captured life in the British colonies brilliantly. So brilliantly that even GIs found themselves thinking of *Kim* in India and those in Ceylon of the mongoose that killed the cobra in "Rikki-tikki-tavi." In October 1944, a sergeant of the 23rd Field Hospital spent an agreeable evening with a British colonial officer in a picturesque valley in northern Burma. "He had a book of Kipling and was one of the few Britishers who seemed to like Kipling as much as we do," he later wrote to his mother in New Jersey. "I recited some Kipling at him so he brought out his book of Kipling verse and he commented that most American officers knew more Kipling than the British."[17]

Reciting Kipling poems may not have come naturally to just any GI, but this British writer, too, had been able to reach a mass American audience with the help of movies. In 1939, *Gunga Din* was released as a film. *The Jungle Books*, Kipling's famous story about a small boy raised by animals in India's jungle, appeared on American screens in 1942. Movies did much to boost the fame of Kipling's characters. Crossing a river in Burma in 1944, a scene of strange familiarity flashed before the eyes of one of Merrill's Marauders. "A small Kachin boy sat silently on the far bank," he noted, "watching over the village cattle as did Mowgli of Rudyard Kipling's tales of this part of the world." By this time, Hollywood had made Mowgli's Indian world so well-known that GIs began to use it as a reference even in the Pacific. "Here I am," a sailor wrote to his wife in Pennsylvania in 1944, "guiding a ship in south seas off a tropical island with flying fish, blue oceans, whitecaps, and floating remnants of coconut palms." It was, he marveled, "like something out of Kipling." Also in 1944, the 592nd Engineer Amphibian Regiment moved camp once again, this time to Dutch New Guinea. Here, young Mowgli easily pushed aside Tarzan, that other enviable creature of the jungle. "[W]e have a forest of immense giants of jungle trees hung with vines and filled with bird calls," a company clerk noted in his journal, "all very much like the movie scenes of Kipling's *Jungle Book.*"[18]

What British writer Kipling had done for the American image of India and Burma with a variety of novels, short stories and poems, American author Pearl S. Buck had accomplished for giant China with one single, powerful book. *The Good Earth* was published in 1931, received the Pulitzer prize, and became a major bestseller. In 1933 it was transformed into a Broadway play, and in 1937 a major Hollywood studio turned it into an Oscar-winning box office hit. *The Good Earth* appeared at a time when there was a remarkable outpour of books inspired by China. Shocked by the shameless aggression of the Japanese, scores of American novelists created an idealized canvas of life in the Middle Kingdom before the violent intrusion. With her novel, Pearl Buck introduced millions of Americans to a Chinese people characterized by uncommon kindness, undivided loyalty, and unshakable patience. Herself the daughter of Presbyterian missionaries in China, she portrayed the Chinese as pioneers belonging to the kind of pure and upright frontier life that existed only in the American imagination. Pearl Buck's Chinese, according to historian T. Christopher Jespersen, were people "whose attachment to the land closely resembled Jeffersonian ideas about a virtuous class of yeoman farmers."[19]

Having learned much of what they knew about this distant region from literary and cinematic sources, GIs sailed into the Pacific with visions so romantic that not even the thought of war could chase them from their minds entirely. The images that the American soldiers carried with them were rooted in long-standing traditions. And they were romantic not only because they were fantasies that had no basis in fact, but also because they were idealizations that gave rise to dangerously high expectations. Following yet another warning about the kind of Pacific illusions created by Dorothy Lamour, for example, one GI pamphlet added: "Let's be fair to the movies, however, and admit that for at least 200 years the same kind of romantic idea of life upon the islands of the Pacific has been standard in America. Until this war these islands have been distant paradises – dream worlds of coral lagoons and coconut palms, hula girls and hurricanes."[20]

Immersed in images like these, it was no wonder that the very thought of crossing the teasing Pacific Ocean could trigger an idealization of the remote. "Of course we do not know exactly where we are going," a college boy from New York City scribbled in his diary with nervous excitement the night before departing San Francisco in 1943, "but we shall probably go a great distance." Later in the war, a Midwesterner, looking back on his travels with the satisfaction of a successful explorer, wrote to his parents: "When I think I'm only 19 and have been 10,000 miles from home, been in 15 states, jungles, Pacific Ocean, Coral Sea, Bismarck Sea, New Guinea where I am now, and God knows where else . . . – guess I'm just bragging but I could still be clerking at Krogers." The expanses tamed and miles conquered were carried as badges of honor in the distant war. "For this was ancient and fabulous China," exalted a 1945 *Yank* souvenir booklet, "this was adventure, this was as far away from the good United States as any man could travel on this earth."[21]

The yearning for the remote awakened a predilection for the exotic. In the weeks before being shipped overseas, a young marine in California relished hanging out in bars patronized by the old hands. "It was there," he said, "that I first heard the romantic island names: Rabaul and Munda and Bougainville, Espiritu Santo, Emirau." The mere sound of them sufficed to make soldiers want a taste of the adventurous. And what better place for excitement than the infinite Pacific Ocean and, above all, the dreamlike South Seas? Traditionally, Europeans and Americans alike had gravitated towards the islands of the South Pacific in their search for paradise. Moreover, these were the islands that had been the favorite setting for boys' adventure stories ever since the genre had emerged in the mid-nineteenth century. When the *Santa Clara* edged towards the Panama Canal in March 1942, rumors flew about, whispering Australia as the destination. "This seemed fantastic to me," an engineer confessed to his diary. "I thought Central America, perhaps South America, would be as far as we would go." More than a year later, another soldier, sailing from Australia to New Guinea, observed in his journal, with an air of grave expectation: "We shall be close to the equator and are heading toward it every hour. It shall be hot as blazes." "[I]s this not," he triumphed, "adventure, bordering on further adventure?" "It was in any case," he confessed, "what I've always dreamed about since the first adventure story I ever read."[22]

But GIs found the Asian mainland to be no less a place of exotic excitement than Pacific islands. After all, tales of adventure much older than even the earliest South Sea stories had been spun from this region. As soon as he arrived in the Burmese theater of war, for example, an American doctor joined the arduous trek to the Salween River as a member of the 22nd Field Hospital of the Chinese Yunnan Expeditionary Force. "On the second day of marching," he noted with disbelief, "we reached an old road that the local people said had been used by Marco Polo." Time and countless patient feet had smoothed the granite pavement since the passing of what was the quintessential explorer in Western imagination. Similar paths in Asia could lead to even more awe-inspiring scenes at any time. On the last day of 1941, a pilot, on a long journey from Burma to the American Volunteer Group of the Chinese Air Force, arrived in the city of Tali, hidden in the Yunnan hills. Here he ran into a group of pilgrims from Tibet. They were quite an unusual sight, with their woolen clothing and fur-lined boots, their heavy packs and long staffs. The men were small, with broad shoulders, and long black hair that covered their eyes. Acutely intrigued by these people from what he called "the land of mystery," the aviator let himself be carried away in his diary. "This is really romance with a capital R," he sighed. "I feel a longing to go back to Tibet with these travelers and see the forbidden city of Lhasa."[23]

Still, forbidden cities never fired the imagination of American soldiers the way virgin nature did in this faraway world. The idea of the West – the horizon where the sun sets – as a land of mystery and romance was at least as old as the notion of this direction as a Utopia, a place where life would somehow be better. An important part of that notion was the longing for the West as a geographical dream world. Even ancient and medieval thinkers imagined the world to the west as one where the climate was benign and delightful, earth fertile, and vegetation lush and heavy with fruit. These were images that barely waned with time. In accounts of their first contacts with North America, sixteenth-century explorers described it as Edenic. When in the early 1800s Lewis and Clark set in motion their expedition to the American Northwest, that part of the globe was still widely believed to be 'the Garden of the World.' Though the two explorers dutifully reported the less rosy realities of the Pacific Northwest, visions of the westward world as an earthly paradise soon took root again in the nineteenth century. They resulted from an avalanche of journals and novels depicting the bounty and kindness of the lazy South Seas, a trend gratefully continued by the movies of the twentieth century.[24]

On the surface, it was hard for American soldiers not to believe in these visions of the unspoiled and generous nature of the Pacific. An elaborate deception set in the very moment the ocean unfolded its calming colors and the sun softened the bodies of tense soldiers. The water had such "an inspiring hue to it," noted a GI who was looking at it from California, that it "fascinates one." Sailing over it on his way to Hawaii a few months later, the same soldier wrote to his wife in Texas, "Its color is such a deep blue that I believe it is a large ink well." The closer one got to the equator, said another soldier, the more dazzling became the ocean's color spell, until it looked like "a gigantic circle of liquid lapis shot through with unearthly blues, greens, and violets – all blending into something too beautiful for a ship of war to swim into."[25]

As for the sun, soldiers could not decide whether it was its rising or setting that was the most astonishing in the Pacific. Whereas the newborn light seemed intent on setting "the world on fire," one soldier observed, the aging light appeared determined to drag the ocean with it "in a final blaze." "No wonder," he reflected, "the Japanese call this and their islands the 'Land of the Rising Sun.'" "I noticed yesterday," said a sailor aboard the USS *Admiralty Islands*, without indication as to whether he was talking about sunrise or sunset, "that several of us were standing in a group just drinking it in – everyone silent and seeming in awe at its magnificence."[26]

Amidst these most wondrous of colors, it happened that schools of frolicking porpoises rushed to keep ahead of the splashing bows, as if to beg the hurried war vessels to take part in their endless play.[27]

Nature persisted in its charm offensive on land as at sea. In their first brief encounters with the islands of the Pacific, soldiers wondered why it had been necessary at all to warn them about the illusions created by Hollywood's movies. Indeed, many an island, north and south of the equator, appeared to be the stunning materialization of these supposed illusions in their minutest detail: whispering palms, bleached beaches, blue lagoons, and a lazy surf. When the moon took over, she made it all look even more unreal. On its three-day flight from Hawaii to Ulithi, a Navy plane loaded with marines made a stop on Majuro Island. The soldiers spent the evening on the moonlit beach, trying to formulate what they felt now that they had discovered paradise truly existed. "But," noted one of them, "how could I have any real response to a tropical island in the moonlight? It was too damn much, too like a movie with Dorothy Lamour; and I could only feel the way I did in movies like that – charmed, but disbelieving." "We all sat a little uncomfortably," he admitted, "looking at the moon on the water, overwhelmed by the virtual existence of romance, drinking our beer."[28]

Majuro was only one of the many places in the Pacific where natural splendor got the better hand of human expression. The fascination with beauty was easily extended to the region's larger islands. "How wild and beautiful," gasped a nurse who tried in vain to take in all at once mountains, jungle, and ocean near Milne Bay, New Guinea. "The water had a long, slow swell," a soldier wrote from Ceylon to his parents in Indiana. "I can't describe the subtle shadings from sapphire to pale transparent green. No paint can do it justice; it can only be seen."[29]

On the mainland of Asia, too, there unfolded scene after scene of natural splendor that appeared not to belong to this earth. "One's first impulse is to doubt one's own eyes," an American surgeon said of the Chinese mountains rising abruptly from the plain of Kweilin. "There simply cannot be real mountains like these! Your mind turns to the illustrations in *Alice in Wonderland* and some of the Walt Disney color films."[30]

Soldiers regarded nature as unspoiled in the Pacific and Asia not only because of its undiluted beauty, but also because of its lavish generosity. The

American image of the world to the west as a bounteous garden was an old one. Thomas Jefferson, for instance, regarded the American Northwest as a land that would "yield an abundance of all the necessaries of life, and almost spontaneously." That arcadian idea was easily transplanted to the South Pacific in the nineteenth century. Patient cultivation and hard labor were thought to be unnecessary on islands where coconut milk and breadfruit voluntarily dropped from trees, and fish could be scooped up with bare hands.[31]

It is not hard to see why even American soldiers of the twentieth century could be fooled into believing the South Sea myth of what one historian has described as the "emancipation from the curse of Cain." GIs who landed on Tami, a tiny coral island off the New Guinean coast, might as well have invaded Paradise itself. Hibiscus and periwinkle bloomed exuberantly. Most of the moon-shaped island was covered with pink, crocus-like flowers. There were dense betel-nut groves. Trees bent under the weight of mangos, wild cherries, and breadfruit. An old frangipani tree delicately perfumed the soft breezes wafting in from the ocean. A marine pilot who had just arrived on Ulithi atoll could now bear witness that indeed on the sand among the soldiers' tents lay coconuts "waiting to be opened and eaten and drunk from." "It was," he insisted, "like Eden."[32]

Both in the Pacific and Asia, animals too appeared to be offering themselves freely for the sustenance of men. The plains around New Delhi stunned GIs with their "thousands of antelope and millions of game birds, ranging from quail to wild peacock." On New Caledonia, deer were so plentiful that "they are regarded as a pest, and may be found grazing with the cattle." All across the Pacific, Americans could be found catching fish with nothing more than empty hooks. When Lindbergh, the famous American aviator, visited Midway Island in 1944, he remarked in his journal that there were "more birds than I have ever seen at one time before." He spoke of hundreds of thousands of terns, canaries, golden plovers, and Japanese lovebirds. Albatross dared to come so close that swimmers could splash them with water. Here, noted Lindbergh, "there has been no retreat of wildlife from 'civilization' – as there was from our westward-moving frontiers during the last century in the United States."[33]

So powerful was nature in its purest form, that soldiers at times felt an almost mystical attraction to it. In the autumn of 1944, the *Lurline* took what seemed like an eternity to cross the ocean from California to New Guinea. "I gazed at it day after day for nearly three weeks," one of the WACs aboard remembered sharply. "I was awed and mesmerized," she wrote. "The cosmic connections absorbed me." With, often for the first time in their lives, not the least barrier remaining between them and nature, soldiers thought it possible, even desirable, to become one with it, to shed their individual skins for an all-encompassing, more meaningful, identity. "I felt great peace and satisfaction," concluded a soldier, looking back at a night of contemplation amidst the elements on Biak Island. "I also felt impersonal, as if I were an object absorbing the natural good of the scene and, in turn, imparting a sense of well-being. I felt at peace." Certainly, no person on earth could wish to create peace with himself more earnestly than a soldier about to risk his life in war. And an Edenic setting could prove surprisingly conducive to the process. It did help, for instance, a soldier on New Guinea prepare himself for the dangerous invasion of New Britain at the end of 1943. "No one should feel unhappy if I do not return," he wrote in his journal, "for I will sink back in the friendly earth and become a part of the blue of tropic waters and the breeze in the palms – a part of the white clouds above green mountains. I will be freed into all the beauty of the earth . . ."[34]

Attraction to the purity of the natural environment seamlessly flowed over into fascination with the people inhabiting it. Troops of the 40th Division, on their way to Guadalcanal from Honolulu, made a stop at the Samoa Islands in December 1943. Their ship stayed at Pago Pago harbor for about four hours; the soldiers eagerly used this time to gaze at the natives ashore through field glasses, observing their every motion as if they were a newly discovered species that needed careful recording. GIs gathered evidence not only for themselves, but also for the loved ones whom they had left behind in the US, and who seemed to have an equally insatiable appetite for exotics. From the island of Espíritu Santo, an engineer wrote to his parents in Chicago in 1943, apparently after much prodding by his family: "As far as the natives are concerned, I haven't come in contact with them yet except to see them at a distance. They look like ordinary colored people but they dye their hair a blond color." A year later, the exasperated soldier wrote home from Kolombangara Island: "I thought I had described the natives sufficiently in previous letters, Dad, but I'll try again."[35]

When the long-awaited close contact with the wildly different other took place at last, it was in the hushed silence of a spell. Almost 50 years later, a GI in his memoirs keenly relived the first encounter with a member of one of the hill tribes of Mindoro in the Philippines: "One day one of these tribesmen, dressed only in a loin cloth and equipped with a bow and arrow, casually made his way along a street in our tented city. He peered in the tents, oblivious to the stares of the GIs watching him. After his curiosity had been satisfied, he drifted away as silently as he had come."[36]

It was tempting to imagine that people isolated from the aggressive demands of modern civilization in their remote idyllic hideaways had been able to preserve a purer life. Westerners had long considered the vast expanses of the Pacific and distant Asia as the ideal setting for hidden shelters, from the Happy Isles of Polynesia to the mountain retreats of the Himalaya. The Tibetan hideout from Hilton's *Lost Horizon* had become so popular that the US Navy steamed into the Pacific during the war with an entire fleet of large carriers in a class of its own called *Shangri-la*. Meanwhile, a B-25 bomber crew spread a strange story on New Guinea. While flying low over the Cyclops Mountains, they had come across a remarkable valley, walled in on all sides by cliffs of a thousand feet – but full of people. "How did these people get into the valley," asked an excited officer. "It is quite apparent that they could not get out. An untouched, untouchable eddy. What a mine of information concerning the primitive and unspoiled." Had these airmen discovered, the officer could not help but wonder, a "New Guinea Shangri-la?"[37]

For one thing, observation soon taught American soldiers that many indigenous peoples had kept in touch with the natural environment in ways unimaginable to Westerners. A military booklet on the New Guinea native told GIs that in "bushcraft, in hardihood, in mobility, he leaves you standing." The skill with which these people listened to and read nature made GIs feel like men robbed of their senses. American troops who landed on Fergusson Island in 1943 came across natives who they claimed had remained virtually untouched by whites. One of them immediately volunteered as a guide. "Like all his fellows," observed an officer, "he was marvelously skilled in jungle signs. He could tell how large a group had passed this way – how many men, women and children; whether they passed leisurely or in haste, in sickness or in health."[38]

Americans also reveled in a native craftsmanship that succeeded in working natural resources with few, if any, metal implements. New Guineans preferred to use their own litters which, made of balsa and split bamboo, turned out to be more comfortable and cooler than either the Australian or American stretchers. Filipino nipa huts, made of nothing but bamboo and palm leaves, were remarkably dry and cool; sturdy villages in New Guinea were held together with vines and bark and not a single nail. Like Lewis and Clark among the Clatsops and Chinooks of the Pacific seaboard, however, GIs were particularly impressed by the locals' knack for the construction of excellent seafaring craft. American accounts ranged from the fine outrigger canoes ferrying equipment to the Buna beachhead in New Guinea, over the stable bamboo rafts carrying troops across Filipino rivers, to the durable Chinese sampans transporting almost anything. Amidst a modern fleet of steel war vessels, one engineer found it worthwhile to spend an entire page of his cherished diary on a meticulous description of New Guinean canoes and their intrepid rowers on the rough seas.[39]

The indigenes had genuinely succeeded in losing themselves in nature by absorbing it fully. As a result, they appeared to impart a sense of well-being that overly civilized people could strive for, but never attain. When the soldier of an engineer regiment strolled through his first New Guinean village, he was "fascinated by the first truly unspoiled people I had ever seen."

It was on this huge primitive island that he became convinced that, though inevitably corrupted in civilized society, "people are born with pleasant instincts." The hospitality of the New Guineans was, he insisted, "so strong and more sincere than ours." While trading with them, he enjoyed watching their "frank faces – faces that had not learned deceit." Neither had these people acquired the least notion of modern time-keeping. And who could blame them, he asked, "[W]hy hurry through a day? It's so wonderful – much too wonderful to split into mechanical fragments of minutes." His was a glorification of the simpler and more primitive way of life worthy of Jean-Jacques Rousseau. But similar feelings were expressed by soldiers in Asia as well as the Pacific. A civil affairs officer who traveled from Kunming to Sian in 1945, for instance, praised the Chinese people in the region near Tibet: "We had very little trouble at any time with thieves. In the country, where the population was unchanged by contacts with foreigners, they were as honest as any people."[40]

What soldiers agreed on most emphatically, however, was that people on these distant frontiers – whatever their particular "pleasant instincts" – appeared astonishingly joyous and content. On Fergusson Island, GIs noted that most locals suffered from skin disease, and that many of their children were pot-bellied. They were obviously malnourished. But, one officer emphasized, they were nevertheless clearly "gay." Such simple people were not afraid of letting that show either. "[W]e always leave them laughing!" noted an ambulance driver on the road from Ledo to Kunming, after another trade stop among Burmese hill people. "Really – these people are always laughing – they do seem to be happy."[41]

Perhaps that is why they seemed to be singing their hearts out, too. The voices of the Fijians were "beautiful," their music was "haunting." On New Caledonia, indigenous dockworkers created a perfect musical harmony, "with no effort, and with no director." "I don't believe," a moved soldier said, after listening to an impromptu Filipino performance, "the N.Y. Philharmonic could have done it any better." One GI thought he had seen enough of the New Guineans to conclude that "[t]heir voices and rhythm were remarkable and far surpassed their ability at writing and arithmetic." "Singing," he had become convinced, "was a natural thing to them."[42]

In fact, these people appeared to be filled with so much well-being that they were not afraid of expressing it even in the most bodily of ways. The uninhibitedness of Pacific islanders in particular had long been part of a Euro-American mythology. After all, born and raised in perfect harmony with a benign and generous nature, unpolluted by civilization, these people could not but represent physical standards. A GI who had come across what he called "pure Hawaiians" in an isolated village on Kauai Island, very much approved of what he saw: "They are a tall people, with straight black hair and very good, white teeth." "The New Caledonia native men – black as the ace of spades," wrote a *Yank* correspondent, "are beautiful physical specimens." Fijian men, too, were described by one GI as "magnificent physical specimens."[43]

With such attractive bodies, Pacific islanders could well afford to flaunt. An officer who arrived at Buna, New Guinea, in early 1943, was struck by the fact that the natives "were everywhere, their sturdy bronze bodies glistening." He was allowed to fasten his glance on one man in particular, who was no less than "a poem of perfectly proportioned muscle planes in gleaming bronze." But there was more to this physical comfortableness than mere exhibitionism. Indeed, the natives' unconcern at nakedness seemed to flow from not having been tainted by original sin. After a hot day's work at Oro Bay, New Guinean laborers undressed, took a bath in a mountain stream, then climbed onto the American truck that would take them to camp – dripping wet and stark naked. "Evidently," mused one GI, "they have not yet learned the acquired habit of being ashamed of their bodies."[44]

Amidst such unrepressed behavior it was the encounter with Pacific women that most soldiers were longing for most eagerly. That encounter was laden with expectation as a result of a deeply-rooted Western mythology surrounding the Pacific, further enriched in recent years by the hula girls and sarong queens of the movies. American military guides did not exactly dampen such expectations. Booklets on the Gilberts told GIs that when the US Congress sent naval officer Charles Wilkes to explore these islands in 1841, "he was amazed at the beauty of the women." The booklets teased the GIs still more with the observation that even today on these atolls it was "not uncommon to see the natives bathing nude." A military pamphlet on Bali told American soldiers that the recent boom in tourism on the famed island was the result of picturesque scenery and ceremonious rituals, "to say nothing of the fact that some Balinese women still wear nothing above the waist."[45]

Prior to their introduction to the seedy night spots hugging military camps in the US, young American soldiers had often not caught so much as a glimpse of pictures of naked women. To be able, then, to watch some of the most beautiful live specimens of the other sex splash and dance in the nude on tropical islands would be the chance of a lifetime. In October 1941, a ship carrying American volunteer pilots to Burma brushed past the coasts of the Dutch East Indies. "What will tomorrow bring?" one airman dreamed in his diary. "Hopefully, a beautiful island and bare-breasted women in the Balinesian tradition!" It was a mirage that refused to evaporate entirely during the war. Three years later and thousands of miles away, amidst the battle for Saipan in the Marianas, soldiers on a landing craft that returned from the beachhead hurriedly updated sailors aboard the USS *Montpelier* about the goings on. They did not just talk war. "They told us," one seaman noted in his journal, "that the girls thought nothing of washing on the beach with no clothes on, some of them were good-looking."[46]

There lived among American soldiers, however, much more than the hope of laying eyes on the women of the Pacific and Orient. The very quality of otherness, of exoticism, had given rise to a mythology of women who were at the same time fiercely attractive and easily available. Moreover, the primitive had long been associated with unbridled lust. Already by the early nineteenth century, all this had turned the Pacific Basin of the American imagination into what Arrell Gibson has called a "hedonistic frontier." The themes of that frontier were not just leisure and physical beauty, but also sexual freedom. During the war with Britain in 1813, for example, when the first US Navy vessel, the *Essex*, entered the Pacific, its captain fired the crew on by promising them that the girls of the Sandwich Islands, later known as Hawaii, would gladly compensate them for the hardships endured while rounding Cape Horn.[47]

Booklets distributed aboard US vessels in World War II continued to play on a similar theme. On Yap Island, the *Guide to the Western Pacific* remarked, "the sex life of the natives has always been somewhat loose according to American standards." This was also true of the inhabitants of the Palau Islands, for example, where girls took lovers as soon as they reached puberty and thought nothing of making their favors available to all. Equally tantalizing images shrouded the Asian mainland, for the Western association of sexual promise with the Orient was much older even than that with the Pacific islands.[48]

Small wonder, then, that the sirens of the deep easily managed to lure young American soldiers with boundless sexual expectations into their tightly-knit nets. "[T]here were," one American observed of his fellow submarine officers in the Pacific, "several schools of thought about fidelity." One group categorically refused to abandon the principle. Another group believed that "when you crossed both the international date line and the equator . . . all bets were off and any pledges made on the other side of those lines were in temporary abeyance." The majority of men, he maintained, fell somewhere in between.[49]

That was exactly what people at home feared, and the American government consequently did what it could to prevent such suspicions from being fueled needlessly. As historian George Roeder has shown, for instance, US officials duly censored any photographs "suggesting that the war might unleash a soldier's sexuality." One of those was a photograph that showed a Filipino nurse who was busy administering an alcohol rub to a bare-chested American. The wounded GI lay on a cot in a church crowded with civilian worshipers. The sensuous Pacific might ignite an American soldier's sexuality anywhere anytime.[50]

GIs certainly did find unbridled sexual release in the whorehouses of the Pacific and Asia. The first stop overseas for many American soldiers was Hawaii. And, like the whalers before them a century earlier, they found it to be a place of utter sexual license. Prostitution was illegal in Hawaii, as it was on the mainland, but the military and the police had always looked the other way, and brothels had existed on the islands for decades. With the war, the number of customers swelled to unseen heights. An estimated 250,000 men a month paid three dollars for three minutes with a working girl. Waits in Honolulu could last hours, spilling into the streets. Brothels switched to production-line methods, with prostitutes not rarely servicing up to a hundred men a day. "The fellas have to line up . .," commented one sailor, "and be quick like a rabbit."

Similar scenes occurred in the South Seas. According to one witness, American sailors and marines in Nouméa, New Caledonia, stood in lines two blocks long, waiting for "prostitutes who were taking care of this mob of men as fast as they could." The fleshpots of the Asian mainland were no less rousing. "There has been much talk lately about the red-light district in Kweilin," a Flying Tiger noted in his diary in June 1942, "wild tales of unbelievable sights." The pilot decided to see for himself, accompanied by a friend. The scene overwhelmed them. Females of all ages, some no older than ten or twelve, stood shoulder to shoulder in the narrow alleys, as if watching a parade. But they were all prostitutes waiting for customers, and – giggling and chattering – they reached for the two Americans, pulling and grabbing them. "[W]e had," the incredulous pilot wrote after his narrow escape, "to dig our heels into the cobblestones to keep from being dragged into a brothel room."[51]

American soldiers had hoped, however, to find in this theater of war more than just unbridled sexual release in anonymous alleys. They wanted from it something infinitely more refined and erotic: the play of the temptress, the abandon of the concubine, the rapture of the harem. After all, they had been led to believe for so long that if such bliss existed, it was where they now served as soldiers. Their military guides again helped remind them of that promise. The 1945 *Guide to Japan*, for example, clearly enjoyed dwelling on the geisha, insisting that "she is not a prostitute, as many westerners suppose, but a highly trained entertainer whose business in life is to make men happy." These were the women GIs had truly hoped to meet in this war – beings created for the sole purpose of pleasing males.[52]

With much patience, and a touch of imagination, some soldiers did succeed in catching at least fleeting glimpses of these enchanting creatures. On Buariki Island, part of Tarawa atoll, native girls, so tells us naval historian Samuel Morison, submissively obeyed American orders to stay in the rear. There, in a deserted village, they quietly nursed marines: "They made palm-frond pillows for the wounded, fanned away flies, brought fresh water and made themselves generally useful." On the Asian mainland, kindred obedient spirits apparently did that and much more. In Singapore, American pilots claimed they slept with girls who entertained them throughout the night, caressing them with steaming towels from head to toe, never even mentioning the word "money." In China, noble peasant girls slipped out of their villages after dark and, without a word, joined Americans under their blankets on the river banks near Chihshui. Meanwhile, their sisters at Tengchung, according to another GI, "decided to offer themselves willingly to the Americans out of gratitude."[53]

This was the simple, primitive life, life as it had been intended to be. This was the world of natural splendor, of unrestrained emotions and uncorrupted instincts, of physical beauty and unrepressed sexuality. No wonder, then, that soldiers felt like guarding against the least corruption of this Shangri-la, resenting the smallest incursion by modern civilization. In New Guinea, one of the least explored islands in the world, a GI was enjoying the sights of a village that had probably not changed much in a thousand years. While observing a woman on her way back from a sparkling mountain stream, however, something suddenly irritated him terribly. "[I]nstead of the clay jar she once carried," the American noted disapprovingly, "she now had substituted a castoff army dehydrated potato can. It sat ugly and out of place atop her kinky head." Likewise, a soldier strolling through a village in Dutch New Guinea was deeply disappointed to learn that the natives here were sleeping on army cots and were using blankets and mosquito nets. "I can't understand why anyone wants to civilize these people," the GI complained, "as they are happy in their own primitive sort of way."[54]

American soldiers had the unique opportunity of seeing some of the world's last virgin areas knowing full well what had happened to all the others. An engineer who worked on the Ledo Road in the Burmese jungle in 1945, for instance, suddenly felt inspired to order "what sounds like a good book on Florida." That the volume's title was *That Vanishing Eden* was probably more than a coincidence. GIs painfully realized that they themselves were the vanguard of the very civilization they liked to imagine they were outrunning. "I caught the island in the passing of an era in its history," a soldier stated regretfully upon leaving New Guinea for the Philippines in October 1944, "for never again will white-sailed trading vessels lazily ply the coast. Never will sleepy ports wait weeks or months for a ship to call, for New Guinea has become part of our shrinking world."[55]

The regret extended from the primitive life of New Guinea's jungles all the way to the simple life of the Chinese countryside. When the chaplain of the Flying Tigers, who had served as a missionary in China before the war, looked around in the provincial town of Kunming, he could only shake his head at the whirling changes taking place. The Western suits and dresses of the newly rich, their glass-and-concrete suburban villas, it all reminded him "of wicked old prewar Shanghai." That they were carriers of the very germs that were poisoning the paradises they so jealously wanted to protect, was too much of an irony for American soldiers not to mull over. A sailor wrote to his wife in 1944 that on Hawaii he had seen how the native people's customs were one by one being "coarsened and cheapened now by war and money." "It made me pensive and sad," he confessed, "for I began to feel that all things are transient and fleeting, and is anything secure?"[56]

But the Pacific and Asia were vast enough to allow American soldiers the continued gratification of imagining that they had broken free from the clutches of civilization, owing to a war that had catapulted them into the world's most distant frontiers. They hurried to shed their old skins and take on new, more natural, identities. From Kipling's *Jungle Books* it was, for instance, only a small step to Baden-Powell's Boy Scouts. "Now I'll believe anything," Mack Morriss cried out in his diary on Guadalcanal in January 1943, "just ran into Louie Kinch." Louie Kinch had been the war correspondent's scout-master when he was a boy in Tennessee. Even without the scoutmasters, however, boys' adventures spontaneously resumed on the many unknown and mysterious islands. Newly arrived on Ulithi atoll, a pilot curiously looked around. All kinds of questions raced through his mind. Where would he live? Where could he go to the toilet? Could you eat the coconuts? Were there natives? "It was," he admitted, "like my first day at Boy Scout camp." An engineer who had just landed on the steamy island of Espíritu Santo was less apprehensive. He immediately proceeded to cut the sleeves off his shirt and remodel his trousers into shorts. "I look like a Boy Scout," the contented soldier reported to his parents. The Americans on this island were apparently behaving like them, too. A month later, the engineer urged his parents to send the Swedish knife an uncle had once bought him because, he claimed, all his comrades were carrying similar knives on their belts.[57]

Primeval islands succeeded in transporting soldiers back to exhilarating times much older than their recent boyhoods. The same pilot who had felt like a Boy Scout upon arrival at Ulithi was soon enjoying swims in one of the atoll's many secluded lagoons for a very particular reason. "I always felt when I swam there that no one had ever gone swimming on that beach before," he relished, "it was sort of a Robinson Crusoe feeling, of being outside human existence, and alone." Submerged in isolation that could be as thrilling as it was disquieting, the Crusoe analogy easily occurred to others, too. In September 1943, a P-38 pilot crashed in the New Guinean interior, some 400 miles from his base in Port Moresby. For weeks he tried to make his way back to civilization without encountering a single soul. He was totally startled, therefore, when one day he came upon the contour of a bare human foot in a river bank. Almost inevitably, that was the very moment he "thought of Robinson Crusoe when he discovered Friday's footprint in the sand."[58]

At sea, soldiers' imaginations liked to drift back to times when freebooters had turned their backs on civilization and had created their own societies and rules. Aboard the *Cristobal* in February 1942, soldiers sailing from New York to Melbourne metamorphosed as soon as their ship broke free from Panama's locks. "Some of the boys are raising mustaches, beards, or just not shaving," observed an MP. "Look like pirates of Capt. Kidd." Sailors played their new roles with fervor. Early in 1944, an officer aboard the tug *Tern* described the crew to his wife. They looked "fierce and exotic," he said, with their deep tans, bushy beards and uncombed hair, their naked torsos and bare feet, dungaree trousers rolled up to the knees. Moreover, they had resorted to a custom that was fast becoming popular among American sailors all over the Pacific: they were wearing "gold or some odd-shaped earrings," on the left side only. "Of course," the officer added, "when we get in port, they get all cleaned up, but out at sea everyone is natural."[59]

Boy Scouts, Robinson Crusoes, buccaneers – in some way they were all different manifestations of one and the same instinct trying to break through the veneer of culture. They were faces of a primitivism that was a recurrent phenomenon in complex Western societies, urging men, as historian Hayden White has put it, "to be themselves, to give vent to their original, natural, but subsequently repressed, desires; to throw off the restraints of civilization."[60]

To step across that defining threshold could be unsettling initially. In January 1945, a group of sailors arrived on the beach of one of the Palau Islands. They checked whether there were women around, stripped, then went about their activities stark naked. One of the men at first felt thoroughly uneasy about it all. "God, what scenes and postures!" he later told his wife in a letter. "There is, to me, something almost ludicrous and ridiculous in an awkward, human, naked body." But it took him less than a day to become somewhat of a believer. "Conversely," he admitted towards the end of the same letter, "it really felt good to strip to the skin and run in the waves, and feel the sun on me and the warm wind." He closed on a naughty note, quickly adding: "I hope that someday we can have a private area where we can cavort in the nude with absolute freedom."[61]

New converts were easily given to zealotry in promoting naturalism. One officer tried to convince his wife that he had seen so many bare breasts in one year in New Guinea, that he did not even pay attention to them anymore. "You know," he lectured, "it isn't human nature for a woman to cover her breasts any more than her lips." As time went on, ever more soldiers lost the self-consciousness even of their own nakedness. It came to the point, for instance, where the *Guide to India* had to warn that in this country people did, in fact, resent exposure of the body and that GIs were, therefore, expected to wear trunks when swimming. A lieutenant of the 43rd Division thoroughly resented the arrival of American nurses near their area in New Guinea in November 1944. "There are just enough of them to be a nuisance," he grumbled in a letter home. "We have had to put canvas screens around showers, latrines, etc – and to wear bathing trunks on the beach. Gone is the life uninhibited."[62]

Stripped of many of their clothes, if not all of them, GIs continued the worshiping of the sun that for many had already started on the trip over.

Soldiers attached remarkable importance to deep tans. Those who were given desk jobs or sent into the jungle, for instance, routinely fretted about their fading color. Tans were, after all, exotic coatings hiding the pallid stigma of the spoiled world they had left behind. When the USS *Admiralty Islands* anchored near an island in the Pacific in August 1944, a sailor caught sight of a colony of naked GIs basking in the warm rays. "Some of them are so brown from the sun," he commented, "that they would almost pass for natives themselves."[63]

That was not necessarily something to be ashamed of. To become native was, in a sense, to tap into the wellsprings of physical and sexual rejuvenation. In August 1944, men of the 244th Port Company, unloading ships at Biak Island, were challenging each other to see who could lift the heaviest weight. A college boy from New York City relished this particular game as much as he did the overall strenuous life overseas that healed the modern split between body and mind. It reminded him of the past, he said in his diary. "I mean," he clarified, "the past when men gathered with men and demonstrated physical strength. The days of pirates, woodsmen, frontiersmen, rugged farmers, etc. Those sorts of men, proud and reveling in their strength. In civilization such occurrences do not happen."[64]

Some months later, in Luzon, Filipino men were talking to this same soldier about the sexual behavior of the Japanese. There were women present, but that did not stop the locals from going into graphic detail and showing Japanese condoms. "That embarrassed me at first," confessed the young American, "but it didn't seem to faze any of them. In fact, the 20-year-old girl proceeded to nurse the baby while talking to us. In a moment, it all seemed quite natural to me, especially in that atmosphere and place."[65]

To allow oneself to become dissolved in wilderness, primitive existence, the simple life, was to participate in the regeneration not only of primal and virtuous society but of original and unspoiled man. And in the Edenic environments of this faraway world, the reflex of wholly abandoning oneself to nature proved highly contagious. In November 1943, men of the 592nd Engineer Amphibian Regiment visited a village in New Guinea. A local missionary accompanied the Americans to help them communicate. The encounter went very well, and when the soldiers boarded their vessel again, cheerful villagers with brightly colored flowers in their hair lined the beach to say goodbye. "We fell into the gay mood," an American wrote, "and soon had these blossoms in our helmet straps." "As we left the inlet," the GI continued in his journal, "the group of brown figures stood knee-deep in water, backed by towering palms and jungle greenness, each fuzzy head topped by a flaming hibiscus, waving a reluctant farewell."[66]

3
Missionaries

The romantic myths of the Happy Isles and *bons sauvages* of the Pacific and the Shangri-las and noble peasants of Asia had been fed by old traditions as well as modern mass media. Where American soldiers' contact with the lands and peoples to the west was of a superficial and fleeting nature, these myths seemed clearly borne out by arcadian appearances and the simple lives of carefree villagers. But encounters with the naked realities of this dreamed-up world, whether momentary or prolonged, just as easily shattered the fragile myths of paradise, leading to a disillusionment as bitter as the expectations had been sweet.

The official military guides played an ambivalent role in the soldiers' volatile opinions of the new frontier. In various subtle and less subtle ways they helped to fan myths like those of uninhibited Pacific islanders and Jeffersonian Chinese peasants. Yet at the same time, they were issuing warnings against overly romantic notions of the region. Fearing perhaps that the GIs might still be lumping together all Pacific islands in the category of 'romantic South Sea,' the 1945 *Guide to Okinawa* thought it necessary to remind the soldiers: "If you were a tourist, you wouldn't put the Nansei Islands high on your 'must' list." Okinawa was, the pocket guide insisted, "NO PARADISE." That same year, it took a military pamphlet two pages and a title in equally bold capitals to inform American forces in the China theater that "THIS IS NOT THE CHINA OF THE MOVIES."[1]

Hawaii posed a particularly stubborn problem for the military. This island group was a part of paradise that the US had made sure to annex in the late nineteenth century. As a result, its virtues had been promoted with special fervor in American novels, movies, songs, and tourist brochures. The stark contrast between the Hollywood version of America's domesticated paradise and the realities of wartime Hawaii caused so much disappointment among GIs that it affected morale on the islands. The authorities decided to attack the problem of disillusion at the root. The Army Information Branch, for example, published a *Guide to Hawaii* that was to be issued to all soldiers en route to the islands. The pocket guide used straightforward language in an effort to debunk several of the tenacious myths of paradise. Still, disappointment with Hawaii persisted throughout the war. Soldiers on the island of Oahu, for instance, gave vent to their frustration by calling it "The Rock."[2]

It was not only in Hawaii that GIs began to see through the Edenic trappings. Against the backdrop of what was a rich and complex romantic mythology, disenchantment became widespread and multifaceted both in the Pacific and in Asia. To begin with, in a region that had been heralded for centuries as one of unimaginable riches and splendor, from the gold of the Solomons to the silk of China, American soldiers were shocked by the poverty they encountered. That the naked natives of Pacific islands had few possessions was part of the expectation and charm. But to the pervasive poverty that haunted Asia's ancient cultures, GIs could respond only with utter disbelief.

US military pamphlets suggested that stagnation was the root of the problem in these once great empires. This explanation, for China in particular, tapped into much older American images of a civilization whose backwardness was the result of a lack of dynamism. The official guides found it all too easy to illustrate this inertia and its inherent contradictions. China had invented gunpowder, for example, yet had fallen prey to all kinds of aggressors. It had contributed enormously to mathematics and astronomy, but its people still adhered to ancient superstitions. It had made great medical discoveries, but disease remained rampant. It had developed advanced irrigation and terracing long ago, yet today's peasants suffered hunger by the millions.[3]

There were similar hints at endemic stagnation to explain India's backwardness. "You might also have been suddenly struck," one booklet pointed out, "that this, the ancient East, was Bible country." Here, too, an Asian culture had reached an admirable level of development, and had then become frozen in time.[4]

Soldiers echoed these opinions. In August 1944, an officer scrutinized the ancient shrines and temples that dotted the Indian countryside as his train rolled from Bombay to Calcutta. "All convinces one of the fact," he wrote, "that this was a civilized country when the natives of the western world were in the stone age." Yet three months later, taking a closer look at the part of China where he was now stationed, he noted: "The Chinese may be the oldest people in the world but have made little change in methods of living." Likewise, what an American surgeon saw while attached to the Chinese Forty-sixth Army in 1944, quickly convinced him that "China could not go on fighting this war in the fashion of the Middle Ages."[5]

Whatever the exact explanation for the backwardness, GIs agreed that the levels of poverty were appalling. The official guides did what they could to prepare the soldiers for this aspect. "In India," warned one booklet, "you will see more beggars with more pitiful faces and misshapen bodies than you have seen before." "You may be shocked, at first," admitted another, "to see how desperately poor most Chinese are." The 1945 *Guide to Japan* pointed out that, even before the war, poverty had been "the common lot" in this Asian country, too, where even city clerks lived in bamboo shacks and used buckets as toilets.[6]

Still, to experience poverty up close – to smell it especially – was much more unsettling than to read about it. In the 1930s, China's population had approached half a billion people. Ninety percent of them were small farmers; two-thirds of those were poor peasants trying to scrape together a living with subsistence farming. Whenever the wind blew in from the distant villages, an officer in Kunming, China, noted in 1945, the air suddenly turned "musty and unpleasant." It was the odor of animals, of charcoal and cow dung fires, of heat and sweat, mixed with the stink of squalor, overcrowding, garbage, and open sewers. It was, said an intelligence officer in a poor *barrio* of Dulag in the Philippines, "the fecal smell of the Orient." The peculiar odor clung to soldiers across Asia. "The Chinese section is quite apart from the British area," noted a Flying Tiger during a stopover in Singapore, "definitely oriental and smelly."[7]

Nowhere, however, did the repugnant smell seem to be worse than in India. One GI called it the country's "most distinctive point." Illusions did not stand the least chance amidst such stench. "According to the Indian Chamber of Commerce here," an ironic private wrote to a friend, "this country is supposed to be the land of mystery, romance and beauty. It sure is a mystery to me where the beauty and romance come in . . ."[8]

It was in India that soldiers were confronted also with some of the most shocking poverty of any of the war theaters. Paupers lined the railroads that rushed GIs to Indian destinations close to Burma. At every stop, disheveled old beggars and crippled children besieged the cars in wrenching scenes that soldiers found hard to stomach. "Mother, I hate to ruin all your beautiful ideas of India," chided an airman, "but I am afraid that it isn't anything like the stories that you read say it is. As a matter of fact, India is one of the dirtiest and most undesirable places on earth."[9]

The squalor spilled over into the Pacific islands hugging the mainland. Americans described the Okinawans as "the most miserable people . . . who inhabited the earth." They were "not very clean personally," and lived in houses that were "utterly filthy." According to correspondent Robert Sherrod, farmhouses on Saipan, in the Marianas, reflected such "sad indigence" that they would have embarrassed "a tobacco road sharecropper."[10]

Those stationed in the region long enough developed such sensitivity to the peculiar smell of indigence that they could detect it as far away as the South Seas. In early 1943, a marine was sent to New Caledonia. Previously, he had served in Burma, India, and China as a Flying Tiger for about half a year. Upon arrival in the South Pacific, the American sniffed the air: "A hot and sticky feeling, a feeling that had become only too familiar was back again. Yes, there were filthy and dirty people as well . . ."[11]

Such repugnant realities fueled a whole series of negative views that contended with the positive Western myths about the people of Asia and the Pacific. Yet those negative views were not necessarily new and original, nor always the exclusive result of direct observation. Quite often, they were rekindled versions of negative stereotypes that had smoldered for decades, sometimes even centuries, in Western thought. They formed part of the contradictory mythologies of otherness that had quite easily combined romantic with derogatory attitudes. The ever-present counterpart of primitivism, for instance, was savagism. If the noble lives of South Sea primitives beckoned emulation, then the darker side of these savages – like that of the American Indians – warranted constant vigilance, if necessary even exorcism. In a similar vein, if European explorers of India had given the West dreams of maharajas and spices, British colonists had added warnings of coolies and religious fanatics. American images of China had also been subject to wild fluctuations, resulting from what historian Akira Iriye has called "the traditional love-hate relationship between the two peoples." Pearl Buck's romantic novels of noble Chinese peasants thus made sure to paper over negative notions of the Middle Kingdom that dated as far back as the arrival of American traders in the late eighteenth century.[12]

The whole concept of the exotism of the region posed a problem in itself. GIs could be attracted to it because of its beauty, its mystique, its sensuality. They could, however, just as easily reject it as outlandish, thus precluding any deeper understanding of the other. Indeed, the extravagance of custom and dress could take the open-mindedness of Americans to its limit – and beyond. The US military tried hard, for example, to prepare soldiers for the eccentricities of the New Guineans: "You'll be able to spot the home locality of a man by his type of loin cloth or his penis covering of shell, gourd, or bark, and of a woman by the cut of her grass skirt or kilt. Such things as body ornaments, tattoo marks, strange hair-dos, and nose plugs will also show where natives come from." Yet in the face of such gaping cultural divides, the exotism of beauty threatened to turn into an exotism of the ridiculous. It gave rise to denigrating descriptions of New Guineans as "oversized roosters with green tails and white headfeathers." "Some of 'em have so many ferns on 'em," remarked one soldier on the same island, "that they look like a bush."

That kind of cultural insensitivity carried the risk of reducing the strange other to nothing more than an object with entertainment value. A lieutenant stationed on an unidentified island in the Pacific tried in vain to catch the ludicrousness of the natives' habits and gestures in a letter to his family. He finally dismissed it all laughingly by saying that there was "a perpetual minstrel show going on."[13]

With behavior turning into performance, natural habitats threatened to become zoos. On Espíritu Santo, word spread in 1943 that "cannibals" lived in the remoter areas of the island. This apparently set in motion a form of tourist activity. "Occasionally," said one marine, "we would make a trip into the hills and take a look at these primitive people with bones piercing their nostrils and ear lobes."[14]

From zoo to circus was only a small step. Flying Tigers training in Burma in the summer of 1941 loved to visit the teak plantations in their time off to look at the elephants that hauled timber. "Their circus memories made this seem a big deal," commented their chaplain, "a bargain, a free treat." But American circuses had put on display more than Asia's exotic animals. The *Guide to Burma* told GIs that, if they were lucky, they might catch a glimpse of "the celebrated Padaung women who are known to our circus goers because of the coils of wire which have stretched their necks to giraffelike proportions." They too could now be gaped at for free.[15]

In observing the locals, American soldiers assumed they could measure intelligence on the basis of outward appearances. In a letter home, one sailor called New Guinea "the jumping off place of the world." He added: "And you might guess about the intelligence of the natives by the pictures I had made with two of them." Extravagant exotism was considered sufficient proof in itself of arrested development. A sailor carefully observed the pierced noses and tattoo marks of the natives on Manus Island. "Rather an unkempt sort," was his instant verdict, "little evidence of civilization."[16]

The shabby look of poverty lead to similar interpretations. In the early 1940s, two US officers who had inspected Chinese forces near Chungking put in a report to their superiors that the artillery officers were of very poor quality. The commander of the battery they had visited, for instance, "was not of a very high order of intelligence." "He was barefooted except for sandals," the officers gave as explanation.[17]

In contrast, later in the war an American surgeon had a chance to observe general Li at Kweilin. Li was larger and taller than the average Chinese; he had a well-rounded head, with a close-cropped military haircut. "He is a handsome man," the doctor said, "with very little of the nasal depression and ocular slant of his race." He looked, in other words, more like an American than a Chinese officer. This obviously facilitated the American's warm opinion of him. "He is a good officer," insisted the surgeon, "and certainly an intelligent man."[18]

If those who looked Western rose in the hierarchy of intelligence quite spontaneously, then those who were able to communicate in the leading language of Western civilization ascended the ladder of esteem even more quickly. American soldiers routinely dismissed natives' estimates of enemy numbers, distances, and water depths as poor and unreliable. They never stopped to think, however, that they expected these people to express themselves in an unfamiliar language and equally puzzling miles and fathoms. The gift of English, therefore, instantly transformed the locals into more intelligent beings by its very virtue of making them intelligible to GIs. "The Philippines are quite different from New Guinea," a fighter pilot told his family. "Several of the people I have run into can speak fairly good English. Some of them are very intelligent."[19]

Like the Greeks who had classified as *barbaros* anyone who did not speak Greek, so to Americans cultural redemption was possible for anyone who spoke English, even on New Guinea. In a mission village, a GI eventually managed to get better acquainted with at least one New Guinean, a boy who spoke English fairly well. Not only was he a "handsome kid." "He is," said the soldier, "one of the brightest of the mission boys and a fine specimen of a native with a bearing much superior to his fellow Fuzzy Wuzzies."[20]

Satisfactory communication remained impossible, however, with many of the locals in Asia and the Pacific. Such a lack of communication precluded a nuanced knowledge of the people, gave rise to various misinterpretations, and ultimately led to the disapproval of much that was misunderstood or not understood at all.

Already in the sixteenth century, French philosopher Michel de Montaigne observed, "each man calls barbarism whatever is not his own practice." The observation was no less true of the American soldiers of the mid-twentieth century. As youngsters in the 1920s and 1930s, for example, they had learned from history schoolbooks that each race had an inherent and distinctive moral character, and that some races were simply morally inferior to others. Such lessons had left their marks. GIs of the 1940s could interpret the absence of inhibitions as a charming aspect of a natural, simple life. But they could just as well read it as a disturbing lack of modesty and, in a broader sense, of morals.[21]

Nudity itself, for instance, risked becoming an irritant, a danger US military guides were aware of and tried to prepare the soldiers for. Over and over again, official publications told GIs that, from New Guinea to China and Okinawa, they should expect naked children, mothers nursing their babies in public, and men relieving themselves in full view. "Though this is a region of considerable nakedness," the *Guide to the Dutch East Indies* tried to reassure, "the people, nevertheless, have their own strict standards of decency and morality, and they rarely expose their bodies completely."[22]

Signs of modesty where the soldiers had not expected them were usually greeted with strong approval. "The men seemed extremely modest in front of us," a battalion surgeon in a New Guinean village told his wife. "When they sat down, they carefully pulled their dirty loincloths down." A lieutenant who arrived in the Philippines in 1945 was satisfied to report to his spouse in Syracuse, New York: "The Philippines (sic) pride themselves on being fully clothed except for shoes and a few even wear those."

Meanwhile, American soldiers did whatever they could to raise the natives' standards of morality. In New Guinea, for example, GIs handed out underwear to naked children and WACs freely parted with their bras. Some soldiers even distributed mattress covers, hoping that the women would cut holes in the tops and wear them as dresses.[23]

Nothing upset Americans more, however, than the natives' blunt exposure of their most private body parts while openly and unthinkingly relieving themselves. Disgusted soldiers reported from India that people relieved themselves in the streets "to their bowels content." As late as the spring of 1945, GIs were shaking their heads in disbelief at the Filipinos' habit of urinating where they stood. "[N]o stop, no stoop, no squint," said an incredulous soldier on Luzon. "When you gotta go you gotta go." Perhaps no American was taken aback more than the officer in a public toilet in Deetah in southeast China. He had just taken possession of one of its holes, when a local woman came in, took over the hole next to him, and started up a friendly conversation in an unintelligible dialect. It left the American speechless and, one might imagine, utterly constipated. Fortunately, there seemed to be less embarrassment in store for GIs heading to Burma. In this country at least, the official guide announced, Americans were to find "a privacy in going to the rear that is supposed to obtain in the best of our western civilization."[24]

There seemed to be many more indications of the lack of morals in this vast region. Sloth was certainly one of them in the eyes of soldiers who came from a society where youthful energy and boisterous dynamism were celebrated and cultivated. "You may think many of them move slowly and take life easy," said the *Guide to the Dutch East Indies*. It cautioned, however, not to "jump to the conclusion that they are lazy." But to soldiers who had been taught that time was inextricably linked with productivity and therefore to be managed and controlled jealously, any careless handling of this most precious of all commodities easily seemed wasteful, if not sinful.[25]

Indolence was perhaps most understandable on the Pacific islands. "Some Europeans will tell you that the native islanders are lazy," the *Guide to New Caledonia* warned. The American booklet, however, preferred to play on the theme of the Garden of Paradise, pointing out to GIs that these people could afford to be laid back because fish, game, fruit, and the drink and food of coconuts – long known in the West as the "lazy man's crop" – were simply there for the taking. Still, their languor could irritate American soldiers, too. On 24 July 1942, an officer watched New Caledonians purchase fresh produce from natives who had arrived by boat from other islands. The scene prompted a scathing comment in his diary: "Too damn lazy to develop any vegetable gardens here and the soil is ideal for them." A report on the Saidor operation in New Guinea, in which American troops had employed countless locals, concluded with a tone of resignation: "The natives cannot be hurried."[26]

If Pacific islanders could still be considered, according to a report on the Schouten Islands, as "pleasantly lazy," then the lethargy of people like the Chinese was harder to condone. A military booklet on the Middle Kingdom summarized one of the most stubborn GI complaints as: "The Chinese won't work. They take it easy." The GIs refused to agree, however, that this was, as the guide claimed, a "fiction." It was not just that they were, as an officer said in 1944, "not very time-conscious." The problem went much deeper than that, all the way to the root of stagnation. "Nothing is ever thoroughly repaired," explained another American officer in 1945, "just patched and repatched, nor is it due to 7 or 8 years of Jap or Sino war, it is just common procedure with these people."

From such observations Americans derived conclusions not only about cultural stagnation, but about racial inferiority. Sailors from a carrier who, at the end of the war, visited a machine shop at Yokosuka near Tokyo Bay, were stunned to discover that the Japanese had been working here from a sitting position. "How could a race that sat down to do their work," an American seaman asked himself, "hope to overcome a people who stood up and moved about while working."[27]

People who lacked a firm work ethic could be expected to resort to stealing. Military pamphlets warned GIs that thieves were at large even in the paradisaical Pacific. In its history of the Marianas, one booklet thought it necessary to mention that in 1521 Magellan had originally named the islands *Ladrones* or 'Thieves,' "presumably because of the character of the natives." A 1943 booklet that instructed American soldiers in how to deal with the New Guineans, told them in no uncertain terms: "Natives are skillful thieves." None of the guides bothered to explain such behavior in a context of differing rules of property, the appeal of unknown Western goods, or sheer poverty.[28]

Whatever the explanation, soldiers learned that opinions of the islanders as disarmingly honest were often thoroughly misguided. GIs who bought coconuts in a New Guinean village in 1943 claimed that the natives had first drained the milk from them. "We had been skinned," bristled one of them, and "felt very much put out at our ignorance of natives." When the natives of Guadalcanal began leaving their mountain hideouts early in 1943, a disillusioned colonel wrote: "They steal everything not tied down." Before long, expectations of islander virtuousness became reversed. "The natives are very well behaved," wrote a pleasantly surprised airplane mechanic on Tanna Island in the New Hebrides in 1943, "and so far they have taken nothing that was not given to them . . ."[29]

The popular image of the Chinese as a people of reliable, hardy peasants evaporated even faster. The grinding poverty of the wartorn country formed a fertile breeding ground for black marketers who were drawn to the wealth of American matériel like moths to a flame. At training centers near Kunming, Americans had to be constantly vigilant as Chinese work-men made off with anything from gasoline and spare motor parts to nails. Local drivers even drained the brake fluid from American trucks to sell it in nearby towns.[30]

American soldiers in the field had similar disturbing experiences. Merrill's Marauders, for instance, lodged chronic complaints about the behavior of the Chinese troops fighting by their side. "For the first time," said one of them in northern Burma in 1944, "we were to experience the Chinese sol-diers' careless habit of making off with everything not tied down or person-ally carried." Much of this was the result of the rickety Chinese supply system. The Chinese central government gave cash allowances to unit com-manders with which to procure food and some of the equipment. But com-manders did not hesitate to siphon money off to their own pockets, sometimes even causing their troops to go hungry. It was just one aspect of what Americans in China came to call 'squeeze.' The word referred to wide-spread habits of embezzlement, extortion, bribes, and commissions – in short, to the kind of chronic corruption through which Chinese of all ranks tried to improve their abominable living standards.[31]

It came to the point where American authorities felt obliged to address what one official pamphlet described as the "seamy side" of China. While some GIs had become witting participants in corrupt affairs (especially black-market operations), there were indications that most Americans were growing increasingly disgusted by the crookedness of Chinese society. The GI guides tried their best to play down the corruptness of America's Asian allies, one booklet in 1944 awkwardly claiming that the Chinese were merely "intensely practical people." But GIs insisted that their 'allies' were just plain dishonest, unscrupulous, and unreliable. "[S]tealing," concluded an indignant pilot after having visited Kunming's vast black market, "was legal in the Orient."[32]

That same lawless atmosphere also spawned unmitigated violence and chronic warfare. The *Guide to the Western Pacific* described the natives of the Gilbert Islands as "a war-like race." It sketched their past in rather fan-tastic pictures of warriors "[c]lad in coconut-mat armor and armed with shark-teeth swords and the tail of the poisonous sting ray." They were said to have "fought each other in frequent wars," and occasionally to have included "the massacre of a few whites in the general sport." For hundreds of years, said a guide to the South Seas, New Caledonia, too, had been "a feasting ground" for warring tribes. Soldiers who cared to examine the island's shell hillocks, the booklet claimed, would come across bleached bones and skulls that offered "a gruesome explanation of the feasting."[33]

In this vast part of the world there often remained nothing more than the harsh natural law under which whomever proved strongest dictated the terms. That seemed to be especially true among the teeming masses of the Asian mainland. American stereotypes of the Orient as a world of endless intrigue and feuding were, after all, much older than Pearl Buck's images of loyal and peaceful Chinese peasants. Amidst the chaos of war, those older stereotypes were easily brought back to mind. In March 1945, troops of the 6th Division were assigned to garrison duty in Manila, which had just been liberated. In no time, one of the battalion surgeons was shoved into the role of assistant medical examiner. An overburdened major quickly filled the newcomer in on the desperate situation: "There's gang warfare going on and we're fishing bodies out of the Pasig River all the time. Everybody is trying to control the black market, prostitution, and various rackets including stealing and fencing. There are political factions vying for control of the system in preparation for independence."[34]

If Americans thought Manila was bad, they found China to be even more chaotic. The Middle Kingdom of factiousness and warlordism lived up to its old reputation. Though Chiang Kai-shek, the Generalissimo, liked to pretend he had everything under control, Americans in the field knew better. Even without encountering Mao's communists in the north, GIs saw enough of China's internal dissension to understand that the tumor was growing larger and uglier by the day. Naval intelligence officers operating on the coasts of southeast China in search of downed Japanese planes could not move around without specially trained Chinese guerrillas as bodyguards. These offered badly needed protection not just against Japanese troops and collaborating forces, but against the local population of whom, according to one American, everyone had turned either "robber, bandit, or pirate." Cliques and clans all over China quarreled and bickered, challenging the central government and its Western ally. In the spring of 1942, for example, American volunteer airmen in Yunnan grew so wary of the troops of a seasoned warlord known as 'the Old Tiger,' that they decided to order pistols and machine guns from Kunming for personal protection. "Hopefully," one American prayed in his diary, "I will not be murdered in my bed."[35]

If factiousness and violence in society at large pointed to obvious barbarism, then the lack of family values was considered to be a still clearer indication of moral degradation. American soldiers were particularly sensitive about the treatment of those they considered to be the weaker, most vulnerable members of the family: children, but also women. Even in the Edenic surroundings of the Pacific, GIs came across evidence of uncommonly brutal behavior towards children. They claimed New Guineans thought nothing of punishing children by charring their faces, and from Bougainville they reported that natives actually marked their children with branding irons. American soldiers who made stopovers in Bali turned away in disgust from ceremonies in which girls were held down to the ground while men forcefully filed their teeth.[36]

Such disrespect for children came perhaps as less of a surprise on the Asian mainland. Ever since the early nineteenth century, reports on the barbaric treatment of children in Asia had filtered through to the US, and evidence of infanticide in China and India had particularly revolted Americans. Recent schoolbooks had presented these countries as increasingly enlightened in such matters, but GIs who had the opportunity of verifying the information on the spot quickly proved their teachers wrong. A pilot stationed at Kunming recalled, "I witnessed many women in inland China, when I was nearly thirty years old, whose feet had been bound long after I had been instructed in school that no longer was there any such binding." By 1945, at least one official guide found it necessary to spend time on convincing the GIs that "the Chinese love children and go to what lengths they can to take good care of them."[37]

The sexual abuse of children in Asia remained a particularly sore point. It too had received much attention in the American press from the earliest contacts of traders and missionaries with this continent. The preference for young girls and boys had traditionally been seen as the most convincing proof of the sexual depravity of Asians. Nothing much seemed to have changed by the 1940s. American volunteer pilots on their way to China in 1941 had barely touched land in Singapore when they caught a glimpse of someone who was said to be the Sultan of Johore and who, the story went, was notorious for his involvement in "the delinquency of minors." Near the end of the war, an American surgeon, involved in the closing down of brothels in Manila, explained to his wife: "They were employing girls of minor age. It's such an accepted institution over here that it is almost shocking in its frankness."[38]

Infanticide, foot binding, teeth filing, the prostitution of minors – all were evidence of a barbaric behavior towards female children in particular. In American accusations of barbarism, the debasement of women had traditionally been a focal point of attention. One of the most persistent images of American Indians, for example, had been that of idle warriors behaving tyrannically towards squaws who lived the lives of overburdened workhorses. Strikingly similar criticisms were leveled against the men of the Pacific and Asia during the war. US military guides tried to prepare soldiers for cultures that treated women like inferiors and expected them to do much of what Americans considered men's work. In New Guinea, women were "shut out" from most important community affairs and forced to do "a lot of the hard work;" in India, wives were "kept more secluded than western women;" while in Japan women were "rigidly repressed" from childhood, and legally were no more than "the servants of men." Only in Burma, clarified one GI booklet, did women "enjoy an amount of freedom unusual in non-European races." Still, even there the education of girls was said to be largely neglected.

Such discrimination and disrespect could only come from men who did not love their wives and daughters. "The Japs don't understand the love we have for our women," Cary Grant said in *Destination Tokyo*, a movie shown during the war. "They don't even have a word for it in their language." The 1945 *Guide to Japan* heartily agreed with Grant's version. "Starved for affection," it told GIs in its section on Japanese women, "they blossom like flowers under kindness and many Americans, who are usually gentle and affectionate with women, frequently wonder how such lovely women can produce such brutes of sons." Nothing irritated GIs more than the sight of women treated as beasts of burden by Asian brutes. When a middle-aged couple entered the American lines on Okinawa in June 1945, high-strung marines shouted at the man to take the huge bundle from his wife's head. A fray ensued when one of the offended marines tried to force the man to be chivalrous while his wife refused to let go of her few possessions.[39]

Gender lines in Asia and the Pacific were blurred in more than one disturbing way. Husbands might expect wives to take on men's roles where it concerned hard labor. Yet men also played the part of women with the least embarrassment. In describing the Chinese theater tradition, for instance, one pamphlet informed GIs that all women's roles were acted by men and that there was thus no point "in sending flowers around to the stage door for the leading lady." But Asian males dressed for the part even outside the theater. For centuries, Chinese men had been laughed at in the West for the gowns they wore and their braided pigtails. In 1944 a correspondent reported from Saipan that in a Japanese command post on Hill 650, soldiers in their hurry had left behind "silk underwear and fine (but tiny) black boots." American soldiers had similar experiences with Pacific islanders. "We were especially interested in the natives who appeared along shore," said a marine during a stopover at Samoa, "and rather surprised to find that the figures in red skirts, riding bicycles, were really young men."

Such blatant shows of effeminacy and transvestism inevitably led to suspicions of latent homosexuality. In 1945 an American officer in the Pingyang district dared not refuse the request from his host, a magistrate, to pose with him for a picture. They did so "like two proper Oriental buddies" – holding hands. The picture shows a grinning, relaxed Chinese next to an American with stiff bearing and forced smile.

Sexual identities were even more confused among Pacific islanders, long notorious in the West for their unashamed acceptance of male homosexuality. When medics of the 608th Clearing Company visited a New Guinean village in 1944, they asked one of the men to perform a native dance. The villager obliged with gusto, decorated his hair with flowers, started beating a can, and in no time was swaying his hips chanting. "Then he circled around one of the men," said a rather embarrassed surgeon, "beating on the can over his head. His movements seemed to have a definite sexual significance."[40]

American alertness to the effeminacy of Asian and Pacific males was in part the reflection of a longstanding Western tradition of representing less advanced cultures as both feminine and childlike. Indeed, American soldiers attributed childlike qualities to the peoples of this region even more freely than they did feminine traits. This should come as no surprise if one knows that from the 1890s to the 1930s, history schoolbooks had unvaryingly taught American children to think of North American Indians, for example, as an essentially infantile race.

The comparison with children literally forced itself on American soldiers to whom the peoples from New Caledonia to the Dutch East Indies and India appeared to be terribly small and fragile. GI descriptions of locals could make them sound like veritable Lilliputians. A pilot of the Tenth Air Force had wanted to take up archery in India but, he wrote in a letter home, "the Indians are puny around here and their bows are like toothpicks in our hands."

If their physical appearance made them look like permanent children, incapable of growing up, then their mental state did much to confirm that impression. They were, for instance, extremely excitable. "There may be a great deal of jabbering and shouting in the village when you first arrive," a GI guide to New Guinea warned with adult detachment. "Keep cool and be patient; it will simmer down." A GI observing New Guinean laborers in 1942 stereotyped them as "chattering like a bunch of monkeys." Western novelties elicited responses reminiscent of the way children received toys. When some natives were presented with lead pencils in a village in New Guinea, they put them in their fuzzy hair, pranced around, and proudly showed them off to the others. "I was again impressed," commented one American, "with their childish simplicity." As late as June 1944, when many a plane had already landed on the strip near Mount Hagen, hundreds of New Guineans were still gesticulating, laughing, and running alongside each new plane that taxied past them.

Scenes of childish naiveté were by no means limited to New Guinea. "The Chinese are as natural as children," said an amused American in Liuchow as he watched them come and go in the midst of an opera, "they do what they want to do when they want to do it." A nurse in India shared the sentiment. In September 1944 she was eagerly awaiting the start of an important Muslim celebration that would break the monotony of hospital life in Assam. "I hope," she told her parents in Iowa, "that we may be able to go watch them for awhile tonight as it should be interesting. These people are childlike in many ways."[41]

Serious work did not interest such people. It was not just that they appeared lazy; they simply did not seem to have the attention span of adults. "They are willing workers . . ," noted an engineer who employed natives on Kolombangara Island, "but some one has to watch them all the time or they will sit down and play." Of the natives of Kusaie Island in the

Carolines, a military guide predicted that no offer of wages would convince them to become laborers. "But," the booklet explained, "if work is organized as a game or other form of competition, they become interested." "If you can sing, sing," a pamphlet on how to keep New Guinean laborers going advised their new American bosses. "They will be tickled to death."[42]

Whereas Americans interpreted less advanced societies as feminine and childlike, they thought of their own civilization as masculine and patriarchal. The downed pilot who was greeted by the mayor and thousands of peasants before leaving their town in the Chinese interior did more than give a short speech and, upon general request, sing a few American songs. Overlooking the mass of small people, the tall lieutenant decided to switch to a more appropriate technique to satisfy their naive fascination with American speech and lore: "Their diminutive side, their innocent curiosity and the firecracker demonstration all combined to make me feel paternal, I suppose, for I proceeded to tell them the story of Little Red Riding Hood, as if it were perfectly natural that I should do so. It was translated for them and they enjoyed it immensely."[43]

Much more was to be done in this region, however, than tickle New Guineans with songs and amuse Chinese with fairytales. The stagnancy, the poverty, the filthy smell, as well as the myriad indications of moral degradation, all combined to convince GIs that here lived people who urgently needed to be uplifted and taught the best principles of American society.

The missionary reflex of GIs was imbedded in a much older and larger Western tradition of regarding the East as a world in need of redemption. Both Edward Said and Akira Iriye have shown how the West, beginning in the late eighteenth century, attempted to force upon the Orient, from Middle East to Far East, its own idiosyncratic visions and interpretations. Moreover, from about the same time, the South Seas began to fall from grace as their abhorrent practices were increasingly emphasized over their idyllism and paradise in the Pacific was thought to be in need of Western salvation after all.

Americans inherited these conceptions of Asia and the Pacific from Europe. But since Americans were convinced that theirs was the most modern and progressive of Western societies, they also believed that their country was the preeminent redeemer nation, the nation that should serve as the ultimate model for other societies. That belief was infused with a strong sense of mission and an optimism that other societies could indeed be transformed in the American image.

Paternalism thus lay at the root of the American attitude towards many different peoples, including those in Asia and the Pacific. From the very beginning, for instance, China had appealed to what T. Christopher Jespersen has called America's "evangelical sense of enlightenment and regeneration," and until the 1940s Americans did not stop thinking of the

Chinese as people who could – and wanted – to be like them. Shortly after Japan had thrown itself open to Western modernization in the 1860s, numerous American advisers were also contributing to the remodeling of this country, whether as professors at the University of Tokyo or as agricultural experts on the northern island of Hokkaido.

Meanwhile, American missionary zeal spread across the Pacific's warmer waters, too. President McKinley once declared, "Our priceless principles undergo no change under a tropical sun." When Americans acquired the Philippines as a colony in 1898, they had a historical opportunity to put these principles into practice. McKinley's call for "benevolent assimilation" fanned a veritable crusading fire among American civilians and soldiers on the islands. They regarded the Philippines, as historian Brian Linn has shown, as a "transfer point for American values and institutions to Asia," and the Filipinos as "the chosen people" who, after a process of thorough education, would act as missionaries for those ideals.[44]

Only to the extent that they mirrored the American way of life could societies truly find favor in the eyes of GIs. In Asia and the Pacific there were few such societies. The *Guide to New Guinea* could not but admit that the natives looked "pretty wild in some places." It, nevertheless, tried to speak in their favor – and to put the GIs at ease – by dishing up some similarities with Americans: "most of them are accustomed to government supervision, probably go to church far more regularly than some of us do, send their children to school, and around the port are a pretty sophisticated lot." The soldiers disagreed, however, maintaining that most of New Guinea looked pretty uncivilized.[45]

In contrast, the Philippines were generally well regarded by the GIs. That these islands had been molded in the American image for over 40 years had much to do with that favorable opinion. The very first glimpses of Filipino towns were often so encouraging that they caused soldiers to feel homesick. Texaco and Pepsodent billboards on the outskirts, Fords and Chevrolets on the roads, jazz bands welcoming the troops. "It was quite a thrill to see real civilization again," an American in Leyte cried out. He was even more thrilled by the fact that the people were "so much like us." They wore Western clothes. Many spoke English. Some had studied in the US and proudly told GIs of their years at the University of West Virginia or the University of Cincinnati. After the filth and smell of previous places, it was a particular relief to see that many Filipinos had also mastered the basic principles of hygiene. "I admire these people," said a sailor who watched civilians at Subic Bay, "they are American to the core and they are so clean and neat – well-starched clothing and the men look like they just stepped out of a barber shop."

"[O]f course," the sailor at Subic Bay hastened to add, "there is also the dirty scrubby native type." Since American soldiers most appreciated the westernized Filipinos, they tended to gravitate to the better educated and more affluent civilians. "These people are so lovely," a sergeant wrote to his mother after attending a local dance. "Of course we're in a place where there are the very highest class Filipinos." The girls dressed exactly like American girls, he marveled, and were actually "more up to date than the Australians."

A military pamphlet assisted the GIs by dividing the population into "five types of Filipino." The categories were shaped by class and ethnicity, and the ranking very much determined by the knowledge of civilized English. At the top of the hierarchy stood the "cultured college graduate," who was in fact able to speak English "a little more correctly than we do." These professionals had the standing of judges, teachers, and pastors in the US and had to be treated with similar courtesy. The non-professional Filipino took a step back on the ladder. His English might not be as polished as that of the professional but, the pamphlet insisted, that did not make him "more a savage than your Uncle Hatfield who works in the feed and grain store." Next came the farmer or fisherman, "who will probably not understand English, but who is also a very civilized citizen." On the bottom rung at last, there were the primitive jungle natives and the Muslim Moros of Mindanao. The guide did not bother to mention whether they knew English. Still, it emphasized that these people, too, were to be treated as friends of the Americans.[46]

Soldiers elsewhere betrayed a similar preference for the better off because of their Western lifestyle. "The cultured ones are very nice to meet and talk with," an American officer in southwestern China told his wife. He therefore hung out mostly with Chinese secretaries and stenographers. "Of course," he noted somewhat ruefully, "even these people of the better class stick to their customs and styles in some cases."[47]

American soldiers clearly saw that in Asia and the Pacific huge masses of people were still waiting for exposure to the gospel of Western civilization. Fortunately, however, the churches of America had already been spreading that gospel for decades in what had been identified early on as a vast missionary frontier. Sweeping westward from the continent, American missionaries had reached as far as the Asian rimland and adjacent islands by the 1820s. In the Pacific Basin, from Hawaii all the way to China and Japan, American Protestants and Catholics had come to constitute one of the most influential forces in sowing and cultivating Western civilization. No other area had attracted more American missionaries than the Middle Kingdom. In large part because of their efforts, for example, America's educational influence had surpassed that of any other foreign nation in China by the 1930s. But in India and Burma, too, American missionaries had played an important role in spreading Western modernization and education. Congregationalists had arrived in Bombay as early as 1813; Baptists were active even among the reclusive Karen hill people, whose languages they converted into written forms using the Burmese script.[48]

GIs thus ran into American missionaries in the most remote corners of the Pacific Basin. The soldiers took much heart from the knowledge that so many agents of civilization had already taken up the region's tremendous challenge. So long as they represented the values of the West, GIs were equally happy to see missionaries who were not American. They welcomed the sight of the many Australian, Belgian, British, Canadian, French, and Irish missionaries. Although military pamphlets warned about possible pro-Nazi sympathies among German missionaries, American soldiers detected little of this, and considered them as just another vanguard of the same civilization. German Lutheran Sisters operating from a town in southwestern China made a point of feeding all American soldiers who passed their station. When they provided men of an OSS convoy with breakfast and a place to wash in 1945, the Americans responded by donating generous sums of money to support the German mission's work.[49]

Symbiosis between American soldiers and missionaries was spontaneous wherever they met. And Western missionaries – or their shadows – were omnipresent. An attack against a suspected Japanese hideout on Eniwetok Island was abruptly broken off, for instance, when GIs suddenly caught the sound of a familiar Christian hymn. Six frightened locals emerged from the hole, their souls and lives intact thanks to conversion. On island after island in the Pacific, missionaries gladly assisted Americans in their struggle. On Guadalcanal, for example, a Belgian missionary cooperated with the 1st Marine Division as a coastwatcher and authority on terrain, while a young Catholic priest from Methuen, Massachusetts, relayed information on Japanese troop movements during the battle of the Tenaru River. New Guinea was dotted with Christian posts, and missionaries hurried to inform American forces about hidden airstrips. Troops in the Markham Valley rushed to clear old turf runways once used both by missionaries and gold miners. So elated were Americans with an excellent airfield site in the Musa Valley that they named it after the missionary of the Abau district who had first pointed it out to them. In the New Georgia campaign, Americans received support from no less than a Methodist missionary bishop from New Zealand, who volunteered to join an advance party to the island of Vella Lavella.[50]

GIs could now see with their own eyes that countless intrepid missionaries had also succeeded in penetrating even the most inaccessible parts of the Asian mainland. "It is very surprising to see a Bible in a native hut," an engineer in the Burmese hills noted as he told his wife that the Baptists had done "a lot by teaching these poor natives about religion." OSS troops in Burma put a torpedo boat at risk for the express purpose of picking up an American missionary at Myebon who was thought to possess intelligence on the Japanese on nearby Ramree Island.[51]

It was China, however, that seemed to be teeming with American missionaries. The *Guide to Shanghai* called the city that was home to the headquarters of more than 20 Christian churches and organizations "the greatest missionary center in China." From there, legions of American faithful had been sent deep into the giant country. Volunteer pilots in Yunnan had an encounter with missionaries who claimed it took 13 days on horseback to reach their station in the mountains. In June 1942, an American pilot crashed in the isolated countryside of the Kweilin area. With sign language he told farmers that he needed a telephone. They led him to the schoolhouse where a village official dialed a number. When the American took the receiver he was dumbfounded to be speaking English with a Catholic missionary who told him he would be glad to take him back to his base.[52]

For the vast majority of American soldiers, Christianity in any form constituted the basic ingredient of Western civilization and offered the most potent antidote to barbarism and savagism. No agent of the West was considered more important than the missionary. In describing white residents, the *Guide to New Guinea* said that the trader, the planter, the labor recruiter, the miner, and the oil prospector had all played "a colorful part" in the history of the island. It pointed out, however, that none of them had been such "highly influential" figures as the missionaries, for they were the ones who had played "an important part in breaking the natives in to civilization."[53]

The missionaries' most vital contribution had been to bring the indigenes better sanitation and health. But they had also provided them with a general education, and taught them to read and write. In doing so, they had helped to spread the English language far beyond Hawaii and the Philippines, even where American soldiers least expected to find it. "Scarcely anyone knows English," said a pamphlet on the Ryukyu Islands south of Japan, "but one may occasionally meet a Christian, educated by American missionaries who worked in the islands, who understands our tongue."[54]

Equally important, God's earthly representatives had introduced Western standards of "decency." On the Marshall Islands, for example, they had introduced "a feeling of shame at nakedness." The Marshallese now wore European clothing, a GI guide pointed out, "often ill fitting and badly matched; but it serves the purpose." On the Carolines, too, they had left behind "standards of morals and behavior . . . very much like our own." The islanders now were "polite" and "modest."[55]

Missionaries were also thought to be responsible for the pacification of this chronically violent region. The belief in the peace-making capacity of the West had prevailed in white America from at least the turn of the century. "Peace has come through the last century to large sections of the earth," Theodore Roosevelt once said, "because the civilized races have spread over the earth's dark places." His message apparently managed to survive two world wars that were largely of Western making. US military pamphlets claimed, for instance, that it was due to whites, and missionaries in particular, that Pacific islanders had abandoned not only "the bloody native wars," but ancient enmities altogether. Some American soldiers were convinced they owed their lives to the moralizing influence that Christianity had exerted on the indigenes. A pilot who crashed in the New Guinean jungle in 1942 was returned to camp by natives "who did not harm him," he claimed, "after learning that he was a 'Jesus man.'" Still, at least one pamphlet could not help pointing to the irony of the situation. "Forced by the whites to give up their old-time feuding and warfare," the GI guide to the Pacific islands said wryly, "the native islanders must have been shocked to find their homes turned into battlegrounds."[56]

The white men's burden was there to be shared. Even those GIs who did not loudly profess to be 'Jesus men' were quick to assist the missionaries in their daunting civilizing tasks wherever they could. Since most American soldiers were Christians, they brought to the region a mass infusion of the valuable faith. Many GIs sailed into the Pacific with the Scriptures or a rosary in their pockets. Even on the transports that carried Americans overseas there was a bible in a sealed container attached to each raft, along with the water cask, to give support to castaways.[57]

Still, American believers sailed to a world peopled by countless millions who were not Christians and who sometimes opposed Christianity. "If you are to get along well with them," advised the *Guide to the Dutch East Indies*, "don't argue about religion." The booklet on India was much sterner in its admonitions, telling GIs to stay away from both Hindu temples and Muslim mosques unless accompanied by a competent guide. Not only was the presence of unbelievers resented in such places, sounded the warning, but Muslims in particular were also known to be "eager to convert the infidel."[58]

Being outnumbered created a disquieting atmosphere for soldiers who had been safely submerged in Christian culture all their lives. "There are very few churches here for us foreigners," wrote a soldier in Calcutta who felt lost on Easter Sunday of 1945. "To the natives every day is exactly alike; you can't tell by their activities if it's Sunday or not." But Christian soldiers refused to retreat to the catacombs. They rallied around their chaplains and clung to each other in regular prayer service and communion. They came together around makeshift altars and in the improvised houses of their own God. "Out near the shore here are the remains of an old, native burial ground," a GI in Dutch New Guinea noted in 1944, "uncovered when our bulldozers scraped off the ground – ironically enough to make room for our Chapel."[59]

Where Christianity had gained footholds among the local population, American forces made sure to aid the missionaries in restoring and propagating the shared faith. In the western Pacific, for instance, many island missions had suffered badly as Japanese occupation forces had evacuated, imprisoned, or executed most Western missionaries. American chaplains hurried to fill the religious void from the very moment the Japanese were driven out. Troops who landed on Cape Gloucester, New Britain, in March 1944 learned that the Japanese had imprisoned the resident Catholic missionary two years earlier, and had torn down the church building. The natives had been unable to practice Christianity since that time. Within days of the liberation, however, US naval chaplains were organizing services on the beach and handing out armloads of rosaries in nearby villages. That same month, a chief on Emirau Island explained to indignant marines that he was the head of a Christian village, but that his people had been unable to practice their faith from the day the Japanese had arrived. Two chaplains of the 4th Marines immediately pitched in. They spent the next two days baptizing, confirming, performing marriage services, and conducting burial ceremonies. "It was all a declaration of the faith of these fine people," commented a satisfied marine.

Throughout the Pacific, American chaplains routinely conducted church services for the islanders, whether in their villages or on military bases. Soldiers gladly assisted both chaplains and missionaries in a variety of tasks. Some thirty men of the 40th Division aided in rebuilding the church of the mission station at Tangarare on Guadalcanal. When it was dedicated in November 1944, 700 islanders attended the ceremony together with numerous American servicemen, including several admirals and generals.[60]

Even in Asia's strongest bulwark of Christianity, GIs felt called upon to help shoulder the flagging faith. In the Philippines, a priest in San Jacinto told an American soldier that only women had remained regular worshippers in his church during the war. The Catholic GI noted with a lightened heart, however, that "when the local men saw the American soldiers attending Mass, they began to be regular members of the congregation."[61]

Yet the mass of American soldiers, whatever their religious creed, turned into the most fervent missionaries only when faced with the filth and disease terrorizing the region. Spreading the tenets of modern science, and in particular the sanitary commandments of the new religion, was deemed more important even than the propagation of the ancient faith.

GIs encountered an appalling disregard for even the most basic principles of hygiene. New Guineans, for instance, lived heaped together in small huts, sharing them with dogs and pigs that scrounged from the family cooking pots. "The Native wasn't affected," remarked one soldier, "although I almost vomited."[62]

Americans were disgusted by the open gutters in Manila that washed raw sewage across the streets and into the river. In the Filipino countryside soldiers learned not to sleep under homes built on stilts or piles if they wanted to avoid being rudely awakened by human excreta raining down. On Okinawa, too, American civil government staff identified the refusal of locals to use latrines as the "chief discipline problem." No soldiers were shocked more by the lack of sanitation, however, than those stationed in India. "They live on rice and curry, eaten with the right hand," a GI reported from Calcutta. "The left is for wiping the rectum. Toilet paper is only for the very rich." Reports from the countryside painted an equally distressing picture. "[T]he water shown you wouldn't let a good clean American dog swim in," a WAC commented on a photograph for her parents, "yet they use these water holes for washing clothes, and also themselves."[63]

Soldiers who left India for the Middle Kingdom at first sight thought the Chinese much cleaner. But a more intimate knowledge of the country quickly proved them painfully wrong. In the crowded cities people were disgustingly dirty, and almost everywhere their toilet habits seemed worse than those of animals. "Evacuation of body wastes is something to be done expeditiously and forgotten," commented a discouraged surgeon at Kweilin, "with no thought of comfort or sanitation." Early in 1944, Merrill's Marauders linked up with Chinese troops near Walawbum in northern Burma. The reinforcement was almost immediately followed by a sharp rise in the incidence of amoebic dysentery. The Americans squarely put the blame on the Chinese and their habit of defecating not only all over the bivouac area, but even in the river from which troops were drawing water to drink.[64]

Much less threatening but equally irritating was the dreadful lack of dental hygiene among the inhabitants of Asia and the Pacific. This was made worse by the habit, practiced from New Guinea all the way to China and India, of chewing betel nuts. Wrapped in leaves buttered with lime, the nuts caused a slight stimulant sensation. But the potent juices also led to rapid decay and discoloration of teeth and gums. The sight of rotting mouths turned the stomachs of many a GI in a region where people did not seem to understand that sane living meant sanitary living.[65]

Americans, on the other hand, brought with them not only sanitary living but something akin to a sanitation syndrome. In the late nineteenth century, modern bacteriology in the US had rapidly spread from the laboratory to middle-class homes and beyond. It had led to a deep-seated germ consciousness and to thoroughly internalized ways of cleanliness. The gospel of germs was still very much alive among Americans during a war that would see the emergence of antibacterial drugs only in its waning days.[66]

Antiseptic measures focused first and foremost on the body itself. Prior to an engagement, American sailors were expected, despite the limited supplies of water that ships could carry, to wash and soap, and then to put on fresh clothes, to prevent infection if wounded. Disinfection of the skin through scrubbing and soaping was practiced with fervor wherever

American troops went. "Wash clothing often and if possible take a bath every day," military pamphlets exhorted from the steamy jungles of New Guinea to the teeming cities of India. Even the tiny language guide written for pilots downed over China regarded "Is there a place to take a bath?" as one of the potentially vital questions. American soldiers used prodigious amounts of soap for toilet and laundry purposes. Troops stationed at Brinkman's Plantation in Dutch New Guinea used a local mountain stream so intensively that it became "milky with soap" – GIs had to walk upstream for at least half a mile to find unpolluted water. A health survey of female soldiers in New Guinea for the first quarter of 1945 found that dermatological conditions were on the increase. The male author of the report suggested that this might be due to "the more delicate texture of the female skin." But he also noted that the growing incidence of skin irritation might be attributed to "the common practice among WAC personnel to shower with soap and washcloth as frequently as three times a day." As late as April 1945, reports from Army divisions in the Philippines were urging the Quartermaster General to send larger quantities of soap.[67]

The antiseptic offensive extended to whatever the soldiers were about to consume. Water was, of course, one of the most important sources of contamination. Boiling it and adding disinfectants were standard safety precautions. Still, soldiers in their urge to be safe rather than sorry preferred to up the doses on their own initiative. "The drinking water is becoming a little clearer," a lieutenant wrote from the Philippines, "but we still put about four or five times the normal chlorine in it."[68]

Anything that so much as touched food had to be sterilized. Before each meal in their camp at Oro Bay, New Guinea, WACs stood in line to dip mess kits and utensils into large containers with boiling water. After they had eaten, they religiously scrubbed them with large brushes, again in scorching soap water, then hauled them through two more cans of steamy water to rinse. GIs who thought of eating in a restaurant in China were told first to ask the proprietor for boiling water to scald dishes and utensils.[69]

American troops made a particular point of erecting latrines that stood their ground as reassuring symbols of Western civilization in the midst of barbarity. In his journal, a captain of the 43rd Division described with affection the "sanitary beauty" of his company's toilets in the dense jungle of New Georgia. They were, he beamed, "masterpieces from hinged-covered, sandpapered seats to heavy paulin tops." Soldiers had been ordered to disinfect them thoroughly twice a day and repeatedly to scour the seats with hot water and soap.[70]

GIs took to cleansing the surroundings with a vigor that surprised even fellow Westerners. In March 1942, the French on New Caledonia turned over to US forces an orphanage for use as a hospital. American medics not only scrubbed every wall and floor with strong solutions of Lysol, they also flushed such copious antiseptic solutions through the toilets that they killed the bacteria of the building's septic tanks. When a terrible stench began to permeate the hospital, French authorities had to be called to the rescue. For a long time after, the amused French kidded the Americans that sometimes too much cleanliness could be unhealthy.[71]

But the Americans were not to be discouraged. Not only did they continue their own war against filth, they even found the energy to carry the sanitation crusade to the indigenes. No excuse for the lack of hygiene was to be considered valid. "Obviously their living standard is low," noted correspondent Ernie Pyle on Okinawa. "Yet I've never understood why poverty and filth need to be synonymous."[72]

Fortunately, Western civilization had already made at least some headway in promoting sanitation. During a visit to a village in New Guinea, a WAC maintained that those children who spoke some English were also cleaner than the others. Soldiers gladly followed in the footsteps of the missionaries. Though in some villages on the island natives were still exuding "a stiflin' obnoxious odor," a private claimed that significant progress was being made elsewhere: "They have been quickly adoptin' lots of American an' Aussie ways an' most of 'em bathe pretty regular now an' are much cleaner." Despite almost half a century of American presence in the Philippines, a female lieutenant who complained about the water shortage in small towns and the fact that she had to wash from her helmet, wrote to her mother: "The Filipinos can learn a lot about sanitation from the US Army engineers."[73]

GIs thought natives everywhere could certainly learn more about dental hygiene. A civilized smile and fresh breath were the first steps to a happier society. When Americans established colonial control over the Philippines in the early 1900s, it was not long before elementary school children started each day with a public toothbrush drill, vigorously brushing their teeth in synchronized movements. In the 1940s, GIs did what they could to continue the mission. Nurses of the 119th Station Hospital in New Guinea never failed to teach the indigenous children they treated how to brush their teeth. Medics of the 608th Clearing Company on the same island tried their best to convince adult natives to abandon the use of betel nut for the chewing of American gum.[74]

Yet GI offerings of soap, toothpaste, and chewing gum drew only lukewarm responses from the indigenes. What truly fascinated them were American medicines. Wherever they went, American soldiers encountered health conditions that were unspeakable. "First visitors to China," warned one GI guide, "are always shocked by the horrible effects of disease on its people." All the enteric disorders were common, venereal diseases were widespread, tuberculars were everywhere, and every type of skin disease known to man covered faces and bodies. "On the surface," said the guide, "the situation looks hopeless."[75]

No Americans were more shocked than those who spent time with Chinese troops. In April 1943 the US military opened an Infantry Training Center in Kunming. The officer in charge described the physical condition of the first Chinese troops to arrive as "appalling." Seventy percent suffered from trachoma, scabies, colds, and intestinal disease, and several died in the following weeks. An inspection in June 1945 of two thousand Chinese soldiers at a replacement depot in Hilanpo, near Kunming, found conditions to be "horrible beyond imagination." "One hundred percent were suffering from malnutrition, T.B., and other diseases," the report stated, "but no medical care was being given." In some places of the compound, the dead had been lying next to the barely living for several days. Even in Chinese military hospitals, sanitation seemed nonexistent. In one ward, incredulous Americans saw with their own eyes how "patients threw uneaten food under their beds, spit where they pleased, and urinated just outside the door."[76]

Health conditions on Pacific islands were not necessarily more idyllic. Military pamphlets warned that even under the swaying palms of the Caroline Islands there festered multitudes of diseases, from dengue, filariasis, and the spectra of typhoid, dysentery, and lung disease to yaws and psoriasis. "There's a world of medicine to be done amongst the natives," gasped a battalion surgeon when surveying the health needs of the New Guineans.[77]

Like the missionaries before them, American soldiers quickly learned that displaying the wonders of modern medicine was the surest way to convert locals to Western civilization. Western medicines were worth their weight in gold throughout the region. American troops in northern Burma, for instance, used medicines as an important part of the payment for the invaluable Kachin hillsmen who fought on their side. A GI who drove an ambulance in a truck convoy from Ledo to Kunming in 1944 led a life of luxury thanks to the most basic of medical supplies he carried. During stops in Burma he bartered aspirin, sulfa, and bandages for the eggs, potatoes, tomatoes, and chickens of the hill people. Business became brisker still when he arrived in China. On the advice of other medics, he headed straight for the Kunming black market. There he instantly sold all the remaining ambulance supplies. Aspirin, iodine, sulfa, bandages, and various odds and ends made him bundles of Chinese bills. The money allowed him to spend some unforgettable days before being flown back to India. "We had girlfriends," the ambulance driver rejoiced, "ate the best food, drank the best booze and had a great time."[78]

In a world where people scrambled for simple painkillers and basic disinfectants, the performance of more complicated medical interventions easily rivaled local magical practices, gaining the Americans much respect. Medics of a unit of the Americal Division on the island of Malekula in the New Hebrides so awed the Nambas by anesthetizing and operating on one of their tribesmen that they spontaneously offered the GIs all the bearers they could spare. On 10 December 1944, men of the 6th Division hiked through the jungle of New Guinea for more than five hours to reach a tribe in the mountains near Sansapor. The village chief had invited them because a few days earlier medics of the unit had saved his only son from the devastating effects of beriberi. The jubilant feast in honor of the Americans, which included excellent food and splendid dances, lasted six whole hours.[79]

Even in China, the ancient empire that had once made such important contributions to medicine, American soldiers became, perhaps more than anything else, bringers of health. The medical organization of the Chinese military existed almost exclusively on paper, and American medical instructors and advisers were attached to various Chinese units in the field. In the North Burma campaign, for example, the US Army provided almost all of the medical aid for the Chinese: three field hospitals, one mountain medical battalion, eight portable surgical hospitals, two medical collecting companies, one clearing company, two veterinary evacuation hospitals, three veterinary companies, one malaria survey unit, and seven malaria control units.[80]

Their cockiness about the superiority of Western science could make Americans arrogantly dismissive of Chinese medical experience. When a GI died from "Chinese encephalitis" at the Christian university hospital of Chengtu, an American nurse lodged a complaint against the American doctors, accusing them of having refused to ask the local personnel for help "because they felt the Chinese doctors didn't know very much." Many Chinese, on the other hand, harbored superstitions regarding Western medicine. In Chengtu, for instance, rumors circulated about the abuse of the corpses of babies and other barbaric practices at the Western hospital. Yet, though American medics often had to tread carefully to make themselves accepted, in China, too, the magic of Western science rarely failed to do the trick. Americans training guerrillas at Shempa in Suiyan province found the Chinese to be very distrustful towards their doctor. When one day the American had no choice but to perform a risky emergency operation on a young Chinese woman, he prayed he would succeed in order not to jeopardize the mission. The woman made a spectacular recovery. "From then on," noted the elated doctor, "I was mobbed by hundreds of patients."[81]

4
Imperialists

American soldiers readily lent missionaries a helping hand in restoring Christian faith and reiterating the scientific gospel of hygiene and health. At the same time, however, they realized that the persistent stagnancy, poverty, and moral degradation of Asian and Pacific societies begged for increased Western intervention and would require large-scale tutelage for quite some time to come.

Still, as imbued with paternalism as they may have been, GIs could not find it in their hearts to condone the blunt colonialism of Europe. "Because the richness of our land has given us a greater opportunity than any other people on earth," lectured the GI guide on the Burma of the Brits, "we should have greater kindness toward others and special consideration for their rights and for their dignity."[1]

American soldiers were unable to look past the European variety of colonialism from the very moment they embarked on their offensive in the Pacific. Its agents rose from the ruins of war wherever GIs showed their faces. US troops in the Guadalcanal campaign, for instance, received invaluable advice and assistance from a major Martin Clemens. Clemens was an officer in the British Solomon Islands Defense Force, a former district officer of the British Solomon Islands Protectorate and, before the war, a plantation manager. Members of both the Australian New Guinea Administrative Units and the Netherlands Indies Civil Administration Units stubbornly clung to American troops as they fought their way across New Guinea and adjacent islands. ANGAU and NICA detachments had only one purpose in mind: to reestablish control over natives and plantations as quickly as possible.[2]

So many colonial estates dotted the islands of the Pacific that at times it appeared as if GIs were hopping from plantation to plantation. Action reports on Papua mention the plantations of Warisota, Duropa, Soena, Giropa, and others; those on Dutch New Guinea speak of the Tadji, Ebeli, and Brinkman estates. On New Georgia, battles raged on the plantations of Lambeti and Piru; on Los Negros on those of Momote and Salami; on Vella Lavella, New Britain, and Manus war enveloped the plantations of Nyanga, Amalut, and Mokerang. In 1942, Americans at Milne Bay, New Guinea, rapidly transformed a large coconut plantation into several badly needed airfields, and a year later, during the invasion of New Britain, they put to good use the well-developed harbor of the great South Seas trading company of Burns-Philp. Meanwhile, most of the Americans who went all the way to India ended up in Assam, where they found themselves hemmed in by Britain's vast tea plantations for the remainder of the war.[3]

Americans had wrested their freedom from a colonial power and tended to sympathize with people who were clamoring for independence. Their Philippine colony had always given Americans an uneasy conscience, and by the 1930s the US had promised the archipelago independence. Nationalist struggles against European colonials never failed to appeal to American instincts. In March 1942, an opinion poll showed that 65 percent of Americans wanted Britain to grant India self-government immediately or at the end of the war. Only 2 percent were not in favor of the idea at all. At the same time, however, white Americans were not ready to bestow equal rights on racial minorities at home and, complicating matters further, the US was fighting a Herculean war on the side of what were Europe's major colonial powers.[4]

Against that complex backdrop, GIs who turned to their official pocket guides for advice on how to approach the issue of European colonialism were bound to find mixed signals. As the US attempted to secure the lifeline with Australia early in the war, French possessions in the South Pacific were among the first European colonies the GIs came in contact with. The *Guide to New Caledonia* claimed that the French were not really colonists but Caledonians who considered the island their home. Still, some pages later GIs could read that there was "no love lost" between the indigenes and the French *gendarmes* without whose permission they could not undertake even something as commonplace as getting a new job or moving house. In the Southwest Pacific, New Guinea's government officials had done an excellent job in civilizing the native, the US military guide had to admit. However, if they were obeyed, the booklet added meaningfully, it was not out of respect, but because they were backed by "the police, the jail, battleships, and soldiers."[5]

The *Guide to the East Indies* presented Dutch colonialism as a case deserving special consideration. The Dutch, it pointed out, had lived on these islands for more than 300 years and considered them their rightful home. "Don't," the booklet pleaded, "start an argument with them about their position in the Indies, or about the colonial system, or that sort of thing." But at the same time, the GI guide mentioned that the Atjehnese on Sumatra had fought Dutch rule for 35 years until as late as 1908, and that

Dutch troops had been forced to remain on the alert in the area ever since. Moreover, it stated that the self-governing status towards which the Dutch had been steering the islands had not placated "the extreme anti-Dutch nationalists," who wanted to "get rid of the Dutch at any cost."[6]

It was the British empire, however, that threatened to pose particularly sensitive problems to American troops. The 1943 *Guide to India* reminded GIs that they were bound for the country at a time when relations between the British and the Indians were very tense. It therefore urged the Americans to steer clear of the controversy regardless of where their sympathies lay. "Your place," it said in no uncertain terms, "is to keep your eyes and ears open and your mouth shut." Yet even while attempting to defuse potential friction with the British ally, the GI guide allowed anticolonial sympathies to shine through, pointing out that what the Indians were trying to do was what the Americans had done 160 years ago. The US thus served as "a source of inspiration" to many Indian leaders. "Our ideals, our way of living," the official booklet boasted, "give them hope for the future."[7]

The war offered Americans a unique opportunity to observe European-style colonialism from within, and they found much to dislike. Indigenous laborers were shamefully underpaid. In May 1943, a lieutenant in a torpedo boat squadron wrote to his parents that the British forced the Solomon islanders to work for a meager 17 cents a day. "'English we no like' is their summating of the British Empire," he reported. Lieutenant John F. Kennedy might have been expected to twist the British lion's tail whenever he could, but he was not the only one by far. The American provost marshal for Assam stopped his complaints about the lethargy of the coolies involved in the construction of new barracks the very moment he learned that these workers were expected to get by on 26 rupees per month and half a pound of rice per day.[8]

Old World colonialism had many ugly faces. Despite the *Guide to Calcutta*'s warnings not to criticize "local politics" in letters home, a WAC bitterly lamented the neglect of the city's poor and the lack of schools. "The British Gov't really likes it that way," she said rebelliously, "because it is too much trouble to help the natives out." Americans stationed among the swarthy islanders of Melanesia had an eerie sense of reliving the dark days of Africans in bondage. The *Guide to New Guinea* explained that almost all able-bodied young men spent from one to four years in the white man's service as indentured laborers. An American sailor caught a glimpse of what this meant for many. He watched as an Australian coconut planter and his foremen had New Guineans clean neglected groves in the wake of the Japanese departure. One of the workers was brought to the Australians for having defecated in a pathway. The boss listened, muttered something, and to the astonishment of the American, a foreman grabbed a stick the size of a broom handle, then thrashed the native's bare back with all his might. After that, everyone went back to work as if nothing had happened. "[S]ome of the natives have not seen their wives for several years," a colonel with the 43rd Division at Aitape wrote to his fiancée, "the Australians keeping them under their thumbs with a system more like slavery."[9]

A blissful ignorance of the nature and conditions of their own country's overseas possessions made it easy for GIs to criticize what they saw of Western colonialism. One of the most widely read history textbooks for schoolchildren in the 1920s and 1930s, for example, barely touched upon the subject of American imperial adventures in the Caribbean and in Asia. Not surprisingly, on the eve of World War II many young Americans had difficulties even locating their country's colonies on a map.[10]

Asked in a survey how they had responded to the Japanese bombing of Pearl Harbor, the main naval base of the US in the Pacific, several American nurses confessed to not having known what the name stood for when they first heard the announcement on the radio. Even some of the country's elite universities had apparently left future soldiers somewhat in the dark about the American empire. A marine lieutenant who had been a junior at Yale at the time of the attack remembered with embarrassment that, when a student had burst in with the news during a play rehearsal, none of the Ivy Leaguers had been able to come up with Pearl Harbor's location. Despite the fact that Americans had been present in Hawaii for over a century and had formally annexed it as long ago as 1898, the 1942 GI guide to the islands thought it wise to remind its readers that a city like Honolulu would be "full of drug stores, department stores, soda fountains, movies, offices, and even Americans."[11]

The military's crash-course education on American colonies managed to fill at least some voids. In November 1944, the USS *McCoy Reynolds* anchored in a bay of the Philippines, America's main colony for almost half a century. The event prompted one excited sailor to fill two pages of his diary with eye-opening information on the islands copied from his GI guide. "The Government of these islands are similar to ours," he concluded in amazement, "in fact modeled after our gov. with executive, legislative and judicial branches." But crash courses did not suffice to take away the endemic ignorance surrounding America's colonies. The Philippines had known Spanish Catholic rule for centuries when the US took control. Still, when a sailor of the USS *Montpelier*, himself a Catholic, mingled with Filipino civilians during recreation on a beach at Lingayen Gulf in March 1945, he was most pleasantly surprised. That evening, the puzzled but approving sailor scribbled in his diary: "It seemed as if they were all Catholics, according to holy medals and rosaries that they wore."[12]

The fact that military pamphlets omitted the existence of the tiny island possession of Guam, also an American colony since 1898, meant that GIs had to discover it all over again. "Mother, this island is only 26 miles long and from 4 to 6 wide," a medic from Kansas wrote. "Guam belonged to America before the war," he continued the report on his exploration, "and there were American schools on it, so most of the natives speak at least a little English."[13]

What discourse had been taking place regarding America's overseas territorial possessions had long been rife with euphemism, even to the point where 'unincorporated territory' had been substituted for the more unpleasant sounding 'colony.' Military pamphlets continued that tradition and fed it to GIs who, in their ignorance, were hungry for and receptive to any kind of information on their country's colonies. There thus emerged a rather rosy picture of America's benevolent imperialism that was in sharp contrast with the cynicism of European-style colonialism. Official guides sidestepped or brushed over most of the thornier issues of America's colonial past. Instead, they highlighted excellent education and spectacular progress in the fight against disease as the most notable aspects of American rule in Hawaii and the Philippines. In fact, the word 'colonization' continued to be skirted, occasionally by means of some very imaginative writing. "You have only to look around to see the result," the *Guide to Hawaii* said unblinkingly, "one of the finest demonstrations anywhere of practical Americanism. Democracy, to the Hawaiians, is taken sincerely."[14]

Ironically, conditions in the Pacific Basin stimulated in American soldiers an imperialist impulse even as they were questioning European colonialism. The history of the frontier had created an expectation of steady expansion among Americans. When the winning of the American West had been completed at the turn of the century, overseas imperialism had seemed like the next logical step. By superimposing the frontier myth on the imperial adventure, Pacific islanders and Asians had become, in the words of Richard Slotkin, "figurative Apaches," and the Philippines "a symbolic equivalent of Boone's Kentucky or Houston's Texas."[15]

GIs felt part of that pioneering tradition and shared in the romantic images surrounding it. They, too, responded to the region's challenges with a missionary reflex and strong paternalistic instincts. "There is a lot of talk about freeing these Islands but really I don't think the people want it yet," a sergeant stationed in the Philippines wrote home in March 1945. "They need us too much for reconstruction and guidance." This to GIs seemed to be the right course, uninformed as they were about the darker side of the American colonialism that had preceded them, and with military pamphlets on the region trumpeting their country's tradition of benevolent imperialism.[16]

Meanwhile, what spurred American soldiers on to accepting imperial responsibility even more willingly was the power vacuum that gaped at them from the ruins of Europe's degenerate empires. On Pacific islands, GIs waded through the soft and rotting coconuts of neglected groves where immaculate and profitable European plantations once had stood. With planes and GIs pouring into India to supply China over the Himalaya, the British in Assam stood by as American authorities requisitioned ever more tea acreage for their expanding airfields. Americans soldiers sensed that the old empires would never be restored to their former grandeur. On New Caledonia, tempers of local officials flared as they expressed grave concerns over the challenges the American presence posed to French authority and sovereignty. Relations with the Dutch in their part of New Guinea were rocky, too. Colonials had to swallow much of their pride and rely almost entirely on the Americans to reestablish the Queen's control. An American officer cooperating with Dutch officials near Lake Sentani in 1944 described their conundrum: "Their task was to impress their authority upon the native population notwithstanding that the native population could readily perceive that the Dutch could not have come back except as passengers." Early in 1944, ANGAU officers tried to stop Americans of the 592nd Engineer Amphibian Regiment from dealing with the natives in a New Guinean village. But a company clerk snapped back at the Australians. "I could afford to be pretty independent," he explained, "as they were using our boat, and I wasn't dependent on them for anything." The Australians were forced to back off. "The Yanks have a way of getting any-thing they go after," the clerk triumphed, "a fact that the Australians both hate and admire at the same time."[17]

Europeans shared the Australians' frustration. They suspected the Americans more and more of going after their very empires. As hundreds of thousands of GIs swarmed over their possessions in Asia and the Pacific, they quite literally appeared to be nudging the original colonists out. With an annoying natural ease, American soldiers penetrated the most cherished colonial retreats of the Europeans. They irritated the British, for example, by taking over their golf courses and patronizing their clubs. The hill sta-tions dotting India and Burma had traditionally been among the most secluded British enclaves. Here colonists had at regular intervals sought to escape heat and humidity – as well as the sweaty colored masses laboring below. Gradually, the stations had been transformed into administrative cen-ters and military garrisons of such importance that Mahatma Gandhi called them "the real headquarters of the rulers." But they were also, of course, excellent centers for American soldiers convalescing or in need of rest and recreation. As the war dragged on, so many GIs were flocking to the hill resorts, from Darjeeling to Maymyo, that the irritated British barely recog-nized even their most precious sanctuaries.[18]

European colonists had treated much of exotic Asia and the Pacific as play-grounds, something perhaps best illustrated by their big game hunting feasts. But these natural preserves, too, were now claimed by Americans, many of whom were hunting enthusiasts, and all of whom had brought their guns. Former American colonials were well aware of the hunting pleasures that lay in store. When the 147th Field Artillery was being readied for duty in the Philippines in October 1941, officers who had served in the islands lectured the men on the conditions they could look forward to. "They painted an appealing picture," noted one historian, "advising the artillerymen to take along fishing tackle, golf clubs, and shotguns, as much sport was to be had." American habits in the Philippines were easily transplanted to European colonies in Asia. In the Indian state of Assam, a lieutenant from Dayton, Ohio, was whisked off to his first big game hunt by a group of fellow officers. The Ohioan killed two wildcats, but missed a boar and a leopard. A captain teased him with pictures of previous hunts that showed not only a slain elephant, but also an immense dead tiger. Big cats had always been among the most sought after trophies in Britain's prewar colonies, from lions in Kenya to tigers in northern India. During the war, however, GIs soon made tiger hunting one of their favorite pastimes in India, and in a matter of years American soldiers replaced British hunters as the Bengal tiger's biggest threat.[19]

With a war that showed Americans to be eclipsing even the greatest imperial powers in Asia, it appeared almost inevitable that the US would henceforth play the role of hegemon in the region. One evening in March 1944, the submarine USS *Jack* carefully cruised on the surface, past the islands of Mindoro and Panay. The men on board were surprised to see that Filipino farmers along the coasts were burning cane fields as if the war did not concern them. "Here we were," a lieutenant muttered, "twelve thousand miles from home, fighting a vicious war in the Filipino's backyard, and they were up in the hills, quietly burning their sugarcane." "I concluded," he wrote resignedly, "that this disparity was the price of power . . ."[20]

As the confidence of American soldiers in their country's armed forces grew, so did their pride in that power and their willingness to pay the price that came with it. GIs realized more than ever that America's burden would not remain limited to its own colonies, a few far-flung island groups in the Pacific, but that eventually it would stretch across the vast expanse of the ocean, even embracing much of the Asian landmass. The war had catapulted their country on a mission so ambitious that Americans overseas had to hark back all the way to the Roman empire for suitable comparisons. In October 1942, correspondent Ira Wolfert watched as Navy construction battalions and Army engineers hacked away at the jungle of the Solomon Islands, built camp after camp, and established lines of communications across thousands of square miles. They labored, he reported proudly, "like ancient Romans." American soldiers played their imperial roles with zest. At the end of 1943, Merrill's Marauders set up a training camp at Deogarh in Rajasthan state. Some time later, a delegation of Indians from the surrounding villages decided to pay an official visit to get to know the newcomers. One of the American officers did the honors and gracefully accepted wreaths of flowers and panniers of fruits and nuts. "Had I worn a toga," he reflected, "the scene would not have been too dissimilar from those encountered by Caesar's legions in ancient times."[21]

American soldiers were not drawn into the huge power vacuum of the Pacific Basin unthinkingly, as if in a mere reflex. They were keenly aware of the interests the region held for them and their country. In the midst of war, the most urgent concern was, of course, one of national security. The attack on Hawaii's Pearl Harbor, and the mad fear of a Japanese invasion of California that had followed it, had left a palpable feeling of insecurity regarding the West Coast flank of the US. An officer of the 43rd Division told his fiancée in 1943 that in the future the US would have to keep certain islands "strongly under our control" and keep them "strongly fortified" so that "they can hold up under any attack in case again any aggressive forces in the South Pacific area attempt to attack the United States."[22]

To a degree that strategy was spontaneously dictated by the perspective of soldiers looking homeward from the Pacific. But it also echoed political sentiments emanating from the US mainland. It was after reading former Admiral Thomas Hart's senate speech, for instance, that an officer of the XXI Bomber Command, stationed on the Marianas, wrote to his parents in April 1945 that the Pacific islands were "mighty important military bases to hold for future protection." Political sentiments were further amplified by some of the military booklets distributed among the soldiers. One of the *G.I. Roundtable* publications, for example, discussed the strategic issue at great length in a 1944 pamphlet entitled *What Future for the Islands of the Pacific?* "There is evidence," it claimed, "that the American people favor taking a much more active part in the affairs of this South Sea region than in the past." "They believe," it continued, "that the requirements of national security and the expenditures made in money and lives demand this."[23]

For one thing, modern transportation had shrunk distances and put even the furthest islands squarely at America's "western doors." Where once steamships had brought the Asian and American continents closer together and had made control over Pacific harbors strategically important, the war showed that "modern clippers of the air" were reducing travel time from weeks to hours, and that possession of a network of island airfields would now be even more vital. The measure of control that the US would be able to bring to the Pacific in the postwar era would determine whether the ocean islands would be "sentry posts of security" or "outposts of possible aggression."

All this was presented, however, not just as a matter of American self-interest, but also as one of world peace. "The United States now bears the major burden of Pacific security," the *G.I. Roundtable* pamphlet noted, "and there is no reason to suppose that it will not have to carry this on through the postwar era." The Pax Americana could take several forms, to be arrived

at in a multilateral framework if possible, in a unilateral fashion if necessary. The booklet suggested, for instance, the creation of a "trans-Pacific
defense belt" stretching all the way from the West Coast to Japan and
Formosa. It imagined this as a chain of fortified islands, with vast runways,
and underground hangars. Another proposal was to fuse practically all the
Pacific territories into a "Confederation of Oceania." That confederation
would be supervised by a governing body shared by all the interested powers
involved. But, significantly, its headquarters would be located in Honolulu,
the capital of America's Hawaiian possession.[24]

If national security was the GIs' immediate concern in the region, they
were nevertheless attuned to the variety of other interests it held. An engineer in New Guinea summarized most of them in his diary in April 1943:
"We are fighting to enjoy the commerce, the natural resources, the wealth,
the good earth itself. We are fighting now for the earth's crust. All wars
have been fought for it. That is the way all empires have grown, no matter
how the history books try to paint it."[25]

The natural resources of the region were, of course, by no means limited
to the gold dust, precious stones, and dribbles of oil that so excited pioneer-
minded individuals. They also encompassed the huge quantities of strategic
materials that were to feed America's giant modern industries, even hun-
grier in war than in peace. The debilitating effect on the US of the Japanese
conquest of most rubber plantations was just one powerful demonstration
of the region's importance in this sense. Time and again the GI guides
pointed to the significance of these raw materials. The high-grade iron ore
of India, for example, which perhaps constituted the largest deposits in the
world. Or its manganese, representing about one-third of global output.
The iron, copper, coal, and zinc of Melanesia. The rich oil deposits, tin, and
other strategic resources of Indonesia. The military pamphlets presented
even some of the smaller islands of the Pacific as industrial treasure-houses.
The *Guide to New Caledonia*, for example, emphasized that some of the
most vital war industries back home relied on the island's minerals, with
many American plane and munitions factories in particular dependent on
its nickel and chrome.[26]

Soldiers were well aware that peace would barely slow America's giant
appetite for resources of all kinds. On New Guinea, a soldier and one of his
comrades, a Kentuckian lumber jack, marveled at the immense potential of
the jungle hardwoods. "Someday it will be tapped," the GI noted, "for we
will be forced to look for just such supplies when we have depleted our
American forests – and we will."[27]

But Asia and the Pacific were much more than regions from which to extract
natural riches. They also represented huge markets where staggering amounts
of products could be sold with tremendous profits. "The Pacific Ocean is so

vast," a sailor reflected in his journal in June 1945, after having gazed at the coasts of Borneo, "that you could put the rest of the world in it and still have plenty of room left over. Europe would only make a small dot out here." Meanwhile, his mind was thinking business. "Someday," he noted, "many of these islands will be up to date with the latest of everything."[28]

Whether driven by individual opportunism or the belief that their nation as a whole needed new markets to ensure prosperity after the war, GIs proved very alert to whatever commercial prospects the overseas territories might reveal. Soldiers fresh from California who approached the New Hebrides in February 1943 watched with satisfaction as natives in outrigger canoes tried to sell coconuts priced in dollars and cents. "It is interesting," observed one GI, "how well known the American dollar is by the natives and its power to purchase things."[29]

The dollarization of the region could only facilitate future commercial dealings that already looked incredibly promising for the US. Go-getting schemes flourished among GIs eager to make up for time lost in the war and haunted by the specter of renewed depression. An officer of the Americal Division, stationed at Cebu during the summer of 1945, noted that, during dances, GIs and Filipinos became invariably engaged in "endless bull sessions" about the archipelago's future development. "The business possibilities here are tremendous," he told his wife in one letter. "I could set you up in the exporting business in about five minutes if shipping were available." His thoughts ranged from candy concessions to cosmetics. In another letter, he wrote to his wife: "I'd love to have the 'Baby Ruth' agency on one of these islands for just about six months and to be able to retire for the rest of my days. And the guy who gets the first five thousand pieces of any type of lipstick in here can retire at the end of the first day."[30]

Yet GIs expected the real bonanza after the war to take place in China. That expectation was part of a much older American fascination with the fabled 'China Market.' It went back to the earliest days of the republic and had continued uninterruptedly until the Japanese had closed the door in the 1930s, even if few American exports had actually materialized by that time. "I am reading a book now by Carl Crow," an artillery officer in China told his wife in January 1945. "It is called 400 million customers, 1937 edition." Of the chapters he liked most he mentioned "Pills for the Ills of China" and "Miss China Discovers Her Legs."[31]

The multitudes of Chinese customers appeared to be begging for much more than American pharmaceuticals and nylons. In May 1942, a Flying Tiger from a hill let his eyes wander over the town of Chanyi. "Behind the rough stone walls and medieval gates of heavy iron," he noted in his diary, "the Yunnanese eat, live, and die in the same way their forebears did in the time of Aristotle." Yet the American believed that change would soon come to Chanyi, too. "As I stood there . . . watching . . . this ancient town," he wrote, "I wondered when the local citizens would build a service station at the west gate. I could see a sign advertising hamburgers." And he was convinced that when that time came, the Chinese would be pumping American gas and eating American beef.

GIs saw especially hopeful signs for their country's commercial expansion in the Chinese buying patterns regarding cars. From Kunming, they triumphantly reported that brand-new Buicks, Cadillacs, and American trucks were leaving the remaining ramshackle British makes far behind them. "European cars," observed one, "are about as common as in the United States." An intelligence officer on the other side of China was happy to note that "all freight and passenger traffic was handled by a fleet of prewar trucks, some Daimler-Benz, but mostly Dodge." When comparing what he found in bustling Kunming with what he had witnessed at sleepy Chanyi, the Flying Tiger had good cause to be optimistic. "We should compare the past with today," he reasoned. "Then one can see the impact of American civilization. I say *American* and not Western or European purposely."[32]

The receptivity that utterly foreign societies showed to American cultural products was even more remarkable. Forty years of American control had left a clear cultural imprint on Filipino society in particular. The GI pamphlet *We Return to the Philippines* described just some of the most obvious effects: "Filipinos enjoy dancing, which is completely Americanized in style. (Traditional folk dances are usually limited to school programs and country parties.) They are ardent moviegoers; before the war U.S. pictures were shown in almost every town in the islands. The average young Filipino you will meet will be completely posted on Hollywood and Hollywood personalities." Local singers gaily entertained GIs with popular American songs, proudly billing themselves as the 'Andrews Sisters of the Philippines' or the 'Bing Crosby of Manila.' Before the war, Manila had earned itself not only the reputation of 'Pearl of the Orient,' but also the label of 'Little New York.' In 1945, Americans committed two cavalry units and several tanks to reclaim the capital's Rizal Baseball Stadium from Japanese troops who had dug in all over the diamond and under the grandstand beyond the third base.[33]

American culture was also forcing its way into territories the US had never possessed. Army Motion Picture Services rushed the latest Hollywood productions to the theaters of the New Caledonian capital Nouméa, while French drug stores advertised that they played the latest American hits. "Baseball is being introduced," ensured the *Guide to New Caledonia*, "limited only by the lack of adequate flat spaces." An officer of the 350th Engineers mentioned that the inhabitants of Emirau Island could barely wait for the GIs to finish their comic strips, and that those on Kolombangara Island got a tremendous kick out of the boogie-woogie and jive. When natives on Los Negros began chanting "Beeng! Beeng!" prior to a movie projection, US Special Services obliged by playing "White Christmas" over speakers fastened to palm trees.[34]

Soldiers noted that even on the vast Asian mainland, American mass culture had been making remarkable inroads. Homesick GIs in Kunming spent many an hour in the *Nan Ping* and *Kun Ming*, two local cinemas where they watched very old American pictures with Chinese subtitles. A chronically bored Flying Tiger, stationed in the same provincial town, was elated when a Chinese doctor – who had studied at Johns Hopkins – promised him old copies of *Reader's Digest*. Some weeks later, the pilot happened upon a copy of Dale Carnegie's *How to Win Friends and Influence People* – in Chinese.[35]

Americans had not won friends in Japan, but there were plenty of indications that American culture had influenced more than a few of its people, too. In a pillbox behind one of Tarawa atoll's seawalls, marines discovered three dead Japanese and a bound volume of the *National Geographic* issues of 1931; the very first article revealed the charms of New Hampshire. Closer to Japan, the traces of American influence seemed only to multiply. In the ruins of Saipan – one of the Marianas, an island group controlled by the Japanese for almost thirty years – soldiers picked through the pieces of Singer sewing machines, but also of Columbia records, pictures of Japanese baseball teams, and jazz piano scores. "An area was cleared of coconut trees so we could sit on logs and watch movies," an amused nurse on Leyte recounted. "Three Japs were caught there watching the movies." This particular story circulated all over the Pacific and was often no more than a rumor. But American soldiers relished the thought of Japanese soldiers risking their lives just to catch a glimpse of America's irresistible dream works.[36]

Finally, there was the earth's crust itself. If Americans had accomplished a measure of success in the past century in extending the fur, mining, mercantile, and missionary frontiers of their continental West into the Pacific Basin, then they had found it much more difficult to transplant the traditional farming frontier to this region. The agrarian frontier that did materialize was limited to one of large-scale plantations that relied heavily on indigenous labor. Hence it was not the settling of lands but resource exploitation and trade that had most significantly defined the Pacific Basin frontier for Americans. Even the GI pamphlets admitted that, regardless of the strategic and commercial benefits that control over the Pacific's territories might offer the US, its lands were ill-suited to attract white settlers after the war.

Still, GIs itched to work the land while they were there. There is a human compulsion, perhaps more so in modern Western societies, to want to manipulate, tame, and transform wilderness to ensure survival and progress. Historian Roderick Nash has shown that Americans in particular carried that reflex with them into the twentieth century as they, by that time, had barely completed the process of building a civilization from raw primal nature. One GI guide, for example, pointed to the striking contrast between the Chinese custom of working with nature in cooperation and the American way of subjugating nature in conflict. "Although they don't do so now," the pamphlet explained, "American farmers do have a tradition of hewing a farm out of the wilderness."[37]

In the untamed wilderness of Asia and the Pacific, that old tradition was easily revived. After reading an article on farming opportunities for returning soldiers in some 24 states and Alaska, a GI farmer from Indiana wrote to his parents: "I guess if there were good land obtainable in the States, some one would have homesteaded it by now. Alaska is a different proposition though, so I think that I will look into it." Soldiers from various parts of the US were on the lookout for better farm lands, and the war allowed them to extend their search all over the Pacific. "This is rugged mountainous country," a disappointed Texan reported from New Caledonia in 1942. "I saw very little tillable land." But a Californian stationed in Hawaii remained hopeful, despite the realization that a white elite of just a few families controlled the entire plantation economy. In letters home, he continued to talk about returning to the islands after the war. "I don't really know what you and I could get into over here, dad," he said in May 1943. "But am keeping my eyes open and right now know quite a few people."[38]

American soldiers knew that the first thing to do upon identifying suitable land was to establish possession by fencing it. They were quite baffled, therefore, to find that many fields in India had remained unfenced, and that cattle in Hawaii was still being kept on the range not by barbed wire but by cowboys. When the 350th Engineers arrived on the island of Espíritu Santo in 1943, one of its officers hurriedly marked a plot of land he intended to make into a garden. He then had a black American orderly put a barbwire fence around it to keep out the wild cattle that roamed the island.[39]

The following step was to clear the land. A few days after the engineer had his plot on Espíritu Santo properly fenced, he wrote that as soon as he had moved into new living quarters, he would "get a bulldozer and push some of the jungle out of the way and plant my garden." Americans had conquered the Marianas by the summer of 1944. But half a year later, soldiers were still being assigned details to clear up the last remains of wilderness. "It just never occurred to me before," said one of them, "how thick vegetation can grow without even cultivation – that is when one has to chop it down."[40]

Next the planting could start and, lacking fresh vegetables in their diet, soldiers took to the task with unbridled enthusiasm. Military regulations in certain overseas locations prohibited sending seeds and vegetation to the US mainland. But a veritable stream of plants found its way from American homes to Asia and the Pacific, and soldiers happily reported to their suppliers the progress of their agricultural enterprises. American gardens in India yielded sweat peas, cucumbers, tomatoes, and corn. GIs in Burma harvested lettuce, radishes, onions, carrots, and turnips. A sergeant of the 23rd Field Hospital in New Guinea told his mother in New Jersey to stop sending seeds. "We've got enough small plants," he wrote, "to start everyone in the outfit with a garden."[41]

The soldiers' farming activities were not simply about food. By regimenting land into fenced areas and pushing the jungle outwards, agriculture was just as much an act of colonization, the garden a form of possession forced on an anarchic natural environment. Simultaneously, agriculture and gardening showed the hand of civilization. They brought culture to a natural wilderness that, like its indigenous dwellers, was thought to be waiting to be developed. GIs quickly learned, for example, to recognize clay paths and flowering borders in New Guinean villages as sure signs of missionary influence. Part of the attraction of the Philippines also flowed from a sense that, as a colony, its wilderness had been forced to retreat. After long stretches of duty in New Guinea and Los Negros, a surgeon breathed a sigh of relief when he entered San Jose on Leyte. "It was nice to see real grass," he exalted, "cultivated fields and trees, other than coconut trees."[42]

American soldiers set in motion or continued the process of cultivation wherever they could. By July 1943, the engineer farmer at Espíritu Santo was proud not only of his variety of vegetables, but also of his rich selection of flowers grown from seeds sent by his parents in Chicago. He had removed the elephant ears and small coconut trees around his tent, which he thought monotonous, and had added color by replanting the area with the more familiar zinnias, snapdragons, and hollyhock from home. Thousands of miles away, a WAC sergeant stationed in a camp near Calcutta selected a picture of one of the prettiest and best kept corners of her post to send to her parents. With the snapshot she intended to show them "that India can be quite lovely, if some attempt were made to keep it up, and landscaped." "Yes," she insisted, "the landscaped parts of India, are much like Florida or southern California."[43]

National security concerns and the manifold economic imperatives forced American soldiers to think about how their nation should ensure its power in the region once they had gained victory. "What should be done about them after the war?" a GI booklet on the Pacific islands asked in 1944 with undisguised imperial arrogance. It suggested various forms of empire. One possibility was to continue the existing imperial system. The Western powers would simply hold their islands under sovereign control; they might even be allowed to annex the mandated territories assigned to them after World War I. In that case, the US would continue on a large scale what GI farmers had begun sporadically, and claim all essential areas it conquered in the Pacific as outright territorial acquisitions. In one instance, the GI guide defined those essential areas bluntly as all "bases and battlegrounds." Elsewhere, it specified that the US would in any case annex all former

Japanese possessions, "regardless of who had formerly owned them." A different option was the creation of an international system of supervision and control for the entire region, in which the US would assume "a vigorous role." Somewhere in between these two what the pamphlet called "extreme schools of thought," arrangements were possible under which the US and other Western powers continued sovereignty over their holdings, but would engage in regional coordination regarding matters of military security, economic development, and commerce. A postwar settlement of that kind might also bring the powers to agree on a "colonial charter" that would determine common objectives for the government and welfare of "the backward peoples in the area." In such an arrangement, too, the US would play a dominant role, and the GI booklet suggested that bodies could be set up for consultation and action comparable to the ones in which the republics of the Americas were engaged.[44]

What the Pacific islanders thought of all this political juggling was of little or no significance to American power brokers. American troops betrayed a similar tendency of not taking the peoples of Asia and the Pacific seriously. If locals were considered as mere pawns to be moved around on US chessboards, then they were just as easily reduced to playthings in the hands of individual GIs. "The commanding officers at Guadalcanal," correspondent Ira Wolfert noted haughtily, "have learned to restrain civilized emotions when barefooted natives come trotting into camp." Patronizing soldiers nevertheless found it hard to resist the urge to toy with people of such unheard of primitiveness and naiveté. "Although we could walk along the beach and pick up all the coconuts we wanted," laughed a medic of the 11th Airborne Division in New Guinea, "it was more fun to pay a native an Australian florin . . . to watch him shimmy up a coconut palm and deliver to us a freshly picked coconut." Bored soldiers aboard ships anchored in Milne Bay amused themselves with flipping coins into the clear water to see New Guineans dive for them from their canoes as if circus performers. Equally bored soldiers in the Philippines thought nothing of putting young boys up to bloody fights – much like gamecocks – with the promise of not more than a few cigarettes for the winner.[45]

But the humiliation of locals could take on much more organized forms. US military authorities accepted or created various systems of separation and segregation. European colonial administrators feared that relaxed contacts between natives and GIs might undermine the carefully cultivated hierarchy of race with its strict boundaries and detailed codes. They therefore imposed all kinds of restrictions on racial interaction. Although conflicts between colonial and US military authorities over treatment of islanders occurred in many parts of the Pacific, American commanders generally helped to enforce colonial nonfraternization rules. Egged on by British authorities, for example, the commanding general on Guadalcanal,

Alexander Patch, issued a memorandum in March 1943 that prohibited GIs to overpay natives, make gifts to them, feed them, or allow them to wander through camps and military areas.[46]

In New Guinea, many villages were declared off limits to GIs. Colonial officials were particularly concerned about GI trading with New Guineans. They predicted it would spoil the locals with the kind of money and goods they had never known before. "We saw little of the natives at first," noted a nonplussed surgeon who arrived in New Guinea with his unit in the spring of 1944. "They evidently were forbidden by the Australians to come to us and do much dealings." In the summer of that same year, American officers caught a GI trading a bayonet on Biak Island off the coast of New Guinea. They instantly assigned the soldier to a grave-digging detail as punishment.[47]

Similar prohibitions on close contacts with natives existed elsewhere in the Pacific. When in early 1943 an American carrier found a new anchorage off the coast of Fiji, a group of sailors was sent ashore to service its planes at an Army air base. In no time, the seamen were hanging out with the friendly Fijians in the evenings. They traded, attended indigenous dances, and drank kava together. But Army military police regularly drove by precisely to prevent this kind of mixing between servicemen and indigenes. Each time, a native lookout had to blow a whistle, after which the Americans would hide in the cane and pineapple fields until the jeep had passed. On the island of Los Negros, natives were allowed to watch the open-air movie shows, but they had to sit on coconut logs in areas that were clearly segregated from the GIs.[48]

Such a policy apparently also applied in the Philippines. In March 1945, personnel of the 23rd Field Hospital went to see *Action in Arabia* in a makeshift theater. The roped off section was for American soldiers only, and guards were posted to keep the locals out. Filipinos could enter this section only with a GI escort; the others had to stand in the back.[49]

Elsewhere, segregation made place for relocation, and indigenes disappeared from sight altogether. On the Micronesian islands, many of which the Japanese had ruled since World War I, all natives were under suspicion without exception. In February 1944, for example, American soldiers rounded up the people of Kwajalein in the Marshall Islands and shipped them all to nearby Enilapkan Island. In the Marianas, especially on Saipan and Tinian, US forces systematically uprooted and transported some 28,000 men, women, and children to internment camps in the rear during the campaign of mid-1944. Marine pilots who arrived on Saipan in April 1945 saw nothing but an empty island on the way to their base. "We drove on, through fields now," one said, "but there were no crops, no natives . . ., no life."

In other areas of the Pacific, too, US military exigencies regularly forced islanders, whose identity and well-being was deeply rooted in the land, out of their ancestral villages. In the New Hebrides, Americans cleared people off Mavea to use the island for recreation and target practice. To make room for airfields, nearly the entire population of Green Island, some thousand people, were put on US transports in February 1944 and sent hundreds of miles further south to Guadalcanal. They remained there for seven months under Allied care. Many were soon reported to be "psychologically dispirited;" 148 died, mostly of malaria. At Ulithi, site of a large Allied naval base, indigenous populations were removed, reshuffled, and finally reconcentrated on just a few of the atoll's islets. Ulithi's Mogmog Islet was selected as one of the fleet's most important recreation centers in the Pacific; its villagers were hurriedly transplanted to Fassarai for the war's duration. Natives had barely completed their exodus from nearby Falalop Islet when Seabee bulldozers moved in and flattened the villages to make room for US runways and camps.[50]

By separating, segregating, detaining, and relocating them at will, US forces appeared to regard the locals as nothing more than pawns to be moved about. At the same time, however, the American military recognized their inestimable value as workers. Seen from that perspective, the peoples of Asia and the Pacific became part of the rich raw materials of the region. If their minds were there to be won and their souls to be converted, then the power of their glistening and swarming bodies begged to be tapped.

Already in the nineteenth and early twentieth centuries, Europeans and Americans had scoured Pacific islands in a competitive search for labor needed to operate the region's plantation economies. Some islanders had been forcibly seized as blackbird labor. Most had entered into exploitative contracts as indentured laborers – close to one million between 1850 and 1942.[51]

During the war, Pacific laborers were sought after more than ever before. Because of the scanty allocation of resources and the long distances involved, US service troops in the South Pacific, for example, were in short supply until at least early 1944. In 1942, an American force arrived in Darwin to build bases for the northward offensive. Lacking service troops and facing a labor shortage in Australia as a consequence of wartime mobilization, it was forced to convert artillery troops into stevedores at the expense of training. A frustrated staff first made plans to import 20,000 laborers from the Dutch East Indies. When the Japanese seized those islands, the Americans thought of requisitioning laborers from India, and they continued to consider that possibility well into the spring of 1944.[52]

The recruitment of island labor to fill service jobs and free combat troops became standard American policy across the Pacific. The US military relied heavily on the Australian, British, Dutch, and French colonial powers to deliver and supervise indigenous laborers. Colonial administrators, plantation managers, and missionaries acted as labor recruiters. During the New Georgia campaign, the commander of the 145th Infantry even received a letter from a New Zealand Methodist bishop instructing the natives of mission posts to help the Americans haul supplies. When not enough volunteers could be found, natives were pressed into service. "'You see, I'm really a slave trader,'" a Dutch lieutenant in a New Guinean village near Hollandia confessed to a GI. "'We are at war. We must have labor for the camps. Of course, we pay them, but they still don't like to work. It's like a tax. I have to see that the chiefs send in enough men. When they don't, we send out and get them. I have some patrols out now.'"

During the peak period of Pacific base operations, American labor requirements exceeded the capacity of many local pools, absorbing nearly all available indigenous hands. In Papua New Guinea, where the need for manual labor was especially pressing, Allied forces employed a monthly average of over 34,000 natives in 1944. This meant that in many villages colonial agents 'lent' all men fourteen and older to US forces after nothing more than a cursory health examination. Whole regions were thus depleted of able-bodied men. "We will take in about a hundred native 'prisoners' . . . for more work," an American engineer involved in construction at the Hood Point airdrome in New Guinea wrote in his diary in April 1943. "It is a wonder that the natives don't rebel and help the Japs. I guess they would be treated worse by them. Here we *make* them work and help us, but al least we treat them reasonably well." Women too were pressed into service for the Americans. In Guadalcanal and New Guinea they carried rations on their backs and hauled baskets full of rock and coral. "The women worked as hard as the men," noted an officer who watched New Guineans clear fields at Milne Bay in 1942. As late as April 1945, a report on the issue of packaging rations, based on the needs of eight US divisions stationed throughout the Pacific, recommended to the Quartermaster General: "if possible identification markings as to contents should be large and plain enough to make sorting by native labor possible."[53]

So dependent on local labor did Allied forces in the Pacific become that they were drawn into vigorous competition with each other for the exceedingly scarce human resource. In New Caledonia, for example, there was a Melanesian workforce of some 5,300. In a 1942 agreement, the French promised to deliver a maximum of 850 Melanesians to the US forces on the island. The labor-starved American military, however, was soon evading the agreement through direct recruiting, employing hundreds of Melanesians more than authorized, and causing yet another bitter clash with French officials. Meanwhile, the Dutch tried to have some seven thousand Javanese immigrant workers in New Caledonia transferred to Australia to be used in their army and support units. They in turn were politely but firmly rebuffed by the French.[54]

US forces employed Pacific islanders in an endless variety of ways. Many young indigenes joined combat units that fought on the side of the Allies.

An estimated 400 men worked as scouts and fighters for the Solomon Islands Defense Force. More than 2,200 Fijians participated in the Solomons campaign as part of guerrilla units or regular infantry troops. In Papua New Guinea, some 3,500 Melanesians served in the Pacific Islands Regiment.

Many more indigenes were given labor and service tasks. They loaded and unloaded ships and trucks; carried water, rations, and ammunition; cleared fields, undergrowth, and jungle; constructed roads, bridges, airfields, and buildings. They took care of laundry, malaria control, and garbage disposal. They served as stretcher bearers and grave diggers. New Guineans were used even as substitutes for tractors and steamrollers, with hundreds pulling ropes to move airplanes and tightly packed barefoot tribesmen stamping earth to level runways.

Many laborers worked for the Allied military for stretches from several months to over two years under the prewar colonial system of indenture. Large numbers of others worked as casual hands or day laborers. Prewar colonial structures combined with the critical needs of war to make working conditions exploitative. Work was difficult, backbreaking, and danger ous. Labor gangs were marched to work at dawn; they returned after dusk. At the height of the war, islanders frequently worked ten hours a day, sometimes more. During the Solomons campaign in 1942, more than two days of rest a month was exceptional.

Although the American military provided its own funds for labor corps operations, prewar colonial authorities insisted on maintaining their own paying scales, which were pitiably low. Workers in the British Solomon Islands Labour Corps, for instance, were paid one shilling or 16 cents a day. In New Caledonia, they earned 46 cents for a 54-hour week. "Had 17 natives assigned to us for any chores we can put them to," an officer of the 6th Division noted stoically during heavy fighting in the Maffin Bay area of Dutch New Guinea. "We are to feed them and provide one blanket each with shelter-half as their pay."

Countless workers fell victim to disease. Pneumonia and influenza incapacitated many. So did dysentery and beriberi, illnesses that resulted from new diets as islanders were forced to eat unfamiliar military rations instead of their traditional Pacific staples. The addition of milk and fresh meat would have been beneficial, but these scarce foodstuffs were reserved for American troops only.[55]

A shortage of service units continued to plague US forces even as they landed in the Philippines in 1944–5. For the invasion of Luzon, for example, the Sixth Army Quartermaster received 40 to 50 percent fewer units than requested. Moreover, transportation on the archipelago was often hampered by heavy rainfall, impassable terrain, poor roads and trails, lack of bridges, and truck shortages stemming from insufficient shipping space.

Not surprisingly, the recruitment of Filipino labor started almost as soon as American soldiers hit the beaches of the densely populated islands. Within the first week of its arrival on Leyte, the 24th Division was hiring Filipinos at an average of 450 a day. They handled supplies on the beach, hauled rations and ammunition to forward units, constructed roads, carried wounded to the rear, and buried casualties. To a greater or smaller degree, most units in the Philippines shared the experience of the 24th Division. During the vicious fighting in the central mountain range of Leyte, the Sixth Army at one time was relying on as many as 8,000 Filipino laborers. In the tortuous advance over mountainous country from Lingayen Gulf to Baguio, on Luzon, the 129th Infantry alone employed about 1,000 Filipinos as carriers. Still during the Luzon campaign, the 6th Division made use of Filipinos even for washing the blood from litters. Meanwhile, behind the front lines, thousands of Filipinos were recruited for labor battalions involved in everything from filling bomb craters to building barracks and hospitals.

Relations with Filipino civilians were generally friendly, and US troops obtained good results in securing the necessary labor by enlisting the support of local leaders, especially parish priests. Still, Filipinos were not always eager to work for the Americans. Some tasks were demanding or outright dangerous. Also, wages followed the prewar Commonwealth Government scales and could be as low as fifty cents a day for general labor. "The danger of paying more," claimed one military pamphlet, "is that the laborer will work one day and then lay off two days to spend what he earned." Women who washed and mended garments for the 7th Division on Leyte were not paid at all: they were told to keep bits of unreclaimed cloth as compensation. In March 1945 even the labor rations were drastically cut in response to the loss of food to the Filipino black market and growing scarcity of subsistence in the US.

Faced by recalcitrant civilians in pressing circumstances, US troops on occasion stopped treating Filipinos as free agents. In the rugged mountains of northern Leyte, armed Filipino guerrillas closely guarded some 300 civilians to prevent them from abandoning the exhausting work of hauling 25-pound loads of rations to the 12th US Cavalry. Meanwhile, a press-gang of the 8th US Cavalry seized all able-bodied Filipinos in sight, forcing the reluctant villagers into service as carriers for the drive to the Diit River.[56]

On the Asian mainland, US policy aimed at avoiding shipment to India of any GI whose work could be done by a local. As a result, Americans swamped the British with requests for dock coolies and workers to build barracks, depots, and airfields. Impatient GIs occasionally fretted and fumed over delays in the assignment of local labor because of colonial red tape and the preoccupation of the British with their own projects. Moreover, American projects threatened to fall behind because the British could not provide enough supervisors, "without whom," an official American historian noted, "the Indian laborer was almost certain to adopt a lacksadaisical attitude toward his work." Despite all this, however, the standard picture in ports and on construction sites within months of the Americans' arrival in India was one of US personnel directing activities and operating heavy machinery, with masses of Indian coolies performing the hard manual work.

For the construction of the Burma Road, that was to link India with China, British authorities furnished swarms of Indian laborers: Pioneer Units of the Indian Army, Indian Tea Association Units organized by the planters of Assam, Indian State Labor Units contributed by the quasi-independent Indian States, tea-garden workers from the Civilian Transport Corps, and contract labor. In addition, the British recruited thousands of Burmese people who were used for the construction of roads and buildings, malaria control, and handling supplies.[57]

American forces in China could, of course, tap into one of the largest labor pools of the world. Chinese authorities were generally forthcoming with labor. But while they handled the challenge with firmness, they did so with little or no concern for the laborer. American naval intelligence officers operating behind Japanese lines in southeast China, for instance, never lacked coolies to carry their supplies. Either Chinese officials, such as magistrates, kindly obliged the allies by furnishing peasants, who owed them regular services under feudal arrangements, or the American officers themselves, under authority vested in them by the Chinese Nationalist Government, impressed civilians to be coolies for the day.[58]

In January 1944, the Allies started a tremendous airfield construction program in the Chengtu area, aimed at stationing B-29s and accompanying fighters. In no time, Chinese authorities mobilized close to 400,000 workers for the immense project. Some 75,000 were contract laborers. Most of the others, however, were conscripted farmers. Within a radius of 150 miles, they were torn away from villages and forced to neglect fields on the basis of 50 workers per 100 households. "The coolies were of all ages, from young children to old men and women," a B-29 pilot of the 444th Bomber Group observed uneasily. "Armed Chinese soldiers were stationed throughout the work area to discourage those who might be tempted to seek employment elsewhere." With nothing more than hand implements and heavy rollers pulled by sheer muscle power, the coolies – all dressed in identical blue jackets and pants – managed to have four B-29 fields and three fighter strips ready for the Americans by as early as 1 May 1944.[59]

Locals were in huge demand not only for hard labor but also as servants. The US military in the Pacific breathed a colonial atmosphere from the very outset of the war as it employed legions of Filipinos as servants. In October 1941, a young Air Force lieutenant from Nebraska felt rather awkward when he had his first meal in the stylish officers' club at Hawaii's Hickam Field. "The tables in the dining room were set for four," he recalled. "Filipino house boys would bring menus to diners for each course, explain course selections, and place napkins in diners' laps." The Navy also had its fair share of servants from the Philippines. While enlisted men were routinely crammed into the malodorous holds of US transports, it happened that officers on deck received excellent meals from the hands of trained Filipino waiters in immaculate white uniforms. Even aboard American submarines, many of the stewards and cooks were Filipinos. "I wish we'd leave so we could find a nice Filippina to do our laundry," a WAC in Dutch New Guinea wrote near the end of the war, after hearing stories of the much more easygoing life in the recently liberated American possession. "That's what they do for the other WACs up there."[60]

In many of the overseas areas, hard dollars and rare goods flaunted in the midst of impoverished millions bought whatever services the Americans could dream of. Away from the combat areas, officers and enlisted personnel alike could afford lifestyles that competed with those of the most seasoned European colonials. "We have native cooks and waiters, all dressed in white," a soldier wrote to his parents in Indianapolis when describing his mess hall in Trincomalee, Ceylon. On Saturday nights, personnel of the 69th General Hospital in Assam employed a punkha wallah, whose sole job it was to operate the canvas ceiling fans by pulling a cord. In more or less permanent bases in India, such as hospitals and airfields, it was the custom to hire personal servants. With five or six to a tent or barrack room, Americans often shared the cost of a local who took care of the communal living space. "We do not do a thing as far as taking care of the place," a WAC sergeant stationed near Calcutta noted complacently while praising the maids or ayahs. "They make the beds, sweep the floors, do all our washing, even our underwear & will go as far as to dress you, if you so desire." "Pity the poor souls who still lead the life of civilians!" a private from Texas jested in a letter describing conditions on his bomber base in northeast India. "Our bearer makes our beds, shines our shoes, sweeps the floor, brings tea and warms water for our baths." This private claimed he made $130 a month. In the Calcutta area, Indian servants charged 30 rupees or $10 for a month's work. Divided by five or six, this meant that Americans in India were being served almost for free. "I'm afraid we've gotten a little spoiled," a nurse admitted after complaining to her parents in Iowa that their ayah had taken a few days off.[61]

Conspicuous wealth went hand in hand with cultural arrogance to create a fitting colonial attitude. In November 1943, an American landing ship lowered its ramp in deep surf in front of a New Guinean village. "The natives," a GI was pleased to note, "immediately saw the situation, and began coming in pairs to the front of the boat where we stood. We put our arms around their shoulders and were on dry ground in a flash." Once acquired, the haughty colonial attitude was hard to shake. After one year in Calcutta, the WAC sergeant was transferred to Chungking, China, in August 1945. "The women who work for us are not as good as our Ayahs," she told her parents, "but they will learn as time goes on."[62]

Indeed, the Chinese were selling whatever services the Indians had performed, and at similar prices. "Life is too easy here," a contented Flying Tiger sighed when describing the "willing 'boys'" of the Kunming base. American pilots on night duty in the Hengyang area in 1942 went to bed knowing that Chinese houseboys would stay awake and alert them with the tinkle of dinner bells at the slightest hint of danger. In 1945, a pamphlet for US forces in the China theater found it necessary to issue a stern warning: "*Handle your servants as humans*: Say 'please' and 'thank you' to your servants, as you would at home . . . Don't assume that you are a member of the master race, and that the Chinese are just here to work for you. This is their country . . ."[63]

Though American troops in many ways tended to regard Asians and Pacific islanders as subject races, they were convinced that many of them liked the US and its people better than any of the other powers that had been exerting control over the region. If Americans had become embroiled in imperialism, they liked to think of themselves at least as imperialists of an enlightened, even sentimental, kind. GIs wanted to believe that the peoples of the region, like children, were responding to the benevolence of their American guardians and tutors with gratitude.

That gratitude, in fact, seemed to predominate in territories that the US had formally possessed for many years and in which it had been able to demonstrate its good intentions most clearly. Not only had the US saved most of their inhabitants from harsh Spanish rule at the turn of the century, but more than 40 years later GIs returned to deliver them from a form of Asian imperialism that had proven to be still more evil. The Chamorros of the island of Guam, for example, did certainly not give the impression that they considered the return of the Americans in the summer of 1944 as a reoccupation. The Japanese had interned thousands of forced laborers in camps at Asinan, Manengon, and Talofofo; countless others had gone into hiding in the hills. US troops found most of them there sick and hungry, but overly joyful at the sight of GIs. All over the tiny island, Guamanians welcomed the former colonizers back with enthusiasm, and many gladly volunteered to help them eliminate Japanese stragglers.[64]

The sprawling Philippine archipelago, however, had been the veritable pearl in the American imperial crown. And military pamphlets confidently stated that this would be reflected in the Filipino reception of the American troops. According to one such pamphlet, GIs could count on two opinions that were "deeply ingrained in the mind and soul of the Filipino." Not only did the Filipino think that the US was "the greatest country in the world," he also believed that the American soldier was "a representative of the finest people in the world." It was obvious why this was so. When the Americans had arrived in 1898, the Filipinos at first had felt that they were "merely swapping masters." This was not surprising, the pamphlet pointed out in what was a rather rare colonial *mea culpa*, as 300,000 Filipinos had died before the US had managed to establish a civil administration. But the guide hastened to add that the US had succeeded in erasing the bitterness of those first years through a colonial administration that was "something utterly new and different to the Far East." Americans had accepted the Filipinos "as equal human beings," had promised them "from the very beginning that they were going to have their *own independent nation* as soon as they were ready for it," and had provided them with "evidence on all sides of our continual good will." Moreover, the Filipinos had now been given "ample time to contrast the behavior of the Japanese soldier with that of the Americans they knew and admired." The GI guide, therefore, thought it "needless to say" that when the Filipinos "greet you it will be as a friend of long standing."

That prediction certainly rang true to the American soldiers who first set foot on Filipino soil in 1944–5. During the landings on Leyte, navigation was instantly hampered by boats full of Filipinos eager to greet the Americans and to supply information on the enemy. Civilians did not even hesitate to jump on US tanks to guide them to hidden Japanese positions. "They are ardently pro-American and feel that they want to do everything to help," a pleased surgeon noted in his diary. At Tacloban, for example, GIs received a tumultuous welcome from Filipinos who crammed the narrow streets and bestowed gifts of fruit and eggs on their liberators. On Luzon, victorious GIs marched under bamboo arches covered with flowers and streamers. Joyous farmers handed out tasty sugarcane candy to troops along every road and trail. In quite a few towns, cheering crowds actually hindered the advance. "The Filipinos almost worship Americans," a moved sailor wrote from Manila Bay, "they seem awfully grateful."[65]

American soldiers were convinced that islanders across the Pacific held them in equally high regard, certainly when compared with Japanese occupiers and European colonials. An official pamphlet pointed to the difference that US troops made for these people, who could now experience "a military rule that is firm but just and that within the limits of security seeks to understand and meet the natives' needs."

GIs believed, however, that the islanders not only appreciated the new regime, but that they also liked the Americans as people. "[I]t seems to be true," correspondent Ira Wolfert wrote from the Solomons, "that, wherever Americans are, the 'natives' like them." This was so because of their egalitarian streak, or as Wolfert put it, "because the American boys squat right down with the people." GIs were quick to give indigenous workers good-natured nicknames, or imaginary first names such as Joe, Dick, or Jimmy. They also made no secret of the fact that they thought it unfair that islanders were paid less for the same work, and gladly augmented their wages with cigarettes, food, and various other goods. In their time off, GIs commonly ignored the nonfraternization rules promulgated by colonial authorities and their own military. In a guide to New Guinea, for example, the Australian author exhorted American soldiers to "be the master" and to maintain a "pose of superiority" at all times. "Don't deliberately descend to his level," the worried Australian implored. Yet on New Guinea as elsewhere, shocked colonial officials watched as freewheeling GIs visited settlements declared off limits, drank local brews with the villagers, and joined in tribal dancing.

Some of this behavior was fueled by overt disdain for colonial authority, prompting European officials to point to the inconsistency between white GIs' tolerance regarding Pacific islanders and their racial bias towards their own colored troops. But GIs also increased their standing with the indigenes unwittingly. In contrast with Western colonials and Japanese occupiers, for example, well-supplied American troops generously gave out cigarettes, clothing, and military supplies. They were unaware, however, that in many Pacific societies, especially Melanesian ones, political stature was acquired through the distribution of resources. Likewise, GIs thought nothing of sitting down with islanders to eat meals, whereas sharing food had a deep symbolical meaning of respect and trust in many indigenous societies. Finally, it was not the physical segregation of black American troops in the US armed forces that struck the islanders but, ironically, the apparent equality between black and white servicemen where it concerned such important matters as housing, clothing, food, and work.

As a result of these and other peculiarities, islanders on the whole indeed felt drawn to American troops. On the New Hebrides, for instance, workers called their American supervisors 'master' – but sometimes also 'brother.' Anthropologists have found that the oral histories of many Melanesian communities in the southwest Pacific contain glowing references to the Americans of the war as egalitarian, friendly, and generous people who were regarded as culturally distinct from Australian, European, and Japanese outsiders. In his study of wartime New Caledonia, historian Stephen Henningham has shown that not only the Melanesian community, but the Javanese and Vietnamese indentured workers, too, generally viewed American soldiers more positively than they did French colonials.[66]

Part II
Frustration

5
Nature

One of the military guides to New Guinea warned GIs in no uncertain terms that on this mysterious island, the Japanese would not be the only, nor even the worst, enemy. "The country itself will fight you with all its forces . . ," the pamphlet insisted. "You must be forever on your guard against this silent enemy, your environment. It is relentless. If you relax, it will get you down." The US military made sure, however, to end on a more assertive note. If the indigenes had learned how to live in New Guinea, then so could American soldiers. "And you should do better," the guide reminded, "for you have with you the advantages of science."[1]

Yet, though the landforms and climates of the other theaters of operation in Asia and the Pacific differed from those of the islands in the Southwest Pacific, most of them would prove to share the one defining quality of New Guinea: the primitive, largely tropical and subtropical environments were determined to offer stiff resistance to Western control in blatant disregard for the authority of modern science.

The natural environment swiftly overpowered the soldiers with the sheer immensity that was endemic to the region. The conflict with Japan was in many ways a battle against distance. GIs received their first taste of the tyranny of space while crossing the Pacific to reach the war. Most soldiers took the slow sea routes. But even those who went by plane felt intimidated by the staggering distances that lay between the war and home. Marine bomber pilots who were rushed from San Diego to Ulithi in the Carolines, first stretched their legs in Hawaii, and then continued their travels for another three days with landings on the islands of Johnston, Majuro, and Guam. "From San Diego we had come six thousand miles," one of the dazzled pilots remarked timidly. "All that way to find a war to fight in."[2]

The challenges of space reminded GIs of some of the greatest American heroes. Charles Lindbergh was one of them, of course. But the memory of Amelia Earhart, the female aviator, popped up even more often. Her story summed up the soldiers' worries. Lindbergh had conquered the Atlantic to receive a hero's welcome in Europe. The Pacific had swallowed Earhart without leaving the faintest trace.[3]

The distances to the war theater were as confounding as they were overwhelming. The voyage across the Pacific threw time in disarray. Hours melted away as troop transports ripped through time zone after time zone. An entire day vanished from the soldiers' lives in a mere instant upon crossing the threshold that was the international dateline. Ships zigzagging across the equator shook up the seasons too. An officer en route to India via Australia wrote in his diary in June 1944: "Since leaving L.A. we've been through Spring, Summer, Fall, Winter, Spring and now we're into Summer again. All in about 47 days."[4]

When at last they arrived at their destinations, many GIs found themselves thoroughly disoriented both in time and space. Anxious soldiers who looked to the stars for reassurance realized with a shock that the long passage to war had not even left the skies intact. Of all the alien constellations, only the newly discovered Southern Cross offered a ray of consolation.[5]

The endless spaces of sky, land, and sea were like vacuums sucking in and absorbing everyone and everything that dared enter them. Skies were volatile and malevolent. The electric flames of Saint Elmo's fire that attacked planes over the Himalaya scared even the most experienced crewmen shuttling between India and China. Bomber pilots talked with disbelief about the powerful currents of the recently identified jet stream that blew heavy B-29s off course at high altitudes, prompting correspondent Robert Sherrod to write that the weather over Japan was "as violent as the nature of the Japanese people." In 1942, a dumbstruck sailor described in his journal how an aircraft from his carrier, the USS *Hornet*, had entered a cloud formation in the Southwest Pacific never to appear again. Not even the wreckage was found.[6]

The Asian landmasses – the monumental mountains and gigantic plains that made up the war theaters of China, Burma, and India – were equally threatening. Of all the B-24s and their ten-men crews lost over the vast expanse of China during the war, some one hundred aircraft have remained missing until this very day.[7]

But if, as Roderick Nash has observed, wilderness designates any environment in which humans feel "stripped of guidance, lost, and perplexed," then the Pacific Ocean was the ultimate wilderness, more disquieting even than the densest jungle. The *Guide to the Western Pacific* informed American soldiers that this stormy ocean was both endless (nearly 70 million square miles) and bottomless (with trenches as deep as 35,000 feet). A historian of the USS *South Dakota* noted that when the battleship returned home from Tokyo Bay in September 1945, after three years of Pacific duty, "it had traveled 246,970 miles – roughly the distance from the earth to the moon."[8]

The inescapable void of the ocean gave rise to much anxiety. On 21 June 1944, the brand-new hospital ship USS *Comfort* sailed out of Los Angeles for Brisbane, Australia. After eighteen days of nothing but sky and sea, the inexperienced American passengers grew so uneasy, and their doubts about the crew's navigating skills so loud, that the captain thought it wise to allay tensions. He announced in the ship's paper exactly when and where they would sight land, praying all the while that he would not err.[9]

Away from the ocean's periphery, islands looked less and less solid. The product of slow volcanic and coral accumulation, their contours porous and uncertain, the pinprick islets and reefs served merely as counterpoints for the vastness of the Pacific, humbly acknowledging the reign of water. Of the 2,000 tiny islands of the Marshall archipelago, for example, not a single one rose more than 30 feet above sea level. The ocean exuded a threatening, stifling atmosphere. The waters "made the earth seem trivial," a pilot on Ulithi observed. "Out here the ocean distances commanded space, and the atoll was a meager refuge, a dot on the vast surface, something you could miss, or lose."[10]

Seemingly supernatural phenomena highlighted the eeriness of the blank and empty ocean. At sunrise or sunset, inexplicable green flashes suddenly set on fire the dark horizon for brief ghostly seconds. At night, bow waves mysteriously emitted a phosphorescence so radiant it made them look like lapping flames. "Of late I have grown increasingly aware what an implacable opponent the ocean is," a sailor operating from Hawaii wrote to his wife. "It is pitiless, relentless, never-ceasing, unconquerable, and restless. Yes, and even treacherous."[11]

To die on such an unforgiving ocean appeared the epitome of a soldier's insignificance. Perhaps no other ritual affected GIs more, therefore, than the burial at sea. The sight of canvas-wrapped, mummy-like figures sliding into their deep watery graves was an unnerving experience. "I'll be over it in the morning after I sleep a while," a shaken destroyer sailor assured his wife after having watched the ceremony on another ship through binoculars. "I suppose you know what a small kid I am really."[12]

The giant gaping grave of the Pacific hungrily swallowed victims until the very last days of the war. On 29 July 1945, the USS *Indianapolis* was torpedoed en route from Guam to Leyte. In a rear area supposedly under American control and teeming with Allied activity, the loss of this heavy cruiser and its 1,200 men went unnoticed for three and a half days. Of the more than 800 men who managed to abandon ship, no fewer than 484 had died in the water by the time the search was called off on 8 August, just days before Japan's surrender.[13]

The waters in which the *Indianapolis* went down were placid. When storms whipped the ocean into a frenzy, human forces were not even needed to help wreak havoc. In the thirteenth century, cyclones destroyed the Mongol invasion forces of Kublai Khan twice in seven years in full view of Japan's shores. So grateful were the Japanese that they called the storms '*Kamikaze*' or 'Divine Wind.' Seven centuries had done nothing to tame the powerful winds of the Pacific. It was the typhoon – described by Melville in *Moby Dick* as the "direst of all storms" – that put most fear in the hearts of American soldiers. This tropical cyclone was the bane of the US Pacific Fleet in 1944–5. Late in April 1944, one typhoon swept through a part of New Guinea where American troops were stationed. "In a few hours," a dispirited engineer noted in his dairy, "nature had caused more damage than the Japanese were able to cause in two years' bombings." A particularly wicked typhoon was that which in December 1944 dealt death and destruction to the Third Fleet while it was in the midst of preparations for the invasion of Luzon. In just two days, mountainous green-water waves seriously damaged seven ships and capsized three destroyers, killing almost 800 sailors. "Later," admitted a sailor from one of the surviving destroyers, "we covered landings at Iwo Jima and Okinawa, which included numerous air attacks, but they seemed like play compared to the typhoon."[14]

The divine winds reverted to their historical roles by becoming truly relentless the very moment enemy forces once again threatened the Japanese homeland. One typhoon forced American convoys on their way to Okinawa for the invasion of 1 April 1945 to alter course, causing delays and minor damage. On 5 June, yet another typhoon caught the US Navy by surprise off the Ryukyu island. The vicious storm again ravaged the Third Fleet, damaging dozens of ships and nearly a hundred airplanes, ripping the steel bow from the heavy cruiser *Pittsburgh* as if it was a mere toy.[15]

If the mass of land and water made steel planes and ships appear fragile toys, then it seemed to reduce flesh and blood to utter meaninglessness. In 1942, a cocky American pilot, stationed near the border between China and Burma, proudly flew his P-40 all the way to the famous mountain barrier to test the brand-new fighter to the utmost. He returned a humbled man. "Looking at those massive, snow-covered spires," the airman confessed, "I respected the magnitude of nature and the magnificence of the Himalayas, and I perceived the insignifance of man."[16]

Against the backdrop of the universal ocean, soldiers suddenly looked so diminutive that they reminded one of crawling insects. On his way to the Solomons in a bomber, correspondent Ira Wolfert sympathized with the men on the ships and islands far below, who were, he wrote, working "heedless as ants." A similar analogy forced itself on a sailor who gazed at comrades moving about on New Caledonia, an island surrounded by nothing but deep blue. "It was a funny sight to see the American sailors all over the high, bare hills," he mused. "They looked like a swarm of little ants."[17]

Nothing more powerfully hammered home the message of a mortal's irrelevance amidst the high seas than to be told bluntly that it was one of the regulations that ships would not stop for anybody falling overboard. In

1944, a British sailor who had died of heart failure aboard a ship en route to Bombay was given a burial at sea. "Just as the sun set, and after a short ceremony," an aggrieved American soldier related, "they slid his body, wrapped in canvas, down a long wooden plank into the ocean. We never stopped or even slowed . . ." "What shall I write you," an officer who had just sailed from California to Hawaii asked his wife, "of the loneliness, the vague disquiet, the awe, the insignificance [the ocean] creates in me?"[18]

With the dead as well as the living being gobbled up by unfathomable empty spaces, it was easy for soldiers not only to sense their insignificance, but to feel abandoned, too. GIs felt as if they were vanishing in Asia's voids without leaving so much as a trace for the loved ones they had left behind. Strict censorship regulations regarding location heightened such feelings. Until late in the war, American soldiers were often not permitted to mention specific islands or ports, only that they were 'somewhere in the Pacific.'[19]

Even without the imposed vagueness, however, GIs found it hard to lift the home front's ignorance of their whereabouts. In the spring of 1944, a soldier of the 40th Division was finally allowed to divulge his exact location in a letter home. It was apparently not enough to bring him back from geographical obscurity, for on 12 July 1944 he had to prod his parents again, this time in an impatient letter: "Have you found New Britain yet?" An equally irritated GI, who weeks earlier had at last been able to tell his family which island of the Marianas he was on, wrote home in August 1945: "Please read my letters carefully . . . I asked you to send a map of Guam and you sent a map of the entire Pacific, Asia etc."[20]

Soldiers were convinced that the American press had also lost sight of them, as the few outdated newspapers they could get their hands on appeared to focus time and again on the war in Europe. Reports from her Marine Corps son convinced even the First Lady that the war in Asia had become "America's forgotten front," both in terms of troop welfare and morale. To bring attention to this problem and to alleviate the situation, Eleanor Roosevelt in the summer of 1943 embarked on a remarkable mission to the still dangerous South Pacific and Guadalcanal. Yet despite such publicized efforts, fear of abandonment continued to haunt American soldiers until late in the war. "It would dampen our elation over the events in Europe," a battalion surgeon spoke for many of his comrades, "because we didn't think they, meaning the leaders in the United States, would pay much attention to us in the Pacific when the war ended there."[21]

The sinister absence of civilization was as disturbing as the region's heart-stopping immensity. Whether on Pacific islands of coral and ash or in the baking deserts, stifling jungles, and dizzying plains of Asia, nowhere could be found much of the mental reassurance of what Samuel Hynes has called "the imposed order of human occupation."[22]

Despite brief glimpses of chaotic Indian cities and quaint Chinese towns, the dominant view from the American front and rear lines on the Asian mainland was that of a universe beyond man's control. In June 1944, fresh troops arrived in India to join American forces at Ledo in upper Assam. One of them described the arduous voyage: "It took about two weeks for this part of the trip – Bombay to the Burma border . . . We rode the rails till there was no more – the end of the line you might say. Seemed like the end of the world."[23]

Civilization had acquired even less of a grip on many of the islands in the Pacific. A GI who arrived in the Southwest Pacific in December 1944 was assigned to an Air Force rescue squadron operating from Morotai Island in the Moluccas. He crisscrossed the area for more than two months before he even saw what could pass for a modern building – a metal shed. In March 1943, after four months at Guadalcanal, the Americal Division moved to Fiji for a long stretch of rest and reorganization. It did not do the veterans much good. "The boys get all the rest needed in two days," one officer complained. "What they need is recreation, bright lights, music, liquor, white women, and a new area. These areas in the islands are all the same. Mountains & jungles; flies and mosquitoes; sun and rain." In December 1943, the men were shipped off once again. This time to the steamy island of Bougainville, where they would stay for more than a year.[24]

After 12 long months in the Southwest Pacific, including duty in New Guinea and New Britain, a GI on Biak Island received a letter from a boyhood friend with an infantry unit in France. The American devoured the information and later that day lamented in his diary: "It is a more interesting war there. When you take a place, it's a town and civilized. Time must pass quickly for them." A sergeant in New Guinea who received a similar letter, told his mother: "I hope that the next place we go to there will be civilized people to meet and deal with."[25]

Many soldiers in the Southwest Pacific pinned all their hopes on the Philippines for that to happen. They longed for action on the archipelago, which they expected – after almost half a century of American control – to offer, as one WAC in New Guinea put it, "at least a semblance of civilization." When they finally made it to Luzon, veterans of the Solomons hollered and slapped each other's backs upon seeing railroads, billboards, and paved streets. On Palawan, men of the 41st Division – who had not seen a town in three years and called themselves the 'Jungleers' – could not get enough even from such simple operations as turning on water faucets and opening doors and windows.[26]

Still, in the end the Philippines, too, were a letdown. Upon closer scrutiny, man's hold on the islands appeared weak and indecisive, with many settlements small and unimpressive, no more than shanty towns. Moreover, war was loosening civilization's tentative grip. A number of sizeable towns on various islands were burned to the ground. The capital

Manila, the 'Pearl of the Orient' that had made so many GIs dream of bright city lights, virtually vanished in a fierce, month-long battle. To an American who flew low over the city after the battle, what was left of it looked like "a gigantic archaeological site in the process of being excavated." From that site, an officer of the 43rd Division wrote home in March 1945: "it being our first taste of ruined cities it has created a feeling of great discouragement and a yearning for home that grows hourly."[27]

GIs involved in island-hopping further to the north did not fare better. By the time Americans managed to take Naha, Okinawa's capital and principal city, it was nothing but a ruin with only one single wall still standing.[28]

Sucked up by the region's immense emptiness, cut off from home and civilization by daunting distances, American soldiers suffered from a tremendous sense of isolation. They worked and fought, Ira Wolfert contemplated as he stared at the ocean from a bomber en route to the Solomons in 1942, "in a loneliness that cannot be imagined." The Solomons campaign starkly confirmed Wolfert's first impression. "Their only company is themselves," the numbed correspondent wrote. "Their only relaxation has to be found in themselves."[29]

That was true of sailors, pilots, and soldiers alike. Aboard ship, the moment the home shore faded, the loneliness thickened. Protective blimps disappeared, then the jolly porpoises, eventually even the obtrusive gulls. "Sea calm, bright blue," an officer reported in his diary from an epicenter of emptiness, "no whales, no fish, no birds, no nothing. Just ocean. Horizon clear." This soldier was sailing from Los Angeles to India. The voyage would take many monotonous weeks, but it at least promised him a destination. Sailors chained to their vessels for the duration of the war were not so lucky, and the salty solitude corroded the nerves of all but the most experienced. When in 1945 Ernie Pyle, veteran correspondent of the European war, joined the crew of a small carrier in the Pacific, he was soon struck by a longing for home much more tense even than that among the veterans in Italy and France. "And nothing to look forward to," he attempted to explain to the home front. "They never saw anybody but themselves. They sailed and sailed, and never arrived anywhere . . ."[30]

Only those actually condemned to year upon year of naval isolation, truly understood what Pyle wanted to convey. "When you are cooped up aboard a small ship," an officer on a tug told his wife in July 1943, "it becomes your whole world and your prison." Fourteen long months later, the same sailor, restless and irritated, wrote from the Central Pacific: "I want to prune, and spade, and milk, and cut grass, and pull weeds, and smell the earth."[31]

Unfortunately, the closest the Pacific Fleet could take its sailors to that bucolic vision was Mogmog. Late in 1944, this tiny islet of Ulithi atoll, halfway between the Philippines and Guam, was transformed into the

US Navy's main recreation center. So crammed with bluejackets was the island from time to time that, according to one naval historian, "from a distance it looked like one of those Maine islands where seagulls breed." One record day, the center entertained as many as 20,000 men, most of whom felt lonelier on trampled and trashed Mogmog than they had been aboard ship.[32]

Mogmog gave sailors a taste of what ground and air units, stationed on hundreds of similar islands, went through. The Solomon island of Pavuvu, for instance, was so small that the 1st Marine Division was forced to conduct field exercises at company rather than regimental or battalion size. In August 1944, the 38th Service Squadron was dropped on the minuscule island of Middleburg, off the coast of Dutch New Guinea. The Air Force unit was kept there for half a year. "Smaller than Alcatraz," a claustrophobic mechanic lamented in his diary in February 1945, "this place has been like a prison." Aircrews could take off at least. But flying through empty skies over equally empty seas before landing again on islands no bigger than a carrier was not much of a relief. Moreover, the strain of constant overwater flying greatly contributed to a mental disorder known as aeroneurosis.[33]

Troops on the Asian mainland were immersed in an equally nerve-racking isolation. On a front not very familiar to the people at home, described by an official chronicler as "an obscure corner of the world previously known only to Naga headhunters," thousands of Americans spent some of the best years of their young lives beavering away at the construction of the Ledo Road in Assam and Burma. GIs stationed in the China theater perhaps received somewhat more attention in the US, but it made their seclusion hardly more bearable. As a 1945 souvenir booklet put it, "cut off from the rest of the world by the Japanese, by the world's highest mountains, by the wastelands of Mongolia," Americans in China too had begun to experience "that walled-in feeling."[34]

Bottomless monotony followed close on the heels of isolation. A battalion surgeon simply titled chapter two of his memoirs of war in the Pacific: "New Guinea: Boredom." Twenty-seven pages the physician needed to detail every baleful aspect of the enervating weariness of life on the steamy island.[35]

During the long empty stretches between action that typified much of the war with Japan, American soldiers fought a desperate – and ultimately unwinnable – battle with poisonous ennui. In July 1943, an officer on the tug *Tern* told his wife that to kill time his men had now turned to making lamps from empty cartridge shells. A few, he added, were carving model outrigger canoes; some were even weaving rugs. En route to New Guinea from Brisbane in 1943, the 58th Evacuation Hospital, which had just completed the long trip from the US to Australia, saw its ship pull into a harbor near Townsville. Though the vessel remained anchored off the Australian coast for seven endless days, the restless troops were not allowed to leave ship even once. One of the unit's surgeons noted in his diary that the men at last "all degenerated to ring making." Dozens of fed up soldiers could be heard rhythmically hammering Australian coins against the ship's iron hull. Those who did not have hammers to make rings out of coins tried spoons. The din continued for hours, until the skipper was driven mad and abruptly put a halt to the recreation of last resort.[36]

Soldiers who spent long months and years in isolated areas developed all kinds of occupational therapies. By far the most frequent off-duty activity was letter writing. A survey of enlisted men in New Guinea in 1943 showed that on a typical day most wrote two or more letters.[37]

The same survey revealed that 60 percent of the men on the island wished to see more movies, preferably upbeat ones – musicals, comedy, light romance. The US armed forces responded by setting up as many mobile outdoor theaters as possible. In April 1943, correspondent Mack Morriss noticed that, even while booming artillery smothered the sound and buckled the screen, riveted GIs were watching *Pride of the Yankees* on Guadalcanal.[38]

In New Guinea, 53 percent of the soldiers wanted their companies to receive good radios or phonographs with records. Reading material was equally scarce. Forty percent of Americans in New Guinea craved more magazines, 19 percent a better assortment of books. On many an island dog-eared magazines and battered books – from popular novels like *The Robe* and *For Whom the Bell Tolls* to the poems of Kipling and Whitman – passed from hand to hand. "Everything in English," an American pilot in Kunming, China, noted in 1942, "is read slowly and deliberately and properly digested." His personal trove included old issues of *The Atlantic* and a particularly welcome copy of *Robinson Crusoe*.[39]

GIs turned to sports and games with a vengeance. All major American sports were popular, though on small islands soldiers were often confined to swimming, volleyball, badminton, table tennis, and horseshoes. Gambling boomed, and soldiers from India to Samoa reported endless sessions of poker, craps, bridge, whist, blackjack, casino, cribbage, pinochle, and bingo.

Troops eventually clung to almost anything capable of puncturing the timeless void that imprisoned them. On Christmas Island, for instance, soldiers painted numbers on crabs, placed bets, then sat around large circles waiting to see which one would crawl out first. "I'm attempting to grow a moustache," a fighter pilot who had been in New Guinea for 10 months proudly announced to his father in June 1943. "It doesn't look too bad I think and it gives you something extra to take up your time."[40]

At some point, however, even the most ingenuous GIs ran out of ideas to break the monotony, finally abandoning themselves to quiet lethargy. "They always seemed to be asleep," correspondent Robert Sherrod observed while accompanying marines from the South Pacific to Tarawa, "in their bunks, on the decks, under the landing boats, on any given surface." A pilot who arrived fresh from the US was struck by a similar languor among the veterans on Ulithi atoll. They were disheveled, undisciplined and, he noted, they "seemed to sleep for astonishing portions of every day."[41]

In the weary sameness, GIs gradually discontinued differentiating between the artificial units of time imposed by modern society. In March 1945, a resigned soldier on Ramree Island, off the coast of Burma, wrote to his parents in Indianapolis: "Thanks for the Easter Card. It will simply be another day, the time passes whether it's Monday, Thursday, this week or that, it's all the same."[42]

The leaden tedium eventually sapped soldiers of their very ability to measure time. In correspondence, they began to confuse days, to mistake dates, or to leave them out altogether. A disoriented sailor aboard the USS *Tabberer* told his wife, in a letter written in mid-Pacific: "I'm leaving the date off this letter until I find out what date this is. I know it is Tuesday cause last night we had chicken salad for supper. We always have that on Monday cause we always have chicken on Sunday. I never know what day it is unless I think of how long it has been since we had chicken. The cook always seems to know."[43]

If the immensity and emptiness, and the sense of isolation that came with it, frayed the nerves of American soldiers, so did the shifting restlessness of the earth they were supposed to conquer and subdue. Its stubborn crust seemed to derive perverse pleasure from resisting military authority every step of the way. With the intimidating Himalaya looming behind their backs, signalmen on the Asian mainland struggled to set up an aircraft warning system for the Tenth Air Force in 1942–3. Hundreds of spotters maintained a visual warning network in the border region between India and Burma. But the Americans managed to introduce radar only in the Assam Valley. The tenacious hills and mountains of Burma refused to accept modern detecting equipment. They made that very clear in a test with the high-tech SCR-516. After months of grueling road construction, it took elephants to transport the heavy components to the intended location. There Americans learned that so many echoes from the mountainous terrain smeared the radar sweep that airplane reflections were completely lost in the glow. Meanwhile, the area's ridges and canyons nervously moved about as innumerable fault planes stirred. In the unsettled and relatively unexplored Patkai Hills of Burma, for example, lonely American engineers wrestling with the Ledo Road were made even more fidgety by frequent tremors.[44]

In the Pacific, American soldiers were surprised to find that many of the islands were mountainous, too. One or more peaks of up to 3,000 feet towered over each of the major islands of the Solomons; Mount Balbi on Bougainville was more than 10,000 feet. From these mountain peaks dropped rugged ridges that sloped towards the sea and made life excruciatingly painful for soldiers. Most notorious became the ridgeline stretching from Guadalcanal's Mount Austen. Here the Japanese made their strongest defensive effort of the campaign. Carrying stretchers up and down the steep slopes so exhausted Americans that litter squads had to be enlarged from the usual 4 to an exceptional 6, 8, or even 12 men. On 2 January 1943, it took 175 litter bearers five hours to evacuate 20 casualties from Hill 27 over a distance of no more than one air mile.[45]

During the Hollandia operation in New Guinea late in April 1944, tanks were brought ashore at Tanahmerah Bay to help troops push inland. On slopes as steep as 60 degrees, however, the narrow hairpin trail that snaked across the Takari Hills stopped the armor in its very tracks. After two weeks of idling, the humiliated monsters were forced to creep back to their LSTs and to rejoin the rest of the 1st Tank Battalion stationed in the Solomons.[46]

In the Central Pacific, hills and mountains resisted control with equal determination. On Saipan, for example, the terrain hampered naval guns in their crucial support of infantry. From the island's center, regal Mount Tapotchau denied artillerymen all sight of targets in the northern half, forcing six spotter planes to stay in the air continuously until the end of the operation. Rock-hard coral played an equally important part in delaying the island's invaders. It took a company of the 105th Infantry on Saipan's southern coast from noon until midnight to advance a mere 200 yards. What slowed them down was not the Japanese, but jagged coral pinnacles jutting up as high as 90 feet.[47]

By the time Americans were fighting their way across the large islands of the Philippines – mountainous northern Luzon in particular – they were relying on thousands upon thousands of locals to help carry equipment in terrain that refused to let any motorized vehicle pass.[48]

Worse than the solid obstacles thrown in the path of soldiers was the brooding mysteriousness that the islands breathed. Upon approaching Guadalcanal, a sergeant of the 29th Marines could not help thinking that the island looked "as ominous as the hidden fire in its belly." Indeed, military guides pointed out that most of the islands Americans were fighting for were the peaks of volcanoes that had pushed up from the ocean floor. The mountains of lava remained visible in varying stages of development. Some still showed their massive peaks and ridges. Other mountains had sunk below the surface, displaying only the coral reefs that had accumulated on their shoulders and that formed the typical atolls of the region.[49]

Even more unsettling to soldiers than the thought that they were clinging to the fringes of volcanoes, was the realization that many of the mountain mouths had, in fact, not yet stopped spewing fire from the bowels of the earth. Military booklets made GIs uneasy with stories of the 50 volcanoes still occasionally active on the Japanese islands, and of the famous

Krakatau in the Dutch East Indies "which blew itself up in 1883 with a blast that was heard 3,000 miles away."[50]

With over 400 active volcanoes in and around Pacific waters, GIs on more than one island were forced to witness firsthand how their angry rumblings merged with the din of enemy fire. On the northern end of the Solomon island chain, American troops executed a landing on Bougainville in November 1943, with smoke and steam billowing high above them, spat into the air by defiant Mount Bagana. In a letter to a local newspaper, a private from Kansas told the macabre story of what had happened to him and his medical unit when their troop transport sailed past a group of islands somewhere in the Pacific in August 1944. Trouble had started when one afternoon officers sighted huge black clouds rushing towards the ship. In a matter of minutes, day changed into night. A thick layer of ash settled on the deck. The ship switched on its navigational lights, soldiers put on gas masks, and chaplains moved among the men to keep them calm. When visibility was down to nil, the transport grounded on a coral reef. Its soldiers were hurriedly rescued by other ships. The transport apparently had fallen prey to what the Kansan described as "a pumice ash storm, resulting from a volcanic eruption."[51]

Yet no volcano intimidated American soldiers more than the one that had given life to Iwo Jima and continued to watch over it jealously. One of the final stepping stones to the Japanese heartland, the island consisted of nothing but molten rock, covered with deep layers of soft ash. Soldiers said that digging foxholes on Iwo Jima was like making a hole in a barrel of wheat. The grayish dust forced even powerful, tracked vehicles to a standstill. There was barely any concealment on the drab island. A sprinkling of trees. Few bushes. No grass. Mount Suribachi itself remained inactive during the war, but jets of steam hinted at the constant threat of eruption, and a foul sulfurous odor rose from a hissing soil that gave some men serious burns. "I can't forget," a shaken marine wrote immediately after the vicious battle for Iwo Jima, "my first impression of the ugly looking volcano, mean looking and dark."[52]

Earth's fiery bowels made the land stretch and heave. While heavy fighting continued on Bougainville in December 1943, a number of tremors and quakes pitched in to rock the island even more. Soldiers were thrown to the ground, gigantic trees crashed, foxholes collapsed. Quivering aftershocks kept the soldiers on edge for weeks. During the battle for Manila, earthquake-proof buildings of heavily reinforced concrete, impervious even to point-blank American artillery fire, reminded GIs of the rebelliousness smoldering beneath much of Asia's crust. So did the *Guide to Japan* when it mentioned that in 1,200 years more than 2,000 major earthquakes had terrorized the enemy's islands, including the great shock of 1923 that had leveled Yokohama and destroyed a third of Tokyo. "Nature," the guide contemplated, "acts as if she resented the artificial forms, into which the Japanese try to force her, by breaking out violently."[53]

But GIs were kept constantly aware of the fact that nature in this region resented not only the Japanese. Earth – boiling and churning – appeared to be still in its formative stages, not ready or willing yet to accept and accommodate people. It gave soldiers the surreal feeling of having been transported far back in time. How far depended solely on the depth of the soldier's imagination. In September 1943, a pilot crashed in the interior of New Guinea. He regained consciousness in 10-foot-tall kunai grass, amidst stifling heat and oppressive silence. "Suddenly," the pilot recalled, "I was on the ground with a feeling of loneliness and of being thrust backward 500 years in time." Even 40 years after the event, a marine vividly remembered that he had thought to himself one morning, upon seeing the mist lift over the Matanikau River on Guadalcanal: "My God, this is what the island must have looked like millions of years ago."[54]

The sensation was not so much that of the untouched, Edenic nature of man's beginnings, but of an environment before history, and beyond time. "From our transport," reported Robert Sherrod, "Saipan in profile looked like a low-lying prehistoric monster, whose spine rose in the center to 1,554-foot Mount Tapotchau." The experience could, in a flash, reveal not only what the earth had been, but what it would someday be again. Such visions left little doubt about the fate of humans in nature's inexorable cycle. Gazing down on Eniwetok, a sailor described to his wife the emotions the primeval atoll triggered in him: "Romance and adventure, but above all a feeling of loneliness, endless time, and insignificance of man. Christ, these islands and palms will be here millions of years after all the Japs and Americans have vanished into fertilizer, and coral animals are the most highly evolved forms of life!"[55]

An enervating climate further deepened the sense of isolation and alienation. Although conditions differed in the various war zones of Asia and the Pacific, most operations took place in an environment of tremendous heat. It complicated the workings of the American military in a myriad of unforeseen ways. Standard lubricating oils in planes on New Guinea ran off, when they did not simply evaporate. Pilots of early B-29 models came to fear take-offs in India because broiling ground temperatures combined with inadequate cooling systems to set motors on fire. Marines on Tarawa discovered that water in metal five-gallon cans that had been filled in New Zealand was almost undrinkable because the heat had dissolved the inner enamel lining.[56]

What affected steel and oil, upset flesh and blood even more. Medical statistics show that in the Central and South Pacific, the number of officially recorded soldiers who fell victim to excessive heat was slightly higher than that in North Africa and Italy. But in the China–Burma–India theater it was 3 times higher, and in the Southwest Pacific as much as 20 times higher.[57]

The intensity of the sun matched the immensity of the region. Steel hulls plying the Pacific Ocean became so hot that sailors could not put their hands on the compartments inside ships without getting burned.

A naval intelligence officer operating in southeast China called the sun "brutal." Without adequate protection it could "raise blisters in ten minutes and knock you flat on the ground." According to a marine on Peleliu, one of the Palau Islands, the sun over the barren coral "bore down on us like a giant heat lamp." Some men's tongues became so swollen they could neither talk nor swallow. Unshaded shells exploded. On other islands, dense vegetation accumulated hot air like a furnace. "Terrible heat that just bears down," an officer on Guadalcanal noted in his diary in December 1942. "Impossible to keep up the pep of the men. Enough to drive them crazy lying in those fox holes for days at a time." Terrible sunburns swelled the skin and colored it scarlet; blisters turned into festering sores. The loss of fluids and salts caused mean headaches, nausea, cramps, exhaustion. Soldiers became mentally confused, some simply passed out.[58]

All the while, American military reports showed a special concern as to the ability of white soldiers to continue functioning in tropical climates. The notion that whites could not be successfully transplanted to torrid zones – humid tropics in particular – because of their degenerating physical and mental effects had become widespread in Europe and the US by the late nineteenth century. To avoid those effects, colonials had periodically returned home to soak up healthier air. Or they had fled to specially built rest centers at higher elevations during the worst of the hot season. It was to shield its soldiers and their families against what was called tropical 'inertia' or 'debility' that the US military, in the first decades of the twentieth century, had constructed mountain resorts at Baguio in the Philippines and Kilauea in Hawaii similar to the hill stations of the British in India and Burma. Women and children in particular had been encouraged to seek refuge in these resorts.[59]

A comparative study of female and male personnel in the Southwest Pacific for the first quarter of 1945 – written by a male – still seemed to suggest that white women were the least suited for the tropics. According to the report, incidences of exhaustion, diarrhea, dermatological conditions, and upper respiratory infections were higher among women than men. The author admitted that the more liberal use of soap by women might explain some of the skin irritations. He also pointed out that since women, unlike most men, were quartered in barracks, increased cross infection could account for the respiratory problems. However, the conclusion of the report read: "It is felt that the tropical climate and the lower inherent physiological degree of stamina possessed by the female, as compared to the male, are contributory factors."[60]

Yet ambivalence about the ability of white males to perform effectively in tropical climates also persisted during the war. "Is there evidence," asked an observer report for the US Armed Forces Far East in March 1945, "that some races tolerate the jungle better than others?" The Eighth Army surgeon thought not. But the chief medical officer of the 25th Division replied that he was uncertain. Although his division had been accumulating experience with tropical climates in Hawaii and the Solomons since 1941, heat exhaustion victims still constituted an estimated 5 to 10 percent of its medical casualties in the Luzon campaign that had started in January 1945.[61]

In most war zones, moisture was as predominant as heat. In the Southwest Pacific, it rained daily, even during the so-called dry season, with coastal areas receiving well over 100 inches annually, and highlands 200 inches or more per year. Across much of Burma, too, rainfall averaged 200 inches a year. Similar conditions existed in those portions of India nearest to China, where most American troops in the British colony happened to be concentrated: many places in Assam had to absorb more than 100 inches of rain each year, one area receiving some 1,000 inches annually.[62]

Rain could pour down with a violence so unrestrained it intimidated even soldiers familiar with the din of battle. "Last night I woke up, and thought an express train was coming into the barrack," a nurse on Goodenough Island told her parents. "The rain made such a tremendous roar, it scared me silly. . . . To attempt to go outside in that deluge, you'd be beaten to the ground by the sheer force of it."[63]

GIs detested not just the rain. A dense, sticky humidity clung to soldiers, covering them with a pearly sweat that could not evaporate. On Guadalcanal, correspondent Mack Morriss noted in his diary: "the air thru which the rain comes down takes on the qualities of the rain and brings the moisture where rain itself could never reach. There is no escape from it in the tropics . . ."[64]

Moisture in its many guises ceaselessly haunted the American forces. Squalls thick like walls obscured signal lights during the invasion of New Georgia, luring several landing forces onto the wrong shores in June 1943. Some months later, in the Central Pacific, they interrupted radio contact between the first waves that landed on Makin atoll and their support ships. Downpours drowned mortar barrels on Bougainville and on several occasions silenced chemical mortar battalions on Leyte. They caused so much damage to the vital Ledo Road into Burma that by July 1943 all traffic on its forward sections had to be halted, prompting a dissatisfied General Stilwell to demand changes in the command overseeing its construction.

Mud paralyzed men and machines. Sudden downpours created quagmires that cut off the 21st Infantry during the landing at Tanahmerah Bay, Dutch New Guinea, in April 1944. Only airdrops and hand-carrying of food and equipment over slimy trails prevented the unit's situation from becoming critical, but the inland advance had to be halted. A year later, amidst rainfall that reached 40 inches per month, even the carabaos the GIs relied on in Mindanao got stuck in the goo.

Flooded rice lands forced signalmen to construct large parts of a communication pole line between Calcutta and Kunming with the help of local boats and elephants. Swamps and paddies beyond the landing areas made sure that all units of the 96th Division fell considerably short of their objectives on their first day ashore at Leyte in October 1944. As late as May 1945, a US Army report on the engineering lessons learned from the Filipino campaign warned: "The rate of monthly precipitation and nature of soils and availability of surfacing material affects tactical mobility to a far greater degree than most commanders realize. More instruction and emphasis are needed in service schools to this respect."[65]

Even if such advice had come in time for subtropical Okinawa, it would scarcely have made much difference. In April and May 1945, far less rain fell on the Ryukyu island than preinvasion meteorological tables had predicted. But then, on 21 May, monsoon winds suddenly unleashed a counteroffensive of Noachian scale. Sheets of rain came down almost without interruption every single day and night until the early part of June. Roads were washed out, bridges swept away, airfields turned into lakes. The motorized Tenth Army came to a standstill. Every road to the front was jammed with mile-long lines of tanks, trucks and jeeps – all clogged and idle. No significant attacks could be mounted. Limited artillery fire persisted, the booming muted by rain, guns instantly disgorging shells that had taken soldiers half a day to haul forward in the mud by hand. Supplies of all kinds dwindled. Troops became hungry. Foxholes filled up and caved in. "Rain," a marine remarked, "became the medium we lived in, a part of our air." Not until the weather loosened its grip on the island were the Americans able to resume their strike towards the heart of Japan.[66]

In one of the region's supreme ironies, nature, amidst moisture that permeated everything, perversely denied soldiers safe drinking water in sufficient quantities. Although sailors made economic use of the precious commodity, fresh water was often in short supply on an immense ocean with few islands and even fewer springs. Ships used evaporators and condensers to add to their fresh water stores from the salty deep. Nevertheless, during the battle of the Solomons in 1942, the USS *Gamble*, for example, was forced to chase rain squalls and once had to send all hands ashore to fill hundreds of five-gallon cans from a spring high up a muddy trail on Tulagi Island.[67]

Ground troops often had a still harder time finding potable water. Modern water utilities were rare, and the few existing ones had often been destroyed, as was the case in Manila. Moreover, local water sources were often polluted and troops lacked adequate supplies of purifying halazone tablets. There was only so much water that units could carry with them onto beaches and into jungles, and it took time for engineer units to establish filtration plants and drill deep wells.

In such conditions, fresh water sources turned into prime military objectives. When US forces in February 1943 found the landings in the Russell Islands unopposed, for instance, engineer patrols immediately pushed inland to find drinking water, a problem at least as pressing as the enemy in these Solomon territories. Action reports on the 182nd Infantry on Guadalcanal in November 1942, on Merrill's Marauders at Nhpum Ga in Burma in March 1944, and on the 162nd Infantry on Biak Island in June 1944, all describe nasty attacks and counterattacks centering on nothing more than tiny, murmuring springs.[68]

Units that failed to find or control such life-giving sources before the water in canteens, cans, and drums had dried up in the scorching heat, could only hope for new supplies or fresh rain. Neither was forthcoming during the first days of the invasion of Peleliu Island in September 1944. On the oven-like coral, panting marines emptied their canteens within hours, surface water was rare, and the few wells thought to be poisoned. At the end of the very first day ashore, soldiers were begging for water "like dying men."[69]

When heat operated on its own, it could mobilize dust so thick and intense it clogged up motors as well as lungs. During dry spells in New Guinea, planes using runways uncoated with bitumen raised clouds so huge they sometimes took as long as half an hour to settle. Air Force commanders complained that the abrasive dust of Assam ground down engine upon engine. Meanwhile, quartermaster truck companies operating between Ledo and Kunming lost increasing numbers of men to what was called dust pneumonia.[70]

It was in alliance with moisture, however, that heat accomplished its most destructive potential. Together, they created an atmosphere of decay that ate away at everything and everyone that dared enter their realm. On 27 June 1944, a lieutenant of the 43rd Division at Aitape scribbled in his diary: "Drazenovick missing in action. Water shortage to drink, no smokes for the men. Mens clothing rotting on them." The officer and his men could not have been in New Guinea for more than a few days, for their division had just begun to arrive from rehabilitation in New Zealand.[71]

In fact, the steamy environments of Asia and the Pacific needed no more than hours to set in motion the destruction of the weakest components of the modern forces challenging them. First they attacked fabrics. Mold clung to cotton clothing and towels, giving off nauseating smells. Large quantities of mildewed sanitary napkins for female personnel in the Southwest Pacific had to be discarded. Rot easily crept into canvas as well as all equipment made of duck and webbing. Most tents, for example, leaked within six months and in another six months were useless. Fungi rapidly spread across footwear, wallets, and other leather goods. Not even the cooler hill areas were immune from attack. A contented soldier undressed and dropped into bed in a high-altitude rest station in Ceylon in June 1945. "When I got up next morning," he noted with disgust, "my GI shoes had green mold around the edges of the soles. It had grown overnight in the dampness." To keep them from getting humid, desperate soldiers before long were stuffing skivvies and socks – as well as personal items such as film rolls – into condoms.[72]

Heat and moisture took only a little longer to ruin much of the more sophisticated and robust equipment. When US communications equipment was put through its first test at Guadalcanal in 1942, the results were discouraging: metal parts of field telephones corroded, insulating materials rotted, batteries smothered. At Nassau Bay, New Guinea, the 41st Division complained that the powder of about 65 percent of its artillery ammunition had to be removed and dried out before it could be fired. By February 1944, it was estimated that 80 million rounds of rifle ammunition for China had been lost to oxidation while stored in Assam. Rust gnawed at the rifles too, and soon GIs were asking parents and wives for wire brushes to stop the metallic cancers from spreading.[73]

The armed forces undertook a frantic campaign of what was called the 'tropicalizing' of equipment. But, although progress was made in waterproofing, mildewproofing, and the like, the American military never succeeded during the war in applying satisfactory protection to materials sent to tropical environments. As late as February 1945, division surgeons on Leyte, for example, complained about the "tropical deterioration" of valuable medical equipment. Due to packaging that was insufficiently moistureproofed, everything from plaster of Paris to gas casualty chests were ruined. Much needed instruments – from scalpel blades to suture needles – had already rusted before reaching their destination.[74]

The heat and moisture that succeeded in disintegrating even sturdy equipment, easily rotted the soldiers' vulnerable skins. Together, they let loose upon GIs across much of Asia and the Pacific an unrelenting army of fungi, bacteria, and yeasts. Whether in the form of rashes, sores, or blisters, infections festered malevolently on knuckles, webs, wrists, feet, ankles, bellies, chests, armpits, and crotches. Soldiers even had to have college and wedding rings cut off to help destroy fungi spreading from the hot, moist tissue underneath. GIs did not bother to distinguish between the hideous infections – they simply placed them all in the same category of what they called 'jungle rot.'[75]

Skin infection remained one of the most common ailments from the time of the Solomons campaign to the battle for Okinawa. In October 1942, a medical intelligence report on Guadalcanal estimated that about 90 percent of the marines suffered from severe epidermophytosis, calling the rate "a vital problem." In 1944, a similar rate was still affecting troops in the Aitape region of New Guinea, for example. But even in the supposedly more healthy Central Pacific, the number of skin infections on an island like Guam in the Marianas could be so high as to overburden medical personnel.[76]

Though not immediately serious, skin ailments were persistent and became disabling if left untreated. Medics had to take care of the infections over a long time, by dabbing them with gentian violet, or by dusting them with a variety of powders (the quantities of bismuth and paregoric mixtures they dispensed, for example, were tremendous). So many marines returned from the Cape Gloucester campaign in New Britain with skin infections that, during morning sick calls on Pavuvu, outnumbered medics saw no other solution than to have them strip and, under supervision, treat each other with cotton swabs dipped in gentian violet. Some were barely able to walk because of feet affected by rot.[77]

Complicity between an energetic earth, furnace heat, and dense moisture spawned landscapes and plant worlds that instantly alienated many an American soldier. After sailing for more than a month from California in 1944, a pilot went on deck and for the first time discerned the Indian mainland. "It was really different even from that distance," he noted in his diary. "There were many hills that looked like they have flat plateaus on them, and in the small valleys were irregular rows of top heavy palm like trees." It was when soldiers came face to face with the tangled mass of tropical vegetation, however, that the feeling of ecological estrangement became acute. From the safety of a training camp, a commander of Merrill's Marauders in 1943 took in the surrounding wilderness of central India, the backdrop for Kipling's *Jungle Books*. "The word *jungle*," the awed officer could not help but confess, "has an ominous sound to the American."[78]

There was no denying that, from a distance, the deep colors and rich curves of canopy looked seductive. But even soldiers who had penetrated the lush wilderness only once would never allow its beguiling surface to mislead them again. Early one morning in April 1943, Mack Morriss returned to Guadalcanal from a B-24 night mission. At dawn, the scenery stunned the correspondent with its coy splendor, but he refused to play the island's game. "The sun hit the land with long, strong rays," Morriss wrote, "and while the shadows gave an emphasis to heights and depth I knew what I was seeing was an outright lie." If there was beauty on Guadalcanal, a marine said, it was "evil beauty."[79]

From abundant warm moisture and perpetual growing seasons had sprung stifling jungles that rose like solid walls along beaches and passageways. It took men of the 21st Infantry on Red Beach 1 an hour to so much as locate the entrance to the trail that would lead them inland from Dutch New Guinea's Tanahmerah Bay. If a soldier stepped five yards off Route 7 in Luzon's rugged jungle terrain, he had a hard time finding the road again. The jungle of New Britain was so dense that assault waves had to hack their way inland once they had crossed the beaches at Cape Gloucester; the first marine casualty was caused by a falling tree. Throughout the campaign on New Guinea, Allied and Japanese forces clung to small enclaves on the coast, leaving the impenetrable hinterland mainly to itself. Because of the dense jungle abruptly rising beyond the shores, 95 percent of the US Army's supply movements in New Guinea had to be made by boat.[80]

In the hot humid wombs behind the jungle walls, romantic illusions of a kind and generous virgin nature quickly evaporated. They gave way to the instinctive fear of a fecundity so unrestrained it threatened to smother soldiers. In New Guinea, each fat heavy leaf that fell sounded like "a light footstep" to a nervous officer who had just arrived from Australia. Thick sprawling roots reaching up to the sky above the island of Espíritu Santo were so overwhelming they reminded an American correspondent of "the flying buttresses of a cathedral." "They say," a soldier on Hawaii noted, "if *one* banyan tree were left to its own devices it would spread in this manner to cover a whole island, killing every other living thing in its path."[81]

Dead organic matter decayed almost as soon as it touched the moist soil, instantly reinforcing an already unstoppable growth. Layers of slimy rot released nauseating vapors that wafted far out to the ocean. To a soldier on deck of a ship pulling into Calcutta's King George Docks, the air was "like a suffocating blanket of acrid-sweet tropical decadence." Long before troops of the 40th Division on the *Matsonia* could even see Guadalcanal, they smelled its "fecal odor." So thick was the odor that soldiers imagined tasting the germs it carried. "Until becoming used to it all I wandered around in a daze," said an American who had just arrived in Burma, "my lips remaining clamped tightly together for fear that the stench that hung in the air would get into my mouth."[82]

What made the putrid air even more sickening to soldiers in the front lines was the knowledge that it contained the stink of rotting human flesh. Battle often did not allow orderly recovery of the dead. Meanwhile, the tropics treated corpses like any other organic material, decomposition setting in as soon as soldiers had fallen. Robert Sherrod claimed that on Betio, one of Tarawa atoll's barren coral islets, "the smell of death under the equator's sun could be detected faintly" less than an hour after the men had been ashore. When the correspondent returned on the fourth day, after a short absence, the "overwhelming, inhuman smell" had become so pungent it made him retch.

The greedy soil of humid jungles hurriedly recycled soldiers like so many leaves, until nothing remained of them but nutrients for more and bigger plants. 'Maggot Beach' is what GIs called New Guinea's Buna area as it wriggled with grubs fattened on soldiers. An officer who passed the spot just weeks after the battle observed that even the bones of the Japanese had already fallen apart. By exposing them to such perversely accelerated versions of life's already short cycle, the region in yet another way reminded soldiers of their utter meaninglessness in nature's grand design.[83]

As if to deepen the surrounding gloominess, multi-layered canopies and dense thickets reduced even the fiercest sun to a dim light. According to an officer on Goodenough Island, troops became so depressed in the jungle's "day-long twilight" that they started felling giant trees just to let in sunlight and chase away the atmosphere of "melancholy."

Moon and stars were no contest at all for the thick growth. Nights brought stygian blackness, making light so unusual and suspect that even the faintest trace of it sufficed to cause commotion, even panic. On the night of 15 June 1944, guards of the 8th Fighter Group, new on Biak Island, placed the whole camp on alert. They had spotted lights near the bivouac and suspected Japanese infiltrators. After hours of anxious suspense, the infiltrators were found to be fireflies.[84]

Nights were made worse by nerve-racking noises that reached frightening pitches at dusk and dawn. Macaws squealed like children. Lizards barked like dogs. Crabs rattled empty ration cans in search of food. Inexperienced American troops responded by shooting at anything from birds to falling leaves.

Yet when the morning light rose again, the jungle fell abruptly and strangely silent. Both in New Guinea and the Philippines, a combat doctor found himself intimidated by the ghastly hush that hung heavy over the jungle's innermost recesses by day. Apart from "gray crows," no birds. Except for some flies and mosquitoes, no insects. No animal tracks, not even on the banks of streams. Nothing but the terrifying sensation of hearing plants grow, swell, and move forward.[85]

Such voracious surroundings could swallow soldiers whole. A few weeks after the arrival of the 6th Division in Milne Bay, New Guinea, for example, an officer of the 6th Signal Company recorded in his diary: "Signal Co. patrol rescued two men from 80th Field Artillery that had been lost in the jungle." Seen from afar, patches of kunai grass might look like "close-cropped lawns." But an unsuspecting soldier at Oro Bay, New Guinea, who strolled into a patch for closer examination, did not return. Having lost his trail after no more than 10 yards, barely able to see the sky through razor-sharp grass 8 to 12 feet high, it took the soldier two frightening hours to free himself. Only on his third day in the New Guinean jungle did a downed pilot at last decide to venture out from the crash site. He located a river, then tried to retrace his steps back to his plane. Despite having marked his trail by cutting into bark and by snapping branches, he failed to find it again. Blind panic seized him, his heart beating wildly, sweat oozing, and for a moment he wanted to run, anywhere. He finally regained his calm – and probably his life – by kneeling down and praying to the Virgin Mary.[86]

Malign vegetation did more than paralyze fearstricken individuals. It expertly hampered and slowed the operations of America's military forces day after plodding day. No matter how much equipment adapted and troops wised up, vegetation's tenacious resistance remained unblinking.

All movement was made tortuous. Troops could labor for hours without making veritable progress and routinely overestimated distances traveled through dense vegetation. On the jungle trails of Guadalcanal, the average march speed for troops was one mile per hour. Off the paths, where trailbreakers had to be rotated continuously, hacking away at kunai grass and brush with machetes and bayonets, half a mile per hour was considered rapid progress. Two regiments of the 32nd Division that were separated by only a few miles during the battle for Buna in New Guinea estimated that they were a two-day march apart. "We were prisoners of geography," General Eichelberger later said.

Beneath the dark canopy, troops found it impossible to determine their own position, let alone pin down objectives. The only means for units of the 305th Infantry to determine their approximate whereabouts in the heavy jungle of Guam in 1944 was to send up flares so that artillery observers could plot their position and radio it to them. In the island's northern tangle, marine units near Lulog mistook each other for enemy troops, exchanging artillery and tank fire. Ten men were down before the mistake was discovered. In the thick foliage of Bougainville, forward observers for mortar units often found themselves no more than 30 yards from the enemy to help bring down fire. But even then they could only detect sounds, not sights.[87]

Dense foliage also thwarted close air support of ground troops. Although consistent air support had been planned for the New Georgia campaign, for example, there was not a single moment during the entire operation when airmen were able to report movements of enemy troops. Moreover, pilots had to be careful not to harm their own troops. The colored panels of prewar exercises were no use when laid out in the jungle. Infantry tried colored smoke and experimented even with black puffs from flamethrowers to stave off attacks from their own pilots. "There is no comfort, no comfort whatsoever," cried an officer, shaken by an incident of friendly fire on New Guinea, "in knowing that the pattern of the jungle has a sameness which invites these mistakes."[88]

Walls of stubborn green caused the military frustration upon frustration. They absorbed the electromagnetic waves of the radios on which blinded troops were entirely dependent. They hampered flamethrowers by sucking up the first burst of fuel and preventing the flame from reaching it. They robbed machine gunners and artillerymen of the visibility necessary to bring full firepower to bear and brought shells to explosion before they hit their targets. They rendered tanks powerless by hemming in their steel bodies and blinding the gunners. During the fighting at Tsamat Ga in northern Burma in March 1944, the 1st Provisional Tank Group tried to rumble out of the jungle by means of a newly discovered trail. Even here, however, tangled vines and branches stubbornly clung to the turrets, slowing the armor so successfully that it took the unit the better part of a day to break free.[89]

Describing the action of the 77th Division near Mount Barrigada on Guam early in August 1944, an official history concluded: "It had been an advance against two enemies, the Japanese and the jungle, and it would be difficult to say which of the two had been the more effective in slowing the American drive."[90]

The jungle insisted on being known as an independent actor. It could decide to cooperate with the Japanese. But it could just as well strike at American troops on its own initiative, without any help at all. "The enemy withdraws," noted a combat artist who sketched marines in action throughout the Southwest Pacific, "but the jungle – unyielding and impenetrable – remains." What made American engineers at Pekoa on Espíritu Santo fight and suffer for weeks in 1943 were not die-hard Japanese troops, but stubborn teak and banyan trees that refused to make room for urgently needed runways. On 4 November 1942, immediately after the landing on Guadalcanal, Seabees began work on an airfield at Aola Bay. Swamps and trees with deep tangled roots put up such fierce resistance, however, that after three weeks of hard battle, commanders at last ordered their troops to retreat. They began anew on a grassy plain at Koli Point.[91]

Merciless and patient, the jungle made casualties without the least regard for rank. Colonel Geerds, battalion commander of the 126th Infantry, suffered a heart attack in Papua New Guinea while climbing one of Buna's muddy trails in October 1942. In March 1944, General Merrill, commander of the famous Marauders, had to be evacuated from the steamy Burmese jungle with heart trouble. Two months later the jungle gave him a second heart attack, spitting him out once more.[92]

The US military increasingly treated vegetation as an enemy in its own right. By 1944, engineers in the staging areas of Hawaii received extensive training in how to tackle tropical growth. An important part of the preparations for the offensive in the Central Pacific was to teach soldiers on Hawaii how to move and fight in sugarcane fields, how to cut passages through them, and how to burn them. When kunai grass that had reclaimed Guadalcanal's Henderson Field resisted burning, the 1st Marine Engineer Battalion regrouped, stormed the fields, and mowed them down with their bayonets.[93]

The hidden force that was at work in the region's tropical vegetation was the same that stirred beneath its waves and crust. But it was the jungle, more than anything else, that turned Americans into animists by reminding them over and over again that it possessed a will of its own. Indeed, trees and grass and vines were so persistently malign that soldiers suspected them of acting consciously. Gazing at the "eerily silent" kunai grass in New Guinea through his mosquito net, a GI confessed to sensing an almost human-like malevolence. "[A]n icy shiver coursed through my body," he told his parents. "I felt as though I was being watched." He was apparently not the only one. Throughout the night, the soldier reported, many a guard blasted away at the grass "in a sudden frenzied fit of fear, brought on by its ghostly appearance."[94]

Still more unsettling than its anthropomorphic qualities were the almost supernatural regenerative powers of the region's vegetation. Sent to Okinawa's Conical Hill at the end of the campaign to round up Japanese stragglers, a soldier remarked: "We didn't find any Japs, but it was surprising how fast the bushes and trees were recovering. As we went through the area in battle I didn't think anything would ever grow there again." Two years earlier, a similar experience in New Guinea had prompted a soldier to reflect more philosophically: "Nature covers the scars of war on her face quickly, but the scars on our civilization will linger longer."[95]

In *The Jungle Books*, Mowgli – Kipling's wolfchild – decides to take revenge on hostile humans somewhere in central India by calling down on them the worst punishment imaginable: 'letting in the jungle.' By trampling their houses and defensive walls, Mowgli's animal allies chase away the inhabitants and open up the village to the jungle itself. Unleashed, wilderness dutifully erases civilization's toehold without leaving so much as a trace.

GIs were forced to witness how the war with Japan was 'letting in the jungle' on a grand scale. With European owners gone, wilderness reclaimed unattended plantations in no time. When, in 1944, marines arrived on Pavuvu Island to rest, they found the sprawling coconut groves overgrown, thick with shoots, and choking with rotting husks that permeated the air with a nauseating stench. It took the Americans weeks to make the area livable again.[96]

Ruined towns and cities underwent a similar fate. "Already," a nurse noted during a visit to Manila in the summer of 1945, "vegetation had begun to take root and was creeping into cracks and crevices of the rubble." Driving through a destroyed town in the Marianas not long after the battle, Ernie Pyle, who had seen plenty of ruins in Europe, was struck by the fact that vines and leaves were already inhabiting the shells that once had been buildings. "[I]t gave them," he reported, "a look of being very old and time-worn ruins instead of fresh and modern ones."[97]

However, GIs who tried their hand at farming, to kill time and grow much needed vegetables, discovered that letting in plants from America was much more difficult. Europeans had not simply settled America, they had transformed much of its ecology into a neo-Europe. However, where European conquerors had run into hardier flora, fauna, and diseases than their own – in the Middle East, Africa, and Asia – they had been much less able to subdue nature and the peoples and cultures rooted in it. American soldiers relearned that historical lesson as they watched how vengeful green masses, born of malign climates, refused to give ground while smothering in the bud plants from abroad.[98]

"There are several unidentified insect and fungus diseases that are not affected by our American insecticides and fungicides that we have available," reported an officer responsible for an Army vegetable garden on Kolombangara Island in 1944, "so it looks rather discouraging." Squirming masses of white worms were eating the roots of his muskmelons, for example, and whatever he tried, the pests could not be controlled. On Guadalcanal's Army farms nothing came to fruition because there were no bees for pollination. The US military went to great lengths to procure significant quantities of the industrious insects, but in no time flocks of ravenous parrots had consumed the imported bees. After several failed attempts, frustrated personnel of the 23rd Field Hospital simply abandoned the idea of having a farm of their own on Luzon. "The wind and storms are too great to plant seed," explained a sergeant. "Also when the dry season is here irrigation is such a problem that we couldn't bother with it."[99]

On Guam, in the Central Pacific, an officer of the XXI Bomber Command grew equally disgusted with the unreceptiveness nature showed American seeds. In the surrounding jungle everything grew "like a beanstalk," he told his parents, and fallen coconuts began "to sprout immediately without even having earth around them." But the vegetable and flower seeds he had received from Missouri died in the unforgiving earth.[100]

With the exception of those who had lived in Hawaii or southernmost Florida before the war, tropical environments were alien to most GIs. Amidst war's suffocating, malevolent vegetation, soldiers therefore desperately searched for more familiar landscapes that could offer solace by transporting them home at least in thought. Early in December 1942, correspondent and Tennessean Mack Morriss, who had left the US exactly one month earlier, longingly confided to his diary while in the South Pacific, "I'm looking forward to seeing cedars again." Having fought his way across Guadalcanal, the Russell Islands, New Georgia, and New Guinea, an officer of the 43rd Division told his fiancée in February 1945: "Never have I experienced such a desire to get home, even for an hour, to feel the cold, crisp breezes of New England, to see a tree bare, gaunt, stripped of its foliage."[101]

GIs had to wait until 1945 to catch brief glimpses of landscapes in which they could recognize themselves again with a minimum of imagination. Soldiers marching through the rolling central plains of the Philippine island of Luzon, for example, felt tremendous relief at being able at last to rest their eyes on scenery reminiscent of Ohio, Pennsylvania, and California.[102]

Ironically, the landscape that brought back more memories of home than any other was that of Okinawa, located near the very heart of Japan. Instead of steamy marshes and anarchic growth, Americans found gentle hills and farmed plains. GIs feasted their eyes on reddish clay and pine trees, on green pastures and Easter lilies. They soaked up breezes that were fresh and invigorating. "You could come from a dozen parts of America," Ernie Pyle noted, "and still find scenery on Okinawa that looked like your country at home." But that was before nature decided to call forth the floodwaters of the May monsoon that turned the island into an unrecognizable mudhole.[103]

What caused the predominantly alien natural environment in which the war with Japan was fought to be still more unsettling was its intimidating fauna. Wild animals had always formed a substantial part of man's fear of wilderness. But nowhere had they fired the imagination and dread of Westerners more than in tropical environments. "Warmest climes," Melville had American sailors in the Pacific say, "but nurse the cruellest fangs."[104]

GIs who learned about the catalogue of cruelties that lay in store for them across the ocean readily agreed with their nineteenth-century predecessors. While the *Kanimblu* sailed for Dutch New Guinea in April 1944, officers carefully briefed their men not only on the human enemy and the area's diseases, but also on the wide variety of treacherous animals lurking in the jungle. They mentioned, among others, "crocodiles up to thirteen feet long in the rivers, constrictors and death adders; mosquitoes, sand flies, black flies, and leeches." "The men," one officer observed, "were grave as they listened."[105]

Although medical statistics indicate that casualties resulting from the fangs of larger land animals were negligible during the war, these creatures instilled a fear far surpassing their real threat. But attacks did take place on occasion, and they could be bloodcurdling. The commander of the 45th Engineers, at work on the Ledo Road, recorded in his diary in June 1945: "tiger killed soldier in Warazup – next night badly mauled another soldier and next night killed native." A nurse in an evacuation hospital at Ledo gave her first dose of the newly developed penicillin to a horribly mutilated GI. "He'd been on guard duty," she explained, "and the tiger really dug into his head."[106]

Isolated incidents like this, often publicized and exaggerated by rumor, kept soldiers on their toes throughout the war. GIs in Assam spent sleepless nights listening to packs of bold jackals scavenging for food around their camps and, according to one officer, howling "like lost and tormented souls in dire agony." Nights on Mindanao in the Philippines were dangerous for soldiers leaving the perimeter of the 167th Regiment early in June 1945, for the guards were trigger-happy. The cause of the tense atmosphere was not Japanese infiltrators, but ferocious boars. "There are a lot of wild pigs running around," a lieutenant clarified in a letter to his wife, "and whenever one gets near a perimeter there is always a lot of firing, in fact you'd think a war was going on." The prevalence of rabies further intensified fears. Military pamphlets exhorted soldiers to seek immediate treatment following a bite by any animal, no matter how slight the wound.[107]

The thought that tropical environments were particularly inimical to whites seemed to apply to both climate and fauna. The carabao of the Philippines, for example, was a generally harmless, domesticated water buffalo. Military pamphlets claimed, however, that the animal was not noted "for his friendliness to white men" because they did not "smell right to him." Before long, of course, rumors were circulating of American soldiers gored by the seemingly tame beasts of burden.[108]

The fierce and exotic character of many of the region's large land animals intensified the feeling of estrangement brought on by landscape and vegetation. "On flights over the Brahmaputra River," noted a pilot stationed in Assam, "I would see rhinos, elephants and other animals which made me realize that we were far from civilization." In the *Guide to the Western Pacific*, GIs could read about the tamarau of the Philippines, or about the archipelago's huge iguana, who was "frightening in appearance, resembling a prehistoric monster." The *Guide to New Guinea* told soldiers about marsupials, giant flying foxes, and big black cassowaries whose kick was "as dangerous as a stallion's." Dutiful readers of the military's many guides to the region probably would not have been stunned had they, in the heart of the jungle, come across unicorns ready to impale them.[109]

Still more frightening were the predators hiding in the deep bosom of that other wilderness, the ocean. Military information on the dangers of the sea read like novels by Jules Verne. GI pocket guides warned swimmers of fish with "poisonous barbs and spines," "powerful" crabs, and capoon eels with "razor-like teeth." The commander of one of the underwater demolition teams at Saipan recalled that his men received "all kinds of scary intelligence," among others about "man-eating clams." The giant octopus never seemed far away.[110]

   Those who laughed away the warnings did so at their own risk. Two new arrivals in the 5th Replacement Depot at Oro Bay, New Guinea, hurried to the beach to take a refreshing plunge in the Solomon Sea. They were just about to end their swim, when suddenly "a huge, batlike thing" leaped into the air, then fell back in the water "with a horrible smacking sound." Convinced that the winged monster would turn on them any moment, the soldiers thrashed back the hundred or so remaining yards in a panic and staggered onto the beach out of breath. The paralyzed men had come eye to eye with the sinister but harmless manta ray or devilfish. Others did not escape the fangs of the deep. "One memorable patient was a young fellow who'd been swimming in the ocean and was attacked by a barracuda," recalled a nurse of an air evacuation squadron at Chabua, India. "His body was encased in a cast from the neck to his feet."[111]

   By far the most feared man-eater of the oceans was the shark, the archetypical symbol of primal nature. On Hawaii, locals could be observed appeasing the shark god by throwing food into the sea in elaborate ceremonies. It did not take long for GIs in the Pacific to understand why. "[S]harks that are longer than a good-sized room," an incredulous sailor of the USS *Montpelier* reported from the Solomons. Those who managed to survive Japanese firepower and abandon their sinking ships could expect no mercy from the ferocious fish. During the battle of Cape Esperance in October 1942, more than 200 men jumped from the burning *Duncan* into the waters of the Solomons. Sharks viciously slashed at the helpless swimmers who desperately clung to anything that could float. When the USS *McCalla* arrived on the scene, its crew found itself "competing with sharks for human lives" and had to use rifle fire to drive off several of the brutes. Some days later, a shark literally heaved himself onto a life raft from the destroyer *Meredith*, tearing away part of the thigh of a horribly burned sailor.[112]

With a few sweeps of their powerful tails, sharks wiped away all illusions of idyllic beaches and placid lagoons. According to the *Guide to New Caledonia*, so many of the predators circled the beautiful South Sea island that of its enticing beaches only one was said to be "generally shark-free." In the hot bays of the Solomons, droves of listless soldiers hung around in their leisure time not knowing what to do. The irony of the situation did not escape Ira Wolfert. "Most of them can't even go swimming in the sea that is all around them," the correspondent wrote, "because of the sharks, barracudas, tiger eels, and sting-rays."[113]

Those who dared take the plunge often did so under armed guard. In the waters of the Palau Islands, sailors from the *Montpelier* were allowed to swim only with three men on deck at the ready with their guns. Each time soldiers on Ramree Island took to the water, one of the Allied ships in the Gulf of Bengal was ordered to watch over them. From the crow's nest, sailors flashed warning blinkers at the first sight of one of the evil man-eaters.[114]

More despised than any other creatures of the wild were the reptiles. Related to some of the most ancient life forms, covered with scales and bony plates, hiding in shallow water or close to the ground, the cold-blooded, treacherous animals awakened in soldiers some of man's most primitive fears. The *Guide to New Guinea* decided to tackle such fears head-on. GIs had to realize that the island's rivers, lagoons, and beaches teemed with crocodiles. This warranted a series of precautionary measures. In the evening, soldiers were to avoid romantic dreaming by the riverside. They were to have lamps or fire aboard frail canoes. They were to splash and make much noise while crossing fords. If, despite all this, soldiers did come under attack, they were advised to "put up a fight." "Poke a stick or a paddle into its eyes," the guide said in all earnest. "Plenty of natives have escaped."[115]

Boy Scout advice was of little use to Americans forced to slug straight through the habitats of the giant armored reptiles. The work of the 6th Signal Company, stringing urgently needed communication lines across New Guinea's Maffin Bay, abruptly came to an end at the Tor River. Each attempt to wade across the stream was repulsed by the angry thrashing of malign crocodiles. The signal crews at long last decided there was no other solution than to use grenade launchers and shoot lines across the river to avoid the fierce animals.[116]

There was, unfortunately, no way of escaping the legions of limbless reptiles poisoning everything from thickets and trees to rivers, paddies, and seas. The slithering serpent, cursed in the Old Testament "above all cattle, and above every beast of the field," had become the most recognizable symbol of evil in Western civilization. Pioneers had carried with them to the New World the legacy of the snake as a creature of corruption warranting persecution and destruction. The still more treacherous shapes in which the serpent revealed itself in the New World had further heightened the colonists' disgust. Celebrated nineteenth-century historian Francis Parkman, for example, demonized the rattlesnake as the "primal curse" of the American West.[117]

But it was in the Pacific and Asia that the symbols of evil proliferated like nowhere else. Military pamphlets derived a perverse satisfaction from exposing them all to the GIs: the coral snakes of the Gilberts; the death adders of New Guinea; the pythons, tree vipers, and rice snakes of the Philippines; the kraits of Burma; the hooded cobras of India. In part because of such alarmist intelligence, GIs demonstrated an inordinate fear of snakes throughout the war, even though medical statistics show that snake bites accounted for an almost negligible number of casualties. On 11 December 1941, following his first air raid in Burma, a Flying Tiger jotted in his diary: "We went out to the trenches near the barracks, but I was more afraid of the snakes than Japanese bombs." From India, a sergeant wrote to his girlfriend in 1943: "You should see the snake hunts that are carried on in and around the cots everynight, worse than an old maid looking for a man."[118]

In the minds of GIs, snakes embodied not just generic evil, but increasingly also the cruelty endemic to this particular region. That is perhaps why fear of the serpent reached a pitch on the eve of the invasion of Okinawa. GIs were told that this key Japanese outpost was guarded by legions of the world's most deadly adders, among which were the habu, the hime-habu, the kufau, and the mamushi. Their bites could kill within minutes and the *Guide to Okinawa* urged soldiers not to hesitate and cut the wound with a knife if no medic was immediately available. "It's amazing the number of people who are afraid of snakes," noted Ernie Pyle while awaiting the invasion aboard a troopship loaded with marines. "Okinawa 'snake talk' cropped into every conversation." Even as the landing ships approached the coast, some of the last instructions shouted by sergeants of the 29th Marines concerned the island's vipers.

Yet, as American troops advanced across Okinawa, they found no snakes. Pyle claimed that after several days, the regiment he was with had killed exactly two specimens, one of which was sent to the command post in a glass jar as a souvenir. Correspondent John Lardner's only explanation was that Saint Patrick had beaten the Americans to the island and had taken all the serpents with him.[119]

The most annoying pests, those that persisted wherever soldiers went, were the insects. In the excessive heat and moisture, they thrived like nothing else. "Insects are enormous creatures," a nurse on Goodenough Island observed, "spiders as big as your fist, centipedes . . . with a bite as fatal as a snake's. You *never* put your clothes on until you shake them thoroughly."[120]

Insects ruled areas in numbers that defied the imagination. In his diary, a sergeant of the American Division described the mosquitoes that had plagued them for three weeks while stationed on a hill in New Caledonia in 1942: "They came in clouds day and night all the time we were there. To fight the mosquitoes we had to wear head nets, gloves, keep our pants tucked in our socks and gloves." Troops on this South Sea island activated smoke pots to help keep the mosquitoes away, and even then could not as much as eat their meals without nets over their heads. GIs who sought shelter in an Okinawan tomb first thought it was smoky inside. "It didn't take us too long," one soldier recalled, "to realize that it wasn't smoke, but clouds of fleas."[121]

Amidst the filth and decay of battle, insects multiplied faster than ever. What stuck in the mind of a marine on Peleliu were the huge blowflies which, though subdued at night, with the onset of daylight "rose up off corpses . . . like a swarm of bees."[122]

Nothing escaped the insects' voracious appetites. Little hard bugs infested the bread of soldiers and sailors alike. In a camp near Calcutta, GIs complained that reckless cockroaches devoured even the gluey spines of their paperbacks. Giant kapok trees crushed tents on New Guinea as they fell victim to ferocious termites gnawing their way straight through the wood.[123]

The pests assaulted human skin with equal determination. "The flies pressed unmercifully against sweaty bodies," noted a revulsed American on Saipan, "and had to be pried from one's eyes, ears, and nostrils." Settling down in a foxhole on Okinawa for the night, Ernie Pyle twice doused his face with mosquito repellent before falling asleep. Only a few hours later he awoke in pain. "It was my face," he wrote. "My upper lip was so swollen I thought I had a pigeon egg under it. My nose was so swollen the skin was stretched tight over it. And my left eye was nearly shut."[124]

Horrific rumors involving merciless insects betrayed the subcutaneous fear the tiny creatures sowed. Pilots of the USS *Suwanee*, about to strike against the Sakishima Islands off the east coast of northern Taiwan in April 1945, were told that so many huge leeches populated the swamps there that they could empty a man's veins in no time. In his diary, an engineer in Burma retold a story that circulated of a pilot downed over the jungle and caught in a tree: "hung down by his feet – couldn't get extricated and was eaten alive by ants and finally shot himself." "[H]ope," he added, "it's not true."[125]

Insects may have stopped short of eating humans alive, but they did transmit an endless variety of vicious germs that caused crippling and sometimes fatal diseases. Mosquitoes carried malaria, dengue, and filariasis; lice and ticks spread typhus and relapsing fever; mites brought scrub typhus; fleas transmitted murine typhus and plague; sandflies triggered a nasty fever named after them.

Fevers constituted by far the most worrisome diseases for the US military. In February 1943, at the end of the Papuan campaign, the disease rate for all fevers in the 32nd Division peaked at 5,358 per thousand troops per year. Medical officers who took the temperatures of 675 soldiers of this division reported that 53 percent of the cross-section ran a temperature ranging between 99 and 104.6 degrees.[126]

A common and particularly mean fever was dengue. Known also as breakbone fever, it caused throbbing headaches, severe joint pains, and bad rashes. Soldiers became delirious and suffered horrible nightmares.[127]

By far the most ravaging fever – and from a military point of view the most debilitating disease – to haunt Americans throughout Asia and the Pacific was malaria. Victims of benign malaria suffered racking chills and fevers, undergoing relapse after relapse. Malign malaria could kill.

What made the *Anopheles* mosquito, the transmitter of malaria, so widespread were the differing breeding habits of the numerous species. Some bred in swamps and rice paddies. Others preferred rivers and streams. Still others could breed in nothing more than rain-filled shell holes or puddles in jeep ruts.

In the early years of the war, losses due to malaria in the Southwest Pacific were staggering. Malaria control units were lacking, malaria discipline among troops was poor, and suppressive Atabrine tablets did not arrive in sufficient quantities or were taken irregularly. In the Solomons and New Guinea, malaria was the most serious medical problem. In fact, malaria on these islands caused more casualties than did the Japanese. On Guadalcanal, the 1st Marine Division suffered 10,635 casualties. Of these, 2,736 were killed or wounded in action; 5,749 marines fell victim to the *Anopheles* mosquito. Decimated combat units on the island allowed only soldiers with a temperature of 103 degrees or more to leave the frontlines. At the start of the New Guinea campaign, malaria claimed four times more Allied casualties than did Japanese weapons. 1943 brought a peak attack rate of 250 per thousand per year for all of the Southwest Pacific. However, stubborn preventive and suppressive measures at last managed to lower the rate to 62 per thousand by November 1944.

But malaria remained a constant military concern. In China–Burma–India, for example, the rate dropped less significantly than in the Southwest Pacific, from 206 per thousand per year in 1943 to 167 in 1944. Seen over the entire war period, the wicked fever caused average noneffective rates of 3.26 per thousand per day in the Southwest Pacific; 3.35 per thousand per day in China–Burma–India; and 4.18 in the Pacific Ocean Areas.[128]

Less common but much more unsettling was scrub typhus. The Japanese knew it as tsutsugamushi or 'insect sickness' fever. American doctors knew next to nothing about the disease, which they had estimated to be quite rare. Spread by tiny red mites that live on rodents in scrub and tall grass, isolated cases of scrub typhus among American troops were first reported in northern Australia and New Guinea in 1942. Baffled doctors watched as the incidence in the Southwest Pacific rose from 935 in 1943 to 4,396 in 1944 and 5,663 in 1945.

The disease, which also afflicted American troops in Burma, proved a formidable opponent. Scrub typhus causes many small hemorrhages throughout the body, including heart muscle and brain. No drug existed during the war that could cure the illness. Victims needed prolonged and intensive medical care. During widespread outbreaks in 1944 on Owi and Biak Islands – outbreaks that felled anyone from privates to regimental commanders – extra nurses had to be flown in to help with the continuous sponge baths needed to bring patients' temperatures down and halt delirium. The majority of the sick were out of action for four to six months. The overall death rate hovered around 4 percent, but a particularly virulent outbreak on Goodenough Island killed one out of every four victims.[129]

The crippling pathogens lived not only on insects. Heat and moisture provided breeding grounds for countless microorganisms – bacteria, bacilli, viruses – that found hosts in soil, plants, animals large and small, and humans. Military pamphlets thus warned against a bewildering assortment of ominous-sounding plagues, from anthrax to hepatitis.

Most troublesome were alimentary ailments, brought on by contaminated food and water. Gastrointestinal diseases, mostly diarrheal in nature, caused soldiers to suffer pain, weight loss, and exhaustion. The highest rate of dysentery, for example, was found in China–Burma–India, especially during the summer season. The rate in this theater peaked at 326 per thousand per year in July 1944, and did not decline significantly until the following year. In an already undermanned theater, an estimated 200,000 man-days were lost from this cause in 1944 alone. During the campaign in northern Burma in 1944, 80 percent of Merrill's Marauders suffered from dysentery. Many simply cut away the seats of their fatigues to stop soiling themselves. But the disease found innumerable victims across the region's many theaters. So many sailors aboard Admiral Halsey's ships suffered from it en route to Saipan in June 1944 that they called their armada 'Bull Halsey's Diarrhea Fleet. Ground troops rarely spoke of dysentery, they simply referred to it as 'the GIs.'[130]

American superiority in medical personnel and facilities was crucial in the war against Japan. It saved many lives and an incalculable number of man-hours. Nevertheless, medical science fought an uphill battle in Asia and the Pacific. To be sure, the challenges in the different theaters were by no means similar or equal. During the first two years of the war, the efforts of the US military were concentrated in the South and Southwest Pacific, two areas that were ridden with disease. In the Guadalcanal campaign, for example, two-thirds of all American forces fell ill. The islands of the

Central Pacific, on the other hand, were relatively free from disease, especially from scourges like malaria and scrub typhus. But here, too, complex threats arose: on a jungle island like Guam, in the form of a dengue outbreak on Saipan, or in the shape of dysentery epidemics in the Gilberts. Of the much larger Philippine islands in the western Pacific, Leyte posed no grave problems of disease late in 1944. During the campaigns in Luzon and the southern Philippines in 1945, however, many of the worst specters, including malaria, returned with a vengeance. In the subtropical climate of Okinawa, disease was easier to control. Still, diarrheal disease rates on the island rose to between 200 and 300 per thousand per year in June 1945, higher even than those of the Sixth Army in Luzon. Meanwhile, American medical personnel in China–Burma–India were faced by a staggering variety of tropical diseases as well as a stunning indigenous ignorance of sanitation on a daily basis throughout the war.[131]

Yet whatever the exact nature of the different disease environments of Asia and the Pacific, they invariably put tremendous pressure on American medical support systems. Calculated per year per thousand troops for the entire war period, the US Army and Air Corps nonbattle admission rate for the more temperate European theater was 464. In contrast, for the Pacific Ocean Areas (which did not distinguish between South and Central Pacific) it was 523, for China–Burma–India 773, and for the Southwest Pacific 807.[132]

Between 1942 and 1945, 83 percent of all casualties in the Southwest Pacific stemmed from ailments. Two percent of US casualties in China–Burma–India in 1944 resulted from combat, 90 percent from disease. Despite increased sophistication of medics and troops regarding tropical and jungle environments, the Southwest Pacific continued to have the highest death rate from disease of all World War II theaters, immediately followed by China–Burma–India. Together, the two theaters accounted for no less than three-fourths of all of the US Army disease deaths during the war.[133]

Commenting on the mushrooming rates of illness in the Philippines in 1945, the official history of the Army medical service in the war against Japan remarked: "Casualty figures suggested that the problem of adequately supporting prolonged high-intensity combat in such a disease environment remained unsolved at the war's end."[134]

In the midst of war it was, of course, impossible to transplant and maintain the traditional Western methods of public health. Moreover, American medical personnel had been trained, by and large, for work in a developed nation and temperate climate. Despite decades of US involvement in Hawaii, Samoa, Guam, and the Philippines, most American doctors and nurses lacked sufficient knowledge of the complex, predominantly tropical diseases threatening their troops in the war with Japan. As soon as the first units arrived in the South Pacific in 1942, for example, it became clear that the common occurrence of multiple infections and the varied symptoms of malaria confused most American doctors. A surgeon of the 608th Clearing Company recalled that as late as the spring of 1944 he and other medical officers in New Guinea were forced to hold informal meetings once or twice a week to try and learn from each other whatever they could regarding tropical diseases. But he admitted that most discussions dealt with no more than "esoteric situations" that some happened to remember from prewar medical journals.

Violent outbreaks of ill-understood diseases like scrub typhus or hepatitis caught medical personnel completely off guard. On Leyte, it took a battalion surgeon of the 77th Division a painfully long time to diagnose a private with hepatitis. When the soldier complained about this to the physician at the field hospital in the rear, the doctor explained that little was known about this "Asian disease" and pleaded with the private not to board the hospital ship, but to stay for another week so that he could learn more about it.

Medical intelligence on this immense and diverse region was often incomplete or faulty or both. Preinvasion plans for Okinawa, for example, elaborately prepared the battle with malaria, schistosomiasis, and scrub typhus, none of which existed on the island. Such lapses in medical knowledge served to heighten the insecurity of American soldiers already bewildered by the complexity and viciousness of the region's diseases.[135]

GIs were made to feel even more vulnerable by the fact that Pacific islanders and Asians seemed to avoid the wrath of nature more easily. By refusing to help set up camp amidst kunai grass, for example, indigenous bearers on Goodenough Island escaped the havoc that scrub typhus brought down on Americans. The bearers had insisted that evil spirits dwelt in the grass. GIs had laughed it away as superstition.[136]

The battle for Myitkyina, which raged from May to July 1944 in the jungle of northern Burma, cost American forces 1,227 killed and wounded – and 980 sick. The Chinese, on the other hand, lost 4,156 soldiers in action, but only 188 to disease. American military analysts pointed to "the very considerable resistance of the Chinese to a contaminated environment." They also, however, ascribed the striking discrepancy in disease rate to the Chinese insistence on boiling drinking water and cooking food, whereas GIs preferred to rely on the chlorinated halazone tablets of modern medicine that unfortunately did not always kill all germs. [137]

But American soldiers could be forgiven for succumbing to the more fatalistic belief that whites inherently lacked the resilience required for life in primitive, tropical environments.

6
Masses

The oppressive floral and faunal fecundity of Asia and the Pacific was matched by a degree of human fertility that appeared at least as aggressive and overwhelming to white American soldiers. Military pamphlets provided GIs with Asian population figures and densities that were staggering: 15 million people in Burma, 72 million in the Dutch East Indies, 389.9 million in India. Java alone, an East Indies island no larger than New York state, supported 48 million people. A booklet distributed in 1945 reminded GIs that the Chinese had continued to fight the Japanese for eight straight years despite the loss of at least five million soldiers and civilians.

If these numbers were intimidating, comparisons with the US were outright disquieting. In an area "a little more than half as large as the United States," the *Guide to India* pointed out, there were packed together three times more people than lived in all of the 48 American states. The *Guide to Okinawa* told GIs that 820,000 people were "jammed" into the Ryukyu Islands, a total area no larger than New York's Long Island. With its 900 people per square mile, the island chain thus surpassed even Rhode Island, "the most thickly populated state in the Union," which counted barely 670 inhabitants per square mile.[1]

Describing the difficulties US engineers encountered during the construction of an oil pipeline from Calcutta to upper Assam, the official history of the China–Burma–India theater noted: "The Westerner, and particularly the American, really does not comprehend the phrase *heavily populated* until he has seen the Indian countryside."[2]

Direct confrontation with these compressed demographic forces brought deeply rooted fears of Yellow Peril rushing to the surface. The nightmare of Orientals as a human flood threatening to wash away Western civilization can be traced back as far as medieval Europe bracing itself against invasions rolling in from the Asian steps. The West's modern formulation of Yellow Peril, however, had its origins in the second half of the nineteenth century, when Asian and especially Chinese population pressures swept emigrants into European colonies in Africa, Asia, and the Pacific and onto the US West Coast. Between 1853 and 1914, at a time when 26 million immigrants arrived in the US, no more than 600,000 Asians (60 percent Chinese, one-third Japanese) settled in California and bordering states. But Americans across the country interpreted this as the vanguard of an Asian army of millions. Fearing the cheap labor of the 'coolie crowd,' and estimating assimilation of inferior yellow races undesirable if not impossible, they united to close the doors to Asians. In 1882, legislation singled out the Chinese as unwanted immigrants. The quota system of 1924 reduced the Japanese influx to a meaningless trickle.[3]

Meanwhile, however, Japan's population pressures had continued to fuel expansion into the Pacific. They had led Japan to gain control of a series of island groups north of the equator, many of them taken from Germany during World War I. Moreover, large numbers of Japanese emigrants had poured into US overseas territories, from the Philippines to Hawaii.

With their focus on the aggression against China since the early 1930s, the American public had lost sight of Japan's expansion in the Pacific. It was the war that made GIs suddenly aware that already long before the attack on Pearl Harbor, Japan had transformed the Pacific Ocean into a poisoned yellow lake that all this time had been quietly lapping against American shores. "It is worth noting," one GI guide revealed, "that the Japs probably know large areas in northern New Guinea and the Solomons far better than the British do." It pointed out that even in this region south of the equator – and under official control of the British, Australians and Dutch – Japanese vessels had been operating for years, "ostensibly to fish."[4]

American soldiers found the concentrations of Japanese in Hawaii still more revealing. In 1943, a *Yank* correspondent returned to the US by way of Hawaii. He had been reporting on America's efforts to stop the Japanese at Guadalcanal. Now he was stunned by "the amazing number of Japs" that all this time had been living unhindered on islands relatively close to America's very coast. "I had expected a mob of service people and a reasonable number of slanteyes," he wrote in his diary. "But it almost seems that the civilian Japs outnumber us; of course that's ridiculous."[5]

It was not. In 1940, ethnic Japanese constituted some 34 percent of Hawaii's inhabitants. Only then came the Caucasians, who made up a quarter of the population. Moreover, in contrast with the West Coast, only 1 percent of Hawaii's Japanese had been interned following Pearl Harbor. Many men of Japanese ancestry, however, had left Hawaii with the US armed forces. "The place is full of Japs, Honey," an utterly surprised sailor from Oklahoma informed his wife in August 1944. "We saw only a few Jap men but the Japanese women just about make up the female population." It was a most unsettling experience for American soldiers who had assumed that the archipelago was their launching pad in the Pacific.[6]

The strike against Pearl Harbor threatened to unleash the pent-up crowds of Asia with a vengeance, and American soldiers wondered if and where the West would be able to stop them. In many ways, Asians – and not just the Japanese – reminded GIs of the persistent insects of the region that proved virtually impossible to control. "Everyone remembers only too well the grim days," the *Guide to New Guinea* said, "when the Japs spread out like a swarm of locusts over the peaceful Philippines and East Indies toward Australia, and eastward into the Pacific Islands." India struck a GI who arrived in Calcutta in 1944 as a "tropical subcontinent anthill that never seems to sleep." That same year, an American surgeon said of Chinese refugees streaming into Kweiyang that they "ate everything in sight just as a swarm of locusts strips everything from the countryside."[7]

It was their tireless, unquestioning industriousness that gave the teeming Asians an uncanny resemblance to ants and bees in particular. To slow the Japanese advance, for example, Chinese peasants had thrown up broad, 15-foot-high earthen mounds across roads. Travelers had to use ladders to climb up and down. During the Salween campaign in 1944, US air forces had to resort to skip bombing to breach the massive walls of earth that girdled the Chinese town of Teng-chung and protected the Japanese troops inside. Parts of the town's ancient walls later turned out to be 40 feet high and 60 feet thick at the base.

Most of these feats – old and new – were accomplished by sheer muscle power. Asians pulled people in rickshaws; they pushed things in wooden wheelbarrows on truck tires. Locals spread the concrete of Bengal's B-29 strips by hand; Chinese crushed stone for the Kunming airfields with hammers, then distributed the gravel in baskets slung from yokes on their shoulders. Long-winding human conveyor belts kept up a steady supply from the fuel dumps while Chinese laborers patiently poured five gallons of fuel at a time into the tanks of heavy American bombers.

Scenes like these confirmed age-old images of the Orient as a bottomless barrel of cheap and mindless labor. The first Asians encountered by marines at the start of the Guadalcanal campaign were not Japanese combat soldiers, but forced laborers from Korea. An American intelligence report stated: "They led a simple, Spartan, obedient and blinkered, but apparently contented cattle existence." Frontline marines bluntly referred to the Koreans as "termites." "You would never forget," said a 1945 *Yank* souvenir booklet for soldiers who had served in China, "the sight of a thousand coolies pulling a ten ton roller over the B-29 fields, mass labor, the kind of mass, machineless sweat that built the Great Wall of China and the Pyramids of Egypt."[8]

More alarming than Asia's already existing multitudes was the high rate of procreation in the region. American sensitivity to this phenomenon had become heightened by social Darwinism and its emphasis on fertility as a weapon in the war between races. In the late nineteenth century, an American philosopher like John Fiske had still been confident enough to contend that the fertile English-speaking whites would multiply faster than the opposition, and that they would spread over large parts of the earth peopled by less vigorous races. By the turn of the century, however, some Americans had arrived at a much more somber view of the future of the white race. Worried by the increased pressures of immigration from Asia, they had come to agree with Henry Adams's gloomy assertion that "the dark races are gaining on us."[9]

Soldiers realized perhaps better than anyone else that numbers were a key to power. It was not surprising, therefore, that GIs showed a marked sensitivity to indications of fertility and population growth. Pacific islanders, for example, convinced them straightaway that Wild Man was indeed "the incarnation of libido." The association of the primitive with unbridled, even apelike, sexual appetite was as old as it was commonplace. Soldiers of the Americal Division who were reconnoitering the island of Malekula in the New Hebrides immediately understood why, when, in its mountainous jungle, they ran into warriors of the Big Nambas tribe. What was truly big on the Nambas was their penis, wrapped in layers of grass and tucked up under a belt so as to give the appearance of an infatigable erection. "It was dyed a bright, flaming red," recalled an awed medical officer, "which against the coal black skin produced a startling effect." In the surrounding villages, the officer ascertained, there were "many children."[10]

Indigenes across the islands happily flaunted their fertility. To an intelligence officer, two of "the most striking oddities" of the many different tribes in New Guinea were the women's breasts – distended and drooping beyond belief by the many nursings – and the warriors' "phallic symbols of startling proportions." A surgeon noted that New Guinea, too, was alive with "innumerable children." A fellow officer who visited nearby Fergusson Island could only confirm that here indeed lived a "fertile race."[11]

The irony in all of this was that throughout the nineteenth century whites had prophesied the inevitable extinction of Pacific islanders. As a result of contacts with outsiders and their diseases, the number of indigenous peoples had indeed dwindled steadily at the time. But as a *G.I. Roundtable* pamphlet pointed out, in the past three decades they had undergone a marked regeneration. Far from allowing their ocean to become a white lake, they had actually brought to some areas overpopulation, forcing European governments to start resettlement programs. The number of whites on the islands, on the other hand, was said to have fallen, in part because of the Great Depression.[12]

Most impressive, however, were the rates at which the Asian populations were growing. Oriental societies quickly convinced GIs that, from a demographic perspective, they were anything but stagnant. In fact, GIs thought they saw plenty of evidence that the white race was being outbred, an ill foreboding of a future in which the Asian capacity for expansion would swell even more.

The results could be felt, a US military pamphlet pointed out, as far as the South Seas. Thousands of Tonkinese and Javanese lived in the region's French colonies, more than 40,000 Chinese were scattered south of the Pacific equator, and over one hundred thousand Indians populated British Fiji alone. Though little new immigration had taken place in recent years, their numbers continued to increase as a result of high birth rates, while they "slowly fused with the island stocks through intermarriage."[13]

The undisputed powerhouse of human reproduction, however, was to be found in Asia proper. In the West, the association of the Orient with sensuality, sexuality, and regeneration has been, as Edward Said has noted, "a remarkably persistent motif." American soldiers carried its imprint, too. "About one out of five women is pregnant," a GI in the Philippines exclaimed. "It seems the Jap occupation didn't stop that. These people go in for production!" But the most riotous fertility was to be found on the mainland. GIs could hardly call that surprising. Had not such scandalous texts as the Kamasutra been written in India? And had not the sexual licentiousness and depravity of China – the polygamists, the concubines, the pedophiles – been exposed ever since the first American visitors had sent their shocking reports? Traveling from Bombay to Kunming, an artillery officer could see for himself the results of these cults of unrestrained sexuality. In August 1944, he wrote from India: "Babies everywhere either visible or invisible. They certainly do not go in for birthcontrol in fact just the opposite." Of course, he explained, this was where a "great amount of their literature is devoted to sexlife." Things proved to be not much different in China. Complaining about the lack of heating in February 1945, the same officer told his wife: "I do not believe that the Chinese, any class, is really ever once warm throughout the winter. Yet they must be occasionally warm as I see they have about as many babies in the summer as in the winter months."[14]

As they closed in on the homeland of the enemy, GIs were reminded also of the tremendous fecundity of Japan's subjects. "Nearly all the women of child-bearing age had babies strapped to their backs," Robert Sherrod reported from the Marianas. "I recalled reading somewhere that Saipan had one of the highest birth-rates on earth." Much like other Asians, inhabitants of the Japanese empire appeared to reproduce without much thought, almost like animals – or insects. A woman on Okinawa abruptly stepped out of a marine cordon, walked to a ditch, and pulled up her skirt. American guards assumed she needed to go to the toilet. Instead, she gave birth. "By the time I had reached her area," a stunned marine recalled, "she had wrapped the baby in a dirty cloth and stepped back through the lines to rejoin her fellow prisoners marching down the road. None of the

Okinawans seemed to pay any attention to her or her new baby. This was sure a different world."[15]

Though GIs ascribed to the peoples of Asia and the Pacific uniformly high fertility rates, the war also confronted them with the fact that between these rapidly reproducing multitudes existed infinitely complex differences, suspicions, and hatreds. The Japanese had loudly proclaimed the liberation of Asia from the West, but the relationship with their supposed comrades-in-arms quickly appeared more one of exploitation than of cooperation. The first indications of this came from Japan's labor troops. While Japanese soldiers routinely fought to the death, with every new battle Americans captured large numbers of Okinawans, Koreans, Formosans, Chinese, Javanese, Burmese, Indians, and Pacific islanders. In Dutch New Guinea, GIs actually came across 120 Sikhs captured in Singapore. Many laborers eagerly surrendered at the first opportunity. Almost all of the 400 POWs taken on the Palau Islands in 1944, for example, were either Korean or Okinawan. Most laborers turned out to have been forced into the military and treated as inferiors. On Tarawa and Makin atolls, for instance, the Japanese had segregated the Koreans and kept them away from all weapons. Some workers had been treated as slaves or worse. The Javanese who had been brought to Noemfoor Island to construct airfields and roads included women and children. The Japanese had given them little shelter, clothing, or food. Those caught stealing had been beheaded or hung by their hands or feet until dead. Of the 3,000 Javanese who had arrived on Noemfoor in late 1943, Americans found no more than 403 alive in August 1944.[16]

Asians whose homeland had been occupied by the Japanese felt an equally burning anger and desire for revenge. On Hawaii, GIs witnessed how the war worsened tensions between the inhabitants of Japanese origin and those with roots in Korea or the Philippines. From the Philippines, a sergeant wrote to his mother: "I don't imagine you can realize how much these people hate the Japs." Even children were throwing stones at the Japanese POWs whom armed American guards were trying to rush out of Manila in trucks. American intelligence units operating in Fukien province had to watch over their Nisei teammates as the Chinese, according to one officer, "felt a bitter hatred against all Japanese, including the American born."[17]

Not all of Asia's hatred targeted Japan. The region had spun its animosities into an endless variety of patterns. General Stilwell quickly came to understand that the Burmese, for example, hated the Chinese at least as much as they hated the British. GIs learned that many Filipinos also disliked the Chinese, many of whom had been on the archipelago for centuries and had acquired substantial wealth. On Leyte, an American heard the Chinese being referred to as "the Jews of the Orient." There did not seem to be an end to the list of acrimony. "Should you see Burmans and

Indians engaging in a brawl," the *Guide to Burma* warned, "don't get into it, and be sure to give them elbow room."[18]

Regional, local, and tribal tensions within embryonic nations caused the situation to be even more kaleidoscopic. In Burma, for example, the Kachins of the hills, like the Shans and Karens, distrusted the peoples of the plains. Having pointed out that on the archipelago there existed at least 250 major language groups, the *Guide to the Dutch East Indies* reminded GIs: "You'll find, too, that the peoples of the Indies are still first and foremost citizens of their own ancestral localities."[19]

To complicate matters further, religion overlapped and crisscrossed many other tensions. Filipinos, for instance, were convinced that their Christian beliefs made them morally superior to the Japanese. "You will hear much," the *Guide to India* said, "about the enmity between Hindus and Moslems." An enmity, the booklet warned, that had been known to result in "clashes."[20]

Yet despite the many indications of diversity, GIs found it virtually impossible to distinguish between Asians who, in a physical sense, all appeared to be identical. Americans often failed to see even the difference between the Japanese and the Filipinos who had been their colonial subjects for almost half a century. On Tinian in the Marianas, a lieutenant witnessed how, one morning, a guard shot one of the Filipino messboys while on his way to the officers' hall. With many Japanese soldiers still hiding on the island, the American had instantly taken the Filipino for an enemy infiltrator. Problems rapidly multiplied when the Americans began fighting their way across the Philippines. As Japanese soldiers slipped into civilian clothes and Filipinos began to dress in captured Japanese uniforms, neither American combat troops nor intelligence units were able to identify enemy spies and saboteurs, who disappeared like fish into an ocean.[21]

The most challenging task by far, however, was to tell the Japanese and the Chinese apart. With many Japanese–Americans behind barbed wire, for example, Hollywood had begun to use Chinese–American actors to play the wartime enemy on screen. The average American moviegoer never noticed the difference. Most American soldiers were unable to distinguish between the two ethnic groups on the basis of either appearance or speech. With American troops training and fighting alongside Chinese soldiers in China, Burma, and India, the US military launched an extensive information campaign aimed at teaching GIs "How to spot a Jap." Famous cartoonist Milton Caniff was hired to solve the tricky problem by means of simple sketches and small text balloons printed in all GI pocket guides to Asian theaters. They contained a series of easy pointers. For instance, if a Chinese was dull bronze in color, a Japanese was on the lemon-yellow side. If a Chinese strode, a Japanese shuffled. If a Chinese had the height, teeth, and eyes of an American, a Japanese showed a marked squint, buck teeth, and legs that were joined directly to his chest. Moreover, the enemy rarely smiled, and his best imitation of an 's' was a hiss.[22]

Though Caniff's cartoons highlighted the physical and moral superiority of America's Asian friends, it is doubtful that they brought much ethnic clarity. Some GIs remained definitely stumped. It took cooks of an American medical unit in China three weeks to unmask a Japanese soldier who all this time had managed to receive three meals a day by walking into camp in a stolen GI uniform and pretending to be one of the Chinese allies. A Chinese-American medic of the 23rd Field Hospital in New Guinea thought it better to be safe than sorry: in big letters he advertised on his helmet that he was indeed Chinese.[23]

American soldiers not only found it hard to distinguish between Asian nationalities and cultures, they also wondered whether, in the end, it was worth the effort. In some places, for example, myriad migrations seemed to have fused people into generic Asians, who were ghastly reminders of the commonality of their race. "It's hard to tell what they are," a lieutenant wrote in a letter on Hawaiian children, "that is, exactly what their nationality is. They're a mixture of Hawaiian, Japanese, Chinese, Filipino, etc."[24]

More importantly, though much discord and division between Asians came to the surface, there always remained the suspicion among GIs of a Pan-Asian reflex of collusion in response to interference by outsiders. That was exactly the kind of fear Japan had gladly been cultivating since the 1930s by stressing the need to liberate the entire region from Western domination and to restore all of Asia to its past greatness. Japanese propaganda warned the West that in this new order hundreds of millions of Asian hearts would beat as one.[25]

This was the nightmare of Yellow Peril come true, and GIs saw too many of its specters to dismiss it as an empty threat. American troops were never able to guess with certainty, for instance, how Asians employed by the Japanese as laborers would respond to an attack. Experience taught that they were liable to surrender at the first opportunity, but that they could on occasion just as well stay loyal and offer fierce resistance. On Kwajalein atoll in the Marshalls, for example, Americans had to club and bayonet Korean laborers into submission. Throughout the war, US action reports continued to talk of Asian laborers as POWs, regardless of nationality.[26]

Despite generally warm receptions, GIs could never bring themselves to trust the Filipinos unconditionally, either. Incessant talk of puppets and collaborators poisoned the atmosphere. An intelligence officer recalled that during the Leyte invasion of October 1944, security concerns reached such a pitch it was decided that only locals with guerrilla identifications could enter US military installations – all other Filipinos remained inherently suspect. Distrust of locals continued to fester during the Luzon campaign in 1945. American intelligence units in Manila, for example, found themselves rounding up gangs of Filipino boys no older than 10, trained by the Japanese to wreak havoc with fire bombs after their withdrawal.[27]

Likewise, during the campaign in Japan's Ryukyu chain, American troops could not be blamed for thinking that, when push came to shove, all Asians were essentially in league with each other. Those who landed on the Kerama Islands came under attack, both on Zamami and Aka, from Korean laborers. Soldiers training for the invasion of the main island of Okinawa had been given to understand that its inhabitants were quite different from the Japanese, and that they had been treated as second-class citizens since their annexation by Japan in the 1870s. Yet to a GI who saw his first civilians on the day of the landing, they looked "little different than the Japanese themselves." What was more, despite the discrimination they had supposedly suffered for generations, many Okinawans were seen fighting with the Japanese. Their reasons for doing so – from indoctrination to intimidation – left Americans cold. The only thing GIs knew for certain was that they were pushing back Yellow Peril in a battle of life and death.[28]

It was the disquieting physical difference of the Asians, and especially their color – whether 'yellow,' 'lemon,' 'mustard,' or 'putty' – that made it so easy for American soldiers to lump them all together, often in blatant disregard for obvious national and cultural sensitivities. Personnel of the 45th Portable Surgical Hospital in Burma, for example, made sure to keep white American and British patients together in a separate ward. Meanwhile, however, they allowed tension to brew in another room where indignant Chinese casualties were put on a large bed of bamboo together with recovering Japanese POWs.[29]

To white Americans who had already used 'gugu' and 'nigger' as interchangeable epithets for their colonial subjects in the Philippines, the awakening of Asians might just as well be read as the beginning of a pan-colored movement. Seen from that perspective, the Asian masses stood to gain allies far beyond their own lands even. "A Filipino told me not long ago," a GI confided to his diary in June 1945, "that a colored soldier told him that after this war the blacks would rise against the whites."[30]

GIs did not need much imagination to see in the Pacific a cauldron of multicolored dissent. "The melting pot reality of these islands," a much impressed surgeon observed in Manila, "was reflected in the faces of the masses and individuals I saw during the sojourn in the city. There were Chinese, Negritos, Hispanic types, Micronesian and Polynesian types, and all sorts of shades of skin color." When troops of the 43rd Division approached New Guinea in the summer of 1944, their transport was met by small boats loaded with what they thought were indigenes trying to sell trinkets. They were flabbergasted, however, when they discovered that the traders were in fact black Americans who – so white GIs claimed – had gone AWOL and dressed as natives to hustle money.[31]

The whirling confluence of colors in the Pacific gave white Americans much to ponder. "Drank my 2 bottles of American Beer," a private of the 37th Division soberly noted in his diary in the South Pacific in 1943. "Had a discussion whether Fijians and Indians are the same as American Negroes."[32]

The war in Asia and the Pacific was, of course, not fought along purely racial lines. The US was allied with China and India. It received support from troops from Fiji and other Pacific islands. It could count on large numbers of Filipino guerrillas. US propaganda gladly played up these realities to neutralize ominous domestic and foreign interpretations of the conflict as a race war.

Yet in an era when many white Americans considered racial integration at home as undesirable, if not unthinkable, such alliances were bound to be uneasy. Opinion polls conducted in early 1943 showed that 88 percent of white enlisted men in US Army camps from coast to coast thought it a good idea to have blacks and whites in separate outfits. One of several urgent recommendations made by Eleanor Roosevelt upon her return from the Southwest Pacific in the summer of 1943 was to relieve the racial tension between white and black American troops in rear areas. That atmosphere did not bode well for prolonged and intense cooperation between white American troops and people who were not only different racially, but culturally and linguistically as well.[33]

To be sure, what made the campaign in the Philippines far different from any other operation in the Pacific was the enthusiastic support American troops received from large guerrilla forces. An estimated 50,000 guerrillas were active in Luzon alone; at least another 75,000 Filipino fighters operated in the central and southern islands. Yet knowing that such local forces existed, the US military failed to prepare for their most effective use, expecting nothing more from them after the invasion than intelligence gathering and certain types of service support. Even in the heat of battle, US commanders in many instances remained reluctant to assign combat missions of any kind to Filipino guerrilla forces.[34]

Some of this undoubtedly flowed from an organized military's weariness about relying on poorly trained and armed irregular forces in front lines. In part, however, it was also a racially motivated suspicion whose roots went back to the American colonial war against the Filipinos at the turn of the century. Brian Linn has shown that while in the interwar period the US Army toyed with the idea of creating sizeable indigenous forces in Hawaii and the Philippines, it never did so, mainly because of its distrust of native citizen-soldiers. Though they did much to idealize their rule in the Philippines, Americans during the war continued to find it difficult to regard their colonial subjects as equals. "Socially," a secret OSS survey observed in November 1943, "the two races have been separated much as elsewhere throughout the Far East." "The Filipino," the report continued, "is . . . at bottom emotionally unstable" and "cannot be expected to support general ideas of justice or right if he has to make an unpleasant struggle."[35]

Misunderstandings and mistrust made relations with the lesser known Asian allies on the mainland even more challenging. Racial prejudice led GIs, for example, to a series of verbal and physical assaults on Indians. Some of these incidents received much attention in both the Indian and American press and caused quite a stir in the host country. It prompted an American officer who was highly critical of Britain's imperial rule to comment that in India "the British color-prejudice seems much less violent than our own."[36]

Cooperation with the Chinese perhaps proved most disappointing. In its GI pamphlets, the US military continually hammered on the vital importance of an alliance with a country that comprised a quarter of the world's population, warning that Japanese propaganda would try anything to break up this friendship. Yet, the better acquainted the GIs became with Chinese people, the more unfavorable their opinion of them. A survey conducted between March and May 1945 among American soldiers who had served in China showed that of those who had had little or no contact with Chinese, 27 percent said that China was not doing its share to help win the war. Of those, however, who had had contact with Chinese soldiers, 53 percent shared that opinion. Finally, of the GIs who had experienced contact with civilians, no less than 62 percent claimed to have lost faith in the Chinese war effort.[37]

Much of the disillusionment was the result of the often lackluster performance of Chinese government troops in the face of Japanese aggression. As late as the spring of 1944, when the Japanese launched a major offensive into Henan province, Chinese troops were routed, in part because famished peasants attacked and disarmed their uniformed countrymen. In 1945, the US military was fighting a losing battle when it tried to dismiss as fiction in a pamphlet for American troops in China the widespread conviction that "The Chinese Army won't fight; they are just sitting around and letting us do it all."[38]

What made matters worse was that, to make the Chinese more understandable and likeable, both the US media and military had been presenting China as the Oriental mirror-image of America since at least the start of the Sino-Japanese War in 1937. The standard GI guide told soldiers that China was a nation of natural democratic tendencies, few class distinctions, and substantial modernization. "Of ALL the peoples of Asia," it affirmed, "the Chinese are most like Americans." GIs were stunned, therefore, to find the real China a medieval country of despotism, corruption, and wretched masses.[39]

Appreciation of the unknown China through a better understanding proved to be a tremendous challenge. "Cultural differences and latent racism," a historian of the few mixed units within the Fourteenth Air Force concluded, "often eclipsed the language problems and sometimes seriously threatened relationships." One of the nurses of the 69th General Hospital in Assam thoroughly enjoyed visits and tea with British soldiers. But she breathed a sigh of relief when told they would be treating GIs and not Chinese patients as had been rumored. "I am certainly glad," she told her parents, "for I have no desire to broaden my acquaintance with our 'Allies' – at least not those."[40]

By lumping together all yellow, if not colored, peoples and dismissing them offhand as unreliable allies, white American soldiers heightened their sense of isolation. GIs grew acutely aware that the region would always resist firm control by whites, not only with its formidable physical obstacles, but also with what historian Richard Drinnon has called its "people barrier."[41]

President Roosevelt had once characterized the Asians whom Japan might be able to mobilize as "1 billion potential enemies." The chilling image lingered. Once overseas, shocked Americans realized how few were the white people holding out in this region against all demographic odds. The *Guide to the Dutch East Indies*, for example, informed GIs that in this sprawling archipelago – with its more than 70 million indigenous people, 1.5 million Chinese, and 30,000 Indians – no more than three hundred thousand Europeans had been ensuring political and economic control. Moreover, with the coming of the Japanese, most Europeans had either fled, been killed, or imprisoned, a fate that had befallen whites throughout Asia and the Pacific.[42]

Anxiously taking stock of their depleted ranks, whites hurriedly gravitated towards whites, regardless of nationality. For a long time, Australia looked like the outpost where the white race would make its last stand in the region. In May 1943, the American minister in Canberra proclaimed the Australians to be America's "natural racial allies in dealing with the problems of the Pacific." Warm relations existed between American and Australian troops at the front in New Guinea. At Buna, GIs gladly shared their few Christmas treats with Aussies. "Your men," an Australian commander told General Eichelberger after the battle of Sanananda in January 1943, "are worthy comrades and stout hearts."[43]

Despite some unavoidable tension and incidents, GIs generally got along well with the civilian population in Australia, too. "When you go to Australia," a gratified sailor noted after a short leave Down Under, "it is like coming home. It is too bad our country is so far away. Our best friends are Australians and we should never let them down, we should help them every chance we get." The task ahead looked daunting, however, even while standing by one another. A captain noted in his diary that in a meeting with engineers in New Guinea in August 1942, General Casey had told them: "We have the help of only seven million Australians. The Japs have the help of 300,000,000. So our job is a big one."[44]

The unifying reflex of whites proved at least as strong in the Middle Kingdom, where modest American forces were hemmed in by some 450 million Chinese whose armies appeared less than keen to halt the Japanese intruders. In this oppressive demographic climate, Western missionary stations became reassuring islands of white solidarity. American intelligence officers operating in southeast China, for example, were welcome guests not only at the French–Canadian and Irish missions, but also at the German stations, all of which they frequented for food, drink, and companionship. The German monastery in Kuangtse was the only place they knew where one could drink fresh milk. "At first it did seem a little odd to stay at a German mission," one officer admitted, "but any possible differences between our two countries were confined to another world and had nothing to do with life in China."[45]

Indeed, in the face of Yellow Peril, Germans quickly materialized into natural racial allies. In Dutch New Guinea, US troops in 1944 liberated a large number of missionaries who had been captives of the Japanese for two years and more. "Several were Germans," noted an officer, "who shared with Dutch and English all their privations without discrimination by their Japanese allies." "By the same token," he observed approvingly, "those German missionaries received from us the same medical care, food, clothing and shelter as the others." Seen from as far away as Asia and the Pacific, the war in Europe appeared to be not only incomprehensible, but an unforgivable act of racial suicide.[46]

GIs not only feared that Asia would smother the white race with its fertile human masses. They also worried that this demographic hotbed, like the region's fecund fauna and flora, would pollute them with its exceptionally virulent diseases. In the West, associations of disease with the dangerous Other – Jews, for example, or blacks – had deep roots. The rise of bacteriology and epidemiology in the late nineteenth century had heightened fears of contamination and led to increased stigmatization in the US of the poor, immigrants, and nonwhites. The decision in 1882 to exclude Chinese immigrants, for instance, was driven by concern over China's potential for exporting not only hordes of inassimilable people, but also innumerable ravaging diseases. China's poverty, filth, vice, and population density were believed to have generated new strains of known diseases so potent they were resistant even to modern Western medicine.

The implications of this menace to public health were horrifying. It suddenly dawned on Americans that – in an ironic reversal of Darwinian logic – an inferior race might well be able to overcome a superior one. "For here," as historian Stuart Miller has noted, "was no normal conflict on a manly level but an underhanded subversive battle involving unseen germs and horrible contagions." Concerns of racial degeneration and extinction thus inevitably crept into the discussion on whether the US should retain the Philippines as a colony following the defeat of Spain in 1898. When racist opponents argued that by assuming such responsibility America would become "contaminated" by the archipelago's "Mongoloid barbarians," they were not speaking merely metaphorically. When Governor General Francis B. Harrison, sent to the Philippines by President Wilson to help prepare eventual independence, visited the Igorots in the mountains of Luzon, he carried with him a cake of carbolic soap, washing himself whenever possible after shaking hands.[47]

The deep-seated fear of catching diseases from racial others continued to haunt GIs in the 1940s. In December 1943, a medic told his mother in New Jersey that a box of native souvenirs, including a miniature boat and two combs, was on its way from New Guinea. "They have all," he hurried to assure her, "been washed and rinsed with an antiseptic."[48]

A number of very specific diseases made GIs shun sufferers with particular anxiety. Americans held their breaths, for instance, upon learning that even in the mid-twentieth century, plague – with all its frightening biblical and medieval connotations – still lurked in parts of India, Burma, and China.[49]

Filariasis, much better known as elephantiasis, also utterly revolted Americans. Causing enormously swollen limbs and scrotums, the disease had long been regarded in the West as the ultimate tropical perversion. Those afflicted by it could expect no tolerance from GIs. When engineers who had agreed to take a group of New Guineans on board their boat in June 1944 noticed a few women with badly swollen legs and feet, they panicked. The women were told to leave immediately. "Soon another woman with the disease was spotted in the loading group," a company clerk recalled, "and I banished her myself by bellowing at her like a veteran."[50]

No disease caused more anxiety, however, than leprosy. Still quite common in the region, GIs returned to it in their writings with almost obsessive regularity. The fear of this ancient scourge, often mentioned in the same breath as plague, was deep-rooted in a society were 'leper' had become a metaphor for anyone who was an outcast. Moreover, as historian Rod Edmond has shown, with the renewed spread of Western imperialism in the late nineteenth century, leprosy had threatened to return to areas where it had long been expelled, as if "to avenge the colonized in a kind of bacteriological writing-back." In fact, it was the fear of leprosy, portrayed by some as a disease that had survived only in "primeval races," that had helped force the decision to close America's doors to Chinese immigrants.[51]

Ostracizing lepers remained a reflex among GIs in the 1940s. General Patch's staff in New Caledonia exploded "with fear and indignation" when they learned that certain lepers were allowed to move about the island freely. The row subsided only when French authorities finally agreed to mark all leprous domiciles off limits. On Leyte, a Filipino guerrilla who was said to suffer from the disease asked American troops for shelter. "He put his hand out," an officer said, "but I did not take it. Bible stories, . . . fear that his presence contaminated the air I breathed – all of these were part of why I ordered him out into the night."[52]

Health fears in many instances led the US military to undertake more systematic racial segregation. Having discovered significant malaria and filariasis counts in indigenous recruits, Army medical officers in the New Hebrides in 1944, for example, cautioned against the use of large numbers of island workers and advised keeping them apart from American troops as much as possible.[53]

The official history of the Army Air Forces' medical service described the presence of indigenous populations in and around installations as "one of the most serious health problems encountered in the Pacific." To attack this problem, airmen were urged not to mingle with natives or visit native villages. Air Force camps were implanted at a distance of at least one and a half miles from any native habitation. Where this proved impossible, the people were often moved to a new area; their old villages torn down and burned. Such drastic measures were often preferable to trying to teach locals basic sanitary principles, the official history claimed, because of "the lack of inherent native intelligence." Meanwhile, indigenous employees, and especially mess personnel, were subjected to "a vigorous standing operating procedure similar to that used in hospital operating rooms." It consisted of "a hot soapy water wash followed by a bichloride of mercury rinse." Native employees also had to use separate latrines and drinking water installations.[54]

Similar procedures were the norm in India, where the US military insisted on building and operating its own food-processing installations, from abattoirs to ice plants. Theater circulars expressly forbade Indian mess assistants to prepare or touch food, and troops made sure to order plentiful stocks of "germicidal rinse."[55]

Of utmost concern to the US military were the debilitating diseases that might spread through sexual contact. If whites were alarmingly under-strength in the region, white women were conspicuous by their absence. White servicemen who complained about the 'woman shortage' on Hawaii, for many the first stop on the way to the war, referred to the shortage of *white* women, as on these islands there was only one white single young woman left for every 83 men. West of Hawaii, the only bastions of white woman-hood were New Zealand and Australia. But most GIs fought their war far from cities like Auckland and Sydney. With only fleeting glimpses of female colonials in Assam and Burma, a sprinkling of missionary wives and nuns in China, and an occasional apparition of WACs, nurses, or Red Cross girls in the Pacific, white women became ghostlike memories. In July 1943, men of the 25th Division, an outfit that had been leading an isolated existence in the Southwest Pacific since December 1942, took to canoes to investigate the beaches of Vella Lavella. They were responding to persistent rumors of a mysterious "white woman" somewhere on the island's shores.[56]

Soldiers desperately tried to keep the fading memories alive. On Guadalcanal in 1943, GIs put together a hugely popular show with "female impersonators of Carmen Miranda & 6 chorus girls." In New Caledonia in 1944, men whistled and growled when Betty Grable appeared on screen in *Coney Island*, touted by one spectator as "a good leg and body show." In January 1945, an officer described the emblems painted on the sides of tank-laden vessels in the invasion convoy for Luzon: "'Miss Fire' personified by an upright, fulsome nude and very female figure. 'Hell's Bell,' equally nude and excessively female, but in a sitting posture. 'Miss Carriage,' of mountainous proportion and contour."[57]

Men improvised means to relieve pent-up sexual tensions. In a history of the 1st Marine Division, for example, Craig Cameron has shown that masturbation was common and that there also existed some form of situational homosexuality. None of this, however, sufficed to calm the burning desire for the companionship of women, and white women in particular. After having censored a batch of sailors' letters to girlfriends and wives, an officer aboard the USS *Tern* wrote to his spouse in June 1943: "Some (all) of the boys are getting sharp (i.e., hot, hard up, carnal urge, wicked, sinful, lustful, ornery, horny, mean, stiff-peckered, hard-on, studlike, bullish, in heat, you name it)." The next day he confessed: "And it is entirely possible I am speaking for myself."[58]

When 38 nurses arrived on the island of Los Negros, a surgeon witnessed how soldiers within minutes "hung around the hospital like dogs." At Base G in Hollandia, New Guinea, servicemen jostled to get the attention of female personnel, pushing against the chicken-wire fence, waving self-made bracelets as bait. Commanders on Pavuvu thought it wise to protect the contingent of six Red Cross workers against the thousands of men from the 1st Marine Division who had just returned from the Peleliu campaign. They put the girls in a plantation house, had a high, floodlit, barbwire fence constructed, and assigned dog patrols.[59]

The girls on Pavuvu caused more resentment than anything else. The marines thought the presence of American women painfully incongruous with what they had just gone through. Worse, though they could not hope to date them, six girls forced thousands of men to change their habits overnight. Burlap sheets were hurriedly draped over the latrines, nude swimming was instantly prohibited. They were not the only soldiers who thought it crueler to be reminded of what they could not have than to be left alone. A soldier who had just run into Red Cross workers on Biak Island confessed: "Seeing all these women suddenly I had the strongest reaction of aversion. They cause more trouble than they are worth."[60]

In this sexually frustrating climate, men began to worry about the fate of their reproductive powers. Many refused to take antimalarial Atabrine, for instance, because of stubborn rumors that it caused impotence. The fear of elephantiasis, too, had much to do with the knowledge that its most common complication was sterility. And even if the tropics should not pollute their genitals, how long before soldiers could put them to good use again? Robert Sherrod reported from Saipan in June 1944 that he overheard GIs in nearby foxholes discuss "whether or not the war would last so long they would be so old they couldn't get married and raise families."[61]

As Sander Gilman has shown, those who experience loss of sexual control and fear of infertility easily project onto the Other exaggerated potency. It offers yet another explanation for the sensitivity of American soldiers to what they regarded as the region's hypersexuality and overfertility. One way for American soldiers to find sexual gratification was, of course, to turn to the hypersexual and overfertile Other. But the relationship with the women of Asia and the Pacific was complex and, quite often, frustrating.[62]

The very circumstances of war inevitably complicated matters. Because the civilians of the Marianas and Okinawa were regarded as potentially dangerous, for instance, most were removed to separate camps. Fraternization was strictly prohibited. Still, relations with native women elsewhere were never a matter of course either. The region's exotism had given rise to a romantic mythology of women who were attractive, lustful, and available. In reality, however, the very quality of otherness more often than not created obstacles that proved difficult to overcome. Beauty, as always, was in the eye of the beholder, and GIs' opinions on the attractiveness of native women in the various theaters of war understandably varied. Nevertheless, disappointment with the physical appeal of the region's females runs as a common thread through the comments of soldiers raised on stories of South Sea belles and saronged Lamours.[63]

GIs searched in vain for the imaginary creatures of South Pacific fame. "In spite of the movies," an officer on Fiji wrote in his journal, "native women don't look like Hedy Lamarr." "There are no women (white) in New Caledonia except nurses and officers," a sailor of the destroyer *Howorth* noted. "The native girls look like hell!" In his diary, a disillusioned *Yank* correspondent, who had been in New Caledonia for two weeks, put it still more bluntly: "If there is a woman even a horny nigger would touch in the whole damn sector, I haven't seen her."[64]

The emphasis of the war south of the equator was in Melanesia, however, and here GIs found the women utterly repulsive. It came as a shock to many that these Pacific islanders resembled Africans. Upon approaching Funafuti Island from Hawaii in March 1944, an info sheet put out by an American crew let troops aboard know: "Recent eye tests notwithstanding *all* female bipeds on this island are black." It was impossible to bridge the divide between white soldiers and dark women who wore nothing but grass skirts, did not seem to bathe, and at 30 already were "shrivelled and unsightly." Vitriolic responses betrayed disillusion and disgust. "For I hate these filthy natives," ran the 'Song of Islands' that circulated among men of the 570th Quartermaster Battalion. "And the litheful, luscious maidens – well you ought to see the cows. All tits and ass, and skirts of grass – a dirty lot of sows."[65]

"[T]he myth of the Pacific war was," a marine pilot noted, "that after a while even the natives turned white and became beautiful." Americans saw the myth for what it was. "Despite the local adage that native girls grow fairer as time goes by," a private concluded, "I'm of the opinion that my two months and more stay here in India is not sufficient to complete this mental bleaching process."[66]

Complex indigenous sensitivities and taboos formed countless additional barriers between GIs and local women. Reality tore most of the myth of the uninhibitedness of Pacific islanders and Asians to shreds. "Natives, however free and easy they may seem to be among themselves," warned the *Guide to New Guinea*, "are likely to resent outsiders interfering with their women." "It will be best to take matters slowly in getting to know the women," advised the *Guide to the East Indies*. "A yoo-hoo in the wrong place, and the local husband or lover might turn out to be a nasty customer." All this was true even in the supposedly licentious South Seas. When the first American troops arrived on Tonga in May 1942, there were no bare-breasted Polynesian maidens waiting for them on the beaches. Queen Salote had thought it wise to instruct her female subjects to withdraw to the interior or to outlying islands for the duration of the Allied military presence.[67]

Matters could prove complicated on the Asian mainland, too. The *Guide to India* told GIs not to stare at or address veiled Muslem or Hindu women. "Many," it insisted rather discouragingly, "will run at the approach of a white man." Chinese girls who dared to be seen in public with American Flying Tigers in Kunming in 1942 found their reputations damaged beyond repair. It caused "savage gripes," observed the chaplain, as the airmen "took the snubs as proof of anti-American feelings."[68]

"Tempers are short," noted a soldier on Luzon in 1945. "Some men are sexually starved; it seems Filipino women don't give much satisfaction. Cases of homosexuality are occurring probably much more than I know about." GIs generally thought the women of the Philippines to be the most attractive of the region by far. But relations with Filipino women other than prostitutes were, remarked a battalion surgeon, "quite confusing." Throughout the American colonial regime, the military had used all legal means to prevent intermarriage and other intimate social relations between soldiers and native women. Moreover, even if a Filipino family gave a girl permission to date an American soldier in the changed wartime climate, customs rooted in Spanish Catholic culture still demanded that she be vigorously chaperoned. It was all too elaborate for sex-starved soldiers who were just passing through.[69]

Cultural and especially racial boundaries made serious relationships, let alone marriages, between American soldiers and native women highly unlikely. But they could not stop young men from having sexual contacts, mostly with women whose favors demanded payment in some form or other. Rates of venereal disease are one way of tracing the desperate sexual odyssey of American troops. Their fluctuations reflect the opportunities for fraternization, the population's health, and the efficiency of control imposed by civil governments and the US military.[70]

In Australia, VD peaked in May 1942 at 45.8 per thousand troops per year, but remarkably successful measures imposed by Australian and American authorities brought it down to 4.2 by November 1944. Elsewhere in the South Pacific, VD was never much of a problem, though its incidence varied from island to island. According to the history of the US Army medical service, VD did pose problems on Fiji and Aitutaki, for example, where "local mores encouraged promiscuity." Still according to the same study, VD was of little or no consequence in New Guinea and elsewhere in the Southwest Pacific, possibly because of "the appearance of the local women." But also because authorities had put villages off limits to prevent the spread of disease, and because many women were hiding in the interior. "They asked us where they could get women," a Tannese who had worked for the Americans in the New Hebrides recalled. "But there were no women . . . If they wanted to steal a woman they said 'suksuk.' They said thusly, this word 'suksuk.' They all wanted suksuk."[71]

In the China–Burma–India theater, constant vigilance was required. In China's rural areas, traveling prostitutes plied their charms near military camps. Or in them. A lieutenant of a quartermaster company stationed near Toppa in April 1945 was put on trial for having "wrongfully introduce[d] into Camp and unlawfully cohabitate[d] with a Chinese native woman, name unknown, who was not then and there his wife." In Burma, commanders had to crack down on GIs who made a habit of entering "villages and individual hutments." Americans on leave after months of isolation in camps in India were irresistibly drawn to the brothel areas of some of the larger cities like Calcutta or Kharagpur, famous for its 'Jig-Jig Lane.' In 1943, the theater counted 2,600 admissions for VD among its 75,000 American soldiers. VD rates eventually were brought down by a rigorous military program that put some of the most notorious brothels out of bounds. By September 1944, the Army Air Forces, for example, had reduced the rate on the Asian continent to 24.5 per thousand from a monthly average of 52.16 in 1943.[72]

Only in the Philippines did VD truly spiral out of control. The islands were plagued by a lethal mix of sex-starved American troops pouring in from the Southwest Pacific, thriving local brothels with heavily infected professionals, and innumerable women forced into prostitution by the destitution of war. By April 1945, rates had skyrocketed to 100 per thousand troops per year on Leyte and Luzon and much higher even in certain pockets.

Military commanders desperately tried to turn the tide with a variety of measures, including shutting down brothels. But soldiers continued to find 'pompom' wherever they looked. In Manila – 'Sin City' – MPs were allowed to ask soldiers for their prophylaxis kits the way they might have inquired after a piece of identification.[73]

VD rates in Asia and the Pacific, with the exception of those in the Philippines, were by no means excessive if one realizes that the 1940 rate for the entire US Army had been 42.5 before a vigorous campaign brought the figure down. But soldiers worried less about VD rates than they did about the virulent nature of sexual diseases in this particular part of the world. Sonya Rose has shown that, in part because of the belief that colored women were especially prone to VD, the US military in Hawaii "provided regulated prostitutes to serve their soldiers in racially segregated brothels." The 'Pink House,' New Caledonia's authorized brothel, was open only to white servicemen. In response to increased sexual tension in the ranks of African–Americans on the island, US commanders in 1943 considered establishing a brothel reserved for black soldiers who would be served by Melanesian women.[74]

What particularly frightened Americans, however, were the venereal diseases of Asia. "[F]earful tales went around," noted a sailor on training in California in the months before Pearl Harbor, "of syphilis picked up in the Orient, requiring long, painful treatment, spinal taps, and eventuating in various kinds of rot and disintegration." Those fears went back at least to the decades of increased Chinese immigration in the nineteenth century. A time, as Stuart Miller has demonstrated, when public opinion had come to believe that Chinese prostitutes were poisoning America with a form of syphilis more potent than the Western variant because spawned by "thousands of years of beastly vices" in "the fleshpots of Oriental lechery."[75]

Military authorities harked back to this theme, and expanded it to encompass the Pacific as well as Asia. "Venereal diseases," lectured the *Guide to Burma*, "are always prevalent in tropical countries." And they were as virulent as they were widespread. The *Guide to the Western Pacific*, after having catalogued the dangers of mosquitoes, snakes, and scorpions in the Philippines, immediately added: "The women, too, are dangerous. There is plenty of venereal disease, of particularly bad types, in the bush as well as in the towns." The *Guide to the East Indies* stressed that these diseases were particularly treacherous to outsiders because "people have built up such an immunity that they may be quite unaware that they can act as carriers."[76]

American soldiers witnessed scenes that made such warnings seem not in the least exaggerated. In December 1944, the provost marshal, on an inspection tour of Calcutta's brothel area in the company of three husky MPs, drove through the "labyrinthian alleyways of Chinatown." "A page out of De Quincey's *Opium Eater*," the stunned officer wrote in his diary. "What filth. What smells and what sights. You could see the sores on some of the girls." Pilots stared in disbelief at one of the wretched Chinese prostitutes in Kunming. "Puss and scabs in her navel and all over her belly," one of them wrote in his journal. "Left breast wrapped in a swath of bandages."[77]

GIs believed that the licentious Japanese soldiers had made VD even more widespread in the region. Asked in a military survey if he had sought sexual contact with local women in the Philippines, a sergeant of the 43rd Division retorted: "I didn't know a Filipino from a Jap. Besides, how would I know they hadn't slept with a clapped Jap." Some thought the Japanese purposely used sexually transmittable diseases to pollute their enemies. "There was a rumor," a hospital technician in Burma noted in his diary, "that there were 500 Japanese women prisoners in this area. All of them were infected with a venereal disease. They were in the area for the specific purpose of infecting our boys."[78]

So intense was the fear of contamination that some could feel polluted merely by laying eyes on willing Asian women. Flying Tigers who visited the notorious red-light district of Kweilin were tugged and pulled at by crowds of prostitutes, but the Americans judged the women too disheveled to make use of their services. Back at their base, however, one of the airmen jotted in his diary that he nevertheless "took a good shower and threw my bush jacket into the wastebasket." A similar sensation grabbed hold of a sexually inexperienced soldier dragged into a Manila brothel by his comrades. One look at the prostitute convinced him that she was "VD personified, as if hordes of syphilis germs were speeding around all over her." He and his virgin friend burst out of the brothel. "We knew we had had a close call," he panted, "wondering if any germs had settled on us. Maybe we should go to a pro-station, 'just in case.'"[79]

In a letter to his brother, however, the frightened GI explained that his escape from the brothel had been spurred also by a story "circulating through the ranks of every outfit in Manila." It was the horrifying tale of a GI who had enjoyed a sexual encounter with "a beautiful white woman" in a fenced compound that he later learned was a leper colony. Such a story was credible because GIs, who understood next to nothing of how the disease spread, often believed that leprosy was in essence a venereal disease. A medical officer in New Caledonia, for example, told the story of a soldier who, after discovering that the girl he had been sleeping with was a leper, turned up at the VD station for treatment. When told that there was no prophylaxis for leprosy, the boy had to be evacuated to the US as a psychiatric casualty. Remarkably, this interpretation of leprosy still resembled the view that had come to life at the end of the previous century. Rod Edmond has shown that, from the 1870s on, leprosy in the South Seas, for example, had come to be seen as "located in the promiscuous sexuality of the culture" and, therefore, as "just punishment for a corrupt and diseased society." It was this "sexualization of leprosy" that had led to its association with syphilis.[80]

The West's horror of leprosy flowed not only from linking the disfiguring and incurable disease with abandonment to South Sea promiscuity and Oriental lechery. Leprosy was moralized also as a retribution for miscegenation. Because the disease was thought to be both indigenous and of a hereditary nature, offspring of racial interbreeding were automatically suspect. Leprosy had thus become additional proof of the theory of white supremacists that interracial unions would produce "weak or effeminate but still dangerous" mongrels and would lead to a precipitous decline of the white population. In the years prior to the Chinese exclusion of 1882, for example, illustrations in the American press had depicted half-castes as monstrous, almost devilish, creatures.[81]

Forced by war to confront the mingling of races in Asia and the Pacific on a scale previously unimagined, miscegenation could not but be on the minds of white GIs. Some of the mongrelization had been voluntary. Military guides alerted GIs to the fact that in the region "marriages between Europeans and the aborigines" were "numerous and socially accepted." "Nine-tenths of the so-called 'Europeans,'" the *Guide to the Dutch East Indies* said rather disparagingly, "are the offspring of whites who married native women." But hybridization also threatened to be the price of defeat, and US war posters showed stark warnings of grinning Japanese soldiers dragging nude white women from burning houses.[82]

GIs were apprehensive of mongrelization wherever they mingled with racial others. An officer on a bus in Hawaii in 1944 could not stop staring at a baby born from a white father and Chinese mother. The experience prompted him to predict in a letter to his wife that global war, the migration of millions of young men, and speedy transportation would eventually bring "many such matings, lawful and unlawful." A master's degree in biology in hand, this American was rather fascinated by such "a big step in the scattering of new seed, new genotypes and the creation of many new hybrids." For others, however, it was a specter that threatened to shake the very foundations of American society. Among the Americans liberated from Japanese prisons in Manila in 1945 were a group of deliriously happy veterans of the Spanish–American War who had never returned to the US. They assured any GI who wanted to listen that one day they would visit home and family again. But in the eyes of one American liberator they were nothing but "a pathetic group." "The truth of the matter was," he noted glumly, "that each had married a dark-skinned Filipino woman and raised a brood of mestizo offspring. They knew their colored families would not be welcomed in Iowa or Maine, or in whatever small town they had come from."[83]

7
Mind

"Japan," the 1941 edition of the US *Handbook on Japanese Military Forces* emphasized, "understands war in Asia and, thus far, has always chosen methods leading to success." For the duration of the war, Americans would be grasping for a better understanding not only of the Japanese, but also of the peoples throughout the region in which the enemy seemed to be moving so effortlessly.[1]

Despite the building tension, American ignorance of Asia and the Pacific had remained widespread in the 1930s. In 1935, for example, no more than twenty people in all of the US were estimated to be concentrating on Japanese studies. Also, in the years before Pearl Harbor, the quantity and quality of press reports coming out of Tokyo were remarkably poor, because many American correspondents had been sent there only after the outbreak of the Sino-Japanese War in 1937. Most possessed little or no background where it concerned Japan.[2]

Not surprisingly, when war broke out, the American public's knowledge of the region was ephemeral at best. A future marine was not particularly impressed by the attack on his country in December 1941 because "the only Japanese I'd ever seen was a little creep who used to stand outside of Stoughton's Drugstore, in my hometown of West Hartford, Connecticut, and demonstrate yo-yos." Four months after Pearl Harbor, a nationwide poll revealed that 60 percent of Americans were unable to locate either China or India on an outline map of the world.[3]

Hard pressed for time and resources, the armed forces could hardly be expected in a time of national emergency to provide citizen-soldiers with the thorough and balanced education that schools and press had systematically neglected in peacetime. Asked after the war what he thought of the Japanese troops, for example, a lieutenant from California replied: "They were not the dumb fools that the U.S. Army had tried to make us believe. We were *not* well instructed in the USA on this subject." Those who were assigned to China felt equally ill prepared. "There should have been a training center where all personnel bound for China would be processed," insisted an

American civil affairs officer who deplored the often strained relations with the Chinese. "Here they would have been told the truth about conditions in China" and "would have learned how to behave themselves." In the summer of 1945, agents of the Counterintelligence Corps were flown into Manila from all over the Pacific to prepare for the invasion of Japan. But the training was hurried as each group of agents had exactly five days to absorb what they could of lectures on such intricate and diverse issues as Japanese government, psychology, geography, and secret extremist societies.[4]

Superficial efforts at education often did nothing more than reinforce stereotypical perceptions. One military pamphlet, published in 1943, called the war task of GIs in India "doubly difficult" because it had to be accomplished in "a complex country, difficult for people like ourselves to understand." Complaints about the inability to fathom either friend or foe in the region persisted until the end of the war. "More than ever," noted Robert Sherrod during the invasion of Saipan in July 1944, "we found that the mental processes of the Japanese apparently functioned in an altogether different manner from our own." "To most Americans," an editorial in the *New York Times* admitted even in the closing months of the war, "the vast and teeming lands of the Orient are still terrae incognitae."[5]

"Remember," said *You and the Native*, a GI pamphlet on New Guinea, "that the language difficulty lies at the root of misunderstanding and friction." Indeed, endless varieties of obscure and hopelessly complicated letter and word systems prevented GIs from acquiring better informed ideas about the cultures and races surrounding them. Military booklets probably discouraged most soldiers straightaway by informing them that nowhere else existed "so many different little local languages and dialects" as in New Guinea, that there were "more than 200 different languages and dialects" in India, and that the Dutch East Indies encompassed "at least 250 major language groups." Lists of emergency words and phrases for American pilots operating from Chinese bases contained not only a section in Chinese, but also pages in Burmese, Annamese, Thai, Shan, Lolo, and Lao.[6]

The US armed forces nevertheless exuded a marked confidence in their soldiers' ability to get a practical handle on even the most difficult languages of the region. "Nobody expects you to learn a language as complex as Chinese," one military booklet assured, "although the glossary at the end of this book will enable you to learn enough to get along." The glossary's meager 15 pages give an idea of what the scope and depth of the soldiers' contacts might have been. Likewise, a US Army pamphlet that informed GIs that on the Marianas the most important language was Japanese, also told them that a close look at manual TM-30-341, plus some self-study, would suffice to master "a working knowledge of the basic language."[7]

In the field, however, things appeared rather more complicated. General Chennault himself ordered the chaplain of the Flying Tigers, who had been a missionary in China in the 1930s, to instruct the American airmen in the Chinese language. "I did try what he suggested," affirmed the dejected chaplain, "but it was like teaching Sunday School in the basement of a nightclub. My language lessons were a washout." Marine officers aboard ships heading for Saipan chose to adopt a more no-nonsense approach to language instruction. Headlined "Combat Language," posters made sure to spell out only those Japanese phrases thought most useful on the island, among others 'Come Out' and 'Don't be afraid.'[8]

Without interpreters, however, American soldiers might as well have been struck deaf, dumb, and blind. Describing the amusements China had to offer, a GI guide readily acknowledged that without an understanding of the language, soldiers would not find much enjoyment in festivals, sports, and games. "You are in something of the same position," the guide tried lightheartedly, "that a Chinese would find himself in were he to venture without a knowledge of English into a Tennessee square dance." But ignorance about totally alien languages could prove devastating to much more than the soldiers' social lives. Several GIs on Okinawa, for instance, strayed into minefields that were clearly indicated by signs carrying big, fat warnings – in Japanese.[9]

Amidst such helplessness, experienced interpreters – whether Asian–Americans, former missionaries, or college people – played numerous vital roles in the region, from intelligence gathering to psychological warfare. During the Japanese siege of Nhpum Ga in northern Burma, for example, sergeant Matsumoto helped his American comrades repulse several vicious attacks by scouting between the lines, listening in on enemy conversations, and relaying crucial information to the garrison's commander. His gift of tongues earned him not only the admiration of his buddies, but also the Legion of Merit.[10]

Linguists, however, remained in terribly short supply. A standard US infantry division in the Pacific, operating with over 10,000 people, could count on only one language team composed of no more than one or two officers and ten enlisted men. From these, division headquarters could spare exactly two people for each regiment, leaving no linguists available for smaller units up front. In September 1944, a US Army report expressed regret and worries over the persistent "necessity for the utmost economy of interrogation personnel." Despite the mushrooming in the US of crash programs aimed at producing quantities of specialists in the languages and cultures of Asia and the Pacific, similar complaints were being repeated until at least as late as the Okinawan campaign in the spring of 1945.[11]

Not only were the words of the peoples of Asia and the Pacific unintelligible, their emotions proved excruciatingly hard to read, too, further sealing their minds to probing American soldiers. Americans were mystified, for instance, by the peculiar ways in which Pacific islanders expressed their suffering and grief. Watching a group of native laborers depart camp in New Guinea in October 1942, an engineer noted that those who remained behind, one moment had been crying and wailing, then suddenly, when ordered to return to work, had "plunged into it with songs and laughter." "It was the greatest display of alligators tears I have ever seen," the officer said disgustedly.[12]

What appeared incoherent was hard to accept as genuine, to the point where GIs suspected islanders of lacking emotions altogether. In December 1944, GIs in New Guinea seemed quite surprised to find among the hapless indigenous refugees who arrived on a nearby beach signs of sincere emotion over even the most traumatic of human experiences. One man had been badly wounded by the same Japanese bullet that had killed the baby still strapped to his back. "The natives have feelings, too," an upset battalion surgeon conceded, "and this one looked really mournful." Of a woman who was helping American medics dress the wounds of her husband, the physician said in a letter to his wife: "She showed so much tenderness and compassion that even the men all remarked on it."[13]

The expressionless Orientals, on the other hand, had long been notorious in the West for their enigmatic character. The blank, imperturbable faces with which they allowed even the whirlwind of war to run its course rendered them still more unfathomable. "Filipinos are very stoic individuals," noted a soldier as his outfit rumbled through Dulag during the Leyte campaign late in 1944. "The oldsters sat or stood at discreet distances from this hell on wheels and on foot, seemingly unmindful of the noise and the stinking exhaust smoke. One old fellow even turned his back to all these horrors of modern civilization and went ahead with his task of slapping and scratching at mosquitoes."[14]

Japanese soldiers appeared so unmoved by even the fury of battle that an occasional hint of emotional response became noteworthy. "This Jap," Richard Tregaskis triumphantly reported about a POW terrorized by bloodthirsty marines on Guadalcanal, "did not have an inscrutable face. Now it was marked by signs of terror obvious even to the Occidental eye." But the exception served only to highlight the rule, upheld even in the face of death. The stony faces of Chinese criminals, brought in for one of the routine executions at Kunming in 1944, dumbfounded an American onlooker. "None of these prisoners," he gasped, "exhibited the slightest emotion; they seemed to be completely stoical."[15]

"Americans," warned the *Guide to the Western Pacific* in its section on the Philippines, "will always feel like a tourist in the islands because no white man can ever get close to or completely understand the workings of the Malay mind." What would always prevent whites from penetrating and deciphering that mind, the booklet asserted, was the fact that the Filipino lived in "a queer dream world of his own," made up of "child-like superstitions and legends."[16]

Not only in the Philippines did American soldiers become entangled in highly spiritual worlds haunted by supernatural beings. On New Caledonia, for instance, GIs were told that, since the indigenes believed that every person was inhabited by a spirit or *ko* that traveled while the human body was asleep, they should never wake their Kanak workers too abruptly.

Some of the native spirits were benign, like those in the form of screaming masks guarding deserted New Guinean villages against the Japanese. Many others that roamed the region, however, were vindictive and predatory. Natives practiced black magic and sorcery, conjuring up infinite rituals and ruses to placate demons or to help keep them away. Kanaks kept fires burning at night to discourage the devil. Papuan carriers refused to follow American troops into many an area they claimed to be the exclusive preserve of ghosts. Igorot bearers in the mountains of northern Luzon appeased spirits by sacrificing pigs and chickens amidst howling dances.[17]

While Burmese hill dwellers contented themselves with wearing magic talismans, Americans received chilling reports on Indian hill people in Assam who worshiped the devil in the form of a snake that had to be fed on human blood drawn from the living brain. So many of the Chinese employed on American airfields jumped in front of fast-moving planes, hoping the propellers would kill the evil dragons following behind them, that tower operators began to give pilots hell for aborting take-off runs to save coolies. One of the patients whom nurses of the 803rd Medical Air Evacuation Squadron were to accompany on a flight from Burma to India was a Chinese shell-shock case. He had almost been bludgeoned to death by uncomprehending comrades who had wanted to "beat the 'devil' out of him." "Their culture and ways were so strange to most of us," one of the nurses lamented, "and we never had an explanation of how to deal with these people."[18]

Among the most prominent of the many spirits were the ancestors. Indeed, natives treated ancestors as if they had never passed away. Hungry GIs in Manila, for example, were irresistibly drawn to the city's large Chinese cemetery, where worshipers left elaborate dishes of choice foods for the dead. By far the most remarkable features of Okinawa were the mausoleums that could be seen from the sea dotting the island. "The Okinawan reveres his ancestors," explained a military guide. "He believes he dwells after death as he did in life." Their ashes were housed in dome-shaped vaults that resembled turtle backs and, some claimed, were meant to symbolize wombs. While the deceased thus lived on in blue ceramic urns, to a soldier of the 77th Division the living in their black kimonos appeared mere shadows of death. Okinawa, he said, was "a gloomy place."[19]

In a world where ghosts and humans mingled freely and faded easily into one another, war became still more unsettling. It was not long before American soldiers were suspecting the living of possessing the powers of the occult, too.

Much of the region, for instance, appeared to transcend temporality. Section 16 of an emergency language booklet for American pilots shot down over China taught the unfortunates how to say, "I want to start now. In an hour. Before noon. This afternoon. Tonight. Tomorrow." But it meaningfully added, in parentheses, "Don't be too impatient. This is the slow moving East."[20]

Despite the brutal convulsions of history, this part of the world had remained serenely unmoved in its geographical and cultural essence. "It was a beautiful land," an officer said of Luzon, "with the emerald of rice growing to the gold of rice ripening, a quiet land that seemed to belong to the long ago."[21]

If the land seemed not to age, then neither did the people who belonged to it. Eternally childlike, they, like ghosts, eerily escaped the curse of time. "He told me that he was married, and had a few children," a B-29 airman said of a conversation with a Japanese prisoner on Okinawa, "I think he was a few years older than myself, but it is hard to judge ages of Asiatics."[22]

It was equally hard to judge if these people consumed food like normal human beings. The fact that battered Asian troops were often forced to fight without supplies or rations somehow came to mean to Americans that they did not need food. General Marshall, in a letter to a British colleague in December 1942, expressed confidence in the fighting ability of the Chinese forces because, he said, the individual soldier had "no nerves," required little in terms of clothing and other supplies, and needed "a minimum of food." Flying from Kwajalein to Roi in June 1944, over islands where bypassed Japs had been left stranded, an Army captain told Robert Sherrod: "Let the bastards stay there until they rot and starve, if it is possible for a Jap to starve, if not, let them die of old age." But a nagging doubt remained as to whether even the latter might be possible.[23]

People who resisted time and hunger might as well have been bodiless. And so it often seemed to American soldiers as they moved among Asians who could be as shadowy in daylight as they were ethereal at night. Despite assurances that about a dozen servants were around, an intrigued American pilot, invited to the house of a European in Burma early in 1942, never caught a glimpse of more than one at a time, "almost as if these servants were accomplishing the job with mirrors, as they moved soundlessly about on their bare feet."[24]

When such people turned against their Western exploiters and became soldiers, they proved formidable enemies. "Subtle and insubstantial," Chinese military strategist Sun Tzu had said as early as the fourth century BC, "the expert leaves no trace; divinely mysterious, he is inaudible. Thus he is master of his enemy's fate." Japanese troops honed this particular art of war to perfection. "We could lick'em," a scared kid told an officer on Guadalcanal in December 1942, "if we could see'em."[25]

That was hard enough during the day, when patient Japanese soldiers lay in ambush for endless hours, fired smokeless rifles, then disappeared without a sound, leaving barely a trace. "[W]hen they removed even empty cartridge cases, and we found only tracks," said a marine on Okinawa, "we got an eerie feeling – as though we were fighting a phantom enemy."[26]

It was in the dark, however, that the Japanese became truly masters of their enemy's fate. From the very beginning, they turned night warfare into one of their specialties. Only through intensive training did the Japanese acquire skills in a method of war for which Americans were ill prepared. Yet GIs were convinced that night skills came natural to an enemy of such chimerical quality.[27]

During the struggle for Guadalcanal in 1942, American ships ruled from sunup to sundown, but, in the words of naval historian Samuel Morison, when twilight came, they "cleared out like frightened children running home from a graveyard." Only later in the war, with the arrival of radar, did American naval forces conquer this "instinctive fear of what darkness might conceal."[28]

The air forces had to overcome similar inhibitions. As late as June 1944, during a tour of the Pacific, Charles Lindbergh complained in his journal that "night flying with fighters has been sadly neglected" and that, in effect, "a complex against it developed."[29]

Ground troops did not even attempt to wrestle the night from the Japanese. "We are daytime fighters," Ira Wolfert reported from the Solomons, "and when twilight comes, we revert to our Indian-fighting past and build old-fashioned squares of defense around each separate automatic weapon." "The Japs move freely at night," noted Canadian observers with the American 27th Division on Saipan in the summer of 1944, "and in many cases talking could be heard and lights seen within their positions."[30]

Advancing units usually halted early enough in the afternoon. Then began the frenzied digging of foxholes, the siting of weapons, the stringing of barbed wire, the placement of trip wires with rattling C-ration cans. To lift at least some of what Ernie Pyle on Okinawa called "the shroud of Oriental darkness," troops stocked up on flares and incendiary grenades, dotted the area with cans full of sand and gasoline, installed searchlights, and relied upon nearby vessels to fire star shells.[31]

None of all this, however, did much to make the night less terrifying. With darkness, the Japanese came alive, haunting the defenders with shrieks, laughter, taunts, and threats in garbled English. They harassed the Americans, charged their positions, and – worse – sneaked into the lines like ghosts. At Buna, in New Guinea, they came so close to the slit trenches that GIs could grab them by the ankles and pull them in. Endless nights of fighting specters left Americans scared, exhausted, edgy, even delusional. Among the nerve-racked men of the 169th Infantry on New Georgia in July 1943, rumors spread that nocturnal raiders were dragging Americans from their foxholes. They used ropes, hooks, and long metal pincers – and wore long black robes.[32]

Yet otherworldly as the fleeting enemy appeared to be, he could not entirely avoid leaving behind traces that exposed him as merely human. So revelatory, so reassuring too, were even the most mundane items abandoned by the Japanese, that no military prohibitions, no warnings of boobytraps, no rumors of enemy stragglers, could prevent Americans from drifting off to poke the objects, examine them, collect them. "Well, naturally," a destroyer sailor wrote to his wife after a visit to Saipan in February 1945, " . . . George and I started wandering about which we aren't supposed ever to do, but always do anyway in spite of regulations. We wandered about inspecting Jap pillboxes and blockhouses and rifle pits." One reason why the Okinawa landings of 1945 were the best conducted of the war was, according to Samuel Morison, that there were no complaints of landing craft crews "going souvenir hunting ashore." Meanwhile, sailors on board one of the larger ships of the Okinawa invasion force threw anything Japanese they could lay their hands on – mainly *kamikaze* debris – into a large box in the bow, to be sifted through later.[33]

Troops in the rear, burning with curiosity, wheedled out of frontline soldiers souvenirs no matter how fragmentary. After having acquainted some of the wounded just back from New Britain in January 1944, a soldier of the 495th Port Battalion in New Guinea excitedly scribbled in his diary: "I have some Jap writing paper brought back by marines and have seen scraps of Jap books and magazines, and bullets."[34]

Bit by bit, the tiny shards brought contours and flesh to the incorporeal ghosts. Some items were rather unusual, like the "pajama-like pants," the "two-toed shoes," or the "little wooden 'pillows.'" Other pieces of equipment proved so practical, however, that Americans were quick to adopt them. GIs in the Papuan campaign snapped up the neat bakelite oil cases the Japanese carried to protect their rifles against rust. Few marines on Bougainville were without the excellent canned heat that came with the enemy's field rations. On Saipan, hundreds of the star-stamped, paper-wrapped kits with toothbrushes, soap, and toilet paper found their way into American hands.[35]

What fascinated the soldiers most, however, were the boxes, cans, kegs, and jars that contained the foods with which the Japanese turned out to have been sustaining themselves after all. "I saw that there were canned pears and peaches and pineapple, goulash, crabmeat, shredded fish and salmon," Richard Tregaskis reported from the Solomons, "hardly the primitive diet on which the Japanese is traditionally supposed to subsist." American troops had little qualms about using the captured Japanese stores. "We are being issued one package of Jap cigarettes a day," a soldier on Guadalcanal noted approvingly. GIs actually became aficionados of certain kinds of Japanese food, such as the canned salmon. When large food stocks fell into American hands on Saipan, Robert Sherrod reported that the soldiers praised the "roast beef with soy-bean sauce" as "a delicacy." He himself admitted: "The beer was excellent (Japs are good brewers), but the non-alcoholic lemon soda was even better."[36]

Soldiers were especially keen to lay their hands on some of the more personal items of the Japanese. On Okinawa, Ernie Pyle saw more than one marine file by with a photo album in his hand. One of them was a corporal from Indianapolis. "In a cave Brady found two huge photograph albums full of snapshots of Japanese girls, Chinese girls, young Japs in uniform, and family poses," Pyle wrote. "He treasured it as though it were full of people he knew."[37]

Whenever the blurred enemy allowed himself to be brought into sharper focus, American soldiers ran the risk of recognizing some of the self in the opposing other. The most innocent item could bring about this unsettling sensation at the most unexpected moment. The sound of Japanese records left behind on Biak. "Funny," observed one GI, "how your enemies' music will make you dislike them a little less." The sight of "Japanese cutie pin-ups" in an abandoned dugout on Okinawa. Smeared sheets of naive, brightly-colored paintings in a blown-out cave on Iwo Jima. "The Japanese soldiers had *children*," a horrified marine realized, "who loved them and sent their art work to them."[38]

Nothing was more unforgiving in its naked portrayal of commonality, however, than a photograph. A battalion surgeon in the Philippines soaked up the meaning of a picture taken from the dirty, bloody jacket of a sprawled, bloated body. "A smiling young man in a Japanese army field uniform was holding a young baby in his lap. Sitting next to him was a lovely young woman with slanted eyes; behind her stood an elderly, sad-looking couple." "God!" the officer's mind screamed. "That could be me!"[39]

Similar feelings were involuntarily shared by some of those who came face to face with Japanese POWs. Upon seeing his first Japanese prisoners in 1945, Ernie Pyle confessed, "they gave me the creeps, and I wanted a mental bath after looking at them." Yet some months later, Pyle reported on an encounter with Japanese POWs on Okinawa: "The Jap corporal had a metal photo holder like a cigarette case in which were photos that we took to be of three Japanese movie stars. They were pretty, and everybody had to have a look."[40]

American troops captured few Japanese alive. One reason for this was that the Emperor's soldiers regarded captivity as the ultimate disgrace, and knew they would be social outcasts if they ever returned home. Those who did become prisoners, therefore, saw no other choice but to embrace their new existence. To the astonishment of the Americans, captured Japanese soldiers thus proved to be surprisingly cooperative, docile, and courteous once they had resigned themselves to their new fate. "[T]hey always stood at the fence, watching us," a US Navy flight nurse remembered of her frequent stops at Kwajalein. "We took their pictures, and they would say things to us, which we thought were kind of sassy." "They're dead pans," a *Yank* correspondent on Espíritu Santo jotted in his diary, ". . . but before we left they had all laughed and cracked jokes and tried to help the doctor with his Japanese lesson."[41]

Much more astonishing to GIs than the occasional human face of the enemy, however, was the discovery that these Asian foes actually shared some of their American culture. Japanese POWs were able to make sassy comments or crack jokes around Americans only because they knew English. In fact, they knew it so well, including slang, that the only defect Americans could detect was a slight mispronunciation of the letter 'l.' Before long, 'Lilliputian,' 'lullaby lane,' and 'apple dumplings' were ringing out across the Pacific in the hope that in the dark these passwords could separate Japanese infiltrators from fellow GIs. But the English of some proved disturbingly flawless. 'Tokyo Rose,' for instance, bombarded American troops with propaganda in an English "whose cultured enunciation," according to one officer, "would not have been out of place in a student debate at Vassar." Quite a few prisoners claimed to have attended American schools and universities prior to donning the Japanese uniform. As early as the Guadalcanal campaign, Richard Tregaskis talked of "yarns about the Japs' ability to speak English, and the alleged fact that many of the dead wore American high-school rings." At home, too, Japanese nationals had apparently been studying English most diligently. One marine was rather surprised, for instance, to find among the few intact books strewn about an Okinawan school "several English grammars and readers."[42]

Together with the English language, America's popular culture had seeped into Japanese society. It was rather baffling, for instance, to receive from a presumed otherworldly opponent propaganda leaflets showing a groggy Popeye on top of a pile of empty spinach cans. One can only guess at the consternation among men of the 1st Cavalry Division on Los Negros in March 1944 when some of the Japanese troops who attacked before dawn could be heard singing "Deep in the Heart of Texas."[43]

Yet, all in all, the experiences of commonality remained too few and fleeting to make the Asian adversary less of a spectral enigma. Combat soldiers actually preferred it that way. It facilitated the task of killing and slaughtering the enemy by preventing thorny questions and doubts from raising their poisonous heads. "The average frontline marine either failed to interpret the signs around him as proof of shared ideas and feelings," Craig Cameron concludes in his study of the 1st Marine Division, "or consciously ignored them." "One of the few Japanese we captured at Okinawa was a Yale graduate," noted a soldier of the 5th Marines. "He spoke perfect English, but we never said anything to him."[44]

What soldiers wanted to avoid by all means was to allow killing to feel like murder. Hence it was paramount to deny proof of shared culture or, better still, to pretend to belong to an utterly different species. Richard Tregaskis observed on Guadalcanal how three Japanese prisoners walked in single file, "while the marines, looking huge by comparison, shooed them along like pigeons." "The Japs," the correspondent wrote, "blinked their eyes like curious birds as they looked at me." Only 20 percent of the veteran enlisted infantrymen of three Pacific divisions acknowledged in November 1943 that the sight of Japanese prisoners had shown them to be "men just like us." Forty-two percent claimed that such close-up encounters with enemy soldiers had made them feel "all the more like killing them."[45]

If combat soldiers sought refuge behind the mental divide and wittingly cultivated it, then US teams designed for the specific purpose of bridging the gap between Americans and Japanese ultimately failed. "[P]sychological warfare units dropped tens of millions of leaflets, made thousands of front-line radio broadcasts and loudspeaker surrender appeals, and conducted hundreds of medium and short-wave radio broadcasts," historian Clayton Laurie sums up, "yet all without significant effect."[46]

Lack of linguistic and cultural expertise forced US psychological units to rely heavily on Japanese–American soldiers. To protect them against capture, however, the valuable Nisei interpreters often had to be kept away from the frontlines. At wit's end, Americans increasingly turned to Japanese and other Asian POWs to help persuade enemy troops to surrender. Two Korean 'bait-boys' who in February 1944 entered a stronghold on Kwajalein for that purpose were tortured by the Japanese inside. Despite such incidents, however, Asian cultural mediators remained indispensable. As late as the Okinawan campaign, the 6th Marine Division reported that "the most potent propaganda messages are those composed by local civilians and prisoners of war."[47]

When left to their own devices, American troops attempted to use the most desperate means to get through to the Japanese. During the battle for Kunishi Ridge on Okinawa, the booming of guns mixed with the wailing of sirens installed on American tanks. Soldiers were told the sinister sound was produced "for the psychological effect it might have on the Japanese." "To me," an incredulous marine bristled, "the sirens just made the whole bloody struggle more bizarre and unnerving."[48]

Although American soldiers found it hard to put together a mental picture of the Japanese, they soon became convinced of one thing: that the enemy was particularly well suited for war in the untamed natural expanses of the region.

Before December 1941, US intelligence had not taken very seriously the possibility of an attack by a country that had only one-ninth of America's industrial output and by a people whose mental make-up was thought not to be conducive to technological know-how. After Pearl Harbor, some of the prejudices regarding Japan's industrial and technological capacities had to be unlearned in a hurry. An officer who entered a naval air intelligence school imagining, like many of his compatriots, that "all Japanese products were second-rate and shoddy," emerged from the training course convinced that "Japan's best engineers and production personnel rivaled the best of any other country's." Likewise, American ground troops steadily gained a healthy respect for enemy pieces of equipment like .25 rifles, Nambu machine guns, and mortars.[49]

Despite such fragmentary evidence to the contrary, however, American soldiers realized full well that, in terms of industrialization, mechanization, and motorization, Japan desperately lagged behind their own country. Armored forces lacked the striking power of Western armies. Japanese infantry had to make do with rifles, machine guns, and knee mortars as they received only limited air and artillery support. Trucks were in short supply. Support services were grievously weak, leading to shortages of rations, ammunition and fuel, and to deficiencies in anything from medical support to road and runway maintenance.[50]

Quality as well as quantity appeared to be a problem. A marine on Peleliu, for instance, thought the Japanese field guns "formidable looking" and "well-made," but he was rather astonished to find that they had wheels of heavy wood reminiscent of the artillery of the previous century. "We thought their stuff was made by Mickey Mouse," a sergeant of the Americal Division summed up his experience. Even the famous fighter plane that for years had been the epitome of Japanese engineering eventually stopped impressing American troops. "At one time," a veteran sailor reminisced in the spring of 1944, "the Zero was the best fighter plane around."[51]

Yet, ironically, GIs believed that from their industrial weakness the Japanese – like Asians in general – derived a kind of resilience impossible for Americans to match. With prodigious amounts of ready-made industrial goods backing them up, American troops were made painfully aware of their degree of dependence on intricate systems of production and supply by Asians who seemed to need next to nothing to keep going. When Americans at Changting airfield declared a B-24 that had become stuck in the mud to be a total loss, excited Chinese mechanics instantly swarmed over the bomber to remove the stainless steel from which they would, among other things, cut watch bands. "The Americans," an intrigued GI admitted, "were learning from the Chinese – let nothing go to waste."

Economy in turn bred the kind of improvisation skills that American soldiers who were raised on stories of frontier ingenuity could only envy. Within months, an American surgeon in China grew convinced that here lived people who possessed a "natural manual dexterity." An officer in southeast China heartily agreed as he watched patient local mechanics, unfazed by the shortages of parts and oil, replace babbitts by bamboo and distill gas from the roots of pine trees.[52]

People so adapt at fabricating things from what happened to be available around them were inexorably drawn to the wealth that nature offered for free. To make fire, Filipinos in parts of Luzon, where no goods had been for sale for almost four years, had switched from matches to a technique in which a plunger was driven into the hole of a carabao horn until the bark tinder glowed. For soap, they were extracting ingredients from cactus roots. "Here again was evidence," noted an American soldier who had once witnessed similar soap fabrication among the Navajos, "that the Filipinos can fall back on their knowledge of how to get along without civilization."[53]

In a like manner, the enemy, lacking sufficient motorized and mechanized vehicles to pull and carry supplies, had made sure, according to a 1944 American manual on Japanese forces, to build most of his equipment "as light in weight as is practicable." Thrown on the defensive, Japanese soldiers, bereft of mines in sufficient quantity and quality, also managed to construct an impressive array of 'homemade' devices from materials as varied as gasoline drums, terra cotta, and wood. US troops in Leyte on several occasions stumbled across Japanese booby traps made from materials as innocuous as coconuts. A nagging voice told GIs that such people would not feel beaten even if the last factory was in ashes and the final supply line severed.[54]

The lack of industrialization forced peoples of Asia and the Pacific to live in close harmony with nature in more than one way. Whether in the hills of Burma or on South Sea islands, for example, GIs could not escape the bizarre rituals of fierce animists. From India, a lieutenant wrote to his wife that he had seen the place where a remarkable religious group, called the Parsees, put out their dead so that birds of prey could tear them apart. They "worship fire, land, and water," he explained, "so this is the only way they can dispose of their dead." While Americans in Kweiyang in 1944 complained about the lack of heat in their quarters, a surgeon noted that the unperturbed Chinese went about their business "as cold-blooded as fish." "After all," the American physician added sarcastically, "Nature prescribes the weather, and who is man to interfere with Nature?"[55]

At times, the symbiosis took on rather shocking forms. New Guinean natives were said to do more than live under one roof with their domesticated animals. "I have even heard," whispered a GI, "that the women nurse the baby pigs."[56]

Mostly, however, American soldiers were much impressed by the ease with which the natives allowed themselves to be led by the rhythms of nature. Despite the fact, for example, that the Dutch had introduced calendars and clocks to the East Indies long ago, the majority of the archipelago's people, a GI guide noted, continued to "depend on the sun to tell time, as their ancestors did."[57]

Nothing of what nature was so kind to offer went to waste, neither light nor food. Of the birds that Chinese guerrillas shot for food, only the feathers remained. American intelligence officers working with them behind Japanese lines queasily looked on as they devoured eyes, brains and, after turning them inside out and washing them, intestines too.[58]

GIs felt particular awe for the natives' sixth sense. Seated in a truck that returned New Guineans to camp at the end of their work day in 1943, an American soldier carelessly let the tall jungle walls on either side of the narrow road slip by. But the natives did not. They, the puzzled GI observed, "kept looking and pointing and talking among themselves, but I never did see one thing along the way to cause their excitement and never learned what was so interesting in the trees." That same year, the 37th Division reported that it was making more and more use of natives at the head of patrols on Bougainville, "as they seemingly can sense the presence of the enemy long before the enemy can be seen or heard by white troops."[59]

The expertise of indigenes was much sought after because Americans believed the Japanese shared in the talents of the peoples of the region to read and understand nature. The stunning feats the enemy troops had performed during the operations in Malaya and Burma, and during the early stage of the campaign in New Guinea, had earned them the reputation of born jungle fighters. As late as October 1944, for example, a military manual found it necessary to stress that if the Japanese had been "highly successful in their earlier jungle operations, on terrain where good roads and railroads are practically unknown, and where every type of natural obstacle exists," this had only been so "because they had trained extensively in jungle terrain."[60]

Despite such exhortations, GIs never entirely rid themselves of the suspicion that the Japanese thrived in the jungle because of innate abilities. "They assumed," Gerald Linderman has noted, "that they as a people were temperamentally at odds, and the Japanese in harmony, with jungle existence." In a report on the Leyte campaign late in 1944, General Krueger pointed out the fact that sometimes limited enemy resistance along a road had sufficed to stop the advance of an entire US division. The explanation was that American troops had shown to be "too roadbound," whereas the Japanese had shown a willingness to disappear into the jungles, swamps and rice paddies, and to "stay there until rooted out."[61]

So close to nature appeared indigenes of this region that they began to take on zoomorphic qualities. When a pilot who had crashed in the jungle of New Guinea crept up to two native hunters and snapped a twig, they "froze in their tracks, like a couple of hunting dogs on point." When, minutes later, he startled a woman of the same tribe, "she started running like a deer." GIs were convinced that Japanese soldiers, like American Indians, could flawlessly imitate animal sounds. On Guadalcanal, "the creak of a beetle or cry of a nighthawk was enough to start aimless shooting." Newcomers in Dutch New Guinea who crawled out of their foxholes in response to pitiful canine howling in a nearby swamp were reprimanded by a veteran sergeant who told them it was not a dog but a Japanese.[62]

It could hardly be called surprising that this was the region where, the *Guide to the Dutch East Indies* did not fail to remind GIs, "the shadowy 'ape man' of Java" had once roamed and "the 'wild man of Borneo'" was fabled to roam still. Somehow, the ape man on hind legs seemed to have been stopped dead in his tracks, his development arrested, his umbilical cord never entirely severed from the wilderness around him. Indeed, the simian traits of people in this part of the world had always intrigued Americans. Already during an earlier war, American colonial troops in the Philippines had been bellowing "the barracks-room song about the tail-less monkeys." It proved all too easy for GIs to transfer such stereotypes to others in the region. Looking for a useful trail with the help of New Guinean guides in 1942, a GI soon found he could not keep up with them: "They swing along like monkeys," he panted, "making better time than they would have on flat ground."[63]

Japanese soldiers, however, seemed to surpass even the Melanesians in tree-top agility. Enemy snipers turned the canopy of steamy jungles into snug habitats. During the battle of Sanananda in Papua, the 163rd Infantry had to establish sniper-observer posts and to booby-trap trees to contain the threat. The marksmen operated just as easily from 40-foot palm trees on coral islands. "By now," Robert Sherrod reported from Tarawa, "all the coconut trees from which snipers had been shot yesterday are filled again with more snipers." Before long, nervous GIs were imagining Japanese in trees everywhere. On Makin atoll, even when they saw no enemy, Americans "fired occasional shots into trees that looked likely [to hold snipers]." Troops on New Georgia reported alarming numbers of enemy tree snipers, but few appear ever to have seen one. A sergeant of the 25th Division remembered one such alert on the island: "Another night there was movement in the trees. Other men had been watching it for a few minutes. Rifles were at the ready, thinking it might be a Japanese sniper. The object was going from tree to tree. It was a large monkey."[64]

Japanese soldiers burrowed into soil as confidently as they nestled in foliage. Sun Tzu's prescript was centuries old: "The experts in defense conceal themselves as under the ninefold earth; those skilled in attack move as from above the ninefold heavens." Yet as of 1942, the Japanese military was following the Chinese strategist to the letter. Indeed, as soon as the Allies in the Pacific managed to contain the Japanese offensive that had followed the strike against Pearl Harbor, and then began to roll it back, Japanese ground forces vanished into the earth. They sank into spiderweb strongholds whose radiating tunnels connected numerous concealed foxholes to large underground shelters. Food, water, equipment, and weapons disappeared with them. On Iwo Jima, a GI noted, "It was a case of one army entirely above ground and the other below." Soldiers on the volcanic island knew that the occasional trembling beneath their feet was caused by earth tremors. Still, no one laughed when one night a sergeant joked that he thought the Japanese were digging below them to blow up the island. Where caves honeycombed hills or stony jungles of coral, Japanese defenders invariably took possession, honing hollows into bulwarks. An American tank crew that fired phosphorus shells into a cave of Okinawa's Maeda Escarpment "saw smoke emerging from more than thirty hidden openings along the slope."[65]

Older images of tireless Oriental hordes as swarming industrious insects surfaced again, causing frustration and concern. "What beats me," bristled an engineer on Kolombangara Island in February 1944, "is why we aren't licking the pants off the Japs. Our equipment is far superior in every way . . . I guess the main reason is that the Jap is a burrowing creature. The coolie has done his work well . . ." Off the coast of Guam, an open-mouthed private of the 77th Division watched an unexpected effect of the pre-landing bombardment in 1944. "The cliffs on the peninsula gradually fell into the sea," he wrote, "opening up underground tunnels that looked like large apartment houses without the front wall. The Japanese soldiers were living like ants underground."[66]

In his underground holes, the enemy reverted to an almost troglodyte existence. The battle for Saipan had been raging for more than a month when Robert Sherrod was drawn to twelve dead Japanese in a field. The scene reminded the correspondent of how few of the enemy he had seen "killed in the open." "Up to now," he clarified, "Saipan had been largely cave warfare." In Peleliu's Umurbrogol Ridge, GIs could "capture a summit and smell rice and fish being cooked by three or four layers of Japanese resting comfortably underneath them."[67]

While, on the surface, American troops pushed forward, conquered, and established control, enemy defiance and resistance continued to fester in what Eric Bergerud has called "an odd netherworld." Okinawan civilians were rumored to be hiding out near Naha in June 1945 long after American troops had taken over. Still, a marine was most startled when one day he "caught sight of a little old fellow disappearing like a gnome into a cave some 400 yards away from our position." The battle for control over Luzon had been raging since January 1945. Yet when the war was declared over more than half a year later, some 50,500 Japanese troops emerged from caves, holes, and crevices in the Philippine island's mountainous north.[68]

On Tokashiki, one of the Kerama Islands near Okinawa, the Japanese commander refused to surrender until months after the battle, and then only when shown a copy of the Imperial rescript announcing the end of all hostilities. He assured his American captors, however, that he could have held out for ten more years. More than a few enemy soldiers did. It was 21 April 1947 when a Japanese lieutenant and 26 men formally surrendered on Peleliu. It was 1949 or 1950 when locals on another of the Palau Islands captured a Japanese soldier with a beard down to his hips. It was still five years later when Peleliu islanders, alerted by the disappearance of food from their gardens, managed to seize "a cave-dwelling Korean."[69]

In a world where man so easily regressed to animalism, the boundary between savagery and civilization became frighteningly shadowy. Japanese commanders routinely issued stern rules regarding personal cleanliness and the construction and maintenance of latrines. However, enemy troops hunkering down in caves for weeks on end, often under intense bombardment, found it impossible to uphold even the most basic standards of hygiene. Through cracks and holes, underground shelters belched noxious vapors of sweat, stale food, urine, and feces. Soldiers of the 43rd Division claimed that on New Georgia "the Japanese positions were easier to smell than see." Landing boat crews operating in the Solomons told sailors of the USS *Montpelier* they could "smell the Japs 25 yards away." Nauseated Americans were quick to interpret these olfactory insults not as the foul smell of war, but as the stench of a primitive culture. "There was evidence of filth and neglect wherever they lived," an airplane mechanic in the Philippines wrote in his diary. "The Japs are evidently the filthiest race of so called civilized people in existence."[70]

Nothing identified humans more readily with primitives, however, than the almost unspeakable practice of cannibalism. For centuries, European travelers had been glad to attribute the taste for human flesh exclusively to nonwhite savages. America, as Richard Slotkin has shown, from the outset of colonization was understood as a battleground between two diametrically opposed lifestyles, that of "Cannibals and Christians." In the Pacific, the uncovering in certain archipelagos of anthropophagous practices had dealt a heavy blow to Enlightenment's illusion of having at last discovered truly noble savages. Moreover, in modern portrayals of the Pacific and Orient, American novelists and moviemakers had dished up potent mixtures of exotic romance and headhunter savagery.[71]

GIs were nervously excited about possible encounters with the world's last man-eaters. American troops in the Solomons jokingly dubbed their force of friendly native bearers the 'Cannibal Battalion.' But the joking abruptly stopped when they found gruesome evidence that among the very enemy they were fighting there were devourers of human flesh on a scale hardly imaginable. American troops came across the first apparent instances of cannibalism – corpses whose fleshiest portions had been cut away – on Guadalcanal in December 1942. It remained hard to believe, however, until stories of Japanese cannibalism in New Guinea, too, began to circulate some weeks later. Men of the 163rd Infantry, who recovered the body of a slain comrade in January 1943, reported that "[f]lesh had been removed from the thighs and buttocks." Many similar reports began pouring in. A private who found the body of a missing American on 23 January stated that "a stew pot in a nearby Japanese bunker contained the heart and liver of approximate size of that [of a] human." Other cases confirmed that Japanese cannibalism extended to the entrails and genitals, and that sometimes even the brains were removed. The victims were Allied soldiers, Asian laborers, native New Guineans, and Japanese soldiers.

The news spread like wildfire. When Charles Lindbergh visited air bases in the Pacific in the summer of 1944, notices on squadron bulletins were retelling the latest necrophagous acts in all their horrifying details. Meanwhile, American troops were reporting instances of cannibalism from Burma, too. But it was during the campaign in the Philippines that the practice again reached a frequency that defied the imagination, with whole squads of Japanese apparently engaged in the hunt for human flesh. The principal reason for the enemy's behavior was starvation resulting from severed supply lines. But GIs did not care for explanations. To them cannibalism was quite simply the epitome of savagery.[72]

Perhaps most frightening of all was that merely from looking at the Japanese, American soldiers would never have judged them capable of anything nearly as horrendous as cannibalism. Most of the Japanese prisoners subjected to Richard Tregaskis's gaze on Guadalcanal, for example, were "well under five feet in height and physically constructed like children." In fact, GIs sometimes made it sound as if they were fighting a Lilliputian army. On New Britain they described the pilot seat of the Zero as "incredibly small." And they found the captured stocks of enemy raincoats on the island to be useless because they "looked like children's and wouldn't reach to the knees of a marine."[73]

Their sudden meekness in captivity conveyed an equally treacherous impression of harmlessness. "The language officer," a marine noted while gaping at prisoners on Okinawa, "acted and sounded more like an elementary school teacher giving little children directions than an officer giving orders to a bunch of tough Japanese soldiers." In death, they could have an almost angelic quality, as on Eniwetok, where a marine compared slain Japanese on the beach to "tired children with their faces in the sand."[74]

The country from which these tiny, fragile-looking soldiers came, said the *Guide to Japan*, had "the charm and delight of the miniature." It was "like a lovely doll's house, almost too fragile and delicate to be true," and had nurtured a culture with a feel for the refined detail. A culture with an "almost religious approach to beauty" and a veritable "worship" of flowers and blossoms.[75]

Indeed, Japanese soldiers at times displayed a delicacy GIs considered misplaced, if not outright effeminate. "Very often, we'd get a photograph off a dead Japanese," said a marine. "Here would be this soldier, sitting in a studio, with a screen behind and a table with a little flower on it. Often he'd be holding a rifle, yet there was always that little vase of flowers."[76]

That beneath this surface of supreme serenity broiled a cauldron of unabated primitive instincts made of the Japanese a Dr. Jekyll and Mr. Hyde kind of people in the minds of GIs. A people "capable in a stroke," as Yuki Tanaka has noted in his study of Japanese cannibalism during the war, "of switching from refined and civilized activity to savagery and barbarity."[77]

American soldiers learned that the Japanese had other dark sides than the taste for human flesh. They also possessed an uncanny capacity to stomach pain. This had long been considered a quality of savagism. American colonists, for example, generally ascribed to Indians an almost inhuman ability to bear torture. The American military's understanding of the Japanese character was not very different. "They can," said the 1945 *Guide to Japan*, "endure hardship and suffering for a long time without out-cry . . . Their women are taught never to cry in childbirth." Soldiers who saw Japanese fight back even after the most horrific bombardments did not need convincing. "I don't know how the Japs can take it," a sailor wrote in his journal in July 1944 following the terrible pounding of Tinian. "They are really gluttons for punishment."[78]

Americans recognized that very characteristic in other Asians, too. Like beasts of burden, they carried incredible loads on heads and shoulders, for instance, without so much as flinching. GIs just could not believe the "admirable, steady, tireless pace" at which Japanese machine gun squads went "clippety-clopping down the trail in the manner common to all Orientals weighted down with heavy loads." Chinese soldiers shared this "half walking, half running trot which never seemed to tire them out completely." "How they do it, I don't know," said an American who watched female carriers hurry along in the mountains of Luzon with loads on their heads at least as heavy as the GI packs, "but it's a long distance and plenty hot . . ."[79]

Somehow, when necessary, Asians appeared able to switch off their senses altogether. In May 1942, the OSS concluded a report on China – studded with distressing statistics on poverty, epidemics, and starvation – with the reassuring note that this was a nation that had an "unrivaled ability to live under difficult conditions." An American involved in caring for Chinese amputees was surprised to find that to these soldiers "it didn't seem to make any difference if they lost a leg or arm, they were always laughing – even the ones who had lost both legs."[80]

Primitive peoples were not only capable of bearing tremendous hardship. They could also inflict pain without the least sign of mercy or remorse. History textbooks had taught American schoolchildren for decades, for example, that their country's Indians, although childlike, were a cruel people given to torture. As American contacts with Asia had increased in the nineteenth century, its peoples had fallen victim to similar stereotypes. Akira Iriye has shown, for example, that cruelty was "deeply etched among the American images of the Chinese" and "rooted for earlier generations in accounts of Chinese torture – the water treatment, the thousand cuts, the killing of Christians by Boxer rebels in 1900."[81]

The onus of cruelty in no time shifted to Japan when it began its onslaught against China in the 1930s, outraging American public opinion by bombing even helpless civilians, as in Shanghai in 1937. By the end of the American war with Japan, public opinion polls showed that people in the US believed Japanese to be inherently more cruel than Germans by a margin of five to one.[82]

No Americans became more rapidly and thoroughly convinced of the evil of the Japanese than those who engaged them on the battlefield. The very first days of the American counteroffensive in the Pacific immediately produced an infamous incident. On Guadalcanal, a patrol of 25 soldiers (one of them with the resonating name of Custer) was mercilessly butchered after having been lured towards the enemy by what was thought to be an attempt at surrender. With each new year of war, the catalogue of cruelties grew longer. Soldiers heard chilling stories of the torture and beheading of downed pilots, the abandonment or cold-blooded killing of shipwreck survivors, the shooting of parachutists in the sky, the use of civilians as human shields. The Japanese were purported to be targeting medical personnel and installations so consciously that hospital tents stopped displaying red crosses, while nurses and medics exchanged the symbols for weapons.[83]

Though many stories of cruelty were confirmed, it remained hard to tell where truth ended and rumor took over. "A favorite sport of the Japs would be," a horrified sailor testified in his diary after listening to Filipinos in Subic Bay, "to take little children and toss them up into the air, then catch them with their bayonets." Many soldiers never saw Japanese atrocities with their own eyes. Remarkably, only 13 percent of frontline infantrymen in the Pacific said they had personally witnessed "dirty or inhuman" acts committed by the enemy, a proportion that was identical among GIs fighting in Europe. When asked, however, if they had *heard* stories from others, 45 percent of the soldiers in the Pacific – nearly twice the number of those in Europe – answered affirmatively. Army surveyors asked themselves whether this larger proportion in the Pacific could not in part be ascribed to the "predisposition to believe evil of the initially more hated enemy."[84]

Whatever their exact sources of information, GIs quickly made up their minds about the Japanese. Asked how he regarded Japanese troops, a veteran of the Americal Division needed exactly one word to formulate his opinion: "sadistic." Yet this portrayal of the Japanese was more than the result of soldiers diabolizing their opponent. It also flowed from a much older inclination to view Orientals as incorrigibly cruel. That is best illustrated by the fact that Americans continued to regard even their Chinese allies as insensitive to the suffering of fellow humans. In 1945, the American command in the China theater was embarrassed to admit that one of the most widespread and persistent notions among its forces was that the Chinese were "extremely cruel" and had "no regard for human life." In a rearguard attempt to dismiss this "fiction," an official pamphlet tried to convince Americans that China was, in fact, a country of "sentimental people," a country where family "always takes care of its own" and parents "love children."[85]

In this region cursed with paradoxes, nothing appeared ultimately more contradictory than the attitude towards life itself. From their military guides, Americans learned that this was a world where "no Hindu would dream of killing a cow" and Burmese thought nothing of building shrines for ants and gnats. But, as a distraught GI pointed out after visiting Calcutta, where Jains had mouths and noses covered with gauze to prevent inhaling and killing insects, "This elevated respect for life was within a few feet of the untouchables dying of starvation or tropical disease, usually both at once."[86]

This was the world where people believed "a tree, or a flower, or a bamboo shoot may house some god." Yet, as almost every American soldier could testify, this was also the world where soldiers recklessly squandered their own lives. American observers in the 1944 Salween campaign, for example, were shocked by their Chinese allies' repeated preference for frontal, suicidal charges over encircling movements. "As a demonstration of sheer bravery the attacks were magnificent," one report said, "but sickeningly wasteful."[87]

No people demonstrated more clearly to the Americans their radically different understanding of life and death than the Japanese. Even in the most hopeless situations, Japanese soldiers refused to contemplate surrender. "Sullen lot," an officer in New Caledonia morosely noted after having seen a survivor of a shipwreck spit at an American medic, "Have had it drilled into them that they must never be captured." When the battle for Tarawa in the Central Pacific was finally over, Americans counted nearly 4,700 enemy dead and exactly 17 Japanese captives. On nearby Makin atoll, stunned GIs looked on as a wounded Japanese officer tried to kick and bite even the medics who wished to help him. In September 1944, a US Army report estimated that the voluntary surrenders in the Southwest Pacific represented no more than 1 percent of all prisoners of war. This estimate included Formosan and Korean laborers, and the report pointed out that if it had not been for starvation, very few Japanese soldiers would have offered to give themselves up at all. After two months of fighting in southern

Okinawa in 1945, the four divisions of the XXIV Corps had taken a combined total of exactly 90 military prisoners. "The Japanese soldier," the US Army history of the Okinawan campaign concluded, "fought until he was killed."[88]

Such an enemy could earn a grudging respect from American soldiers. "Clever, courageous little bastards," Robert Sherrod let slip when Japanese on Tarawa turned out to have infiltrated American lines at night in an action they knew would cost them their lives. Looking through field glasses at enemy soldiers in the Philippines who refused to take cover even when American shells were falling all around them, a lieutenant could not but admit in a letter: "You have to admire the guts of these little Japs sometimes."[89]

More often, however, the unquestioning ease with which Japanese appeared to snuff out their own lives went far beyond the kind of courage that Americans could comprehend or approve of. A group of some hundred enemy soldiers, cornered at Marpi Point on Saipan, bowed to US marines watching from a cliff, stripped off their uniforms, bathed in the ocean, and put on new clothes. They spread a huge Japanese flag over a smooth rock. Then they put grenades against their stomachs and – one by one – pulled the pin. Such ceremonies were impressive, the defiance of the gestures shocking. Still, Japanese soldiers seemed to be proving a point only to themselves, as Americans were unable to grasp the logic behind a nation committing suicide.[90]

GIs were forced to witness how, with nauseating frequency, lonely Japanese soldiers sacrificed their young lives in actions that made not the least difference. On Tarawa, Robert Sherrod watched as a Japanese – naked except for a loincloth, but armed with a grenade – threw himself under an American tank that was storming a pillbox. "The grenade does not even blow the tank's tread off," he reported, perturbed by so purposeless an act. "The tank lumbers over the Jap, still firing." When during the Leyte campaign the Japanese for the first time launched *kamikazes* in large numbers, Americans found it hard to believe that the enemy was now even treating highly-trained pilots as expendable coolies. "[T]hey crash their planes against our ships," an incredulous sailor scribbled in his journal after hearing about *kamikazes* for the first time in November 1944. "[T]he pilot," he gasped, "stays in the plane also." Curious Americans on Okinawa examined the *Baka* bombs, tiny suicide planes filled with explosives and powered by a rocket. They could travel only one way. "It made me sick to look at it," an airman said. "A machine for killing pilots."[91]

Most sickening, however, were the scenes of wholesale slaughter when infantry attacks degenerated into desperate suicidal assaults. On 2 February 1944, General Corlett's headquarters on Kwajalein warned: "Be alert for counterattack at anytime day or night, it's bound to come. The Jap makes his suicide counterattack at dawn on the day after his cause becomes hopeless."

Exactly one year later, Ernie Pyle, en route to the war in the Pacific after years of covering the European conflict, made one of his first stopovers on Kwajalein. "Our Seabees," he noted soberly, "couldn't dig a trench for a sewer pipe without digging up dead Japanese." Similar scenes were repeated over and over again. After just two days of battle near Henderson Field on Guadalcanal in October 1942, Americans buried 941 Japanese in a tiny sector known as 'Coffin Corner.' One night's counterattack in July 1944 cost the Japanese on Guam an estimated 3,500 men. Americans were able to fire howitzers at the attackers point-blank. Thirsty marines could not use the Fonte River for drinking water, so polluted was it by enemy corpses and blood.

The Japanese preferred killing comrades to letting them fall into enemy hands. In the spring of 1945, for example, 200 soldiers were found dead in a Japanese hospital in Bayombong, Luzon. Healthy soldiers who found themselves cornered did not hesitate to put an end to their own lives. In a Saipan ravine that GIs renamed 'Harakiri Gulch' lay at least 60 soldiers, their hands ripped off by grenades, heads gone, gaping holes where the abdomens had been.[92]

Most difficult to understand was that, when American troops approached Japan's home islands, even civilian subjects of the empire joined in what one GI described as "a terrible, self-destroying orgasm." Hundreds of Saipanese waded into the ocean to drown. Others leapt from the cliffs of Marpi Point to the jagged rocks below. On the Kerama Islands, scores of families used grenades, knives, ropes, and razor blades to kill themselves. "We yelled at them to stop," remembered a distraught GI, "but it did no good. Old men were cutting the throats of small children and young girls."[93]

Such was the carnage across the Pacific that American troops were often baffled by what to do with the bodies. While battle raged, it was simply impossible to remove them all. Americans who slipped on the ridges of Okinawa's Shuri Line slid to a bottom sludgy with mud and decaying enemy corpses; buddies had to help them get rid of fat maggots crawling from pockets, belts, and leggings. When battle died down, the piles of enemy dead were hurriedly and unceremoniously done away with. The mass burial ground of thousands upon thousands of Japanese killed on Tinian had to be fenced in to keep out scavenging animals. On New Britain, dead Japanese were dumped in big holes blown by dynamite. Three days later, bloating corpses, spreading a terrible stench, defiantly pushed up the earth.[94]

Americans might just as well have taken on ghosts from the far beyond. "He fought to die," a sailor aboard the USS *South Dakota* summarized the gaping existentialist divide, "we fought to live."[95]

"What could ever prompt a man with even average intelligence to take his life and take so many lives as that fellow did today? What is behind it all?"

The question the radioman of the USS *O'Bannon* asked after having witnessed a vicious *kamikaze* attack on the invasion fleet off Mindoro in December 1944 burned on the lips of many a soldier in Asia and the Pacific.[96]

Some thought it was impossible for Westerners to understand. A GI who had just heard about a bloody but futile suicide raid on a Leyte airstrip believed, more than ever before, that the Japanese had "a mind of their own." The implication was that, in sharp contrast to Westerners, the Japanese (like other Asians, and primitives in general) were not rational people. In his first weeks of covering the war in the Pacific, the best explanation famous correspondent Ernie Pyle could come up with in 1945 was that Japanese soldiers were "thoroughly inconsistent in what they did, and very often illogical." "It would take another Jap to figure out why," he dismissed the radioman's question.[97]

There were soldiers, on the other hand, who believed that the answer was quite simple and that it had nothing to do with Japanese motives and values whatsoever. In his study of the 1st Marine Division, for example, Craig Cameron has found that throughout the war, rumors circulated identifying liquor and narcotics as the enemy's driving force. Richard Tregaskis was present when marines in a jungle clearing on Guadalcanal stumbled onto stacks of boxes with a strange substance. "Opium," a marine immediately confirmed. The correspondent later had the label deciphered as a blood-coagulating agent. Still, even long after the war, a veteran maintained that the "Banzai charges were 'Saki' and drug led."[98]

Whether artificially induced or not, on more than one occasion Japanese behavior certainly appeared to be mad. According to a US Army history of the campaign, by the end of June 1945 about half the enemy troops who continued to resist in southern Okinawa "were fighting in a daze, and rape was common since the soldiers felt that they had only a short time to live." "I've come to the definite conclusion," an infantryman in the Philippines told his mother that same month, "that these Japs are all either crazy or bomb-happy."[99]

Sander Gilman has documented how common it has been for racial stereotypes to be infused with images of psychopathology. Indeed, similar procedures were employed to taint the Japanese enemy in official publications destined for American servicemen. The 1942 *Guide to Hawaii* announced, for instance, that it would begin by describing life on the islands before the Japanese "went berserk." Offering a possible explanation for the frenzied soldier Americans had so often seen storming their lines as if invulnerable, the 1945 *Guide to Japan* noted: "In moments of stress he is likely to become panic-stricken or hysterical."[100]

Hysteria was only one of a variety of mental disorders suggested by the *Guide to Japan* to shed some light on the enemy's strange behavior. The Japanese male allegedly suffered also from an acute "feeling of insecurity." This had many complicated sources, but in part was rooted in his childhood, a stage in life where his parents were said to have alternately spoiled and neglected him, thus creating a boy given "to fits of temper, yelling and screaming." Step by step, the military guide thus revealed the complex genesis of the crazed banzai warrior. As one could have suspected from his hysterical fits, the Japanese was a person plagued also by immense frustration, someone who "underneath his calm, almost poker-face exterior" was in fact "a bundle of quivering nerves." This mental state was created by a government and society that "curbed [him] no matter which way he turns." So relentless was the repression that a Japanese was not permitted "to give way to any emotion such as joy or sorrow" and was denied "the great relief of violent laughter or tears." When such repression did not allow at least certain outlets, mental derailment was virtually unavoidable. Unfortunately, in Japan there were "no valves except those provided by war or other moments of great excitement." Unrelieved repression and frustration, together with "the constant compulsion to kowtow to superiors," thus produced people with a nagging inferiority complex. People "who seek by bullying weaker persons to convince themselves of their own strength."[101]

The US military's crash courses on psychopathology by no means guaranteed a more coherent picture of the enemy. "They're little, warped-brained savage animals with the complex of suppression," one adherent of pseudopsychology ventured on the subject of suicide pilots, "but they have fear, like any one else." "Their fear is worse," the GI continued his murky diagnosis, "for there's that phobia of having nothing to live for – the inferiority complex they try to overcome."[102]

Since madness was obviously not easy to dissect, it was often more convenient to accuse the enemy of plain stupidity. "If the Japs had the equipment and intelligence the Germans have," a lieutenant in the Philippines told his mother in April 1945, "they would be tough to beat." That the Japanese were not intelligent soldiers was demonstrated most vividly by their lack of imagination and flexibility. Training, said an American manual on Japanese forces, was thorough but rigid, inhibiting "initiative" among enlisted men and "originality of thought and action" among officers and NCOs. "Your enemy can't think as fast as you can," General Shepherd reminded marines on Okinawa when he urged them in May 1945 to take advantage of cover and maneuver rather than to try and "outslug" the Japanese. Robert Sherrod, too, was wont to ascribe the spasms of massive self-destruction to the enemy's unbending, inferior mind: "He had never been taught to improvise and his reflexes were hopelessly slow; if his plan of battle failed . . . he was likely, under pressure, to commit suicide. He didn't know what else to do."[103]

The sanctity of authority, more than anything else, had caused the Japanese mind to ossify. "We tell our youngsters, 'think for yourself,' . . . 'you are on your own,' 'it's up to you,'" explained the *Guide to Japan.* "The words the Japanese hears from the cradle to the grave are 'obey,' 'obey,'

'obey.'" It was the military, above all other institutions, that had perfected "blind and unquestioning subservience to authority," to the point where each soldier was reduced to "an efficient cog in the machine" and conditioned to "carry out instructions to the letter."[104]

Paradoxically, this meant that Japanese soldiers were likely to behave suicidally in battle with or without officers. In the Solomons, Ira Wolfert maintained that it was the Japanese cadre that stoked fanaticism and that "soldiers in direct contact with their officers keep trying to kill our men even in the last extremities." However, if in the confines of their units they were like lambs led to the slaughterhouse, then "split up," as one of Merrill's Marauders in Burma claimed, "they were like chickens." Without leadership, the *Guide to Japan* asserted, the soldier falls victim to "blind despair," "[h]is mind just shuts down." When an officer was "killed off or lost," a marine on Iwo Jima corroborated, "they did not have the intelligence to carry on without him but only knew one thing and that was Banzai and to die for the Emperor."[105]

Some squarely put the blame for the enemy's suicidal behavior on the Emperor, apex of the chain of command, whom GIs knew was worshiped like a divinity. After having lived through yet another *kamikaze* raid off Leyte, a sailor aboard the destroyer *Howorth* wrote: "[T]hose Nips must give their hearts and souls to the 'Imperial Bastard'. . ."[106]

American soldiers grasped at anything their military guides could offer them to help rationalize Japanese stoicism in the face of death. The "spirit of the warrior" and "hero worship" cultivated by a militarist society. The extolling of "warlike ventures as 'divine missions'" and attack as a "mystic virtue." The disgrace and humiliation capture would bring to families back home.[107]

From at least 1944 on, manuals also urged GIs to remember that the Japanese soldier was told that Americans "torture prisoners" and that he therefore "may prefer death to pain and suffering." Civilians were fed similar "Tokyo propaganda" about Americans, the *Guide to Okinawa* warned, "so you can expect them to look at you as though you were a combination of Dracula and the Sad Sack – at first anyway." "They are firmly convinced that we plan to pull their toenails and hair out by the roots and slice them to pieces a little at a time," a sailor in the Philippines wrote to his wife about the Japanese. "That is humorous but tragic too. Perhaps they would quit if they realized we aren't atrocious as they are."[108]

In the end, however, a preferred explanation among GIs for the enemy's suicidal tendency was neither psychological, sociocultural, nor religious, but demographic: the Japanese were reckless with life because they had it in excess. That was, after all, a truism for the entire region. George Roeder has shown, for instance, that long before the war, American media had been depicting Asian death, especially mass death, much more readily – and gruesomely – than death in the Western world. This was partly so,

Roeder posits, "because of cultural assumptions that life was held more cheaply in the East than in the West." Modern media's powerful images had only reinforced those assumptions.[109]

Entering Calcutta on the Hooghly River in April 1944, a GI watched as a body floated by, fat vultures calmly picking its entrails. The scene was, he stated, "our first introduction to the cheapness of life in this part of the world." American soldiers could now see for themselves that profuse fertility and unbridled procreation had led to a mind-boggling devaluation of life. "One was forced," a revulsed soldier told his parents in Indiana after a Red Cross tour of Calcutta, "to view the out-of-control over-population and its results: starvation, disease, and the reduction of life to a cheap and worthless commodity."

If, according to a military manual, it was wrong to say that the Chinese were cruel, then it was true that they "look at human values differently from the Americans." "As someone once said," the manual added, "*There are so many people in China.*" In Calcutta, where, in the words of one GI, "disease does away with thousands of them a month," Americans had to step over the corpses of beggars no one hurried to pick up from the sidewalks. In Bengal, they were forced to look on as the famine of 1943 took the lives of an incredible 1.5 to 3 million people. Coolie gangs on American airfields in China did not always bother to stop even when workers became entangled in the ropes pulling the heavy stone rollers. Chinese commanders could remain stoic even when wounded or sick soldiers "died in the ditches and the dogs ate them."[110]

Could GIs really be surprised then that the Japanese, forced by their own overpopulation to search for more living space, were squandering lives to attain that goal? It was during the second day on Tarawa, a Pacific atoll crawling with suicidal Japanese defenders, that it suddenly dawned on a startled Robert Sherrod that this was in effect what the enemy's strategy by 1943 had boiled down to. The Japanese, he realized, were trying "to make us grow sick of our losses" while they themselves were going to "hang on under their fortifications, like so many bedbugs." "They don't care how many men *they* lose," the correspondent assured, "human life being a minor consideration to them."[111]

Despite his strenuous efforts to fathom the enemy on Tarawa, Robert Sherrod still found his logically contrived answers coming up short more than half a year later, amidst the fury of Japanese self-annihilation on Saipan. During the last days of June 1944, he watched as Americans one last time yelled for a deaf enemy to abandon a cave, blew it up with TNT, then sealed the entrance with a bulldozer. "We never found out what was in the hole, whether there were any Japs or many Japs." "But I thought," the correspondent wrote, his analytical capacity exhausted, "many questions in fighting the mysterious little Japs must forever go unanswered."[112]

Not only the Japanese, but ultimately almost everyone in this region, from the New Guinean tribes to the Chinese masses, proved too enigmatic for Americans successfully to decipher. Their refusal to have their minds invaded and mapped, infected American soldiers with the nagging doubt as to whether people who could not be understood could ever truly be controlled.

This was all the more frustrating because, on the surface, these people certainly appeared easily led and well managed. GIs came upon many a wondrous scene in Asia confirming deeply rooted images of a servile, kow-towing race. "Most of the locals had never seen an Occidental before," said an astonished American officer operating in the Pingyang district of south-east China in 1945. "The elders would stand beside the trail and bow respectfully when I walked past – always being scrupulously careful to cover the aggressive right hand with the passive left."[113]

Most astonishing was that, once defeated, the enemy himself turned out not to behave altogether differently. "A good many of the Okinawan civil-ians wandering along the roadside bowed low to every American they met," observed a rather nonplussed Ernie Pyle. "Whether this was from fear or native courtesy I do not know, but anyhow they did it." The instinc-tive submissiveness to authority was remarkable. One moment the Japanese were ferocious soldiers determined to fight to the death, the other they were exemplary docile captives, willing to share information freely, volun-teering even to work for the Americans. There were disquietingly few Japanese in the prison pens on New Britain when an engineer of the 592nd Amphibian Regiment arrived on the island late in December 1943. One of them, however, "smiled at everyone and bowed."[114]

In death, as in captivity, Japanese soldiers knew how to yield to superior force. "You instantly recognize the spastic convulsion and rattle," a marine on Okinawa said of a soldier he had just shot at close range, "which in his case was not loud, but deprecating and conciliatory, like the manners of civilian Japanese."[115]

At first sight, too, the peoples of Asia and the Pacific, like children, appeared easily taught. To a lesser or greater degree many of them had, for example, adopted the West's languages, products and dress, lifestyles and religions. But closer contact allowed more careful scrutiny. And it revealed to GIs that even after many centuries, the West's administrators, educators, and missionaries had not managed to penetrate much deeper than the skin.

Following the Meiji Restoration of 1868, Japan had thrown itself open to Western-style modernization in dramatic fashion. Experts from all over Europe had been invited to advise on matters ranging from law and educa-tion to the organization of Army and Navy. Dozens of American teachers, mining experts, railroad engineers, and agricultural specialists had been lured to the archipelago with the promise of lucrative contracts. The West's new pupils turned out to be exceptionally gifted. By 1905, Japan's spectacular metamorphosis had enabled it to defeat Russia. White empires in Asia and the Pacific had not stopped trembling since.

Yet despite all this, the *Guide to Japan* told GI observers nothing new in 1945 when it contended that westernization had merely exerted a superficial impact on the enemy. "The changes, on the surface, were fabulous," the guide wholeheartedly agreed. "But underneath in their thinking, in their inner life and attitude, the Japanese rejected the ideas and ideals of the western world in favor of the ancient ways. The surface acceptance of western techniques has fooled many Americans. We have expected that because the Japanese adopted a constitution, automobiles, western clothes, baseball, the movies, chewing gum, electric light, airplanes, machine guns and battleships that their mental processes would be the same as ours. They are not."[116]

Japan had solicited instruction from Europe and America, and it had done so barely fourscore years ago. In the Philippines, however, the West had been forcing its lessons on the people for some four centuries. Moreover, at the dawn of the twentieth century, the US itself had taken over in the archipelago where Spain had left off, polishing the insular societies in its own image. Indeed, by the time US military pamphlets had finished describing the Filipinos, GIs could be forgiven for expecting them to look like slightly more exotic copies of themselves.

We were, said a sergeant from Texas who arrived in Leyte late in 1944, anticipating "a Westernized and Christianized culture within the fringes of the Orient." For members of a counterintelligence unit, this NCO and his comrades appeared rather taken aback by the actual conditions on the island. They were surprised to find people who, after almost four hundred years of strenuous Western civilizing, were "still close to the Malayan-Polynesian migrants who were there ancestors." People, too, who showed nothing more than "thin veneers of the Spanish and American."

The very act of communicating posed insurmountable problems. "Americans claimed that in one generation they had taught 25 percent of Filipinos to speak English," the Texan sergeant noted, "a figure greatly exaggerated on Leyte." The counterintelligence people were accompanied by Filipino soldiers from Manila, recruited in the US to serve as Spanish interpreters. But to the Americans' astonishment, even the language of the original conquistadores, whose influence reached almost all the way back to medieval times, proved to be of little help in large parts of Leyte. "In the *barrio*," the exasperated NCO readily admitted, "my investigations usually ended at the blank wall of noncommunication."

Meanwhile, even amidst the most deadlocked dialogue, Filipinos preserved their obedient smiles and subservient courteousness. But American soldiers could not help but wonder what message they could possibly be expected to bring to people who, beneath docile appearances, had kept hearts and minds closed to the Western message for so long. "I walked among them, sympathized with them," said the intelligence man from Texas, "all the while feeling alien among people who had been under the same flag with me for forty years."[117]

Especially discouraging for American soldiers was the realization that Christianity, considered by many of them the most important ingredient of the Western message, had not shaped the peoples of Asia and the Pacific as significantly as they had expected either. For over a century, various Christian denominations had been sustaining firm crusades in the Pacific Basin. All that time, Americans, too, had been following the exploits of their missionaries, stretching all the way from Hawaii to China, with keen interest.

On the surface, European and American missionary efforts again appeared to have borne fruit. In most of the small islands and coastal regions where the war in the Pacific was fought, for instance, GIs found Christianity to be widespread. Their military pocket guides warned them, however, not to be deceived. Twelve different mission bodies, Catholic and Protestant, were said to have over half a million converts in the Solomons and New Guinea. But the *Guide to New Guinea* informed GIs that Christian natives still practiced magic and sorcery and continued to worship spirits, including those of their ancestors. Protestant missionaries had been converting the Marshallese from their pagan beliefs since the 1850s, claiming over four-fifths of the islanders as followers. But the *Guide to the Western Pacific* doubted if "the principles of Christian morality" had exerted "a far reaching effect" among people who had simply ignored Protestant ranting against smoking, drinking, and casual sex. Congregationalists declared all of the twelve hundred natives of Kusaie, in the Carolines, Christians, but the islanders nevertheless refused to believe that spirits did not inhabit their cloud-wrapped mountains. On Yap, too, according to the same guide, despite hard work by Spanish and German Capuchins as well as Protestants, the natives remained "pretty thorough-going pagans."[118]

GIs who stayed long enough in one spot to observe the indigenes more closely discovered for themselves that missionaries in the Pacific had inflated the size of their flocks and that many so-called converts were nominal Christians at best. "Cannibalism had all but died out among the coastal tribes, but was still practiced ritualistically in the mountains," a chemical officer in New Guinea noted early in 1943. "These folk had been under missionary influence for years, but it had not bitten deeply."[119]

Quite often, indigenes had cannibalized Christianity itself, salvaging that which fit their precontact beliefs, ignoring the rest. When the same chemical officer moved on to Dutch New Guinea in 1944, he attended a local service in a village near Lake Sentani. He was informed afterwards that what he had partaken in was a Dutch Reformed service. "But a Dutchman might not recognize the fact," the flabbergasted American admitted, "even if he understood the language." Rome had not necessarily fared better in the South Seas. "He and the other villagers were Catholics," a puzzled surgeon noted after talking with a village chief on New Caledonia, "but did not go to church." GIs were soon questioning whether indigenous peoples either understood or cared for even the most basic principles of Christianity. "The majority of the natives working here on the farm are Seven Day Adventists," a cantankerous engineer on Kolombangara Island wrote to his parents in Chicago. "Maybe they propose to be of that faith just to get out of working on Saturdays. Personally, I think that they are 'wicked,' meaning that they have no religion at all."[120]

In Asia the situation was even more discouraging. Though thousands upon thousands of missionaries had heroically hurled themselves into the Chinese masses, their religious fervor barely seemed to have scratched the surface. In Changting, in southeast China, an American officer learned that missionaries used to lure hungry newcomers with handouts of food, prompting cynics to dub them 'Rice Christians.'[121]

Even in places like the Dutch East Indies and the Philippines, where Christianity was widespread and deeply rooted, the religion had often been so thoroughly modified as to be barely recognizable to the faithful of the West. Nearly 80 percent of the Filipinos were said to "belong" to the Roman Catholic church. Yet an American intelligence officer observed: "My experience with rural Filipinos led me to believe they have, after all these years, only a thin veneer of Christianity over a strong inner core of animism."[122]

While Christians in the East Indies paid lip service to the principle of the one and only God, they made sure not to break off contact with the ancient spirits dwelling in the archipelago's innumerable sacred haunts. One such site was "Goenoeng Djati," venerated by most Javanese. "Desecration of such a place," cautioned the *Guide to the Dutch East Indies*, "might even lead to a popular revolt all over the island and to the killing of American troops."[123]

The inhabitants of Asia and the Pacific – forever smiling, bowing as by instinct, always nodding in agreement – bent in the wind, but only so far. Like the generations of missionaries and colonizers before them, American troops were soon experiencing for themselves that the locals were neither easily taught nor managed.

The limits of Western instruction could be painfully obvious. Some failures were none the less telling for being localized. A medic of the 11th Airborne Division watched as "the more modest" members of the American military rushed to the moral aid of topless indigenes in a New Guinean village with brassieres and mattress covers for Mother Hubbards. Days later, the medic chuckled, proud native women strutted about, their breasts protruding from holes cut in the dress; the brassieres slung from their shoulders, filled with shells and other possessions.[124]

Other defeats had major implications, however. The US tried hard during the war, for example, to exert among China's polarizing nationalist and communist forces what Frank Ninkovich has called "a benign liberalizing influence." But no Americans could see more clearly that these efforts were quixotic and doomed to fail than the very military advisers and liaison officers stationed in the ancient Middle Kingdom.[125]

Not only as missionaries, but as bosses, too, Americans discovered that they had to tread carefully. Though neither Melanesian laborers nor Asian coolie gangs had much say in whether they wanted to work for the GIs or not, they demonstrated through numerous acts of passive and active resistance that their contribution was not entirely unconditional. Engineers building a crucial jeep track from Dobodura to Simemi during the key battle for Buna in November 1942 relied heavily on New Guinean carriers. When the natives refused to go so much as near the rumbling front, however, there was no convincing them: vital American combat troops had to be pulled out of the line to carry the supplies. Months later, on Guadalcanal, American troops faced similar problems under Japanese bombardments. "Natives all quit work," a quartermaster officer scribbled in his diary. "Won't go into dugouts which they believe are graves. Therefore taboo. Has increased our labor problem tremendously." The problems the 96th Engineers encountered with indigenous labor in New Guinea were chronic. "[T]hey tried to pull every trick imaginable," a captain lamented, "feigning illness and fatigue." Worse, his unit's work on much needed piers and bridges was seriously hampered by the widespread desertion he chronicled in his journal during much of 1942 and 1943.[126]

The antlike coolie gangs of Asia were not as malleable as they looked either. On Assam's airfields absenteeism was common during the numerous religious holidays and, on occasion, the laborers, many of them women, simply refused to work while rain was falling. By the end of 1942, the whole construction program, deprived of heavy American machinery, had fallen far behind schedule. According to an official US Army history, construction of the B-29 fields in China in 1944 was punctuated by "some serious riots caused by disgruntled workers whose only desire was to go home." When in March 1945 food shortages forced the US War Department to cut the labor ration in its own colony, angry protests erupted across the archipelago; unrest in Manila's vital Base X culminated in strikes and mass resignations.[127]

The Okinawans might be bowing to American soldiers, Ernie Pyle noted, but they did so "with Oriental inscrutability." GIs became increasingly convinced that the humble composure of the Asian served to hide a rebellious mind, the courteous gestures to obscure a clenched fist. Much more poisonous even than a lack of understanding was misunderstanding. Each word, each move, each act of the Asian that violated American expectations was inevitably interpreted as additional proof of the dishonesty, slyness, and treachery he had been accused of by the West since long.[128]

In the long fight against the Indian in America, colonists had decried his preference for secrecy, his love of surprise, his unmilitary use of concealment. American schoolbooks had denounced him for "making war without declaring it." In one violent stroke, the Japanese at Pearl Harbor again brought to the surface all these primal fears. And they made sure to keep them alive in the American soldiers up to the very end of the war.[129]

Long before the Indian wars in America, Chinese strategist Sun Tzu had axiomatized, "All warfare is based on deception." The Japanese could not have agreed more. Dressed in American uniforms, they took a battalion of the 20th Infantry by surprise during the battle for Lone Tree Hill in Dutch New Guinea. On Butaritari, they placed snipers among Gilbertese natives, then drove them towards American lines. On Guadalcanal, they attempted to draw fire by clapping together sticks of bamboo. On Angaur, in the Palaus, they fired artillery and mortars principally while American heavy weapons were booming, tricking GIs into believing that friendly rounds were falling short.[130]

Sun Tzu had said, "When near make it appear that you are far away; when far away, that you are near." The Japanese never lost sight of the principle. During the Papuan battle of Buna in 1942, they made it a practice to rotate their weapons among hidden positions, time and again giving inexperienced Americans the impression they were surrounded. On Okinawa in 1945, Japanese artillerists were said to conceal their gun flashes by building bonfires in front of their positions.[131]

Sun Tzu had said, "avoid the enemy when his spirit is keen and attack him when it is sluggish." The Japanese followed it to the letter. In northern Luzon, they sneaked back into previously cleared minefields and replanted them. In the town of Caibaan, in northern Leyte, they waved a white flag; when approached, they opened fire, wounding five men. During the battle of Vella Lavella in October 1943, a group of American PT boats picked up 78 survivors from the Japanese destroyer *Yugumo*; one of them killed a sailor of PT-163 who was giving him a cup of coffee.[132]

Never did the Japanese allow American troops to let their guard down. Not for one moment did they allow GIs to believe that the enemy could ever truly be brought under control. As early as the Guadalcanal campaign, Americans were seeing to it that the enemy dead were "shot again." "[J]ust to make sure," correspondent Richard Tregaskis explained. Late in 1944, somewhere between Leyte and Mindoro, the USS *O'Bannon* hauled a lone Japanese survivor from the sea, the first enemy the crew had ever seen up close. "He smiled and winked and said 'Me Help,'" a sailor wrote. "He caused quite a commotion aboard ship. There were enough rifles and pistols on the little guy to scare him to death." By that same time, infantrymen of the 96th Division on the island of Leyte were suffering from the same nervous insecurity. "Each of us developed a weariness, a perpetual crouch and a fear of what lay just ahead," said a lieutenant. "It was quite similar to our childhood fears of what was in the closet. What we knew or had experienced of the Japanese fighting man to this point was that he was suicidally devoted – as an individual – to killing Americans. He was incomprehensible to the American mind. In our minds his devotion kept each of us fearful and alert to his seemingly haphazard actions."[133]

If unabated distrust of the Japanese enemy could be a life-saving reflex, then the growing feeling that Americans could not place much reliance on Orientals as allies created a dangerous atmosphere of suspicion and skepticism. "The Chinese do not naturally make a direct approach to anything," an American surgeon complained in 1944. "They are masters of indirection, deviation, and insinuation." The Chinese vexed Americans with their stubborn refusal to argue with others or to criticize them openly. What the Chinese regarded as politeness, Americans considered to be a lack of frankness, sometimes mistaking, as Wesley Bagby has noted, "agreeableness for agreement."[134]

Such misunderstandings were rife not only in China. Soldiers operating in America's own colony, for example, felt frustrated by what an official Army history described as a "tendency of the Filipinos to say 'yes' to everything." Not only did it frustrate cooperation. It also appeared all too clearly to confirm preconceived notions of Oriental duplicity and deceit. In March 1945, Americans in San Fernando, Luzon, released a number of local Hukbalahap guerrilla leaders after they had signed an agreement promising loyalty to the American and Commonwealth governments. As he watched them walk away, an American officer vented his misgivings about the deal: "They had done what they thought we wanted, had said what they thought we wanted to hear, in characteristic Filipino fashion. In the same Filipino fashion they could regard the agreement as a piece of paper and forget it."[135]

As the war unfolded, the rise of America's military strength in Asia and the Pacific became meteoric; the pushing back of Japan, merciless; the reestablishment of white control in its stead, frenzied. Still, American soldiers could never rid themselves entirely of the nagging feeling that they were fighting a losing battle in what was an unfathomable world.

The region's guileful yea-sayers were disquieting enough. But even more worrisome were those whom the disruption of war now provided enough confidence to bare their clenched fists against the West. No matter how much the Japanese were showing themselves to be imperialists, too, their call to throw off the yoke of the alien West inevitably took root in soil made fertile by many decades and centuries of exploitation. Signs of this became obvious to Americans very early in the war. As the golden sun set on the tranquil countryside around Rangoon in February 1942, the enthralled chaplain of the American Flying Tigers remarked that "the land-scape was pure *National Geographic*: thatched villages and crumbling Buddhist shrines, clusters of bamboos and palms, busy farmers in the rice fields, elephants bathing in the river." Meanwhile, however, the Japanese were closing in on the capital and, within days, the deceptive quiet was ripped apart as Burmese nationalists rushed into the open, plundering, sab-otaging – and sniping at isolated Westerners. "I could not hope to under-stand," admitted the shocked chaplain, who before the war had worked in China as a Protestant missionary, "the stresses and hates the war was begin-ning to uncover beneath the picturesque surface."[136]

The war brusquely wiped away the West's carefully woven delusions of power and control. "The natives are used to us, as white men," asserted a pamphlet drawn up by Australians for GIs operating in the dark heart of Melanesia, "they feel we belong, whereas the Japanese are in every respect strangers . . . Therefore, their natural inclination is to side with us." Several pages later, however, the Australians felt obliged to caution that hostile New Guineans might nevertheless be encountered near where the enemy was. "They may be working with him and they may have been promised rewards for capturing you." An American pilot who crash-landed in the New Guinean jungle in 1943 was taken prisoner by such hostile natives. He had to shoot his way out of their village, he later recounted, very much "like in Custer's Last Stand."[137]

The power vacuums so feared by rival imperialist powers were gusts of fresh air to peoples who had suffered suffocating oppression for so long. "Today I made my first trip to what is generally called the native village," a GI noted in his diary just after having entered Dutch New Guinea in September 1944. "No Dutch were present, nor have I seen any since coming here. So apparently the whole administration is up to the native soldiers, who looked neat and intelligent and entirely capable of the job."[138]

In many island societies, the American military itself, knowingly or not, contributed to undermining the fragile hierarchies of power. Its tremendous material wealth and exorbitant salaries, the deeply egalitarian message of white GIs sharing food with natives, the stunning sight of uniformed and armed African–Americans, all this caused Pacific islanders to question the former colonial order and its social inequities. In April 1943, upset French colonials in New Caledonia reported that the Kanaks "were behaving in an arrogant fashion since the arrival of the American forces."[139]

Throughout the region, budding self-confidence went hand in hand with growing nationalist self-consciousness. Traditionally, nationalist struggles had never failed to appeal to American idealistic instincts. Charles Weeks has shown, for instance, that whenever friction arose between Tongans and Europeans, white American soldiers "inevitably" sided with the Tongans. In the Southwest Pacific, European colonial authorities attempted to restrict interaction between islanders and American servicemen in part to prevent, in the words of anthropologist Lamont Lindstrom, "the circulation of anticolonial and other dangerous knowledge."[140]

Traditionally too, however, Americans had dreaded any revolution that smacked of radicalism. Nationalist movements could be "a dynamic force," but only, cautioned a GI pamphlet, "if rightly guided." But GIs who witnessed the convulsions of war firsthand, increasingly feared that Asians might be embracing what one State Department official in April 1945 described as "ideologies contrary to our own." In the summer of 1942, for example, frustrated Indian nationalists turned violent, denouncing not only the British, but their American stooges, too. At the height of the riots, American commanders had to restrict their troops to the camp areas to avoid clashes. Two thousand engineers who disembarked at Karachi in July had to be rushed to safety – bullets in their rifles – through streets lined with signs screaming 'Americans, Quit India.'[141]

What worried GIs even more than riotous nationalism, however, was its unholy alliance with communism. Among the scarce English reading material that a Flying Tiger in Kunming managed to scrounge in 1942 were five Shakespeare comedies, *The Book of Common Prayer*, and *A Debate on Communism* – a pamphlet, noted the intrigued American, "with footnotes in Chinese." By 1945, it was painfully clear to American troops that communism was refusing to remain a footnote in the region's history for much longer. On 29 June, an American of the 311th Fighter Group noted in his diary that the people of the town in China where he was stationed were "growing icy towards the G.I.'s. Something must be in the wind." On 16 August, he sounded much more alarmed: "Our barracks has been alerted for base guard tonight & tomorrow in case anything starts????!!! This China revolution looks like it might flare up right in our faces here in the north."[142]

Much worse was that, by this time, the bolshevist cancer appeared also to have spread to America's own territories. GIs who pushed into northern Luzon in 1945 found the crowds sullen, even belligerent. American flags were nowhere to be seen, but from many a bamboo pole hung banners displaying hammer and sickle. As they gave each other clenched-fist salutes, husky young men icily ignored the GIs. Within weeks, communist Hukbalahap guerrillas, who had opposed the Japanese invader from the outset, were also raiding American arsenals and sniping at US Army vehicles. So disruptive did they become in the Sixth Army area, that when a counterintelligence officer received the assignment to restore law and order, he thought it "sounded very much like a Japanese peace and pacification campaign."[143]

But GIs were doubtful whether they would be more successful than the Europeans at rescuing the crumbling Occidental world order – political, economic, or cultural. On and around Del Monte's plantation airstrips in Mindanao, American troops were forced to inhale the gagging stench of the once sweet fruits of colonization: millions of pineapples that had been rotting away since the arrival of the Japanese. They heard Hukbalahaps in Luzon demand 'Land for the Landless.' In Luzon, too, they saw priests on their knees, scrubbing away at the hammers and sickles smeared on the doors of ancient Spanish churches in blood-red paint.

With their lightning strike against Pearl Harbor, the Japanese had ignited a revolt in the region that neither they nor the West could have hoped to contain. As an officer from Texas rummaged through an abandoned Filipino school in Leyte, he picked up one of the American schoolbooks desecrated by the Japanese. "It seemed as much out of place," he observed, "as the Japanese propaganda book in which faces of Filipino children had a Japanese look. Tools of conflicting cultures, both had been left to disintegrate."[144]

8
'Going Asiatic'

While disembarking on Christmas Island in 1942, personnel of the 204th General Hospital were mockingly welcomed by veteran American truck drivers. "But never fear," they yelled, "by the time your replacements show up a year from now, you'll look and act like the natives who inhabit this God forsaken island."[1]

Fears that unbridled wilderness and unmitigated primitiveness would bring on cultural regression and native contamination had haunted Americans from colonial times. Abruptly transplanted from old civilizations to cultural deserts, communication with homelands fickle, European settlers in the New World had fought hard to uphold traditions of religious order and social organization under the tremendous pressures of an environment in which neither God nor King felt much at ease. They had chosen to be frontiersmen, not savages. Despite falling into ambush after ambush in America with close-order formations maneuvering in the open the way they had done in Europe, for instance, colonists refused to adapt to Indian-style warfare for a long time. They considered it barbaric and feared it would turn them into brutish beasts not much better than the natives themselves.[2]

When frontiersmen eventually began to push as far west as the Great Plains, those who inhabited the settled agricultural communities further to the east were soon voicing concerns that the unforgiving West might cause people to turn into lawless, nomadic brigands. The Great American Desert reminded those who lived on the East Coast and in the European mother-land most sharply of the menacing Asian steppes and their hordes of apoc-alyptic horsemen. As early as 1775, in the discussion of the Ohio Valley, Edmund Burke argued that if the British government prevented further set-tlement west of the Allegheny Mountains, American frontiersmen there "would wander without a possibility of restraint" and consequently "would change their manners with the habits of their life." In short, he warned, they "would become hordes of English Tartars."[3]

The specter of what the vast expanses of landed and watery wilderness in Asia and the Pacific could do to even the most civilized people clung to

Europeans and Americans until deep into the nineteenth century and beyond. During the exploration of the South Pacific, for example, Westerners became utterly fascinated by tales of the ignominious beachcombers. Whether sailors who were shipwrecked or had jumped ship, or whether mutineers or escapees from convict settlements, all of them had turned their back on civilization and abandoned themselves to island life and native mores without restraint. By having done so, they came to represent, in the words of Rod Edmond, "a 'heart of darkness' vision of regression," thus scandalizing both colonists and metropolitans.[4]

For the growing numbers of American soldiers who were stationed in Asia as a result of the increasingly assertive designs of their mother country around the turn of the century, worries of cultural backsliding in the oppressive ecological, demographic, and mental environments of the region were so common that they found their way into the military lexicon. Among American troops in China, for instance, comrades applied the label 'gone Asiatic' to anyone who had lived in the country long enough to have mastered some of the language or to think nothing of wearing Chinese clothing. Most of all, however, they used the expression for those who had gone far enough over the edge to marry an Oriental. Most men in the Pacific Army guarding the colonial possessions of Hawaii and the Philippines signed up for a two-year period and then returned stateside. But there were those who reenlisted for overseas duty and formed what Brian Linn has described as "a cadre of semipermanent colonials, to whom the Pacific Army was both home and career." Inevitably, they, too, were characterized by the two-year transients as 'having gone Asiatic.'[5]

Similar fears of cultural regression haunted GIs unabatedly during the war with Japan. Before long, the expression 'going Asiatic' reverberated through the region with renewed meaning. As long as troops adapted to the environment superficially and in the most practical of terms, there was no danger. There was nothing wrong with engineers trying their hand at bamboo sheds with nipa roofs, with cooks adding coconut yeast to biscuit dough, with infantrymen protecting their guns against rust with shark liver oil. Neither could one point a finger at the company commander of the 43rd Division who, in the course of the campaign in sweltering New Georgia, confessed in his journal to "becoming something of a nudist over here, seldom wearing more than a pair of low cut sneakers and home made shorts," and who admitted even to having "adopted a new type of underwear – the Jap loin cloth." "It's comfortable," he argued, "and they're easily washed." On the contrary, the troops' willingness and ability to use new and strange surroundings to their advantage was seen as evidence of the best of American frontier heritage, something to be proud of. "We're getting real native like," a boisterous sergeant in New Guinea who had mastered the craft of making utensils from bamboo let his mother in New Jersey know. "We tied the bamboo in a big pack with the vines hanging from the trees and than carried it on our shoulders."[6]

In copying native dress and habits, however, there were lines not to be crossed. Those who did could count on being denounced by their brothers-in-arms as 'having gone Asiatic.' A marine on Pavuvu Island in 1944 claimed the expression was used to indicate "a singular type of eccentric behavior characteristic of men who had served too long in the Far East." A soldier in Ceylon gave his parents in Indiana a vivid illustration of exactly how eccentric GIs who had been longtime residents of this island had become. "Around here," he wrote in July 1945, "you see fellows wearing shirts and loose pants made from bright yellow, blue, or orange silk parachutes. Some men wear sarongs of gingham, like the natives. An order came out recently clamping down on this type of garb. Things had gone too far."[7]

Boredom forced sailors cooped up in hot vessels for months on end to flee in an eccentricity no less outrageous. By January 1944, so many would-be pirates aboard the USS *Montpelier* were having their ears pierced and rings put through them that officers had to ban the practice altogether. "Some of the fellows," a resigned sailor observed, "must be becoming 'Asiatic.'"[8]

Much more worrying than changes in outward appearances, however, was the looming danger that the vicious overseas environment would awake primitive instincts that beneath the cracked veneer of civilization lay dormant but not dead. This caused concern as far away as the home front. In a letter to her husband in August 1943, First Lady Eleanor Roosevelt wondered if jungle warfare was not "making savages out of American youth." She traveled all the way to the South Pacific that summer for the answer to her question. When she arrived, however, she found the marines to be far from happy with her visit. The reason was a stubborn rumor that she had said they had become "savage killers," ravaged by tropical diseases, who would have to be quarantined in the islands before they could ever hope to return home.[9]

The First Lady's alleged comment piqued troops in the Pacific not only because it made them feel abandoned, but also because it said out loud the doubts that soldiers harbored secretly. Would not the hot humid wilderness indeed dissolve all civilized restraints? Early in 1943, the USS *Nassau* anchored off the coast of Fiji. To prevent the crew from being driven crazy by the heat and boredom, a liberty party was sent ashore every day for a few hours. But a sailor who was part of a shore patrol accompanying one such group had to watch impotently as a sudden tropical downpour instantly washed away all discipline, causing the liberty party to disintegrate. Rollicking soldiers dashed about in the rain, rolled in the mud, and disappeared into the jungle. Chasing the wayward sailors through the underbrush, the exasperated shore patrolman panted, "Where they were going, God alone knew. Back to nature, I thought."[10]

Would nature's dissolution of discipline also eventually unleash the repressed Wild Man lurking within? Fears of that kind certainly smoldered. Fear of runaway violence, for example. A marine on Peleliu to whom a comrade showed a hand just severed from a Japanese corpse, found barely breath enough to gasp, "Have you gone Asiatic?" But there was fear also of uncontrollable sexual drives. An entranced officer watching New Guineans dance to the sounds of snakeskin drums readily confessed that "an intangible, disturbed, primitive chord deep within us responded." To a captain invited to a similar dance on a beach near the village of Hula on the same island, it was more than he could stand: dozens of young girls "wiggling like a snake, running their hands over their bodies with their bared breasts quivering like over-hard jello." "It was enough to make a white man forget he was white," the officer ashamedly wrote in his diary. "So I just didn't watch them."[11]

American soldiers were branded as having 'gone Asiatic' not only when lost to exotic eccentricity or primitive savagery. A private who joined the 25th Marines as a replacement in 1944 noted that when veterans spoke of comrades who had "gone Asiatic," they meant they had "cracked up."[12]

Psychological breakdown, usually termed war neurosis or battle fatigue during World War II, was responsible for one of the American military's most vexing problems in Asia and the Pacific. Neuropsychiatric disease formed the leading cause of so-called nonbattle disability separations. Of all war theaters, the neuropsychiatric rate was highest in the Southwest Pacific at almost 44 per 1,000 average strength per year. In the Pacific Ocean Areas (Central and South Pacific combined) the rate was lower, but still slightly over 34.

The medical services were ill prepared to handle such large numbers of neuropsychiatric patients. Physicians were unfamiliar with many of the mental afflictions and often misdiagnosed patients. Psychiatrists were scarce. For instance, although psychiatric problems were also common in the China–Burma–India theater (14.8 admissions for psychoneurosis per thousand per year, 2.68 for psychosis), by the end of the war there were no more than 21 psychiatrists in the entire region, serving almost 200,000 troops. It took the US War Department until November 1943 to establish the position of division psychiatrist, desperately needed for forward-area treatment.

An additional problem was that medical channels tended to shepherd "puzzling or incomprehensible cases" all too easily to the rear, and from there all the way home, unduly weakening many a unit. In 1943, for example, of the 23,000 casualties evacuated to the US from the Army hospitals of the South Pacific Area, no less than 28 percent were diagnosed with neuropsychiatric disorders. Only very gradually did the military switch to keeping patients who suffered from mild to moderate cases of stress-related ailments as near to the front as possible for treatment. The new policy was the result of experience showing that rest (brought on by barbiturate sedation if needed) without complete removal from the war zone made many such patients fit for service again within a matter of days.[13]

Many of the most common psychological problems in Asia and the Pacific were caused not by the pressures of combat, but by the strain of prolonged living in almost total isolation. "And another enemy out here," Ernie Pyle explained to his readers on the American home front, not long after he arrived in the Central Pacific in February 1945, "is one we never knew so well in Europe – monotony. Oh, sure, war everywhere is monotonous in its dreadfulness. But in the Pacific even the niceness of life gets monotonous." Pyle reported that on the Marianas, where even the last Japanese stragglers had now been rounded up or killed, "the days go by in their endless sameness and they drive men nuts." Things were by no means easier for the landlocked forces in Asia. According to the chroniclers of the India-based Tenth Air Force, for example, ground personnel found the tedium of life in Assam "almost unbearable."[14]

Nerve-racking climatological conditions made the weight of monotony still heavier. "A sense of futility spread among the CIC agents," an officer in Leyte noted at the end of 1944, "futility and depression from living and working day after day in heat and dampness that mildewed the soul." As the weeks and months and years piled up, soldiers were overcome with fatigue, listlessness, and indifference. In his journal, a company clerk, who had been in New Guinea since October 1943, described the distressing state he was in barely three months after his arrival on the island: "Sometime since arriving here, I had quietly acquired a strange disregard for things – complete apathy, as complete as any such state of mind could be . . . Being shot at didn't seem to be especially alarming to me, and I could stand guard for hours in the rain without feeling any special discomfort. In fact, I had ceased to feel anything at all. One day just telescoped into another." Conversation with fellow soldiers inevitably grew stale. Before long, there remained nothing even to write home about. A study of a cross section of enlisted men in an inactive tropical area overseas found a marked decline in letter writing between the thirteenth and eighteenth month. By November 1944, the company clerk of New Guinea, now in the Philippines, threatened to give up the very journal he had been keeping dutifully ever since leaving the US almost two years earlier. "[A]s I feel," he wrote, "it has dropped into an uninteresting repetition of dull days."[15]

Sailors condemned to staring at empty horizons from floating prisons hot as furnaces did not fare better. The USS *Montpelier*, 607 feet long and about 50 feet at its widest point, left Philadelphia for the Pacific in December 1942. By July 1943, according to one sailor, many of the men, none of whom had received more than a few hours of shore leave a month, had definitely become "Asiatic." Chronic forgetfulness was a sure symptom. First, men forgot what day it was. Then they could not remember what they had done in the morning or what they had eaten for lunch. They found themselves in the washroom ready to brush their teeth without toothbrush or paste, or on deck asking for a match for the already lighted cigarette between their lips. After a while, minds on occasion could go completely blank, with sailors finding themselves in parts of the ship not knowing what they were looking for nor how they had gotten there.[16]

Soldiers and sailors suffering from such conditions were said not only to have gone 'Asiatic,' but also to have become 'pineapple crazy' or 'rock happy' (terms already coined before the war by the Pacific Army in Hawaii), to be suffering from 'bush fever,' or to have gone 'jungle happy.'[17]

Whatever the name, apathy and memory defects were just a few of a series of striking symptoms. Efficiency declined. By the end of 1943, it took ground personnel of the Thirteenth Air Force in the Pacific, for example, twice as long to complete a given unit of work than it did earlier in the year. Accidents in machine shops, on runways, and in the air increased. Discipline deteriorated. In comparison with more recent arrivals, company punishment in inactive tropical theaters increased significantly among men with two or more years of service.[18]

As perfect copies of empty days seamlessly glided into each other in end-less succession, utterly bored soldiers grew increasingly moody and irritable. "You can sense it in the letters," a lieutenant and censor of the 169th Infantry noted in New Guinea in November 1944. "Worries about home affairs become magnified, lack of feminine companionship becomes unbearable, petty annoyances assume large proportions, the specter of a coming campaign becomes terrifying."[19]

"The intense concentration of self in the middle of such a heartless immensity," Herman Melville had exclaimed in his eulogy of nineteenth-century whalers in the Pacific, "my God! Who can tell it?" A century later, the ceaseless introspection forced upon GIs by the region's boundless emptiness proved no less torturous. "We get too much time to think," a pilot in New Guinea lamented in a letter in 1943, "which brings on brooding and that isn't good."[20]

Soldiers became abnormally excitable. "A nervousness has come over me, a feeling which I cannot quell," an officer in Dutch New Guinea told his fiancée in Connecticut in 1944. "I cannot sit still for long, my arms, my legs, my body has that restless, nervous feeling, a feeling that does not have an outlet, yet might be relieved by loud screams."[21]

A report on WACs stationed in Ceylon (84 percent of whom had been on the island for more than a year) found that 44 percent suffered from increased nervousness and depression. A battalion surgeon of the 6th Division claimed that by the end of 1944 depression among his men in Dutch New Guinea had become "endemic."[22]

Some turned suicidal. During his visit to the Pacific in 1944, Charles Lindbergh noted that a game called Russian roulette had found acceptance among American troops, but that incidents were hushed up and officially reported as accidental discharges. "Sometimes I envy those who fell early in the [war]," a dejected soldier in Dutch New Guinea confessed in his diary in August 1944. "At least they have rest and freedom. We have neither, and little hope of it in sight."[23]

Combat instantly wiped away the wear and tear of isolation and boredom. But it unleashed many new mental pressures that were no less ravaging. In the war with Japan, the classic stresses of battle were compounded and magnified by an unearthly environment and the enemy's ghostlike tactics. A soldier of the 1st Marine Division on Guadalcanal in 1942 saw three or four men go "crazy" in his platoon alone; they had to be led away trembling, wailing, screaming. Many other soldiers came out of the campaign with glassy eyes staring into nothingness. In his diary, correspondent Mack Morriss referred to it as "the Guadalcanal, or 1000-yd, stare."[24]

The most spectacular occurrence of psychological breakdown in battle took place among troops in New Georgia in 1943. The gloomy Solomon island exuded eeriness. The lugubrious jungle exhaled a sickening smell of damp decay. Foliage stirred with the black shapes of bats with wing spans of up to three foot and bodies large as squirrels. The 43rd Division had been given time to get used to tropical environments in New Caledonia, Guadalcanal, and the Russell Islands. It had, however, not yet experienced jungle combat when it set foot on New Georgia late in June 1943. In less than two weeks, the division came apart at the seams. Treks and clashes in the dense, hilly jungle quickly wore the soldiers down. The enemy's ceaseless nocturnal tactics of harassment fueled feverish anxiety. Agitated imaginations did the rest. Slithering crabs became Japanese infiltrators. The stench of jungle smelled like poison gas. The phosphorescence of rotting logs was mistaken for enemy signals. Outrageous rumors spread like wildfire. Troops panicked. Almost 16 percent of battle casualties were later estimated to have been caused by friendly fire. Lack of firm leadership aggravated the situation as it allowed mental breakdown to become contagious. The 169th Infantry fell victim to mass hysteria. An officer on the Munda trail looked on as droves of cases of what he described as "war neurosis" flooded the collecting stations on 10 July. They were "sobbing or moaning and shaking like men with the palsy," their eyes "empty of expression," their faces "loose and flabby like an idiot's." In the course of July, the New Georgia Occupation Force, made up of the 25th, 37th, and 43rd Divisions as well as Navy and Marine Corps units, suffered an astonishing 1,750 neuropsychiatric casualties. Fifteen hundred of those came from the 43rd Division, and 700 of those from the 169th Infantry alone.[25]

Though the events on New Georgia were rather exceptional, the incidence of mental breakdown remained high until the very end of the war with Japan. Neither tropical climate nor jungle terrain complicated the Okinawa campaign in the spring of 1945. But in this long and bitter battle, the enemy not only remained as entrenched, fanatical, and unpredictable as ever, he also resorted to furious *kamikaze* attacks and heavy artillery fire in a way rarely seen before. With the realization that each new advance made the war worse came a feeling of utter exhaustion and deep hopelessness. According to official Army historians, neuropsychiatric cases were "probably greater in number and severity in the Okinawa campaign than in any other Pacific operation." About 1 in every 7 admissions was for causes "loosely termed psychiatric." In three months, an estimated 3,000 to 4,000 soldiers on the island stumbled into overcrowded field hospitals, their minds broken by war against the Asian foe.[26]

With rotation home during the war unthinkable except for a happy few (mostly small groups of aviators, or sailors on ships returning stateside for quick repairs and refitting) and furloughs to homelike Australia and New Zealand exceedingly rare, Americans sought temporary escape from the harsh realities of war in Asia and the Pacific by other means.

When asked in official US Army questionnaires long after the war with Japan if drug use had been a problem in their unit, most veterans resolutely replied in the negative. The response of a former sergeant of the 132nd Infantry, "We would not have recognized drugs if we had seen it," was typical.[27]

Yet depending on the definition of drugs, the answer proves rather more qualified. Medicinal substances, for instance, occasionally found use outside their traditional prescription. In January 1945, a battalion surgeon of the 6th Division, anxiously awaiting the invasion of Luzon, told his wife that he planned on taking a dose of Amytal the night before going into combat. Late in February, amidst heavy fighting in Luzon's Shimbu Line, the combat doctor was already admitting in letters home to taking "big doses" of the same substance at night because his nerves were now "really on edge." Liberal barbiturate therapies remained acceptable perhaps, but the use of opium-derived morphine for any other reason than killing physical pain could not be tolerated. A corporal of the 1st Marine Division noted tersely: "1 Corpsman used morphine out of medic kit to sleep – afraid of nights – evacuated."[28]

If barbiturates and morphine remained the carefully guarded preserve of medical personnel, however, then all kinds of narcotics had been circulating quite openly throughout Asia and the Pacific for centuries. Already in the 1870s, amidst fears that the country was being overrun by Chinese hordes, the American press had been sounding the alarm on "the damning influence of the opiumpipe." Not surprisingly, many GIs suddenly found themselves face to face with substance abuse in the reputed lotuslands: prostitutes in Honolulu shooting heroin, Kachins in Burma smoking the bitter brownish residue of poppies, an occasional opium pipe in the pack of a dead Japanese. Narcotics were so plentiful in a city like Calcutta that one military report direly forecast the addiction of wholesale numbers of GIs.[29]

It never came to that either in India or other theaters. Still, though most soldiers would have agreed with a private of the 5th Marine Division who dismissed drugs as "scary stuff," the region's readily available narcotics did find their way into the fringes of America's armed forces. Rather than take the tablets their own doctor prescribed to combat diarrhea, for instance, naval intelligence officers operating in southeast China "much preferred a Chinese potion that was loaded with chloroform and opium" and that was "most delectable to take." A soldier on Okinawa claimed he saw a sailor trade "a dozen dirty pictures" for "a stained little Japanese flag" and what he took to be "a small quantity of opium."

The punishment for possession of narcotics could be harsh. Dishonorable discharge and confinement at hard labor for one year was the sentence for a private of the 748th Railway Operating Battalion in Assam, found guilty of introducing into camp two ounces of ganja, a substance described by one of the witnesses as a "weed the Indians smoke that makes you high."[30]

There was, however, a much more popular way of 'getting high,' one that was socially acceptable among Americans and carried punishment only in exceptional circumstances. "Alcohol was the drug of choice," remarked one marine. "We were pretty innocent about others."[31]

The military itself provided alcohol. A couple of bottles of weak beer now and then for enlisted men; small monthly allowances of hard liquor for officers. But such modest quantities were by no means sufficient to satisfy strained nerves. Some asked – and received – liquid moral support from the home front. "Yes, I got the two bottles of Scotch," a lieutenant in the Philippines told his mother, "and I would like about 20 more if possible."[32]

GIs discovered countless other ways of procuring more of the desperately needed substance. Brand-name liquor could be bought, albeit at exorbitant prices. New Caledonian French charged $20 for a bottle of whiskey in 1943; that same year, locals in India demanded $19.50 per fifth. On Biak Island in 1944, some men of the 495th Port Battalion got drunk on liquor that sailors of the merchant marine were selling at $40 a pint.

Potent native potions, on the other hand, cost almost nothing. For a few rupees, GIs in India and Ceylon could drink rum-like arrack from hollowed-out bamboo tubes. It was known as "booze by the yard." Tuba, a drink in the Philippines and Guam made from palm-tree juice and possessing "the potency of double strength TNT," was available "in gallons." In China, dirt-cheap rice wine and a sorghum-based drink called mao-tai soon earned themselves the nicknames of 'White Lightning' and 'Green Death.' Outright lethal was the bootleg liquor sold by Filipinos as regular 'whiskey' for no more than a dollar a bottle. When a soldier of the 37th Division approached Manila in February 1945, a huge military billboard on the outskirts read: "Deaths From Poison Liquor to Date – Total: 48."[33]

If liquor could not be bought, then one way or another GIs made it themselves. They built stills with tubing taken from wrecked Japanese planes. They stole dispensary alcohol and mixed it with fruit juice, first filtering the alcohol if tinted with iodine by pouring it through a loaf of bread. Soldiers were willing to try any concoction that promised to take their minds off the hardships of war with the Japanese. On the island of Los Negros, a surgeon of the 58th Evacuation Hospital noted in his diary on 12 June 1944 that three soldiers had died that day from "eating canned heat which had wood alcohol in it."[34]

As the war dragged on, forgetting became ever more urgent. In March 1945, various units came together at Guadalcanal's Cape Esperance to practice landings for the invasion of Okinawa. At the end of the exercise, hundreds of tense officers descended on the clubs at Tulagi before leaving the Solomons. "Several passed out from an excess of spirits," one lieutenant noted soberly, "and had to be carried down the steep hill to be dumped into launchers and carried back to the ships; unable to climb rope ladders, some of them were hoisted aboard in cargo nets." In their own way, substance abusers too had gone 'Asiatic.'[35]

Part III
Fury

9
Human Rage

The more the far western frontier frustrated American soldiers' control, the more it fueled their fury. The more Asia and the Pacific's nature and people demonstrated a capacity to absorb violence, the more GIs abandoned themselves to destroying their environment before it would succeed in destroying them.

Rage peaked, of course, in the face of the enemy, during the ferocious battles that punctured the long stretches of unbearable nothingness and uncertainty. During an American counteroffensive in Luzon's Kembu sector in June 1945, a worn-out signal officer of the 6th Division scribbled in his diary: "All day spent getting wire communication to our wild Infantry. They have really smelled blood and aren't to be stopped." A year earlier already, a US Army survey of infantry divisions in the Pacific had found that when the going was tough, thoughts of hatred for the enemy helped 35 percent of officers and 32 percent of enlisted men "some," and 46 and 38 percent of the respective servicemen "a lot."[1]

No single service possessed the monopoly on hatred for the enemy. On a transport off the coast of Luzon in December 1944, for example, soldiers and sailors alike responded with unmitigated joy when they saw a burning Japanese fighter tumble towards the ocean. "As soon as he hit the water," one witness observed, "a tremendous yell split the air, and we continued cheering, me included." Two months later, amidst the apocalyptic battle for Manila, a lieutenant of the 11th Airborne Division wrote to his mother: "Nothing can describe the hate we feel for the Nips – the destruction, the torture, burning & death of countless civilians, the savage fight without purpose – to us they are dogs and rats – we love to kill them – to me and all of us killing Nips is the greatest sport known – it causes no sensation of killing a human being but we really get a kick out of hearing the bastards scream."[2]

Hatred of the Japanese foe routinely burned out of control, respecting not the least boundary. Soldiers found it impossible, for example, to switch it off just like that in the face of a violent foe who suddenly changed into meek victim. "This is the first outfit I've seen," correspondent Mack

Morriss penned in his journal while with the 35th Infantry on Guadalcanal in January 1943, "that was more willing to take prisoners than to go on killing." The battle had been raging for almost half a year then.[3]

Hapless casualties did not necessarily fare better. On New Britain early in January 1944, a soldier of the 592nd Engineers watched as berserk marines one morning went out to examine enemies slain at night. "I found that any atrocity the Japanese commit can be matched by Americans," he wrote. "Our marines are Japanese fighters of long experience and long memories. Wounded soldiers simply had their throats slit by the long knives carried by every marine raider." Half a year later, the same engineer, now stationed in Dutch New Guinea, noted in his journal: "There is but one law here, KILL, KILL, KILL!"[4]

Rampant rage failed to be extinguished even by orders from above. In a desperate effort to obtain prisoners for intelligence purposes, the Americal Division had to encourage its soldiers with the award of a case of beer or a bottle of whiskey for each Japanese captured alive. In July 1943, the military in the Southwest Pacific conceded in a confidential intelligence memo that "it took the promise of three days leave and some ice cream to bring in the first live prisoner."[5]

Without enticements, GIs stopped bothering about the capture of foes deemed too treacherous to run the risk, too fanatical even to appreciate the attempt. "Early we would be rewarded for prisoners," a sergeant of the Americal Division remarked dryly, "later when the stockade was full and info not needed we killed them, as they did us." Commenting on the rapidly approaching end of the European war in the spring of 1945, an officer in the Philippines wrote, "the big difference is that the Germans don't fight to the end while the Nip rarely surrenders and frankly it's O.K. with me as the deader they are the better I like it."[6]

Such attitudes made efforts by American psychological warfare units to convince as many Japanese as possible to surrender a losing proposition. In March 1945, the Psychological Warfare Branch in the Southwest Pacific received persistent reports of Japanese in the Philippines who were allowed to come into the open waving surrender leaflets only to be mowed down by American troops. A psychological warfare officer attached to the X Corps in the Philippines wrote to General Fellers that "if something isn't done about the attitude of our men and officers toward taking prisoners and giving them a chance to be taken, we may as well pack up and quit trying."[7]

If a live Japanese was not worth more than a case of beer, then dead ones had no value at all. On the one hand, repeated suicide attacks caused enemy bodies literally to pile up. At the end of the Japanese counteroffensive on Guadalcanal in October 1942, for example, over 1,500 decaying bodies lay in front of the 1st Battalion, 7th Marines, and the 3rd Battalion, 164th Infantry, alone. On the other hand, chronic shortages of military mortuary details and civilian labor made the burial of enemy dead

throughout the Pacific more a question of waste disposal than graves registration. Before long, the hurried bulldozing of shallow mass graves for slain
Japanese was a routine operation.[8]

More than once, combat troops were told to pitch in. They found the
burial of enemy dead not only demeaning, but utterly unnecessary, had it
not been for the stench and swarms of bluebottles they bred. "My first
assignment in our new company," said a soldier of the 306th Infantry on
Leyte, "was a 'sanitation detail' – burying the Japs. There was a convenient
shellhole nearby, so we dragged them, guts trailing behind, into the hole and
threw just enough dirt on them to keep down the smell." On Guadalcanal,
GIs shoved the loathed task on to Japanese POWs; on Roi Island, the handling of Japanese corpses was left to the natives.[9]

Quite often, dead Japanese simply remained were they had fallen; their
remains, at best, hurriedly sprayed with sodium arsenite. On the small
island of Wakde, off the New Guinean coast, shooting had stopped on
20 May 1944. On 16 June, an officer commented in his diary: "Inspect
Signal installation on Wakde Island. Many dead Japs still not moved to the
mainland to be buried." "No one would move a dead enemy," the officer of
a bomb disposal company on Okinawa noted. "If it was in the road, they
just ran over it until it was flattened out and then the dust covered it."[10]

In the end, even the grisliest evidence of enemy dead left GIs stone-cold.
As he traveled from camp to the work area in Luzon's fiercely contested
Cagayan Valley in June 1945, a private of the 112th Engineers noted in his
diary: "Counted 3 dead Japs along road, but smelled plenty more." About a
week later, he mentioned, with similar matter-of-factness: "Counted over
15 dead Japs along road; about 5 fresh ones." On 27 June, a compact entry
on the same passageway read: "Did not see any dead Japs along road – but
smelled dead ones at about 20 places."[11]

Yet the enemy dead were not always simply ignored. They were desecrated. American soldiers on Okinawa were seen urinating into the gaping
mouths of the slain. They were "rebutchered." "As the bodies jerked and
quivered," a marine on Guadalcanal wrote of the repeated shooting of
corpses, "we would laugh gleefully and hysterically." They were mutilated.
"All of the skulls are minus their teeth," a horrified engineer said of the
countless unburied Japanese on New Georgia, "because souvenir hunters
use them for bracelets." They were interested in more than bracelets. Some
Americans had pouches tied to their belts. In them, they carried small pairs
of pliers to be used for extracting the enemy's gold teeth, as if they were
just another kind of Oriental riches, there for the taking. Less sophisticated
scavengers used knives, or they smashed the skulls with rifle butts, if they
did not simply kick the teeth out.[12]

Although America's armed forces expressed disapproval at such behavior,
James Weingartner has shown that their "half-hearted measures were not
likely to halt practices as popular as they were gruesome." As late as the

Okinawan campaign, sailors who found the lower leg of a *kamikaze* who had crashed into their ship were cleaning the bone and crafting it into souvenir rings without the least inhibition. On the island itself, squads of the 77th Division, sent out to eliminate snipers, returned with rifles as well as ears to document missions accomplished. A corporal of the 6th Marine Division on Okinawa claimed he actually saw "some Nip bodies that had been scalped."[13]

Blind rage failed to distinguish not only between the living and the dead, but also between soldiers and civilians. American forces dealt harshly, for example, with natives suspected of cooperating with the Japanese. A private of the Signal Corps decried the rough handling of suspected Burmese collaborators by an OSS unit to which he was attached for some time: "Going into villages, interrogating people, often kicking their teeth in. Executions were summary and brutal. Machine-gunning and things." During the campaign in New Britain early in 1944, a man from Tauali village was said to have wounded a marine lieutenant with a Japanese rifle. The American response was swift – and indiscriminate. "I did not learn if any natives were killed," an Army engineer wrote in his journal, "but have an idea they must have been. Anyway the village was burned to the ground by the marines after the incident."[14]

As soon as American forces heard that Japanese troops had managed "to corrupt" a community, an unflinching Admiral Halsey recalled of war in the Southwest Pacific, "we would bomb the village." An English translation of leaflets dropped on Bougainville in January 1943 read: "A serious warning from the big white chief . . . The village of Sorum has been disloyal . . . and has helped the Japs. We have now bombed them. We also bombed Pidia, Pok Pok, Toberoi, and Sadi when they helped the Japs. If any villages help the Japs we will bomb them and destroy them altogether." But uncorrupted Melanesians fell victim to indiscriminate American bombing just as easily. One historian of the naval air war concluded that in the Southwest Pacific "little thought was given to warning the pilots of the presence of friendly natives."[15]

The difference between combatants and noncombatants became even less meaningful as American troops closed in on Japan. Reports on enemy casualty figures for Luzon and the southern Philippines simply lumped together the Emperor's soldiers and victims from among the almost 40,000 Japanese civilians on the islands consisting, among others, of government officials, businessmen, farmers, and their wives and children. On the Marshall island of Kwajalein and the Mariana island of Saipan, the US military routinely talked of frightened civilians entering their lines as "surrenders" and of those herded into stockades as "prisoners."[16]

On 20 April 1945, when Okinawa's Motobu Peninsula was declared cleared of enemy troops, the Tenth Army announced that all civilians in occupied sections of the island, irrespective of age or sex, were to be interned. They were prohibited from moving about unless accompanied by armed guards. Meanwhile, civilians who continued to roam Okinawa's battle areas were in mortal danger. "Shoot the bitch, shoot the Jap woman," a lieutenant of the 11th Marines suddenly heard some of his men scream at the top of their lungs. Shots rang. An Okinawan woman struggled to her feet. She tried to pick up her baby. More shots ripped the air. The mother crumpled. "When I could leave my post and go down behind the road," the officer recalled, "none of the men there would own up to having fired."[17]

Many more Okinawans were unintentional victims of the Americans. Fear of horrific bombing and shelling during the day forced civilians to move about at night, inevitably drawing the full wrath of edgy GIs alarmed by the slightest noise. "In the morning," a chronicler of the battle noted, "the perimeter of their night positions was strewn with as many dead goats, rabbits and civilians as Japanese soldiers." A pilot, awakened by rifle fire in the night, rushed to where the commotion had come from. One of the air base sentries had shot at a noise. The body of a man in rags was found some distance away. "Perhaps he wasn't even a Jap, only an Okinawan, hiding and hungry," the airman wrote. Still, although he "felt revulsion at his deadness, so ugly," he admitted he could muster "no fellow-feeling at all. He might have been a dead dog, hit by a car and thrown to the side of the road." "The burying procedure was simple," observed a private of the 96th Division who was assigned to a mortuary detail for Okinawan civilians after the battle for Kakazu Ridge. "We rolled them over into nearby shell holes or ditches and covered them with dirt."[18]

Many women on Okinawa came to wish the Americans had just killed them and dumped them into a hole. Instead, the enemy brutally violated them, showing not even the least mercy. Marching south, men of the 4th Marines passed a group of some 10 American soldiers bunched together in a tight circle next to the road. They were "quite animated," noted a corporal who assumed they were playing a game of craps. "Then as we passed them," said the shocked marine, "I could see they were taking turns raping an oriental woman. I was furious, but our outfit kept marching by as though nothing unusual was going on."[19]

Wartime rape serves to sharpen the aggressiveness of soldiers. It also helps to steel the male bonds between warriors, hence the frequency of gang rapes in war. But rape just as much reflects a burning need to establish total dominance of the other. That is why enemy women are quite commonly sexually abused in front of fathers, husbands, or brothers with the express purpose of increasing also the humiliation of the male foe. That drive for indisputable control, to be accomplished in part through demeaning, was undoubtedly what moved US marines, for example, to rape almost all women of one of the villages on Motobu Peninsula.[20]

Exactly how many Okinawan women were raped by American troops will never be known, as the victims were either too ashamed – or too frightened – to report the crime. The estimate of one Okinawan historian for the entire three-month period of the campaign exceeds 10,000. A figure that does not seem unlikely when one realizes that during the first 10 days of the occupation of Japan there were 1,336 reported cases of rape of Japanese women by American soldiers in Kanagawa prefecture alone.

Remarkably, to be of Oriental appearance was sufficient reason for women on Okinawa to run the risk of rape. When, for example, Korean 'comfort women,' brought to the island by Japanese forces before the battle, fell into American hands, some of them, too, were forced to succumb to GIs.[21]

In their frustrating attempts to gain dominance over their environment, American soldiers also turned violent against the natural surroundings that continued to resist and harass them every step of the way. Some of the violence was committed rather unthinkingly. Americans on ships, for instance, routinely used flying fish for target practice. Military pamphlets discouraged the killing of the many magnificent tropical birds, but soldiers took aim at them from pure boredom. Some of the destruction, however, was deliberate. Sailors reveled in the killing of sharks, the predators they despised as much as they feared them. In the Central Pacific, men on the USS *Tern* caught one with a big hook and bacon as bait. "They hauled him up on deck and hit him with an axe," an officer wrote. "Of course everyone wanted some of the teeth." Serpents, too, potent symbols of wilderness and its treachery, fell victim to relentless persecution. It did not matter if they were poisonous or not. "Natives beat the bush daily to frighten snakes away," a nurse in India said, "but the GIs enjoyed killing them and placing them near the mess hall so we had to see them." The skin of a 15-foot snake proudly adorned the mess hall of the 7th Tactical Fighter Squadron in New Guinea. On that same island, a company clerk typed one of the letters to his parents on the back of a python skin.[22]

On occasion, the GIs' anger with nature's never-ending pests became virtually uncontrollable. "Capt. Carroll . . . pushed us back, unslung his rifle and blazed away," an infantryman described the discovery of a coral snake on a New Caledonian beach in 1943. "We all had a shot or two, and each shot that hit would cause the snake to pop into the air." On the island of Pavuvu in 1944, hordes of giant land crabs refused to let marines get some rest after the furious battle for Peleliu. "Periodically," one marine recalled, "we reached the point of rage over these filthy things and chased them out from under boxes, seabags, and cots. We killed them with sticks, bayonets, and entrenching tools." "We must fight vermin constantly," asserted an officer on a ship where war had just been declared on cockroaches, "else it will contaminate and harm us."[23]

Viewed as a whole, the many frustrations caused by the ecological, demographic, and mental environment of Asia and the Pacific contributed more
than their fair share to the growing brutalization of American troops.
Simultaneously, however, the rage building in GIs against anyone and
anything standing in the way of victory over Japan was sustained also by
hardening hatreds born form multiple sources.

In the very first place, the war with Japan was a clash not between intol-
erant cultures, religions, or races, but between incompatible powers and
economies laying claim to the same region. Old salts told newcomers to
their ships of how, long before the war already, Japanese crews had shouted
at them, "Yankee, we sink you," whenever they passed each other in port.
That the opening shot of this imperialist war had been fired by the
Japanese, GIs would never forget. As one by one the USS *Enterprise*'s aircraft
returned after the stunning American victory at Midway in June 1942, the
mood on deck, according to one bluejacket, was "triumphant," the ship's
crew "hysterically excited." "We were exultant," the sailor wrote, "not just
at the revenge for Pearl Harbor, sweet as that was, but at our renewed sense
of power and superiority over the Japanese fleet." Throughout much of the
war, a popular record among GIs in the Pacific from one side blared
"Remember Pearl Harbor," from the other "Let's Slap the Dirty Little Jap."[24]

For some GIs, America's imperialist ambitions formed the true heart of the
conflict. "Let's forget the things we learned as children about fighting wars
for the four freedoms," a captain of the 96th Engineers in New Guinea lectured in his diary in 1943. "Who in here believes that we are? . . . We are
fighting now for the earth's crust. All wars have been fought for it. That is
the way all empires have grown, no matter how the history books try to
paint it. And we are not going to stand by and let Japan take from us the best
part of the earth's crust. That means we are going to fight back like hell."[25]

A zero-sum struggle so bitter meant that GIs were willing to accept even
the destruction of what they wanted to save, rather than concede it to the
Japanese. In 1942, when the same captain of the 96th Engineers was stationed in a part of New Guinea that was as enchanting as it was fertile, the
"sweet smelling, almost nauseating flowers" reminded him of "a fairy
land." "And here were we," he thought, "ready to instigate plans which
would soon destroy it." Then, in an afterthought, "Well, better us than the
Japanese."[26]

At an underlying level, however, the conflict with the Japanese was also
undeniably cultural in nature. Following the decade-long economic and
social turmoil of the Great Depression, and a string of military defeats in
the wake of Pearl Harbor, Americans came to interpret the war as a judgment of the national character. In his study of the 1st Marine Division, for
instance, Craig Cameron has shown that, from the outset, the American
counteroffensive on Guadalcanal in 1942 was cast as a "cultural mission,"
"an ideological struggle to preserve the American way of life."[27]

Liberty, republicanism, democracy, faith in progress as embodied in industrial achievement were all aspects of an American self-image that the war brought into sharper contrast. Another such aspect was individualism. Dug in on Peleliu in September 1944, moisture dripping from trees in the darkest night ever, panic suddenly seized a soldier of the 5th Marines. "I had the sensation of being in a great black hole and reached out to touch the sides of the gun pit to orient myself. Slowly the reality of it all formed in my mind: we were expendable." "It was difficult to accept," the marine later wrote. "We come from a nation and a culture that values life and the individual."[28]

This was a trait the Americans came to appreciate ever more in the face of a nation and culture that squandered lives in a most shocking fashion. By the time American planes returned from the battle of the Philippine Sea on 20 June 1944, a breakneck darkness had already engulfed Task Force 58 that had launched them earlier that day. Refusing to abandon his crews, Admiral Mitscher for once threw caution to the wind: every vessel in the huge armada switched on every single light it had, guiding the aviators home with a beacon of brilliance. "A great job was done by everyone to save our pilots' lives," a thoroughly satisfied seaman cheered that night on the USS *Montpelier*. "The Japs would never do anything like this."[29]

Patriotism and national chauvinism deepened with every new year of war. "Mom, I'm telling you," a private of the 1st Marine Division proselytized in 1943, "there's no place in the world that can compare in any way with the United States. I never realized that until I had to leave them. I have seen other countries; the customs and the people who make them up, and I wouldn't swap my heritage as an American for anything in the world." Only 8 percent of infantry officers surveyed in the Pacific in the spring of 1944 admitted to a "lack of conviction about what they were fighting for," significantly lower than the 22 percent recorded among their counterparts in Europe around the same time. In October 1944, GIs came together in the tropical darkness of Biak Island to release some tension watching a show. "At the end of the film," a soldier wrote in his diary, "there was a shot of the American flag fluttering in the breeze, and there was not a sound from the audience. It was a strange, dramatic kind of silence. For some reason it would have seemed ridiculous to cheer."[30]

The cross was at least as important a component of American identity as the flag. Among Americans in uniform, the significance of religion increased. Although 18 percent of GIs from all theaters surveyed at the end of the war claimed the Army experience had decreased their belief in God, 60 percent said it had strengthened their faith. Seventy percent of enlisted infantrymen and 62 percent of infantry officers questioned in the Pacific in the spring of 1944 acknowledged that prayer helped them a lot when the going was tough. This made prayer the single most important source of support in combat, more important even than the strong bonds with other men in the outfit.[31]

American soldiers, meanwhile, also considered Christianity one of the most potent forces of redemption for the infidels of the barbaric Far West. "You can put aside all notions of dealing with a primitive people when you get into the Philippines," a GI pamphlet assured. "The Filipinos are a people with 400 years of Christian culture behind them, first Spanish, then American." The Japanese, however, appeared to have declared war against Christianity's powerful influence in the region. GIs were shocked, for instance, by evidence of the enemy's mistreatment of missionaries and his desecration of churches. On strongly Catholic Guam, the Chamorro population first saw their cathedral turned into a jail for Americans, then into a Japanese entertainment center. "At the native church," a marine in the Russell Islands reported, "we found that the enemy had used for toilet paper the Church of England's song books."[32]

Americans were convinced that the religious alternative Japan threatened to replace Christianity with was far inferior. The *Guide to Japan* emphasized that Buddhism, one strain of Japanese religion, had "no moral code, no idea of sin in its teachings." Neither could the enemy find in Shinto, Japan's native religion, "any moral code." This was made worse, according to the same military booklet, by the fact that Japan had wittingly hampered the spread of Christianity from the very moment Saint Francis Xavier had introduced it there. As a result, the Japanese, "unless he has happened to have come in contact with westerners," had no idea "of what we consider right or wrong," nor "the slightest conception of what 'liberty' and 'freedom' mean."

Instead, Shinto made the Japanese "mix up men and gods in their thinking." Not only was the country's state religion responsible for the deification of the Emperor, it had convinced even ordinary Japanese that they had divine origins. No wonder then that the Japanese were "a nation which once despised us as softies and weaklings, a people who believed they were gods while we were but mortal men – a country who believed it had a divine mission to rule the world." In a propaganda film on Japan, tailor-made for GIs but released only in the last days of the war, a Japanese general was quoted as having said, "The sword is our steel bible."[33]

The war against Japan, at yet another level, was thus also a head-on collision between rival Gods. Late in July 1944, a dismayed sailor, who watched the fury of battle on Saipan from a distance, noted in his journal: "The Jap Government really feeds its people with a lot of lies. They tell them that it's an honor to die for the Emperor and that he is God." A few weeks later, en route to America for ship repairs, the same sailor wrote: "It is the happiest time in a person's life, when he returns to the U.S.A. The Greatest Country in the World, God's Country." Marines on Peleliu agreed without so many words. They stripped dead Japanese of all the green-rubber, pocket-sized folding bags they could find, threw out the personal photos and papers, and replaced them with treasured Bibles and New Testaments.[34]

A war that pitched so many starkly antagonistic cultural and religious values against each other was easily cast as a veritable clash of civilizations. Commenting on the recent revelations of the brutal ways of the Emperor's troops during their conquest of the Philippines, *Yank* in February 1944 was able to conclude only that the Japanese "doesn't want to live in the same world with our kind of civilization." An enemy who could not even contemplate coexistence was bound to ask no quarter. He would be given none either. There would be, warned the GI magazine, no "settling for anything less than complete victory."[35]

Racially inspired hatred further stoked the flames of fury. Forty-two percent of veteran enlisted infantrymen in the Pacific, surveyed early in 1944, admitted to feeling all the more like killing Japanese soldiers after nothing more than having *seen* enemy prisoners. This is probably the best evidence available of how contempt based on sheer physical otherness helped escalate the fight with Japan into what John Dower has described as a "war without mercy." The finding becomes even more striking when one knows that only 18 percent of their counterparts in Europe gave the same answer in November 1943 regarding contacts with German POWs. "God bless the whole world," a corporal of the 5th Marines wrote to his father at the end of 110 days of frontline hell on Guadalcanal, "and I'm looking forward to the days when Italy and Germany are licked so that the whole might of the allied nations can be thrown in to crush Japan and the swines that are her sons, fighting to rule the white race."[36]

American soldiers had deep sources of racial prejudice to draw from: contempt of blacks, but also of American Indians, of Asian immigrants, and of colored peoples encountered in the course of imperialist adventures in Latin America and the Pacific Basin. Craig Cameron has uncovered striking parallels between the racial attitudes of marines who fought Hispanic rebels in the Caribbean in the interwar period and those who battled the Japanese on Guadalcanal in 1942–3. Stuart Miller has documented the degree of racial hatred for the Filipinos rampant in American troops who replaced the Spanish on the islands at the turn of the century. In 1944, a military pamphlet thought it wise to warn GIs that the Filipino had "a deep racial pride as you yourself." It also thought it necessary to add that his pride was not misplaced but "well founded on centuries of Christian culture."[37]

Racial scorn easily combined with cultural and religious disdain to form a poisonous brew. In his review of thousands of censored military photographs taken during World War II, for example, historian George Roeder, in sharp contrast with what he found on the war against Japan, never encountered any evidence of GIs taking body parts of European soldiers as trophies.[38]

That same explosive mix could blow up just as well in the faces of colored peoples in Asia and the Pacific who did not belong to the enemy camp. An American sailor who visited the Gilbert Islands mentioned that many villages had been declared off limits to servicemen, and that it was announced that strict disciplinary action would be taken against "any man who molests or tries to molest the natives." En route to Burma by train, a horrified officer of Merill's Marauders discovered that some of his own soldiers were taking pot shots at cows as well as their Indian owners – or what the men called "the wogs." Although the *Guide to China* warned GIs not to assume an "air of white superiority," instances of American "heavy-handedness" when dealing with the Chinese created an increasingly tense atmosphere in official circles in Chungking and among the people at large. Incidents between Americans and Chinese increased throughout the war. By the summer of 1945, reports were mentioning affrays, stabbings, and shootings. "There was lacking," the official Army history of the China theater noted stoically, in a discussion of the predicament of American liaison personnel, "the sense of fraternity with and close support by one's own people."[39]

Deep-seated racial contempt convinced many GIs that the war in Asia and the Pacific went beyond a clash of civilizations. They came to believe that this overseas Far West was, in fact, as Frederick Jackson Turner had once described America's continental frontier, "the meeting point between savagery and civilization." In his volume on the Guadalcanal campaign, naval historian Samuel Morison quoted a sign at fleet headquarters in the South Pacific that screamed: "KILL JAPS, KILL JAPS, KILL MORE JAPS!" Morison, who himself had been in the Pacific during the war, commented: "We were fighting no civilized, knightly war . . . We were back in the primitive days of fighting Indians on the American frontier."[40]

Much earlier already, Americans had applied that same Indian analogy to Asians other than the Japanese. During the pacification campaign in the Philippines at the turn of the century, imperialists simply substituted 'Filipinos' for 'Apaches.' In response to the Boxer Rebellion in 1900, *Harper's Weekly* had put the Chinese on the same footing with the Filipinos and excluded them, too, from the "peoples of the civilized world" because their racial makeup, despite their long cultural history, was still characterized by "tribal" qualities.[41]

Indeed, almost half a century later, GIs did not have to be fighting the Japanese to relapse into that kind of reasoning. Americans of the 341st Bomber Group, on a visit to the Taj Mahal, watched in astonishment as a man carried a dead child to the Jumna River, tied a sinker to the corps, then heaved it into the water. Huge black turtles instantly tore the little body apart in full view of the Americans, who hurried away in disgust. "This display of heartlessness," the unit's chaplain observed, "embittered our men against the Indians for a long time after that, and won many sympathizers for the British." In the mind of the clergyman himself, such "callousness in the treatment of the remains of their loved ones stamped the Hindus as a subcultural species."[42]

From branding people as uncivilized, savage, and subcultural, it was only a small step to despising them as being subhuman and bestial. "The people," a WAC who had just arrived in India wrote to her parents in August 1944, "are thin and emaciated looking," and they "wash in the river along with their cows which are sacred, & their horses." Within a mere three months, she had concluded: "Although the Indian & Chinese people are supposed to have the oldest civilizations, they have really not advanced from the animal stage."[43]

No Asians deserved such a verdict more in the minds of GIs, however, than those who kept hurling themselves against American might like "a mad dog." Asked in a postwar Army survey how he had regarded Japanese troops, a former sergeant of the 132nd Infantry curtly replied: "Our hatred for the Japanese increased. We thought of them as the lowest form of life. So what did I think of them as people? They were not people." "If the Japs were not like animals," a sailor, frustrated by the prolonged battle for Saipan, noted in his diary in June 1944, "they would have given up a long time ago because their cause is hopeless." "The Japs," a lieutenant of the 160th Infantry wrote to his parents on 26 January 1945, amidst vicious cave warfare in Luzon's Zambales Mountains, "live like rats, squeal like pigs and act like monkeys."[44]

Such foes asked to be hunted down like dangerous game. Ferocious German shepherds and Dobermans snarled and barked frenziedly aboard the USS *Kittyhawk* in the autumn of 1942. "These were guard dogs going to Guadalcanal," a sailor noted, "to smell out Japanese soldiers – God help them – in the jungle." Some thought that even dogs were too good to use on Japanese soldiers. "Killing a Japanese was like killing a rattlesnake," recalled one marine general. Others preferred to compare it with the destruction of still lowlier pests. Robert Sherrod quoted a veteran marine en route to Tarawa as saying that getting the enemy out of his holes would be "like pulling a tick out of a rug." A marine on Okinawa stared at a dead Japanese soldier in the middle of a muddy road. "He had been mashed down into the mud by tank treads," he observed, "and looked like a giant squashed insect."[45]

It is important to note that many American soldiers were already imbued with loathing for the Japanese long before they ever set foot in one of Asia and the Pacific's war theaters. At the end of 1943, Army psychologists found that 38 to 48 percent of the men of a newly activated infantry division, then in training at Camp Adair, Oregon, agreed with the statement, "I would really like to kill a Japanese soldier." Only 5 to 9 percent of them indicated agreement when that same statement was applied to a German soldier. Likewise, 67 percent of infantrymen in training in the US in 1944 said they wanted to see the Japanese nation "wiped out" after the war, whereas 29 percent wanted a similar fate to befall the German people.[46]

Remarkably, however, when the latter question was put to enlisted men *in the Pacific* that same year, the percentage agreeing with "wiping out" Japan was down to 42. Although this revealed a substantial degree of vindictiveness among veterans, feelings of hatred towards the Japanese among trainees in the US were thus shown to be significantly higher. Such a brutal attitude in the ranks of GIs who had yet to experience the first shot fired in anger, should be explained in part as a reflection of emotions permeating the home front at large. The shock of Pearl Harbor and the sweeping victories of the Emperor's troops early in the war, together with a long tradition of racial prejudice towards Asians in general, had produced a virulent hatred and fear of the Japanese that ran through all levels of American society. Throughout the war, American media ruthlessly portrayed the Japanese people as fanatical, diabolical, and treacherous. Articles, movies, songs, cartoons, and advertisements kept up a savage barrage of messages dehumanizing the Asian opponent.[47]

The climate reached a point where even American forces in the field were loath to let down the home front in its bloodthirsty clamor for revenge against the Japanese. Military authorities, for instance, routinely censored photographs from the front lines that showed GIs treating wounded enemy soldiers. Even a photograph of an American interpreter consoling a Japanese child on Saipan was deemed inappropriate for home viewing. In April 1945, a medic gave his parents in Kansas a description of the work he had been assigned to do on Okinawa in a ward for civilians and Japanese soldiers. At the bottom of the letter he scribbled: "P.S. You needn't tell people that I am nursing women or Japs. I'm not particularly proud of it."[48]

While contempt of the Japanese had deep roots in American society, and continued to be fueled by the home front, US military authorities also played an important role in fanning the flames of hatred. Official publications bombarded new recruits with inflammatory imagery. A booklet entitled *The Jap Soldier* made sure to tell GIs that marines fighting in the Solomons had reported the enemy to exude "the gamey smell of animals." Another War Department publication unabashedly likened Japanese soldiers to poisonous snakes. "Our training led us to believe," a private of the 5th Marine Division admitted, "that they were less than human."[49]

So successful had the indoctrination of men of the 1st Marine Division been, that when in the early stage of the Guadalcanal campaign they met not the ferocious Japanese troops they had been led to expect, but only Korean laborers, marines unleashed their pent-up hatred against the harmless coolies instead. "Contacts with termites were also witnessed," one intelligence report mentioned derisively, "and more of these laborers might have been taken alive if eager Marines had not shot them as soon as spotted." General Vandegrift and his lieutenants nevertheless explicitly continued to sanction "ruthless precautions" on Guadalcanal in order to sustain morale within the division and keep up its aggressive spirit.[50]

Inciting men to unrestrained contempt for the Japanese was by no means limited to the shock troops of America's military. Admiral William 'Bull' Halsey, one of the more outspokenly racist commanders of the Navy, went aboard the USS *Montpelier* on more than one occasion. Each of his visits left an indelible print on one of the ship's medical officers: "He was a character. You could never forget him, because he certainly deserved the name Bull. He was a short, stocky man and swaggered across the deck. Whenever he spoke about the Japanese, it was in very strong terms and he inspired everybody in hatred of the enemy."[51]

Still, in the final analysis, neither the frustrations arising from the agonizing physical and mental environment of Asia and the Pacific, the acrimony springing from cultural and racial competition, nor the contempt unabatedly stoked by home front and military suffice to explain the complex process of barbarization in the war with Japan. To understand fully the rage grabbing hold of GIs in this conflict, one also needs to weave into the analysis the psychological mechanisms triggered by the very phenomenon of battle itself. For no matter how much words, images, and thoughts deformed the Japanese foe into a diabolical and bestial creature, the physical partaking in the butchery of what at close range remained a human being, to many did not come easy. It was never wise, for instance, to contemplate the enemy dead for too long. "No one said a word," a soldier of the 164th Infantry noted as his platoon marched past six dressed skeletons on Bougainville. "We just pushed on down the trail. As we moved on I was thinking about their mothers. How sad, they gave birth and men take it." For a soldier to stop and think about the enemy he had just killed with his own hands could be downright devastating. For a sergeant of the 29th Marines, the taste of real combat came on Okinawa. He killed his first man on Motobu Peninsula in April 1945, shooting him point-blank. "I don't know," he later said, "how long I stood there staring . . . A feeling of disgust and self-hatred clotted darkly in my throat, gagging me . . . Then I began to tremble, and next to shake, all over. I sobbed, in a voice still grainy with fear: 'I'm sorry.' Then I threw up all over myself."[52]

A replacement for the 5th Marines was thrown into his first battle on the island of Peleliu in September 1944. He could not tell what was more revolting, the sight of enemy dead, or of veteran marines pawing their pockets and packs for souvenirs. "I hadn't budged an inch or said a word, just stood glued to the spot almost in a trance . . . Would I become this casual and calloused about enemy dead? I wondered. Would the war dehumanize me so that I, too, could 'field strip' enemy dead with such nonchalance?" In his memoirs, the mortarman answered the question himself: "The time soon came when it didn't bother me a bit."[53]

In the fury of battle, even the stubbornest moral objections died a thousand deaths. One of the first forces to which they fell victim was, of course, self-preservation. Faced by an enemy whose notoriety for ruthlessness and treachery grew with every new day of war, 'kill or be killed' came to be applied all too easily to any Japanese in uniform. Including those with their hands up, always suspected of faking surrender. Including even the slain, often "rebutchered" simply because GIs feared from experience that they might be feigning death. "It did not necessarily reflect racial hatred or any hatred," noted a chronicler of the Okinawan campaign, "many simply knew the job had to be done."[54]

Yet, for many, it was the lust for revenge that gave this most basic of human reflexes a still more violent twist. "The Japs had to be killed anyway because of how they fought; there was no other way," said a soldier who operated a flamethrower on Okinawa. "But," he added, "what made you *want* to do it was your friends. When you saw their corpses day after day, your hatred – oh God, *hatred* – built day after day. By June, I had no mercy for a single Jap who wanted to surrender." When asked in a survey early in 1944 what kept their men fighting when the going was tough, 18 percent of the officers of an infantry division that had fought in the Central Pacific believed that it was sheer vindictiveness, twice as many as their counterparts in divisions in Europe at that time. Army soldiers, marines, sailors, none were immune to it. In August 1942, the cruiser *Vincennes* was one of several American ships sunk during the battle of Savo Island. Survivors were rushed to New Caledonia. "Her crew ask to guard Jap prisoners," a Quartermaster officer on the island noted in his diary, "guaranteeing that in a short time there won't be any."[55]

Every new step forward on the path of barbarization could be justified as nothing more than retaliation in kind. "They used explosives and dum dum bullets in their long rifles," a marine wrote to his father at the end of the Guadalcanal campaign, "so we cut the end of ours off with bayonets so that when they were hit the bullet would spread making a hell of a hole in them. You had to beat them at their own tricks." With 13 percent of infantrymen in the Pacific in 1944 claiming that they had seen Japanese atrocities, and 45 percent that they had heard of them, such reasoning was rampant. On 19 December 1942, an officer of the Americal Division on Guadalcanal wrote in his diary that marines had become "absolutely blood thirsty," not only because they had seen many comrades killed, but because they "have run across evidence (plenty of it) which would indicate that the Japs are torturing their prisoners." On 24 January 1943, he noted that by now "Army fellows" as well as marines were proving to be "blood thirsty," because they had found on the enemy items taken from Americans on Wake and the Philippines (including, allegedly, the diary of a marine's brother). Still worse, they had good "reason to believe that the Japs are going cannibalistic." "When you see some of your own men who after being killed were dug from their graves and eaten by the Japs," a lieutenant on Leyte wrote to his mother in December 1944, "you lose any pity you ever had and kill with the greatest pleasure."[56]

What dulled the GIs' senses most dangerously in combat, however, was the seemingly icy contempt of Japanese soldiers for their own lives. On 7 July 1944 an estimated 3,000 screaming enemy soldiers, some armed with nothing more than bayonets fixed to poles, hurled themselves against American troops on the island of Saipan in the biggest banzai attack of the war. "It was like the movie stampede staged in the old wild west movies . . . These Japs just kept coming and coming and didn't stop," one officer recalled. "It didn't make any difference if you shot one, five more would take his place." Slaughter on that scale, repeated time and again in Asia and the Pacific, made killing more tolerable not only by making it look unreal, but by lending it an abstract hue that blotted out faces and made people look like cattle earmarked to die.[57]

The blind fanaticism of the Japanese gradually convinced American soldiers that mass destruction was the only answer left. How could one expect to make such people surrender by means of words? "I am not certain as to what effect it ever had on the Japanese," Admiral William Leahy stated. "The best psychological warfare to use on these barbarians was bombs, and we used bombs vigorously." How could one hope to convince them to lay down arms by making them see reason? "During the war we learned," Robert Sherrod said, "that killing them was easier than teaching them."[58]

A savage war thus escalated into a war of extermination, if only because impatient GIs grew increasingly convinced that killing as many Japanese as possible was literally their only way out of the Asian morass. "Our job is a dirty one, slow and plodding and exterminating lots of Japs . . ," a lieutenant of the 160th Infantry, mopping up the enemy in Luzon's Zambales Mountains in his third year overseas, told his parents. "When I observe a deceased Jap, I feel nothing at all. As far as we're concerned, they're to be hunted down and put away like gophers. To me he's just one Nip nearer to getting home."[59]

There was a chilling logic in massacre. Off Luzon's coast, a destroyer sailor who longed to be reunited with his wife, wrote at the end of 1944: "I want the war to end soon. I pray often that God will do something about it. I don't necessarily want to kill ALL the Japs, just enough to make them see that they can't win." Since marking the days – if he could remember them at all – seemed to lead nowhere, he finally pinned his last hopes on counting bodies, faithfully sharing his desperate calculations with his spouse. 8 March 1945, off the coast of Iwo Jima: "There was only 27,000 there to begin and we have accounted for 14,000. Add another 3 or 4,000 for those blown to so many pieces they can't be counted and we have two thirds of them whipped." 1 April 1945, D-Day, off the coast of Okinawa: "There are 55,000 Nip soldiers on this island and half a million civilians. The soldiers mostly will be killed by our troops and I hope the civilians commit hari-kari like on Saipan." In the heat of battle against a suicidal enemy, the reservoirs of pity dried up fast.[60]

Minds were further eased into accepting their brutalization when the ranks they were part of acquiesced in much of the savagery committed. In November 1943, the USS *Montpelier* was attacked by some 70 enemy planes. Its crew downed some of them, then continued firing at the few Japanese who had been able to save themselves by parachute. It was a flagrant violation of the laws of war. "The men were blasted out for doing this," a sailor noted in his journal. "They were told not to waste ammunition in such a way. They were also told that it was good shooting." During briefings, just days before the invasion of Guam in July 1944, news was announced to the 4th Marines of presumed atrocities perpetrated by the Japanese on Saipan, another of the Mariana Islands. Details mentioned the beheading of American prisoners; some countrymen were said to have been skinned alive. "When it was announced that there would be NO PRISONERS TAKEN on this invasion," a corporal remembered, "a cheer went up from the guys." Troops who had just captured the island of Peleliu received the following message in October 1944 from Admiral Halsey: "The sincere admiration of the entire Third Fleet is yours for the hill blasting, cave smashing extermination of 11,000 slant-eyed gophers. It has been a tough job extremely well done."[61]

Combat soldiers were much less concerned, however, about letting down generals and admirals far to the rear than comrades on their very side. And in the front lines, patience with squeamishness wore exceedingly thin. Shame and disgust threatened to overwhelm a marine who killed a Japanese at close range on Ngesebus Island in the fall of 1944. But then he suddenly checked his emotions. "I felt like a fool," he said, "and was thankful my buddies couldn't read my thoughts." In the summer of 1944, Robert Sherrod watched as marines on Saipan tried to dislodge the enemy from a cave. They had tried bulldozers; they were now bringing in TNT. Their sergeant was getting agitated. "One of the Marines kept talking about coaxing the Jap or Japs out of the cave," Sherrod noted. "He said, somewhat wistfully: 'I wish we had somebody that knew enough Japanese to fetch him out.'" "He said this," the correspondent added, "in a low voice, so the sergeant did not hear him."[62]

Up front, snappy commands from lowly NCOs could prove more murderous than the hyperbole of a high-ranking 'Bull' Halsey. On patrol somewhere in enemy territory, a private who had taken point suddenly found his path cut off by a Japanese. The enemy had his hands high and appeared not to carry a weapon. "My sergeant told me to shoot him," the marine recalled. "I refused, someone else dispatched him to the Shinto gods."[63]

Moral objections hardly had a chance to resonate amidst the unabating pressure from peers. A soldier of the 1st Marine Division remembered what he described as "one of the rare occasions I ever saw compassion expressed for the Japanese by a Marine who had to fight them." It took place while battle raged in Okinawa's Shuri Line. Men from his unit stumbled across a

Japanese soldier in a ditch. He had no way out and was gravely wounded, yet infuriated Americans kept firing at him. For one marine, it was too much: he called out, deploring them to stop. The only thing his comrades did, however, was snap back at him angrily, completing the kill.[64]

Meanwhile, mercy for the enemy turned out to be at least as rare a commodity among the indigenous people fighting alongside US troops. Natives who helped mop up the Japanese on Biak Island could choose to bring in captives, but they could also decide to return with the enemy's ears on a piece of string. According to at least one American, Filipino scouts on Leyte "took delight in the slaughter." They severed the heads of Japanese victims with their big bolo knives, then hung the trophies from poles with ropes of hemp. American airmen who watched a parade in Kunming late in 1941 were treated to colorful paper dragons interspersed with Japanese prisoners – emaciated, dirty, and "jerked along by collar-and-leash affairs." From the Middle Kingdom's southeast, a frustrated naval intelligence officer, eager for information from downed Japanese airmen, reported that "the Chinese killed an enemy flyer as soon as his plane stopped rolling."[65]

Amidst such pervasive barbarization, there remained nowhere to go for the overly scrupulous. A revolted infantry intelligence officer commandeered two GIs to help him remove a Japanese pilot who had been left to rot between a Filipino refugee camp and the 77th Division area. The enlisted men despised their assignment. Insulted graves registration personnel refused to accept enemy dead under any circumstances. "I was stuck," said the conscientious American officer, "with a dead Jap, two angry soldiers, and no authority to appeal to."[66]

"Is there," a despairing infantryman of the 7th Division in Leyte insisted on knowing in the fall of 1944, "going to be reborn in the soul of America the passion for the Christian faith our fathers knew when they hacked a nation out of a wilderness . . .?"[67]

American soldiers abandoned themselves to rage against the wilderness of the furthest West, and the savages in it, as this appeared the only way that remained to safeguard the civilized values they stood for. But rather than regenerate, they regressed amidst the unmitigated violence. In December 1942, a Quartermaster officer of the Americal Division had a chance to talk with some of the notorious Raiders, just back from seventeen days of operating behind Japanese lines. In his diary, the officer expressed surprise at the fact that most of them were boys no older than 16 or 17. And he added: "The 'Raiders' are more like the American Indians than Human Beings."[68]

While preparing for the invasion of Emirau Island early in 1944, men of the 4th Marines in a clearing on Guadalcanal came across at least a dozen skeletons of Japanese soldiers. "Before long," one marine wrote, "skulls were decorating the posts around tents and other areas of camp." One might not have been surprised if Kurtz had joined them shortly, for the scene appeared to be taken straight from Joseph Conrad's *Heart of Darkness*. "It's so very difficult for me to explain, to say the things I want to, my thoughts are so disconnected." These words were written in a letter sent from the Mare Island Naval Hospital by a marine who had fallen casualty to battle fatigue on Guadalcanal. "Of course I'm not insane," he tried to reassure his parents. "But I've been living the life of a savage and haven't quite got used to a world of laws and new responsibilities."[69]

By accepting the terms of savage war as laid down by the Japanese foe, by applying them with a vengeance even, GIs had become what they loathed. They had, in yet another way, 'gone Asiatic.' In July 1944, Charles Lindbergh, from the safe distance of Australia, reflected on the GI behavior he had been confronted with during his tour of the Pacific: "They treat the Jap with less respect than they would give to an animal, and these acts are condoned by almost everyone. We claim to be fighting for civilization, but the more I see of this war in the Pacific the less right I think we have to claim to be civilized. In fact, I am not sure that our record in this respect stands so very much higher than the Japs."[70]

That is not to say that human rage in the war against Japan ever managed to silence the voices of reason and conscience entirely. George Roeder has rightly pointed out that if, in trying to understand so complex a phenomenon as war, accounts that sanitize it are inadequate, so too are those that speak only of war's brutalizing effect. To illustrate his point, Roeder, in his study on American censorship during the war, quoted from a letter written by a marine caught up in the atrocious battle for Saipan. The corporal described how the sight of many dead Americans had made their blood boil. Then he wrote: "When we were heading for Garapan, we all talked about how we were going to kill any jap we saw. Young or old, male or female. But, we really changed our minds when tattered, terror and hunger stricken kids, the age of Harvey, Linda, and even carrying babes as young as Bobbie, came out of holes and caves waving a torn white rag. Well this was really a sight that put a lump in your throat. The killing was confined to those japs who preferred dying for their emperor rather than surrender."[71]

Yet even those few lingering echoes of moral outcry were destined to be drowned out by the din of industrial violence and the blast of technological destruction. Forces too crude to distinguish between innocence and guilt, too impersonal to be bothered with right and wrong at all.

10
Industrial Violence

The Japanese called it *seishin*. In Western parlance, the US War Department's *Handbook on Japanese Military Forces* lectured, the closest equivalent to this alien concept was "spirit," something the Asian opponent regarded as a "mystic virtue which can overcome material weapons in profane hands."[1]

Since the Meiji Restoration of 1868, Japan had, of course, been undergoing spectacular transitions as a result of its sudden, warm embrace of Western modernization and industrialization. At the same time, however, the nation had stubbornly clung to ancient traditions and what it considered to be its unique qualities. In the militarized society of the 1930s, the looming clash with the West had made an even clearer outlining of Japan's cultural essence an undertaking of vital importance. Inevitably, the nation's reemphasized self-definition was molded in sharp contrast with the existing image of the fated nemesis. In fact, authorities told people that 'The Pure Self' could be attained only by expunging foreign influences.

The most harmful of these influences were easily identified. Despite its remarkable modernization and industrialization, a resource-poor Japan knew all too well that it could not even begin to match the productive capacities of the West. After all, Japan's conflict with the West in Asia had arisen from the very dispute over which of them was to benefit from the region's rich raw materials. Not surprisingly then, it was rampant materialism that was singled out as the West's most despicable influence. A cartoon published in a Japanese magazine in 1942 personified Japan as a woman combing the dandruff of Anglo-American influences from her hair. Words identifying the dandruff spoke of individualism, selfishness, worship of money, hedonism, extravagance, and materialism in general.[2]

On an everyday level, people were told that 'The Pure Self' was to be set free by austere living. Taken to its most extreme conclusion, Japanese soldiers were taught that near-perfect purification and – in the process – victory could be attained by sacrificing their very lives. GIs would do well to remember, the 1941 American training manual heeded, that "the Japanese seem to feel . . . that it is more important to have spirit . . . than men or weapons."[3]

The war thus polarized the self-images of both sides. If the Japanese emphasized spirit as their unique quality, then what Americans considered to be a crucial aspect of their own exceptional identity was progress as embodied in material wealth. GIs successfully competed with Japanese savageness, but they were incapable of matching something as incomprehensible as Japanese spirituality. Instead, they became increasingly proud to be betting everything on exactly that which their enemy envied as much as he despised it: America's renowned industry and technology. "As far as the length of the war, I don't see how it can stop in less than three years," a soldier in the Solomons wrote to his parents in Massachusetts in May 1943, "but I'm sure we can lick them eventually. Our stuff is better, our pilots and planes are – everything considered – way ahead of theirs and our resources inexhaustible . . ." That lieutenant John F. Kennedy overestimated the time it would take to defeat Japan by at least half a year even while lauding his country's industrial might was strong testimony to the GIs' apprehension of Asian spirit.[4]

The weight of US industrial production was staggering. So was the development of American logistics, the science of supply. That is far from saying that there were no supply problems in Asia and the Pacific during the war. Not only was the US involved in a global conflict, with its armed forces everywhere displaying voracious appetites, but early on the decision had been taken to assign troops opposing Germany a higher supply priority than those fighting Japan. Moreover, the extraordinary physical difficulties – climate as much as distance – often defeated even the most Herculean efforts.[5]

During the early stages of the war especially, when the Japanese Navy was still a major hazard, US troops were at times forced to get by on a shoestring. As late as January 1943, the 32nd Division in New Guinea, which had begun to arrive on the island in September 1942, complained of shortages in the supply of something even as vital as antimalarial medicine. But, although shortages in forward areas occurred throughout the war, the overall supply of American goods increased so overwhelmingly with each new year that it all but smothered the enemy. Nurses of the 20th General Hospital in India received so much of the antimalarial drug Atabrine later in the war that they could afford to use some of it for dyeing their barrack curtains yellow. When engineers involved in the construction of airfields in Bengal in 1944 found Indian cement scarce and inferior, even that substance was imported in large quantities all the way from the US. By mid-1944, the huge numbers of typewriters circulating in the Southwest Pacific, an area without local manufacturing sources, led to the establishment of a spare parts depot in Brisbane, Australia, where the many worn-out machines were to be rebuilt. Early in 1945, yet another depot was organized for this purpose in Manila.[6]

The needs of America's armed forces were prodigious. And they grew with leaps and bounds. Average poundage per soldier on the attack transports heading for the Gilbert atolls Tarawa and Makin in November 1943 was more than 1,300. The supplies required for the Leyte operation in the fall of 1944 were astounding. The War Department estimated that, for the landing period alone, a force of 150,000 men would need 1.5 million tons of general equipment, 235,000 tons of combat vehicles, 200,000 tons of ammunition, and 200,000 tons of medical supplies. After that, 332,000 tons of equipment would be required every 30 days. When early in 1945 considerable numbers of Americans were flown from the India–Burma theater to China, it was calculated that each GI necessitated the monthly delivery of 62 tons of supplies via air or tortuous land route.[7]

Meanwhile, steady increases in supplies only served to heighten the soldiers' expectations. In November 1943, an excited engineer guzzled a cold orangeade beneath the canopy of the hot New Guinean jungle. It was his first iced drink since leaving Australia, made from water stored in a Liberty ship in the bay. He smacked his lips, then lamented in his diary, "I don't know why an ice plant has not been erected at Oro Bay, because anything can be built in this army if it is needed and wanted by the right people."[8]

By the time of the Okinawan operation in April 1945, seemingly everything possible was provided for the nearly 200,000 troops involved. In medical supplies alone, for instance, the Tenth Army, for the assault phase, received 25,000 litters, 50,000 blankets, 100,000 cans of footpowder, 100,000 iodine swabs, 30 million vitamin tablets, and 7 billion units of penicillin.[9]

The foodstuffs piling up for the American forces were at least as spectacular. In July 1942, a quartermaster officer of the Americal Division in New Caledonia wrote in his diary: "distributed 70000 lbs of fresh beef. The quantities that we are dealing in are astonishing. Have now over a million lbs of flour." The official Marine Corps history of the battle for Iwo Jima claimed that, by the end of the campaign, Americans on the beaches of the tiny island had unloaded "enough food to feed the entire city of Columbus, Ohio, for an entire month."[10]

Although local procurement was vital in India and China, and crucial contributions were made by Australia and New Zealand to provisioning troops in the Pacific, highly mechanized American farmers had few problems filling the gigantic, evergrowing orders they received from their country's military. However, getting the many different food items to the proper places in the proper quantities at the proper times was much more difficult. During the Guadalcanal campaign, when a still powerful Japanese Navy reduced American ships to blockade-runners, hungry troops became grateful for the dried kelp, noodles, and wormy rice they captured from the Japanese. Once America began to rule the waves, however, the major quartermaster problem that remained in the Pacific was the frequent scarcity of certain food items at advance bases and in combat zones. This was particularly true in New Guinea as the giant island of jungles and mountains did everything in its power to hamper unloading and distribution. But if combat soldiers ever went hungry, it was only for short periods. And if there were scarcities of certain foodstuffs, troops hardly starved; they simply took more from the mountains of other items. A nurse of the 35th General Hospital at Lae, New Guinea, for example, remarked that at one time they "ate canned chili and canned spinach for a month."[11]

In fact, the only thing American forces eventually had left to gripe about was the monotony of their fare. And even that was being remedied where possible in ways that sometimes took the soldiers themselves by surprise. In December 1943, men of the 495th Port Battalion in New Guinea unloaded the coolers of the USS *West Point*. Among the treats the ship disgorged were apples, grapes, lemons, grapefruit, pineapple juice, chicken, liverwurst, and salami. "It was funny, really funny," said one GI, "to stand in line and wait to see what would come out next. Then, all of a sudden out came a box of frozen strawberries! Can you imagine having frozen strawberries in New Guinea?" Earlier in the war, men of the 45th Engineers had been forced to shoot water buffaloes if they wanted to taste fresh meat while working on the Ledo Road in Burma. But in February 1945 the unit's commanding officer mentioned in his diary: "had American ground hamburgers tonight, shipped from USA and received frozen – what next?"[12]

By the end of the war, the nature of the complaints listed even by infantry divisions up front would have outraged Japanese forces reduced to starvation in many an outpost. In April 1945, the Quartermaster General received a report from the US Army Field Forces in the Pacific Ocean Areas. Based on a study of eight divisions, the report intended to provide suggestions to make the B ration "more palatable." It pointed out that troops were growing sick of the corned beef hash and the meat and vegetable stew, and that they wanted to see more of the components containing spaghetti, vienna sausage, macaroni, and pork luncheon meat. Soldiers complained that there was never enough of the following either: sauces, spices, relishes, pickles, olives, salad oil, mayonnaise, mustard, onions, ketchup, and cheese. More chocolate was desired, too, "not of the Tropical Hershey variety of which the men are tired – but of the Rockwood, or Peters-Caylor-Kohler type." Where it concerned hard candy, the report concluded, "A substitute for Charms is badly needed."[13]

Spectacular advances in industrial and agricultural production had been feeding a cult of the machine in American society for a long time. GIs knew they had to thank their country's unrivaled mechanization for the abundance of goods and food lavished upon them even as soldiers in so distant a frontier; they were convinced that it was the American machine that eventually would bring them victory in so merciless a war.

On day one of the landing on Betio Island, Robert Sherrod, ducking low, creeping along the edge of a pier, bumped into a stalled bulldozer. "This, I reflected," the correspondent noted disparagingly, "was the American way to fight a war – to try to get a bulldozer ashore, even before many men had preceded it." More were to follow, demolishing bunkers, sealing caves and holes to prevent reoccupation at night, burying the enemy alive. By the end of the battle for Tarawa, Sherrod was a convert, too, calling the dozer "a fine weapon."[14]

An infatuation for many, machinery became a veritable aphrodisiac to others. "Honey," a sailor wrote to his wife after having seen his first B-29 bomber on Iwo Jima, "you can't imagine how huge they are until you see them. Their tail assembly alone stands as high as a house. And are they beautiful. Next to a woman the B-29 and the P-51 fighter are the most beautiful females we have out here."[15]

What GIs wanted in a beautiful piece of equipment was sturdiness, not the toylike quality of Japanese and other foreign tools. US infantry divisions, for example, emerged from the campaigns in the Solomons and New Guinea convinced that even in jungle environments heavy machinery – artillery, tanks, engineer equipment – was more effective, reliable, and durable than equivalent lightweight matériel. In India, American military personnel took over operation of the Bengal and Assam Railway on 1 March 1944. By the end of that year, 238 powerful US engines made up almost two-thirds of the railway's locomotive power. By that time, too, 6,500 commodious American freight cars, with twice the capacity of the local four-wheel cars, were busily rumbling through eastern India. In the Philippines, one of the main tasks of American engineer units following closely behind the infantry was to shore up bridges as soon as possible. They worked around the clock, first to strengthen bridges sufficiently to carry two-and-a-half-ton trucks, next to reinforce them to 20-ton capacity to hold the M-8 tanks, then to bring them to 36-ton capacity for the M-10s.

GIs could not get enough of their country's wonderful machines. From the South Pacific came shouts for more tractors, cranes, shovels, and dump trucks. In the Southwest Pacific, troops clamored for more tractors, graders, cranes, concrete mixers, ditching machines, and welding equipment. When tanks got stuck on the Admiralty Islands in March 1944, soldiers simply sent D-7 bulldozers after them and forcefully dragged them through the jungle to where they needed them to be.[16]

"Of all the noisy places on the various planets," a soldier from an engineer regiment in Leyte wrote in his diary in December 1944, "this war on this world has them all beat! Noise, noise, noise, twenty-four hours a day, seven days a week – trucks roaring, bulldozers snorting, jeeps rattling and blowing, boats leaving the shore, guns firing, planes roaring overhead, generators running, and most of these all at one time. If one thing stops, there is a new sound to take its place. Every nerve in your body screams for quiet, and, even in sleep, you are aware of noise."[17]

The quantity of fuel needed to keep this sea of machinery humming was mind-boggling. For the capture by the combined services of the five-mile-long island of Iwo Jima alone, one source estimated it to include 4,100,000 barrels of black oil; 595,000 barrels of diesel oil; 33,775,000 gallons of aviation gasoline; and 6,703,000 gallons of motor gas.[18]

America's huge industrialized army inevitably left thick trails of waste as it crept forward. Despite the fact that the supply of troops on Guadalcanal had been difficult during the early months of the campaign, even the large bomb craters on the island were said to be filled with tin cans by the end of 1942. Around that same time, New Guinea's Port Moresby was already booming into a major base, with new roads, airfields, and harbor facilities. It came to resemble what Army historians described as "a frontier town." Latrines were erected on the beach. Countless ration cans lay discarded all over. Refuse was dumped in open pits, garbage hurriedly burned. Insects swarmed to the stink, spreading diarrheal disease and malaria. Where organization improved or hard island surfaces prevented rubbish from being buried, large garbage barges took it out to sea and dumped it by the tons. Ships contributed their fair share to the pollution of bays and beaches. Oily bilge water was pumped overboard. Saltwater flushing systems carried sewage straight into the ocean. "The water in the bay is a sickly green," a destroyer sailor off the coast of Leyte wrote to his wife, "filthy with the toilet wash of many many ships."[19]

Abundance brought not only heaps of filth, but also an appalling carelessness with goods of all kinds. "Things are dropped while being unloaded from the ships – anything from a gasoline field range to a case of canned goods," observed a soldier in Oro Bay, New Guinea, in November 1943, "and seldom is anything fished up from the bottom." In the six months that the 6th Division operated in New Guinea's Sansapor area in 1944, it accumulated 1.5 million pounds of canned meats that its men disliked and refused to touch. A year later, it was signaled to the Quartermaster General that infantry divisions in the Pacific were receiving "too much Barbasol brushless shaving cream." "At a minimum," the report stated, "25% is always thrown away."[20]

If the Japanese military recklessly squandered valuable lives, then America's armed forces showed little concern about the wastage of replaceable goods. Poor planning and the inevitable chaos of war at times caused pinching shortages, but in certain areas they could just as well lead to so much excess stock it threatened to overwhelm. "We have all been doing a lot of shooting lately," an engineer in New Guinea wrote in his diary in the fall of 1943. "Cases and cases of ammunition are available. You take what you want and go out and shoot at anything except one another. We had some good shots at white cockatoos, but no one hit any." In June 1944, men of the 608th Clearing Company in New Guinea, together with soldiers of several other units, were told to line up. As hundreds filed by, truckloads of brand-new equipment – helmets, gasmasks, clothing – were forced upon GIs who looked puzzled because they already possessed all of these items. "Some of the men protested," a surgeon wrote to his wife, "but they were told to take the stuff and move on, and throw away what they didn't need or want . . . I figured at least $15,000 worth of stuff was thrown away." "This is not an isolated example," he added. "There are many worse stories . . ."[21]

Meanwhile, a spasmodic supply of food could give rise to what quartermasters referred to as the 'feast-and-famine' cycle. From one day to another, scarcity could turn into glut. To get rid of excess stocks of perishables, each GI at Oro Bay, New Guinea, from 22 to 24 November 1943 was "daily served nineteen eggs and bountiful portions of beef and butter." "We got a huge load of fresh meat this afternoon," wrote a lieutenant of the 160th Infantry in New Britain in May 1944. "Evidently they had too much over in New Guinea so shipped us the rest. Five-and-a-half hogs for 150 men at 150 pounds per hog. As we have no cooling system, we have to be rid of them by morning." The reefer *Autauga*, plying vessels in the Pacific with fresh foodstuffs in 1945, followed orders when forcing customer ships to take equal amounts of fruit and meat, even though crews preferred apples and oranges as they lacked refrigeration to store the meat. Weary sailors complied, then heaved entire cases of soon-to-be-spoiled beef and ham over the side and into the ocean.[22]

As much of the packaging and storage proved inadequate, the tropical climate caused heavy losses even of nonperishable foods. In mid-1943, inspections at Port Moresby, New Guinea, revealed that no more than 10,000 of the 541,000 pounds of canned corned beef, less than 5 percent of the canned tomatoes and raisins, and only some 30 percent of the margarine, canned orange juice, and dehydrated vegetables remained fit for consumption. In March 1944, condemnations at the same base amounted to 2,143,000 pounds, or 16 percent of all the food examined. For all of 1944, the total loss of nonperishables in the Southwest Pacific may have run as high as 25 percent.[23]

Neglect made the life of much of the mechanical equipment at least as short. Salt water and volcanic ash wore out brake shoes on trucks operating on beaches within ten days. For each hour of operation, LVTs and DUKWs required an estimated two hours of maintenance. As lack of time and spare parts made such upkeep unthinkable, however, it was often easier to order new vehicles. Shortage of service personnel made salvage operations fare much worse even than repair activities. As late as May 1945, a US Army report on the lessons learned in the Leyte campaign concluded: "Conservation of property and hence shipping continues to be a major problem with our expanded army. It requires continual effort to utilize all material to the maximum, including salvage, in order to conserve property."[24]

With the end of the war, such concerns evaporated entirely. Trash produced by the immense American naval base on the island of Santo in the New Hebrides had initially been dumped on a deserted beach. As time went by, the beach became too small, so bulldozers began pushing the rubbish into the water. Before long, the garbage started to rise above the ocean's surface, so bulldozers flattened it, smoothing the surface with sand and coral. When, after more than three years of hustle and bustle, the order was given for the base to be dismantled in August 1945, American trucks lined up on the giant garbage platform for weeks on end. They dumped astonishing quantities of equipment: office furniture, refrigerators, machinery. At the end, to speed things up, trucks were not even emptied anymore. Motors running, they were sent to the bottom of the ocean together with their loads. A 1946 topographic survey of Santo revealed that the tiny island had grown by about ten acres.[25]

The resources and productive capacity of the US overpowered friend and foe alike. In February 1944, the USS *Montpelier* lay at anchor in the Solomon Islands' Purvis Bay. Sailors were regularly sent out in barges to dump the ship's trash on a nearby beach, where it would be burned. "There were about ten natives pawing the trash," a bluejacket noted on one such trip. "They retrieved clothing and anything that they could make use of. A few children about seven years old were with them." What Americans on Santo called a garbage dump was a treasure trove to indigenous people. In the summer of 1945, islanders dug through the rubbish day and night, hauling away anything salvageable in trucks, swarming over the dump even from canoes.[26]

So wretchedly poor were people in India that the stunning contrasts provided by American wealth left GIs torn between compassion and contempt. A member of the 311th Fighter Group gazed through the window as his train rolled from Bombay to Kanchrapara late in November 1944. Fellow countrymen tossed candy, biscuits, dextrose, and bruised fruit to the countless beggars hugging the rails. "Whether it was rotten or not made no difference to them," the airman wrote in his diary. "They would eat anything. We threw cans and paper and wood boxes out. Nothing stayed on the ground very long. They picked up everything."[27]

Despite the prodigious needs of their own military, American supply lines actually managed to spew out food for others, too. In planning for the invasion of the Gilbert Islands, for instance, Service Force Pacific Fleet also provided enough beef and flour to feed 30,000 indigenes for one month. Air Supply Service dropped tons of rice, pork link sausages, peanuts, spinach, peas, fruit bars, sugar, salt, and vitamin pills in support of Chinese allies operating in northern Burma. Each of the four American divisions that landed on Okinawa on 1 April 1945 carried 70,000 pounds of rice and soy beans intended for civilians made destitute by battle.[28]

America's steamrolling plenty wallowed on and on, bit by bit crushing even the formidable spirit of the Japanese foe. In June 1945, a battalion surgeon of the 20th Infantry treated a Japanese medical officer in the mountains of northern Luzon. He described the encounter in a letter to his wife. "When I dressed a slight flesh wound of his and used half a packet of sulfa powder, he was amazed that I left it and he folded the packet carefully and placed the remains into his pocket. He muttered with deep feeling, 'The Americans have so much, we have so little.'"[29]

With Americans strengthening air and naval superiority in the Pacific at a merciless pace, raw materials no longer reached Japan in sufficient quantity, industrial production failed to compensate for equipment lost, and logistical lifelines to troops overseas were severed. As late as 1944, infantry divisions stationed on Guadalcanal were still engaged in mopping up Japanese soldiers trapped on the island. Most often, however, the only enemies captured were those cornered by cooks while trying to steal food from unit messes. In December 1944, not a single shipload of food reached the Japanese in Luzon. In response, the *14th Area Army* cut its ration from three pounds daily to nine-tenths of a pound, but in many units soldiers were lucky if they obtained as much as half a pound of rice per day. Japanese troops were forced to scrounge food from long-abandoned Filipino gardens. By June 1945, there was not a pig, carabao, or dog alive in the sector of the *Shimbu Group*. Most troops were eating roots, bark, and grass. Some threw themselves on human flesh. In the course of July, for every man killed in combat, the group lost nearly 10 men to starvation or disease. To persuade the enemy to lay down his arms, US psychological warfare teams throughout Asia and the Pacific increasingly stressed the good treatment awaiting those who surrendered. Propaganda leaflets raining on jungle and coral pictured Japanese prisoners smoking cigarettes while ogling plates piled up with hot food.[30]

GIs gained confidence not only from the immense amount of matériel backing them, but from its quality, too. The lightweight, miniature versions the enemy used to counter American weapons were almost laughable. An officer in Luzon was comforted by the sound of "our own baritone rapid-fire machine guns" barking back at the "high-pitched staccato, woodpecker rat-a-tat-tat of the Japanese machine guns." Light Japanese tanks were instantly identified by the toylike "tinny clank-clank" of their bogey wheels. To the heavier armor of the Americans, the enemy seemed to have no rational answer. "The Japs screamed and hollered, and actually beat on the tanks with their fists and knives," a captain told Richard Tregaskis of the landing on Tanambogo Island near Guadalcanal.[31]

As American forces tightened the noose around the have-not nation, acute shortages developed for almost all imaginable materials basic to industrial activity. "We left behind," a marine who fought on Iwo Jima noted with obvious satisfaction, "what seemed great quantities of *metal*: cartridge cases, ammo boxes, etc. They left behind wooden boxes attached to a carrying pole with straw ropes."[32]

Nothing confirmed the soldiers' trust in America's industrial edge more, however, than evidence of superior mobility. Asia appeared literally frozen in its tracks. Among American Air Force personnel in China, motor-vehicle accidents formed the most important cause of noncombat injuries, something that was ascribed mainly to the poor condition of roads. On the relatively large island of Saipan, primitive infrastructure delayed the movement of supplies away from beaches so much that units were forced to supplement motor transport with bullock carts. Despite ceaseless work by American engineers and Filipino pick-and-shovel crews, progress on Leyte remained seriously hampered by the poor quality of roads leading to the interior of the island.

Locals had a hard time growing accustomed to the heavy traffic imposed by the Americans. "Here you find people wandering all over the street and you get burned-up about it," a GI guide to China noted. "Why are the Chinese like that? The Chinese are like that because . . . the reactions of most of the country folk and many of the city people are geared to a slow way of life – sedan chairs, wheelbarrows, pack animals and rickshaws." The appreciative grins of four Chinese soldiers, whom Flying Tigers told to hop into the back of their truck near the village of Wenshan, melted within minutes. "After but a few miles of this careening and constant jarring," noted one of the pilots, "it became evident that Oriental boys were unaccustomed to vehicular motion." They vomited all the way to their destination. A WAC told her parents in April 1945 that people traveling in bullock carts near Calcutta halted in the morning, slept until dark, then continued their journey again at night, when the traffic from the Americans was less heavy.

By late 1944, an alarmed General Wedemeyer reported that in all of Free China there were only about 2,000 trucks left in good condition. The situation was so critical that he sent an emergency request for the 5,000 lend-lease trucks already on order, and asked for an additional 2,000 two-and-a-half-ton 6×6 US Army trucks. Washington responded by promising to deliver no less than 15,000 vehicles by the end of 1945.[33]

GIs never even thought of taking seriously the vehicles sent into battle by the Japanese. On Guadalcanal already, they mocked the bantam "Nipponese versions of the Chevrolet." Japanese trucks captured in New Guinea's Wakde-Sarmi beachhead had to be abandoned because they failed to climb the steep slopes beyond. Whereas a US Army division could count on 2,125 vehicles, a Japanese infantry division could expect no more than 500. By the time these divisions clashed on the plains of Luzon in 1945, none of the Japanese units had even its authorized number of crucial vehicles. Lack of fuel and lubricants paralyzed what little the enemy had left on wheels.[34]

American soldiers felt secure in the knowledge that their country could match and beat the quantity and quality of any of the enemy's military machines. Only once in the war did the Japanese manage to shake that confidence to the core, and then it took suicide pilots to do so. The first large-scale *kamikaze* attacks occurred during the invasion of the Philippines in the fall of 1944. To Americans the spectacle appeared utterly surreal.

Which is probably why they were inclined, at first, to accept even the weirdest rumors surrounding the phenomenon. The pilots were believed, for instance, to wear white robes and black hoods. "Some," Robert Sherrod noted, "said they were manacled to their cockpits." The American correspondent, who witnessed the first suicide attack in January 1945 while with the Third Fleet southeast of Formosa, thought such scuttlebutt hardly surprising. "Nothing could have been more awesome," he agreed, "than to see a human being diving himself and his machine into the enemy; nobody except the Japanese could have combined such medieval religious fervor with a machine as modern as the airplane."

The West had long shuddered at the thought of a time when Asia's human masses would manage to harness industrial and technological muscle. In the Japanese *kamikaze* an apparent disregard for all too readily available human life now seemed to have fused with the power of the machine into an almost unbeatable weapon. By the time of the Okinawan campaign in 1945, *kamikaze* attacks were coming over in rumbling waves. The first one counted no less than 355 suicide planes. Those that followed in the next three months counted 50 to 200 aircraft each. "The strain of waiting," recalled one correspondent, "the anticipated terror, made vivid from past experience, sent some men into hysteria, insanity, breakdown." *Kamikaze* attacks at Okinawa sank 26 vessels and damaged 164 others, killing and wounding thousands of sailors. Yet, in the same battle, Americans destroyed some 4,000 Japanese aircraft, 1,900 of them suicide planes. Even in Okinawa's darkest hours, GIs knew that for each plane sacrificed by the enemy, several more were rolling from America's factories.[35]

Americans spontaneously ascribed much of the apparent industrial and technological backwardness of the region to the inherent mental deficiencies of its peoples. The comforting cliché that Japan's industrial progress was the result of importation and copycatting, and not of any natural inventiveness, remained alive even during the very war in which the Asians proved to pose a frightful challenge to the combined Western powers. The capture of American-made vehicles at Buna, of trucks at Sanananda with US Army markings (probably brought over from the Philippines), of 1938 Model V8 Fords at Wakde only served to confirm that view. GIs made sure to mention such finds in letters home. "It is a funny thing," an engineer on Kolombangara Island wrote to his parents in February 1944, "but a lot of Jap vehicles have instructions for oil change and spark plug clearances printed in English even though the same name plate states that it is a Japanese make made in Japan." On Tarawa atoll, Robert Sherrod examined the cabin of a bullet-riddled enemy truck. "Though they are Japanese-made, the dashboards of the trucks have their instruments labeled in English," he noted, too. "Here is an example," Sherrod continued, "of the Japanese tendency to imitate: the 'water' thermometer dial is in the centigrade of the French, as is the 'kilos' of the speedometer; 'oil' and 'amperes' dials might have been taken from either the Americans or the British, but the fuel indicator is labeled gasoline instead of the British 'petrol.'" Meanwhile, GIs never entirely abandoned suspicions that behind the most lethal enemy bombing raids or artillery barrages hid Japan's European allies. As late as the Okinawan campaign, there were occasions where they believed "Nazi artillerymen were commanding the Jap batteries."[36]

Such suspicions were part of a much older tendency to regard nonwhite peoples as more emotional than logical, and thus as less apt at developing, mastering, and applying science and technology. The Chinese people had long been considered the perfect illustration of this phenomenon. Why had the Middle Kingdom, despite a number of revolutionary inventions, not been able to escape stagnation and, eventually, foreign domination? Not only because many notable inventions had come about by chance rather than design, but because the Chinese – in contrast with the Europeans – had not known how to put them to work. They could have used gunpowder to conquer the world – they used it for fireworks instead.[37]

American soldiers arrived in China with echoes of such presuppositions still in their minds. "Working around machinery," the 1944 handbook for American troops in China warned, "you discover that drivers and mechanics sometimes neglect the upkeep of cars or mishandle pieces of machinery. Your normal reaction is explosive." But, the handbook continued in patronizing defense of "the average Chinese," "He simply hasn't had that background. He can probably outlast you in carrying a load at two ends of a pole or in tilling a Chinese field or he can probably carve or weave more and better than you. He has the background for patient handicraft. But not at this stage for mechanical precision. So don't expect too much."[38]

GIs never did. Liaison officers groaned as Chinese soldiers wrecked one vital artillery piece after another through misuse or lack of maintenance. Personnel in Assam moaned when month-long efforts to train some 1,400 Chinese as truck drivers for the Ledo convoys ended in dismal failure. Such incidents were singled out as proof that what the Chinese lacked was not only experience and training, but even the least mental receptiveness to the logic of technology and scientific management. The Chinese who did possess that 'Western' quality were so few they were worth mentioning. An American surgeon at Kweiyang was happy to shower praise on Marshall T'ang of the Thirteenth Army: "In daily association with him for many months we found him to be highly intelligent and quick in making decisions, a Chinese who thought more like an American than any that we had found."[39]

"In war, numbers alone confer no advantage," Sun Tzu had said. "Do not advance relying on sheer military power." Had they known the ancient Chinese strategist's writings, American soldiers would have shrugged off his advice as hopelessly outdated. For GIs derived their pride – and sense of superiority – almost entirely from the way their military managed and applied America's material and technological might. It was a feeling that easily gave rise to condescension towards those who appeared to lag behind. "The commanding officers at Guadalcanal," wrote Ira Wolfert, "have learned to restrain civilized emotions when barefooted natives come trotting into camp. Exactly what the natives think of a civilization their first contact with which is the mechanized war bursting around them, remains locked . . . beneath their . . . skulls."[40]

To many soldiers the temptation to demonstrate exactly how much sway the shiny machinery gave them proved irresistible. An engineer, invited by a pilot to join him in a flight over the New Guinean coast in his dive bomber, wrote: "He hedge-hopped all along the beaches, scaring natives who were fishing and nearly taking off the roofs of houses in their villages." So frequently did planes 'buzz' villages in New Caledonia (stampeding cattle and cutting telephone lines in the process) that by the end of 1943 even the French acting governor was complaining about it to American authorities.[41]

When James Cook discovered Hawaii, a GI guide explained, the islanders, who worshiped many gods and had never seen a white man, believed the British captain to be a chief god or *Lono*. Americans did not find it hard to imagine themselves divine replacements of the Brits. In fact, divine power was exactly what several Melanesian peoples ascribed to the GIs. Americans were widely regarded by them as friendly, but also as violent. Their overpowering machinery and supplies, next to which even the material goods of the Europeans and Japanese paled, was considered irrefutable proof of the supernatural origin of their force. After the war, several island peoples adapted their most ancient oral traditions to incorporate a mythical land by the name of America. Many others adopted 'cargo cults,' believing that material wealth, and the power that came with it, could be obtained through ritual worship.[42]

Subjects of the age-old civilization of China knew better than to explain Americans as divinities, but that did nothing to undermine the GIs' profound sense of exceptionalism – and superiority. "I laughed as I saw the ancient means of cultivation," an American fighter pilot bragged as he took off from his Yunnan base in 1942 and looked down on the "coolie boys" plowing the terraced rice paddies with buffalo and "wooden scraper." "Again I found myself pitying these earthbound creatures. I said to myself: 'When you reach the end of that paddy, I'll be many miles from here.'"[43]

At the outbreak of the war, the Japanese had horrified Americans by dismissing them as decadent weaklings and by appointing their own kin sons of divinities. Gradually, however, that strident tone annoyed GIs more than it worried them. As they beat back the Imperial ships and planes that had once struck as far as Pearl Harbor, and found themselves pushed forward by infinite numbers of sturdy machines made in the USA, their sense of material achievement buried the enemy in contempt. In June 1944,

Robert Sherrod quoted a defiant General Hale on Kwajalein as saying, "But what have they done to retaliate for all we've done to them in the past year? Where is their carrier strike against Honolulu? I don't think they've got anything to do it with . . . Besides, the Japs can't build like we can. They haven't got anything that can touch the bulldozer."[44]

The bulldozer did more than build. Reports detailing enemy casualty figures increasingly cautioned that they did not include the Japanese dead in bunkers and caves – erased by the blunt blades of America's earth-scraping machines.[45]

By noisily grinding them into the earth, American bulldozers reduced the Japanese to the level of the stubborn fauna and flora around them. Beyond understanding and out of control, gloomy refuge of a savage enemy, wilderness, too, was to be plowed under. The first and most vital step in establishing dominance over nature was to chase away darkness and its many ghosts. To prevent the enemy from using the cover of night for infiltration and counterattacks, Americans kept the front lines lit with ever greater quantities of naval star shells. Canadian observers with the 27th Division on Saipan in 1944 noted that illumination projectiles were being used "on a lavish scale." "Most of the night was like daylight," Robert Sherrod reported from the Mariana island. With one ship to a regiment, by the time of the Okinawa campaign the US Navy was providing night illumination on the same basis as gunfire. Towards the end of that campaign, star shells were furnishing so much light that drivers claimed they did not have to turn on headlights.[46]

Americans in no time marked territory wrestled from the enemy by fierce lights of all kinds, often in blatant disdain for the nearby Japanese. Even while Finschhafen, New Guinea, was still suffering occasional night bombardments, one soldier in January 1944 claimed that "the harbor looked like the middle of Broadway at Christmas." A few months later, on his way to Sansapor in Dutch New Guinea, a battalion surgeon noted, "We passed one of our islands not far from Japanese territory last night and the lights were as flagrant and the glow of the sky as bright as Chicago's skyline as seen from Lake Michigan." "Two or three miles of the shore line was lighted up like a city," wrote an airplane mechanic whose ship had dropped anchor in Bougainville's Empress Augusta Bay in July 1944, "but we could see artillery fire in the distance, 12 or 15 miles away – after dark."[47]

In May 1945, marine dive-bombers on Okinawa began to fly at night. "Any light – a truck's headlights, a fire, a lighted doorway," remembered one pilot, "was to be fired on." As he looked down after take-off, American territory was lit up for miles. "It might have been California, or Memphis, or Pensacola. But the lights stopped suddenly in a ragged east-west line below Naha, and from there south the island was as black as a night sea. It was like an allegory – the good side full of light, and the evil side covered in darkness."[48]

A war of extermination was launched not only against darkness, but also against the vermin lurking in the shady wilderness. Men of the 608th Clearing Company in New Guinea, driven mad by the clouds of flies emerging from mud in the spring of 1944, at last were forced to take drastic measures. "We dug up 200 square feet of the ground," commented an exhausted GI, "digging down two feet, and filled that in with coral rock so we could add sand onto that and then keep it well oiled and raked."[49]

Steadily, however, the desperate struggle against pests evolved into a chemical war, with soldiers backed up by an arsenal of the most murderous weapons. "Trapping, poisoning, and burning or burying rats should be practiced," warned a September 1944 report in preparation for the invasion of Leyte. In February 1945, another report on the Philippines concluded that at least ten pounds of poison would be needed per thousand men per month to win the battle against rats in the islands. But of all the noxious creatures, it was insects, not rodents, that increasingly pushed American troops to retaliate with weapons of mass destruction. Soldiers armed themselves individually. With cans of insect powder liberally distributed by the military. With Freon bombs and pyrethrum sent from the home front. With Skat to blast mosquitoes. With Flit to annihilate bugs devouring jungle gardens. Heavier and heavier equipment was brought in for the war against pests. Things got so bad in the Burmese jungle during the monsoon season that surgical technicians had to stand by during operations in portable hospitals with hand pumps, at frequent intervals spraying the bugs that cluttered overhead lights. While stationed in Hawaii in the summer of 1943, the 40th Division had to call in fumigating trucks to fight bedbugs, running mattresses through the contraptions every two weeks.[50]

As neither powders, aerosol sprays, nor fumes managed to subdue the plagues, the US military began to seek retribution against flies and malaria-carrying mosquitoes through more aggressive chemical agents released from the air. The first reported account of planes spraying insecticides relates to an operation in February 1944, when L4-Bs dusted an area near the Markham River in New Guinea with Paris Green, a bright green powder, copper-based and highly poisonous. It was a colorless, odorless, water-insoluble agent, however, that became the most popular insecticide by far. Having cut loose from the labyrinthine kunai grass in which he had been lost for two hours at Oro Bay, New Guinea, a GI breathed a sigh of relief. "And," the satisfied soldier noted, "for an hour afterward I was constantly sprayed with DDT to rid me of the vermin." Oblivious to its toxic effects on humans, American forces sprinkled, sprayed, and poured DDT wherever they could. They applied it to captured enemy supply dumps, corpses, human feces. They used it in latrines, messes, and garbage areas. Planes released it in mixtures of diesel oil, lubricating oil, and gasoline.[51]

Reports on the first experiments from the air in the spring of 1944 talked of A-20s in the Pacific spraying "on the basis of a half pound of DDT per acre." Beachheads on the Palau Islands, Iwo Jima, and Okinawa were being treated as soon as the first landing waves had hit. On Peleliu, teams with portable sprayers were already ashore on D-Day. After having been "treated to the 'wonders of chemistry'" by a low-flying bomber several days earlier, an airman in the Marianas told his mother in February 1945, "The whole time I've been sitting in the tent writing this letter tonight, not a single insect has come in, with the light on and no screen door."[52]

In China, strenuous efforts were made to spread DDT over all ditches and rice paddies within a half-mile radius around each American base. In the two last months of 1944 alone, B-25s discharged 2,474 pounds of the newly developed chemical over airfields and bases in Assam, Burma, and southern India. Malaria control units in Leyte used DDT liberally in their systematic disinfection of all Filipino houses near American bases. Beginning in April 1945, C-47s doused the city of Manila with the agent in repeated three-day periods.[53]

And yet, despite all this, the battle against pests remained an uphill one. Dense jungle canopy and decaying vegetation on forest floors made much aerial spraying ineffective. In the summer of 1944, for instance, scrub typhus still managed to paralyze entire units on Owi and Biak, islands near Dutch New Guinea. Chemical processing companies had to be rushed in. Normally responsible for impregnating clothing for gas warfare, the specialist units feverishly switched to the miteproofing of uniforms with an emulsion of dimethyl phthalate, 100 gallons of which were needed per 1,000 men per month across New Guinea.[54]

While ever more fungicides, germicides, miticides, and insecticides were thus being dispensed by ever heavier equipment, plans for large-scale herbicidal warfare were accelerated too. Although never used, by 1945 the US military was seriously considering, for instance, the possibility of replacing explosives with ammonium thiocyanate in order to destroy the tropical vegetation that so vigorously continued to aid and abet the Japanese.

By the summer of 1945, chemical agents were on their way to the B-29 bomber bases in the Marianas for the express purpose of destroying food crops on the enemy's home islands. Only the end of the war prevented the destruction of Japan's rice plant, declared just another pest for no other reason than that it sustained a loathed enemy.[55]

The vicious conquest of earth's crust created gaping environmental scars. There was a limit to what even the most potent poisonous agents could accomplish. So American troops threw themselves against nature with muscle and mechanical power, too, hacking and slashing at it with the determination of a people for whom the memory of wrestling civilization from wilderness was all too vivid. In September 1944, more than half a year after the battle, Charles Lindbergh visited Roi, one of Kwajalein atoll's tiny islets.

"War is like a flame," he observed in his journal. "Where it sweeps, life disappears, the birds and the trees with the Japanese. We come with bulldozers and scrape over the surface until it is barren as a gold-dredged area."[56]

To create fields of fire, bulldozers uprooted dense undergrowth of brush and scrub. To deny snipers cover, they erased cane fields. To restore neglected airstrips, tractors mowed down kunai grass. But it was the jungle's tangled mass of vegetation that posed the most formidable challenge. A colonel in the Russell Islands wrote home, more with the voice of a colonial pioneer than that of an officer of the 43rd Division: "The jungles cannot be compared to the wildest forests in America. It rises an impenetrable wall, and every foot must be chopped, then burned and the task of planting commenced." Faced by this daunting foe, GIs fell back on their most powerful industrial arms. From the island of Espíritu Santo, an officer of the 350th Engineers, a poultry farmer in civilian life, described the wonders of American heavy equipment in building a supply depot. "The first thing that I had to do was to clear away a hole in the jungle to put the building so I requested a bulldozer and there it was in the morning. Next I wanted to put a post right where a huge coral rock happened to be so I sent for an air compressor and jack hammer and in a few minutes, it was out of the way. Then there was a big stump that had to be removed so I put the 3 sticks of dynamite under it and touched it off with an electric cap and that obstruction was scattered all over the jungle." "This is a great experience," he told his parents, "and I am learning a lot."

Tracked vehicles in no time managed to subdue environments thought untamable forever. On New Georgia, bulldozer operators continued to plow away even while under fire, protected by steel shields salvaged from wrecked enemy landing craft. In mountainous northern Luzon, American bulldozers forced roads through countryside in which the Japanese had been able to use only horses. For 2 months, 400 men, 6 bulldozers, 2 clamshells, and 20 dump trucks worked to carve a supply base out of Bougainville's virgin jungle. When they were done, they had cleared an area the size of "four large city blocks."[57]

Still more heavy machines were unleashed against the environmentally sensitive atolls of the Pacific. Tiny as the islands were, they acquired tremendous military significance as nature's "stationary aircraft carriers." Before they could fulfill their vital roles as launching pads against the enemy, however, they were to be thoroughly transformed. Supply depots and repair shops had to be built, ditches to be dug, roads to be constructed. More importantly, an array of smooth but hard airfields and runways was needed. Atolls abound in coral. The coarse substance is formed by the skeletons of minute spherical animals feeding on plankton washed in from the ocean, all part of a complex and fragile ecosystem. But engineers learned above all that coral was a perfect material for construction, ideal especially for the surfaces so badly desired by the air forces. Power shovels,

bulldozers, earthmovers, graders, and rollers feasted on coral that was quar-
ried, crushed, flattened and, where necessary, coated with asphaltic concrete. "I have seen," an airplane mechanic on Middleburg Island wrote in
September 1944, "the big diesel tractors pulling the earth-moving scrapers,
operating in water along the shore to a depth of as much as five feet."
Where reefs resisted quarrying, explosives were rushed in. When an Air
Force lieutenant arrived on Tinian in December 1944, the pace of engineers
constructing B-29 strips was frantic. "Their operations went on 24 hours a
day. The trucks hauling coral to construct four parallel landing strips on
the north end of the island were timed to arrive at intervals of seconds,
and no interruptions were allowed."[58]

GIs were determined to beat back the enemy from an untamed frontier
whose full potential he, nor the region's former inhabitants, had been able
to unlock. "Now the beaches swarmed with men and machinery," a GI
exalted as his ship pulled into New Guinea's Hollandia harbor in July 1944,
"roads were being built; camps erected. Probably more work had been done
in a few short weeks than the Japanese did in their more than two years of
occupation of this port." Ernie Pyle arrived in the Marianas early in 1945.
"Furious building was going on," he reported. "Planes arrived on schedule
from all directions as though it were Chicago Airport." "These islands," the
correspondent was content to predict, ". . . will never return to their former
placid life, for we were building on almost every inch of usable land."
   Flying in from Iwo Jima, a marine pilot, who touched down on Okinawa
when the battle was only a few weeks old, was hit in the face by the
"American energy and bustle." "It looked more," he gasped, "like a construction site or a highway project back home than like a battlefield –
slashes of raw earth everywhere, bulldozers, steamrollers, cities of tents and
temporary buildings, heaps of supplies." Markers on the road lining the
island's west coast soon proclaimed it the 'US 1.' "The way Americans can
build," Ernie Pyle estimated in the first week of the Okinawan campaign,
"this island can be transformed in two months. Before long it could look
like Guam or Pearl Harbor."[59]
   In their fury to force order on nature's unyielding chaos, American
troops went so far as to redraw the very contours of the stepping stones to
Japan. An airman in the Marianas was awestruck when, for the first time in
two months, he was able to leave camp again in March 1945. "I could
hardly recognize the geography," he told his parents in Missouri, "since so
many hills had been leveled and cuts made for the highway." Forced by
the Japanese, the Palauans had labored an entire year to build a single
airstrip at Airai. Following the invasion of 1944, Americans hewed a string
of airfields and bases from the archipelago in a matter of weeks. A Palauan
woman recalled that when she returned to Angaur, the place where she was
born, "It was a different island."[60]

11
Technological Destruction

Asia and the Pacific's tenacious resistance to control provoked not only heightened aggression by means of industrial tools, but also an escalation in the attritional use of military weaponry. The steady merging of the rage of humans with arms geared towards wholesale destruction increasingly enabled furious wishes of extermination to be executed in cold blood.[1]

It was the power of explosives that US troops harnessed first and foremost. American soldiers realized early in the war that the Japanese had difficulties bringing sufficient firepower to bear. Despite horrific naval bombardments by the enemy early in the Guadalcanal campaign, by February 1943 Mack Morriss was able to note, "We think his artillery is his most misused weapon – and I think he lives in fear of ours." Manuals on Japanese troops taught GIs that they possessed excellent mortars, but that their artillery was "deficient in number, caliber, and technical training." GIs in the field acknowledged this time and again. Marines on Saipan assured Robert Sherrod that the Japanese – routinely lobbing no more than three or four rounds into American lines with antiquated guns, then halting – did not know how to use artillery. In March 1945, a battalion surgeon in Luzon's Shimbu Line wrote that Japanese artillery prevented him from sleeping at night. But he added: "Thank goodness, they are rather poor with it and also have a lot of duds."[2]

Not only was Japanese artillery generally weak, as the protracted war eroded Japanese naval surface and air strength, so too did it hamper the production and supply of ammunition. For every ton of organic high explosives produced by Japan in 1944, US industries delivered nearly 26 tons. By 1945, Americans were matching every enemy ton with slightly more than 61 tons. Among American troops in the European theater of operations the rate for wounds caused by shell fire and flak was 55.25 per 1,000 per year. In the Southwest Pacific this rate was 15.47, in the Pacific Ocean Areas 11.36, and in China–Burma–India 2.18.[3]

From the outset of the war, American public opinion considered overwhelming firepower the best way of defeating Japan in the shortest time with the fewest casualties. The day after the attack on Pearl Harbor, a car-toon in the *Chicago Tribune* showed a teeth-clenched, muscled sailor walk up to a giant gun aimed at Japan. In his arms were two bulging bags of powder. They were labeled: "War without Mercy on a Treacherous Foe." The newspaper's caption was the military-industrial formula for victory: "Throwing in an Extra Charge."[4]

As the war dragged on, American forces overseas clamored for ever more extra charges. By the end of the campaigns in the Solomons and Papua New Guinea, early in 1943, GIs were convinced that what they needed to penetrate the jungle and destroy pillboxes was more and heavier artillery in the form of 105 mm and 155 mm guns, 81 mm mortars instead of 60 mm pieces, and medium Sherman tanks rather than the light Stuart armor. Before long, they were receiving all of this in quantities the enemy could hardly imagine. In defense of Hill 700 on Bougainville, for example, American artillery between 8 and 13 March 1944 supported the 37th Division with no less than 13,000 81 mm mortar shells, some 10,000 75 mm rounds, and almost 21,000 105 mm rounds.[5]

Meanwhile, naval gunners also began to flex their muscles with grim determination. During fire practice conducted by the USS *Montpelier* near the New Hebrides in January 1943, a sailor wrote, "the concussion is ter-rific. It makes the inside of your throat and chest feel like it was being ripped out." On the morning of 25 July 1943, naval gunfire in preparation for the 43rd Division's offensive against New Georgia's Lambeti Plantation reached a density of 70 rounds per 100 square yards. A dissatisfied Admiral Wilkinson later claimed 200 rounds had been needed.[6]

As the offensive in the Central Pacific got underway, it was decided to subject Japanese defenses to saturation bombing before landing troops. The first main objective was Tarawa atoll in the Gilberts, where Betio Island was large enough to support an airfield. One of the ranking naval officers is reported to have announced: "We do not intend to neutralize it, we do not intend to destroy it. Gentlemen, we will obliterate it." In some three hours, 3,000 tons of shells and bombs were dropped on Betio's 291 acres. Yet when troops reached the shore, the majority of the enemy's dug-in weapons were still in operation. The hurried conclusion was that future amphibious operations, in the words of historian Ronald Spector, "required more – more of everything."[7]

Intense preparatory bombardments for the Marshalls campaign lasted three days instead of three hours. On 1 February 1944, day of the landing, 7,000 14-inch, 8-inch, and 5-inch naval shells, 29,000 field artillery rounds (fired from nearby islets), and aerial bombs as heavy as 2,000 pounds plowed into Kwajalein Island alone. Although defended at least as heavily as Tarawa, Kwajalein atoll was taken at a much lower cost in lives.[8]

From that time on, the expenditure of explosives broke new records with almost every new campaign closer to Japan. Iwo Jima underwent 10 weeks of bombardments from air and sea prior to the landing on 19 February 1945. On D-Day itself, ships fired a staggering 38,550 5- to 16-inch shells into the island's 8 square miles. Two days later, Robert Sherrod reported from one of the supporting vessels that the fleet's salvos were still hitting the island "as fast as typewriter keys beating against a sheet of paper." Even then, however, troops had to fight for the heap of volcanic ash yard by yard for over a month.[9]

When troops were finally poised to enter the snake pit itself, they could count on fire support that appeared inexhaustible. In the three hours preceding the landing on 1 April 1945, Okinawa's beaches were ripped open by almost 45,000 shells of 5-inch and larger, 33,000 rockets, and more than 22,000 mortar shells, launched from a fleet of 200 vessels. "The power of the thing," Ernie Pyle wrote, "was ghastly." In addition to suffering merciless air attacks, Okinawa was pounded by tremendous artillery power massed on nearby islands. An average of 75 field guns to every mile of front was lined up in the morning of the landing. They dropped 19,000 rounds on the enemy's lines in just 40 minutes. "We fired for four nights straight," remembered a gunner whose 531st Field Artillery blasted its first salvos at dawn of the first day, "with practically no rest, except an hour or two which we caught during the night." Yet when the smoke lifted, the Japanese, deep in their caves and tunnels, appeared anything but crushed. The commanding general of the XXIV Corps Artillery later said he doubted the morning barrage had killed as many as 190 Japanese, or one for every 100 shells.[10]

Infantrymen became so accustomed to massive fire support that commanders feared they were growing too dependent on artillery. Because the dense jungle of New Georgia refused to reveal the opponent's location, GIs attacked the terrain instead, saturating even areas free of the enemy with mortar shells. Observers in the Philippines reported that when troops encountered more than minor resistance, they tended to fall back and call for fire support, prompting General Krueger, commander of the US Army combat forces on Leyte, to complain that the infantry expected artillerymen to do their work for them.[11]

American troops came to rely on large quantities of explosives in countless other ways. Impatient engineers routinely cleared jungle areas by dynamiting trees. By the time of the Biak and Kwajalein operations in 1944, GIs were using TNT charges of up to a thousand pounds to seal caves suspected of harboring stubborn Japanese defenders. Underwater demolition teams blew channels through coral to allow landing and supply craft to reach beaches. On Saipan, for example, divers placed some 105,000 pounds of explosives in a reef to blast a passage for tanks. GIs across the Pacific eventually thought nothing even of employing blocks of TNT to catch fish. When crocodiles hampered bathing and swimming in the Solomon Islands, marines used so many hand grenades against the armored reptiles that orders had to be issued prohibiting the expenditure of explosives for this purpose.[12]

The effects of so much explosive power were astounding. The combined fury of naval, air, and artillery bombardments made Kwajalein Island look to one observer "as if it had been picked up to 20,000 feet and then dropped." "The beach itself," wrote a marine who had landed on Peleliu in September 1944, "was as desolate a place as I ever hope to see. It reminded me of some last war picture of a flat waste in France, after a prolonged shelling." As far as two miles off shore, the rumbling concussions ravaging Corregidor in March 1945 made the USS *Montpelier*'s steel tremble.[13]

Firepower targeted landscape as much as humans, as blasts blew away vegetation and churned earth to get at the fanatical foe underneath. By the third day of fighting on Betio, the islet was "bare except for the stumps of the trees." "For approximately the depth of two city blocks back from the shore," observed a soldier on New Britain's Yellow Beach, "not a leaf remained on a tree in what had once been dense jungle." All that was left of lush Wakde Island, off the coast of Dutch New Guinea, was "a strip of yellow desert – misplaced in a blue tropic sea." At Munda, so many trees of New Georgia's dark jungle had been reduced to "naked sticks pointing upwards" that only the night could offer GIs relief from the sweltering sun.[14]

Before long, Americans believed that explosives gave them the very power to change earth at will. When in the spring of 1942 the Mauna Loa erupted on the island of Hawaii, and lava flowed towards the city of Hilo, B-17s were sent over to drop bombs in the crater and divert the flow. The effort had little effect, but if spewing volcanoes were hard to rein in, Americans found it ever easier to blast earth's quieter folds into obedience. Lone Tree Hill, for example, a misnamed coral mass in Dutch New Guinea's Maffin Bay, covered with dense rain forest, paid a terrible price for harboring the enemy. In the Army's official history of the battle, fought in the late spring of 1944, a footnote to the description of the natural setting cautioned: "The past tense is used in this paragraph because the entire cast of the terrain in the Lone Tree Hill area was changed during the next two months by continuous artillery and air bombardment." "There's no use giving you a sightseer's guide to the Nansei Shoto," the GI *Guide to Okinawa* said with resigned arrogance, "because after the navy and the air forces have blasted the way for a landing on those islands, they just won't look the same."[15]

A power that could move mountains inevitably wreaked horrific devastation on mere mortals. In the first days of the Leyte invasion in October 1944, American fire was allowed to fade slightly only after dark. After the landing, a blurred sentence in a Japanese soldier's captured diary, translated by 7th Division intelligence, read: "I feel alive during the night and dead during the day." Still, no matter how great their losses and how numbed their minds, Japanese troops seldom refused to crack under fire. On 6 June 1945, Admiral Ota from Okinawa sent a communiqué to his superiors in Tokyo. In it he apologized for not having been able to defend the Empire more successfully.

But he stressed: "Fierce bombing and bombardments may deform the mountains of Okinawa but cannot alter the loyal spirit of our men."[16]

For civilians not steeped in military honor, American firepower brought nothing but suffering. In the Marianas, Tinian Town was reduced to "a maze of concrete foundations and open-top cisterns." Garapan was such a mass of rubble that street fighting in the Saipan town proved near impossible. Suicidal resistance from Japanese troops in the concrete heart of Manila eventually forced American commanders to order their artillery to level everything except churches and hospitals if they were known to contain civilians. Even that last distinction could not always be made. With some 12,000 rounds, roughly 230 tons of explosives, Americans all but razed Intramuros, the ancient Walled City of Manila. On Okinawa, Americans dropped leaflets telling civilians to identify themselves by wearing white to avoid being strafed and bombed. Naha, the island's largest town, was laid to waste; villages and towns like Kakazu, Dakeshi, Kochi, Arakachi, and Kunishi leveled to the ground; Shuri, ancient capital of the Ryukyus, struck by at least two hundred thousand rounds, transformed into a "crater of the moon."[17]

From at least as early as the Gilberts campaign in 1943, overburdened American medical units proved inadequate to care for wounded civilians. As a result of the prelanding bombardment, during the first days of the Leyte campaign, medics treated more Filipinos than they did GIs. In the 7th Division sector, for example, 75 percent of the medical facilities of the sole clearing company in operation were used to care for civilian casualties.[18]

The rows of dead formed even more horrifying spectacles. Some 22,000 civilians on Saipan died. An estimated 100,000 civilians lost their lives in the battle for Manila. Figures on Okinawa's civilian casualties range from 80,000 to 160,000, one third of the population. Although the causes of death varied, many fell victim to indiscriminate firepower, or what the Okinawans called the "typhoon of steel."[19]

Horrific as the effects of these artificial typhoons were, the sense of power they conveyed could be exhilarating to American soldiers. As a forward observer watched from his LST how the heavy naval and air bombardment tore the invasion beaches of Noemfoor to shreds in July 1944, he experienced "a sort of fierce exultation in my breast." "It gave me a beautiful feeling," he wrote, "to see such a display of might and to know this is only a fraction of the power America possesses." But also, he confessed, "a feeling of satisfaction to know that little yellow men are in there taking the brunt of this – a part payment for some of the suffering and agony they have caused."[20]

Stiffened with enough bile, power-induced adrenaline proved frighteningly murderous. An artillery lieutenant of the 43rd Division was pleased with the amount of close support he had been able to give "our boys" when the going had been tough in Luzon. "We were constantly in demand," he wrote, "and fired thousands of rounds." "I'm becoming," he noted coldly, "something of an expert at mass killing."[21]

Neither distance nor thick steel separating American soldiers from the hated foe could quell such rage. When feeling low, a sailor aboard the destroyer *Howorth* forced himself to picture what it would mean for America, and its women in particular, if Japan claimed victory. "And consequently," he wrote to his wife, "I get a joy out of being the man that holds a piece of iron in his hands that helps kill them. I don't shoot a gun, no one does the actual firing on here. We *all* do it." By the time he was involved in the battle for Iwo Jima, the same sailor had but one regret: "I only wish I were in close enough to see their bodies and parts of bodies go sky high when our shells hit."[22]

Despite the tremendous destruction that blast was able to wreak, American troops feverishly searched for still more efficient ways to subjugate the unyielding enemy. Relentlessly, US military technology began to harness one of nature's most primitive and vicious forces – fire. Flames had cast a spell on man from the very beginning and continued to do so. In the winter of 1945, GIs from a quartermaster unit paid a guided visit to Calcutta. "The biggest event of the day," a lieutenant wrote to his family, was a stop at the "Hindu burning grounds." "There we actually saw several bodies being consumed by fire – it wasn't exactly a pleasant sight, but I was so interested that I didn't pay much attention to the unpleasantness." Spontaneous fascination with fire's all-consuming power had always gone hand in hand with instinctive fear. GIs unfortunate enough to witness one of the many accidents with white phosphorus ammunition, initially intended mainly for smoke screens, would never forget the horrors brought on by its burning chemicals. Early in 1944, an explosion startled men of the 244th Port Company in New Guinea. They rushed to where the blast had come from. There they found a GI splattered from head to toe with the chemical of a phosphorus grenade. No one knew how to put out what was searing its way through the soldier's flesh. The blankets they wrapped the victim in caught fire. The soldier burned to death at their feet. The horrible scene left the men "physically ill and shaken" for days. "It was sights like this," reflected a marine who saw a similar thing happen to an American soldier on Iwo Jima, "that made a man wonder if mankind were really civilized that he had to use such tools to understand himself."[23]

Yet, increasingly, tools of fire were exactly what American troops preferred to use against all that was threatening and incomprehensible in the alien environment of Asia and the Pacific. For fire was much more than a weapon of destruction. It was also a means of purification. Nothing cleansed front lines and camp areas more radically and thoroughly from their noxious pests, for instance, than scorching flames. To eradicate once and for all the Hawaiian bedbugs terrorizing Schofield Barracks, desperate soldiers of the 40th Division at last resorted to burning them out of the mattress coils. Troops on Owi Island lit aviation fuel to rid their tent areas of hordes of large red ants. On Leyte, furious infantrymen poured gasoline from five-gallon cans into their foxholes, igniting the flammable puddles with matches to exterminate clouds of mosquitoes. One dark night on Guadalcanal in 1945, armies of huge land crabs suddenly descended from the hills as if on command. Before they reached the sea, they overran the camps of marines preparing for the invasion of Okinawa. The veterans fought back. Gasoline was rushed in. Before long there rose from the battlefield "flashing bursts of flames."[24]

The situation was much more desperate in New Guinea, however, when in the summer of 1944 a deadly form of typhus swept through the ranks of GIs on the main island and offshore islets. Found out to be transmitted by mites hiding in dense undergrowth, the only way to eliminate the pests that had shown to withstand even DDT was to unleash a fire war. All bivouac areas were cleared, and for weeks dark clouds billowed from brush, grass, and dead wood systematically torched. It was in parched terrain that scrub typhus was eventually halted.[25]

But dense canopy and undergrowth hid creatures slier and deadlier than even the most venomous mites. Japanese soldiers had turned camouflage into a science and an art, making the best of an environment often as alien to them as it was to their enemy. Americans were left with only one powerful answer to the natural screens that explosives failed to wipe away. As early as the Guadalcanal campaign, GIs were burning grassy planes and dense vegetation to allow infantry and artillery to spot attackers in time and bring down firepower on them unhampered. In 1944, both the 27th Division and the 2nd Marine Division, training in Hawaii for war in the Marianas, diligently studied the methods of setting fire to sugar cane and moving through the blackened fields. But even before these troops set foot on the islands, many of their cane fields were, noted Robert Sherrod, "burning merrily." Yellowish clouds swirled over Saipan's cane, ignited by the US Navy with phosphorus shells, now increasingly used for incendiary purposes. Two days before the invasion of nearby Tinian, P-47s dropped fire bombs that contained a mixture of gasoline and gel – the first napalm bombs used in the Pacific war. Although they, too, failed to burn the islands' hardy trees, which had been resisting both phosphorus and thermite, napalm's spectacular effectiveness against cane and underbrush assured its increased use.[26]

If flames could lick through the thickest underbrush and wipe out even microscopic mites, then surely they could force their way into the ports, slits, and vents of strongholds impervious to blast. Surely they could also incinerate the most stubborn enemy within. No matter how deep-seated the human dread of fire unleashed, GIs found themselves ruthlessly sucked in by the hopeful logic of flame.

The American portable flamethrower, holding five gallons of fuel, made its first successful combat appearance on 15 January 1943 at Guadalcanal. It eliminated three particularly stubborn bunkers within half an hour. That some Japanese soldiers actually tried to flee the inferno impressed the Americans at least as much. To have found a weapon that could apparently scare the enemy before it killed him was deemed remarkable. As if Japanese were not earthly creatures who shared the natural fear of fire, but demons who could be exorcised by extraordinary means only.[27]

From that day on, American reliance on the flamethrower continued to grow. "All men fear fire," a chemical officer in New Guinea observed early in 1943. "But there are degrees of fear." And he was convinced "the Japanese fear was beyond normal." Half a year later already, the flamethrower was used on no fewer than 54 occasions in the first 6 weeks on New Georgia. Fuel thickened with napalm soon enabled the flames to be thrown as far as 50 yards. When even mechanized flame weapons could not reach into the caves of Peleliu's Umurbrogol Pocket in 1944, engineers attached long hoses to fuel tanks, activated booster pumps, and sprayed the Japanese positions "much as firemen direct water on burning buildings." "All night," a marine on the island wrote, "occasional shifts of wind blew the nauseating smell of burning flesh our way." When, suddenly, his ears caught "muffled screams" soaring from a stronghold with the flames, he took much courage from them. "Even the stoic Japanese," he was pleased to note, "couldn't suppress the agony of death by fire and suffocation."[28]

Whereas tropical humidity made many devices malfunction in the Southwest Pacific, the enthusiasm for the flamethrower in the Central Pacific soon knew no bounds. Each Army division slated for the Marianas in 1944 received 141 portables, each Marine division 81. By 1945, a marine division could count on no less than 243 sets. "They have a lot of cut up country in the rocky edges of the island and a lot of holes to hide in," a sailor wrote to his wife during the battle for Iwo Jima, "but you know the Marines and the Army. They just love those new flamethrowers." And he hastened to add: "I do too." Before the rains set in on Okinawa, flame tanks alone had spit 75,000 gallons of burning fuel at the enemy.[29]

Fire's indiscriminate power permitted American troops to define the enemy rather broadly. In the process of consuming pests, vegetation, and soldiers, flames easily engulfed civilians, too. They had already devoured Indian camps all the way from the Narragansets to the Cheyennes in North America's frontier war. They had just as greedily licked at Filipino villages and crops in America's colonial war. Half a century later, they continued to eat their way through settlements across Asia and the Pacific. In January 1944, an officer in New Britain was shot by an inhabitant of Tauali. Marines retaliated by burning the village to the ground. Likewise, OSS units raiding behind Japanese lines in Burma punished "unfriendly" villages by setting fire to them. A company of the 305th Infantry in Leyte pushed into Abijao on 30 December 1944. It snuffed out weak Japanese resistance, then torched the Filipino town "to prevent its reoccupation." When snipers in buildings at Nafutan Point opened up on the 1st Battalion, 105th Infantry, GIs responded by burning the Saipanese settlement to the ground, "flame throwers joining in the arson."[30]

Constant fear of ambushes and snipers led to an almost systematic torching of Okinawan houses – or 'huts' as Americans preferred to call them. Even flame tanks were called in to set fire to villages. Early in June 1945, 81 mm mortars brought a blistering barrage of white phosphorus shells down on the village of Tera. Marines uncovered few enemy soldiers in the area afterwards, but they did find numerous dazed and mutilated civilians among the ruins. "You can't use water on it," recalled a medic who saw too many Okinawans smolder with phosphorus, "just Vaseline, but the Okinawans didn't have any – or anything else. So lots of them just burned and burned." Men of the 96th Division chose to put at least one of them out of his misery with a bullet. Even the war against Japan was never entirely without mercy.[31]

Whereas the scarcity of flamethrowers among Japanese troops seemed to confirm their pathological dislike of fire, American soldiers constantly lived in fear of poison gas, the one weapon they thought particularly suited for so treacherous, and ever more desperate, an enemy. After all, the Japanese were known to have used toxic gas in the Chinese war, and American posters denouncing this had made sure to show victims with horrible skin wounds.[32]

The atmosphere surrounding this weapon of mass destruction was nervous from the very beginning. The 40th Division arrived in Hawaii in September 1942 to help defend the islands. "All of them," a lieutenant wrote to his parents in California, "even the smallest kinnygarden kids, carry their gas masks with them." In the first months of the battle for Guadalcanal, on several occasions the Japanese sent over smoke screens accompanied by false yells of 'Gas!' An airplane mechanic on Fiji, readying himself for the move to Guadalcanal in July 1943, wrote in his diary: "We have tested our gas-masks again in a gas chamber and are well prepared for gas attack." While masks and impregnated clothing rapidly disintegrated in the heat and humidity, one gas scare followed another in the Pacific. "Radio Tokyo has inferred that Owi Island is to be subjected to a gas attack," Charles Lindbergh wrote in his journal in August 1944. "There is a general overhauling of gas masks and other equipment."[33]

As the Americans inched ever closer to Japan, tension surrounding gas war mounted. "Will the Japs use gas?" an engineer in New Guinea wondered after having listened to a lecture from a chemical warfare officer in April 1943. "In the immediate future I think not," he replied. "Before the end of the war, absolutely." Polls published by the Army in January 1945 showed that two-thirds of air service personnel in the Pacific thought it a distinct likelihood that the Japanese would use gas against American troops. Soldiers boarding C-47s in India for the trip over the Hump to China early in 1945 were subjected to severe weight restrictions, but gas masks were not among the items they left behind. For the invasion of Luzon in 1945, GIs had their masks waterproofed; they were also issued gas capes. Marines destined for Okinawa tested and retested their masks. They packed special hoods, designed to crouch under if "sprayed with mustard gas." In the first week on Okinawa, a gas scare broke out in the 383rd Infantry when GIs saw exploding Japanese mortar shells release "a queer greenish smoke." Battalion commanders had to intervene to calm the line companies and set them straight.[34]

Unknown to American troops, the Japanese in fact became less willing, and less able, to use gas as the war wore on. The threat of retaliation from an enemy who increasingly dominated the air was one factor; diminishing resources and facilities to produce and distribute war gases another. Ironically, amidst unabated fears of Japanese poison attacks, it was the Americans who saw the taboo on gas war erode in their own minds. The US had not signed any international agreement outlawing the military use of gas, but public opinion as well as military leaders had emerged from World War I with a strong aversion to the horror weapon. Moreover, after Pearl Harbor, President Roosevelt made it clear that the American policy concerning gas war would be one of retaliation only. Yet among American troops in the Pacific the thought of initiating a gas war was being entertained at least as early as the Guadalcanal campaign. In October 1942, when news from the Solomon island filtering into South Pacific garrisons was grim, rumors about all kinds of emergency measures flew back and forth. "Also claim," said an officer in New Caledonia, "to have in Australia a new gas that can be sprayed from a plane at 20,000 ft. However all the experts feel that gas warfare wouldn't be too effective in this Island Warfare because of the shifting winds."[35]

With apparently only a fickle breeze separating the enemy from American poison gas at the outset of the war, soldiers, as the war grew ever more ferocious, were easily swayed to take the escalating exterminationist logic of blast and fire yet one step further. Troops engaged in desperate cave warfare on Biak in 1944, for instance, were treading a thin line when they set gasoline on fire in tunnels for the express purpose of producing "harassing fumes." That line had virtually vanished when they also began placing smoke pots in windward cave openings. To be sure, none of these smokes, designed for the purpose of creating protective screens for troops, were classified as poison gas. But chemical officers knew full well that in enclosed spaces they were just as lethal.[36]

By the time American troops were fighting frighteningly costly battles on Japan's very doorstep, ever louder voices rose in favor of using poison gas outright. Both the media and certain military leaders had been clamoring for it since the bloody battle of Tarawa in 1943. Unknown to public and troops, a report on the subject of poisonous chemicals to be used against Iwo Jima had already been drafted by June 1944. It talked of severing all of the enemy's communications before inundating the entire island with gas. The plan was never executed. But on 4 May 1945, a private of the 8th Marines on Okinawa wrote to his parents, well aware that the winds might shift against him: "Seems the end is in sight in Germany. If they would only use gas, it would be over here. Tho it is bad, it isn't much worse than white phosphorus."[37]

Desperate measures were needed in a desperate war. Indeed, despite America's tremendous industrial weight and technological superiority, the war in Asia continued to look like a war without end. Euphoria in Europe did nothing to change that harsh reality. "Guess people back there are celebrating V.-E. of Germany," a private wrote to his parents on 28 May 1945. "That's good news, but my war's over here." Two weeks later he lay dead on Okinawa.[38]

"What was distressing," said a surgeon on garrison duty in Manila when the news of Germany's surrender arrived, "was the fact that it was as bad as we had expected – that every inch of Germany had to be conquered before the war would end." That did not augur well at all for the war against the fiercely fanatical Japanese. Meanwhile, Allied successes in the Old World also reawakened anxieties of abandonment among American troops on the far western frontier. GIs in Asia and the Pacific were haunted by the thought that people at home, eager to get their lives back on track, would forget about them as they slogged away forever. As Allied armies raced towards Germany in September 1944, a disquieted sailor wrote home: "I sincerely hope that the American people realize that when Germany does collapse that the war then is only half won, for we will still have a long way to go in the Pacific. I fear, 'though, that most of them will assume it's all over and with a big celebration will expect to return immediately to normal peacetime living." Late in June 1945, a lieutenant aboard the USS *Rolette* implored his family in Tennessee, as well as the American public at large, not to become too optimistic and to let down their guard, as it risked dragging out the war even more. "They won't quit when their little islands are blasted to bits," he warned. "They have vast production centers in Manchuria and Korea. Check in a history book and see how long they have had those areas under control. They have not been sitting idle during that time."[39]

Soldiers could not even begin to fathom the time it would take to conquer all of the vast expanses occupied by Japan. En route to the US in August 1944, after the battle of Tinian, a sailor of the USS *Montpelier* calculated in his journal, "When we come out here again . . ., we should hit Borneo, Java, Bali, Singapore, Philippines, China and of course Japan."

"It won't be long before Burma is mopped up," a soldier in Ceylon tried to sound upbeat in May 1945, "then there is Thailand, Singapore, Sumatra, Borneo." Apart from the invasion of Japan, nothing was more worrisome to GIs than the prospect of a large-scale campaign in monstrous China. As late as the summer of 1944, General Stilwell admitted to the American press that he could see no change in the high quality of the Japanese soldier in his theater of war. Disheartening news of enemy advances in China continued to reach American troops in the Pacific until early 1945. "This week all hands were given cholera shots," a nervous sailor in Subic Bay wrote in June 1945. "Cholera is very common in China." On 7 August 1945, distressed men of a port company in Luzon considered the distribution of pamphlets on China "a logical indication that operations will begin there shortly, and that we may be included." "There are rumors," one of them wrote in his diary with sunken heart, "of a strike next month."[40]

But it was the bloody struggle for Japan's "little islands" in the Pacific that had most American soldiers transfixed. On these islands more than anywhere else, Japanese soldiers were vividly demonstrating how material abundance was to be negated by the power of will. "They built underground so well," Robert Sherrod said of the Japanese on Iwo Jima, "that they all but nullified our superior firepower. We could bomb and shell until our guns sizzled and our pilots dropped." Worse still, ever since the *kamikaze* strikes, there existed among GIs a fear of even deadlier enemy combinations of spirit and machine to come, dreadful Japanese versions of the *Vergeltungswaffen*, to be used against Americans as they approached the homeland. In the fall of 1944, rumors on Biak Island whispered that 15 American bombers had been downed over Borneo by "a new Jap interceptor." "There are always stories cropping up about secret weapons," one soldier on the island noted nervously. Troops on Japan's doorstep were astounded to find enemy artillery suddenly much improved and deadlier. In the battle for Okinawa, they encountered Japanese guns in greater quantity, size, and variety than in any previous Pacific campaign. It was artillery, in fact, that contributed in a large measure to the high number of combat fatigue cases on the island. Some months earlier already, on Iwo Jima, Americans had been fired at not only by more rockets than ever before, but by spigot mortars as big as 320 mm. "It seemed odd," noted a suspicious Robert Sherrod, "that the miniature-loving Japs would suddenly come up with so prodigious a weapon."[41]

Whether by spirit or machine, the Japanese, while falling back, were extracting mounting casualties from the Americans. 'Home Alive in '45,' the optimists had once believed. On 15 July 1944, at the end of the battle for Saipan, a sailor wrote in his journal: "We lost 2500, 2000 missing and 13,000 wounded. Every campaign our casualties get higher." "Mom," a radioman of the USS *O'Bannon* wrote in November 1944, "these Japs will never cry for peace, they have to be beaten to their backs then stomped.

I never saw such fools in my life. That is why they predict a long war out here and it will be, we have an awful long way to go yet." 'Out of the Sticks in '46,' claimed a revised prediction. Total American losses on Iwo Jima early in 1945 were close to 27,000. 'Hell to Heaven in '47,' ran a new, more desperate cry. The capture of Okinawa in mid-1945 cost more than 49,000 American casualties. 'Golden Gate in '48' now sounded the GIs' best hope. American forces in the Pacific lost more lives in the battles of the first six months of 1945 than they did during the previous three years in that theater. In May 1945, estimates in the American press began to insist that half a million to a million more GIs would die before the war in the Pacific was over. "No one who was not there," a sailor of the USS *Suwanee* later wrote, "will ever understand how fatalistically we viewed the invasion of Japan."[42]

With B-29s pounding Japan from Iwo Jima, and American troops firmly on Okinawa, Ernie Pyle wrote: "One main question asked over here now is, 'How long will the Japs hold out?' There are all kinds of opinions, but nobody really knows. We don't know because no one in his right mind can pretend to understand the Oriental manner of thinking."[43]

Made weary by an enigmatic foe who appeared to have on his side both space and time, American soldiers desperately grasped at reinforcements of any kind as the gaping emptiness pulled them in ever deeper. In July 1944, rumors in a squadron of the Thirteenth Air Force insisted that Japanese troops were being rushed to the Manchurian border in response to Russian mobilizations. "This," an excited lieutenant wrote in his diary, "sounds too good to be true." It was, but hopeful Americans never abandoned the close monitoring of Soviet moves. "I can hardly wait," a sailor on the USS *Admiralty Islands* told his family in January 1945, "to buy each day's paper to see how far the Russians are from Berlin." Meanwhile, a destroyer sailor, caught up in the bitter struggle for the Philippines, was looking still else-where for support. "The British fleet is on its way out to help now," he assured his wife as much as himself, "and I think China and Britain will furnish the ground forces to retake China, that is if Germany folds soon."[44]

Although they feared that victory in Europe might cause a letdown at home, soldiers in Asia and the Pacific logically assumed it would send much needed additional troops their way. That is why they were anxious to see war on the other side of the world come to an end as soon as possible. So anxious, that on 18 March 1945 wild celebrations erupted on Iwo Jima when word was leaked that Germany had surrendered. By the time the news was found out to be premature, several soldiers had become casualties of their own jubilant barrages. Sobered troops instantly returned to the dangerous task of mopping up Japanese soldiers still holding out on the northwestern part of the island.[45]

When, almost two months later, tidings of the Axis surrender in Europe were officially confirmed at last, of great expectations among GIs in the Pacific War quickly remained only the most cautious optimism. American veterans of the European war made it clear that the only place they wanted to go was home. Moreover, readying them for the war against Japan and shipping them to the Pacific would take months at best. America's allies, too, appeared rather lackadaisical in diverting their energies to Asia and the Pacific. The day after the news of Germany's surrender, yet another false rumor of a Soviet attack on Japan made the rounds, this time aboard the USS *Dayton*. "I'll be surprised if she has at this early date," a lieutenant hoped against hope, "but disappointed if she doesn't in the near future." Two days later, a galled airman in India told his parents, "I am in favor of letting the [Brits] finish off the Japs, then they can say that they helped." On 12 May 1945, a soldier reported from faraway Ceylon: "After Germany's surrender the news here has tapered off to the same old thing. Maybe the European armies will be sent here . . . At least there is talk of returning even though it may be a matter of years for us."[46]

Where American soldiers ultimately looked to for a speedy deliverance from the evils of war in the heart of Asia was the sky. In August 1943, not long after his boat, PT-109, was sunk by the Japanese while on patrol off the Solomon Islands, lieutenant John F. Kennedy wrote: "When I read that we will fight the Japs for years if necessary and will sacrifice hundreds of thousands if we must – I always like to check from where he is talking – it's seldom out here." In the same angry letter, however, he took comfort: "Perhaps all of that won't be necessary – and it can all be done by bombing."[47]

As US bases multiplied, from the coral islands to the fields prepared by Chinese coolies, and as Japanese aircraft dwindled, soldiers and sailors drew courage from American planes roaming the skies with ever more impunity. From their wings and bellies they showered the hostile environment below with increasing quantities of anything from high explosives to DDT. If some GIs imagined aircraft one day spraying poison gas if necessary, then experiments with fire rained on front lines from the air became reality as early as July 1944, when P-47s dropped napalm bombs on Tinian not only to destroy vegetation, but also to burn to death Japanese soldiers in open trenches and dugouts. From that summer on, the use of fire bombs against tactical targets rapidly escalated. What had once been a novelty, American ground troops soon grew inured to as fighter-bomber aircraft routinely came to the rescue with M47, M50, and M69 incendiaries, aimed at enemy strongholds, motorized vehicles, troop concentrations, and military stores from altitudes no higher than 50 to 100 feet. Fire bombs filled with napalm-thickened gasoline proved especially effective. They were in great demand from the mainland of Asia to the smallest islands of the Pacific. Used in combination with regular incendiary and high explosive bombs, napalm lay waste, for instance, to many a town in Burma and China suspected of storing, in its wooden buildings, supplies useful to Japanese troops. During the operations in the Philippines, American air forces over the island of Luzon alone dumped on the enemy a total of 1,054,200 gallons of gasoline thickened with napalm gel.[48]

Few GIs wanted to know where the almost 70,000 gallons of napalm ended up that failed to be placed on target in Luzon – or whether the other million gallons managed to distinguish between Filipino civilians and Japanese soldiers. Likewise, few raised questions about what happened to its inhabitants when 20 percent of the Chinese town of Paoching was destroyed by American fire bombs early in 1945. American troops had witnessed the effects of indiscriminate bombings amidst the fury of war as early as the Solomons campaigns in 1942–3. They had stopped asking questions long since. For two days in a row, American planes bombed villages on the Solomon island of Malaita. No Japanese troops were near, but at least 24 indigenous people, mostly children, died. "The whole village was on fire," inhabitants of Laulasi Island later recounted. "People just ran naked and swam to the nearest islands, to the reefs and to the mainland." Enraged islanders from Santa Isabel threatened to cease their intelligence activities in the Solomons unless the Allies guaranteed there would be no more bombardments of their villages. "In reading the reports," naval air historian John Lundstrom has commented, "I get the impression that little thought was given to warning the pilots of the presence of friendly natives. They had leave to attack everything they thought might be military objectives without determining whether the Japanese were actually present."[49]

When American aircraft were at last able to carry destruction to the very heart of the enemy's empire, callous neglect of noncombatants at and near the front quickly made way for a ruthless targeting of civilians. By the summer of 1945, carrier-based planes as well as fighters and bombers belonging to the Fifth Air Force were flying tactical sorties over Japan. They attacked airfields, factories, railroads, bridges, and what was described as "other such targets of opportunity." Some reconnaissance fighters reported having strafed civilians in fields and roads. When the Japanese government announced that men and women, old and young, would be called up for home defense, the Fifth Air Force's intelligence officer was swift to declare in July 1945 that "the entire population of Japan is a proper Military Target . . ., THERE ARE NO CIVILIANS IN JAPAN." "We are making War," he grimly defended the decision, "and making it in the all-out fashion which saves American lives."[50]

Already much earlier, however, GIs had begun to believe that it was the indiscriminate strategic bombing of Japanese cities that might succeed best in reducing American casualties by weakening, perhaps even breaking, enemy resistance. On 14 June 1944, B-29s of the XX Bomber Command launched their first strike against Japan from airfields in China. More than 60 of the brand-new, ultraheavy bombers attacked the large iron and steel works at Yawata on the island of Kyushu. Two days later, news of the feat of the "Super Flying Fortresses," as one sailor called them, reached the USS

Montpelier off the coast of Saipan. It gave the crew a tremendous boost on the second day of furious fighting for the Mariana island, as "a big cheer went up when the announcement came over the loudspeaker."[51]

By November 1944, the Mariana Islands themselves had been transformed into launching pads for B-29s that could now reach Tokyo and all other important cities of the Japanese island of Honshu. But neither from China nor from the Marianas did B-29 precision bombing of key industrial targets prove very effective. Then, under the new leadership of General Curtis LeMay, the XXI Bomber Command on the Marianas switched to incendiary attacks against Japanese cities in January 1945. By destroying entire city sections, B-29s could get at factories, home-based workshops, and military installations in one sweep, simultaneously putting tremendous psychological pressure on the enemy. As up to 80 percent of construction in Japan's compact urban areas consisted of wood and paper, fire was deemed the perfect weapon for mass destruction.

On 4 February 1945, 69 bombers dropped nearly 160 tons of incendiaries on Kobe and destroyed 2.5 million square feet of the city. A sergeant from the 23rd Field Hospital, enraged by evidence of Japanese atrocities committed against helpless Filipinos, wrote to his mother on 22 February: "I hope to HELL that Tokio and all of Japan and EVERY Jap is completely destroyed in return for the destruction and sufferings they have caused. There can be no pity on the Japs and that goes for women and children . . . Tokio should be completely demolished even if it has to be finished by Engineers after the war is over. A pile of bricks and graves which once was Tokio should be the Monument to this Second World War."[52]

His prayers began to be answered within days. On 25 February 1945, 172 B-29s attacked a section of Tokyo with 453 tons of fire bombs, burning some 27,000 buildings. It was early in March when the Japanese capital fell victim to 279 B-29s in the most devastating fire raid of the war. American soldiers eagerly tracked the escalating destruction rained down by the awe-inspiring bombers. "TOKYO burning after 1000 tons of incendiaries dropped on 10th," the commander of the 45th Engineers in Burma scribbled in his diary on 12 March, "claim 15 acres at least destroyed." Impressed though he was, the engineer seriously underestimated the damage done to Tokyo, which in the night of 9 to 10 March had in fact been hit by more than 1,600 tons of fire bombs that destroyed some 15 square miles of the city, consuming 250,000 buildings, and killing almost 90,000 people. *Time* magazine called it "a dream come true," as the raid had proved once and for all that "properly kindled, Japanese cities will burn like autumn leaves."[53]

An airman in the Marianas excitedly perused the clippings his parents had sent regarding the Tokyo inferno caused by the XXI Bomber Command to which he belonged. Here was a man at last, he wrote of General LeMay, on the day American troops landed on Okinawa, who "wasn't afraid to take

260 The GI War against Japan

the responsibility for seemingly radical tactics." In doing so, he had "won a great victory – and with even fewer losses than ever."[54]

So systematically were LeMay's new tactics applied to other Japanese cities in the wake of the Tokyo success, that by the end of March stocks of incendiaries were exhausted. New ones were rushed to B-29 bases within weeks. In May 1945, the first raid of 500 bombers was launched against Tokyo, leaving more than half the capital gutted. In mid-June, when all of Japan's largest cities had been virtually destroyed, the American offensive switched to provincial centers as its main targets, eventually destroying or damaging almost 60 of them. "It doesn't seem," a nurse in India wrote on 21 June, "as though there could be much of their mainland left to bomb, with the terrific pounding it has received." But the bombing not only continued, it was given a wry psychological twist. On 27 July the commander of the 45th Engineers in Burma correctly described the new strategy in his diary as "announcing what cities are to be razed next to the Japs: then going ahead and doing it a day or two later." He added matter-of-factly: "11 cities have been so announced and we took six of them today."[55]

On 6 August 1945, American bombers took Hiroshima. Three days later, they took Nagasaki. On 15 August, a B-29 crew member on Tinian described to his wife the mission he had flown over Japan just the other day. "It was much the same as the others only they threw up more flak than we had seen before. We hit the Hikara Naval Arsenal and as usual erased it from the Jap industries." Amidst the numbing escalation of destruction from land, sea, and air, it took time for the extraordinary fury of atomic bombs to stand out. In the wake of the nuclear attack that would divide the twentieth century into two radically different halves, an American aboard the USS *Ingersoll* wrote in his journal: "Today dawned foggy, another air-strike day on Honshu, with four-on, four-off. The papers were full of the new atomic bomb. It's cool again, cool enough for a blanket cover at night. No strike was launched because of the fog. We stayed around the launch area. I lost my fountain pen." In some American soldiers, the special nature of the nuclear devices apparently did not register at all. An airplane mechanic from the 38th Service Squadron kept a diary for much of the war. He wrote detailed entries on his stay on the Philippine island of Palawan throughout the months of August and September 1945. He announced the Japanese surrender. He described the joy at hearing the news. Not once, however, did he mention any of the two atomic bombs.[56]

American soldiers had followed the production of ever more destructive weapons with vital interest – from 500-pound M76 incendiary bombs (popularly known as 'Block Burners') to B-29 'super bombers' (twice as heavy as B-17s, with a bombload capacity of no less than 20,000 pounds). The single bombs pulverizing Hiroshima and Nagasaki to GIs signaled another significant step up the ladder, but not immediately the crossing of a threshold. The initial comparisons, for example, were inevitably conventional. On 3 August 1945, a sailor noted the radio had reported that 820 B-29s had dropped

6,600 tons of bombs on Japan in "the largest raid in history." On 6 August, another sailor wrote in a letter: "Everybody on the ship is quite excited today about the big bomb that was dropped on Japan yesterday and which was equal to 2,000 B-29 bomb loads." The day after, an aviator aboard the aircraft carrier *Cowpens* noted in his diary: "Received word of new atom bomb today. Should shorten war considerably if brought to front in quantity soon."[57]

Only as more precise information on the new bomb began to seep through in the hours and days after Hiroshima did soldiers gradually begin to understand that a weapon had been created that signaled a radical departure in warfare. During a test in New Mexico, it was supposed to have "*vaporized* a steel tower," one incredulous soldier noted, while people 150 miles away "thought there had been an earthquake." Before long, 'uranium' and 'radioactivity' were the buzz words among GIs. On 9 August, an artillerist described the bomb to his wife as "incredible" and "futuresque," "something in the nature of a miracle." There were rumors that the bomb disabled anything powered by electricity. "Heard that anyone entering the area for years after the explosion," an infantryman whispered in a letter home, "will be killed by the energy generated in the air." "It looks," commented a sailor, "like H.G.Wells predictions are very close to coming true." Meanwhile, faulty sources blew up what were already horrific casualty figures. Men of the 311th Fighter Group in China heard that 150,000 people had been killed in Hiroshima. From Chinese papers they learned that the second atomic device had incinerated 630,000 Japanese in one flash. "It is said to have made the first bomb obsolete," one pilot noted. "So it must have been a new type."[58]

Things were moving so fast now that stunned soldiers began to believe the end of the war nearer than they had ever dared hope. When word spread of the attack on Nagasaki, officers pressed against each other in the wardroom of the USS *Wilkes-Barre*, "eagerly awaiting news of the damage wrought there." Reports detailing the city's unfortunate fate electrified American soldiers. "Newspapers, usually shoved under your nose by insistent little newsboys, are harder to find in Manila than American whiskey," a private wrote on 10 August. "I can't remember such excitement and hopeful speculation." Elated rumors claimed that Japanese leaders considered bowing to American atomic pressures. As soldiers awaited official news of the Japanese surrender the mood turned giddy, anxious, and furious all at once. "Darling," a nerve-racked sailor wrote to his wife on 11 August, "please forgive me if I seem to be in a mood. It's just that so much depends on this decision." Three days later a private in Luzon wrote in his diary: "Now that the end is so near, we are all aroused to a new pitch of hate and want to see the Japs utterly smashed if they do not end it soon."[59]

The private's ink was barely dry when the Japanese ended it at last. On the morning of 15 August 1945, men of the 20th Infantry in northern Luzon received orders over the artillery radio to cease firing. "At 0830 a sudden, heavy silence descended upon all of the mountains," a battalion surgeon recalled. "It was almost a religious experience to feel the silence." Soldiers choked in the first rush of emotions. "It is now all over," a sailor wrote. "It is almost too much to comprehend. Honey there is so much on my mind that just at present it is just one big jumble. I will sign off for now and wait till things settle down a bit so that I can write an intelligent letter." Within hours a chain reaction of wild celebrations set off. Manila erupted into "an orgy of drinking and dancing." Soldiers ripped off buttons and chevrons. Men were killed by reckless firing. "It was," a pilot on a Pacific island remembered, "an hysterical, frightening night, a purging of war's emotions."[60]

As the exhilaration ebbed away, however, more sober thoughts took over. The American atomic machine – a frightful device fusing blast, fire, and poisonous gases all in one – had at last managed to bludgeon the Japanese spirit into submission. Few Americans regretted that. Polls held between 10 and 15 August showed that as much as 85 percent of people in the US approved even of the use of the second atomic bomb. Had surveys been organized among American soldiers in Asia and the Pacific, that percentage could only have shown to be higher. "Boy," a surgeon on Cebu Island exhaled in his diary the day the enemy surrendered, "you feel like you have been given a reprieve from the electric chair. We were really sweating out that invasion of Japan. Now it is all over. I bet we have saved at least a million casualties." His words could have been those of almost any American soldier over there.[61]

Yet, it also occurred to GIs that the technological price for victory had been high. So high, in fact, that suddenly it appeared to have mortgaged their own and their children's very future. "Granted that it is terrible if misused," a naval lieutenant tried to reason, "so is fire or water or electricity. I don't see why with a little intelligence and a sense of moral values the force of the atom can't be as potent a weapon for peace as for war." But it was no use sounding lighthearted about atomic bombs. After all, intelligence had not been able to prevent the second world war in half a century. And total war had made a mockery of every moral value imaginable. "Once again," a soldier in the Philippines lamented, "we have the vicious circle of powerful, new, destructive weapons and more intricate defenses against them, until this frenzy of diabolical invention shall backfire into the faces of all humanity. As other eras have had their rise, peak and decline, perhaps we are reaching the peak of our machine age and beyond lie the black pits of decline."[62]

With the powerful guns of the USS *South Dakota* silenced at last, a sailor had "time to soberly review and reflect upon the implications of the war's end." "It has many," he found, "and a lot of them are unpleasant . . . Not the least disturbing factor is the first hand knowledge of what desolation and death . . . can be wreaked on civilians, and that the next war, if any, will see still more civilians involved. Maybe us; atomic energy is free."[63]

Asia's ghosts were stirring again even before the ashes had turned cold.

Notes

List of abbreviations used in the Notes

ADP	The Americal Division Papers, US Army Military History Institute
BP	The George Bartholomae Papers, US Army Military History Institute
CC	The Margaret Craighill Collection, US Army Military History Institute
CP	The Lloyd A. Corkan Papers, US Army Military History Institute
CWP	The Charles W. Whalen, Jr. Papers, US Army Military History Institute
JAG	Judge Advocate General
MWP	The Martha A. Wayman Papers, US Army Military History Institute
Q	Questionnaire
SC	The World War II Survey Collection, US Army Military History Institute
SP	The Richard Selee Papers, US Army Military History Institute
USMHI	US Army Military History Institute, Carlisle, Pennsylvania
UT	The World War II Collection, University of Tennessee, Knoxville

Preface

1. Pyle, *Chapter*, 3.
2. Spector, *Eagle against the Sun*, 383.
3. Thorne, *Allies*, 728.
4. Ibid., 729.

Chapter 1: Pioneers

1. For these twin experiences of frontier and immigration and their impact on US foreign relations in general, see Hodgson, "Immigrants and Frontiersmen," 525.
2. Zika, "Dogs," 168, SC and Hynes, *Passage*, 163.
3. Slotkin, *Environment*, 15–16 and Linn, *Guardians*, 65.
4. Slotkin, *Gunfighter*, 278–9.
5. *Guide to Australia*, 1, 3, 7, and 13.
6. Sabel, 14 Jan. 1943, UT.
7. Kernan, *Line*, 9.
8. Brion, *Lady*, 13 and 62.
9. Clark is quoted in Allen, *Garden*, 316. Kernan, *Line*, 7.
10. Mathias, *Jive*, 56.
11. Brion, *Lady*, 64 and Morison, *Naval Operations*, vol. VII, 91.
12. For the role of whaling in America's penetration of the Pacific, see Heffer, *Pacifique*, 69–70.

13. A more detailed account of the origins of this ritual can be found in Rediker, *Devil*, 186–9.
14. The example of the XXIV Corps is from Cannon, *Leyte*, 40–1.
15. Demott, 29 July 1944, UT.
16. Kernan, *Line*, 41 and McBride, *Good Night*, 131.
17. Fessler, *No Time*, 49–50.
18. Shellback card in the file of Stephens, SC.
19. Fahey, *Diary*, 241.
20. Hynes, *Passage*, 111; Lucas, *Letters*, 12; and Mathias, *Jive*, 62.
21. Tramposch diary, 8 Nov. 1944, UT.
22. McBride, *Good Night*, 218 and Lucas, *Letters*, 181.
23. Hall, *Love*, 41 and Fahey, *Diary*, 257.
24. Sledge, *Breed*, 24.
25. *Guide to Burma*, 16; *Guide to India*, 27–8; and *Guide to New Guinea*, 7 and 9.
26. Smith, *Triumph*, 450, 547, 627, and 639.
27. Toliver, *Artist*, 118.
28. Zimmer letter, 4 Aug. 1944, SC.
29. *Guide to China*, 13, 30, and 44.
30. *C.B.I. Pointie Talkie*, 18 and Maule, *Letters*, 308–9.
31. Frillmann and Peck, *China*, 154–5 and Powell, *Surgeon*, 71.
32. Roeder, *Censored*, 83.
33. For Guadalcanal, see Miller, *Guadalcanal*, 45; for Bougainville, Morison, *Naval Operations*, vol. VI, 280 and 290.
34. *Marine Corps Operations*, vol. III, 28.
35. Crowl, *Marianas*, 406; Cannon, *Leyte*, 235; and Dod, *Engineers*, 588.
36. Dod, *Engineers*, 457 and *C.B.I. Pointie Talkie*, 34.
37. Caldwell, *Secret*, 139 and 163.
38. Miller, *Guadalcanal*, 43.
39. For New Guinea, see Smith, *Approach*, 244 and 290–1 and Dod, *Engineers*, 188–9; for Tarawa, Winters, *Elements*, 221–4; for New Georgia, Miller, *CARTWHEEL*, 170; and for Leyte, Cannon, *Leyte*, 250.
40. Slotkin, *Environment*, 16. For a definition of "mental map" and its significance in US foreign relations in a broader sense, see Henrikson, "Mental Maps."
41. Wolfert, *Solomons*, 135 and Tregaskis, *Guadalcanal*, 43–4.
42. Kahn, *Tedium*, 60.
43. Wolfert, *Solomons*, 63 and Burns, 6 Jan. 1943, ADP.
44. Owens, *Hell*, 67; Young diary, 27 March 1945, SC; and Pyle, *Chapter*, 110.
45. For the Far East as ethnocentric geographical label, see Huntington, *Civilizations*, 47. For the Far East as American Far West, see LaFeber, *Clash*, 3–5 and Drinnon, *Facing West*, xiii and 279. Lieutenant General Miles is quoted in Flint, "Pacific Frontier," 139.
46. Morriss, *Diary*, 25 and 28; Drea, "Patience," 24–5; and Calvert, *Submarine*, 136–7.
47. *Guide to Hawaii*, 4 and 27 and Lane, untitled memoir, 38–9, UT.
48. Kahn, *Tedium*, 239.
49. *Guide to Shanghai*, 21 and *What You Should Know about China*, 15.
50. Smith, *With Chennault*, 33–5 and 41.
51. Caldwell, *Secret*, 163–4 and 168.
52. Toliver, *Artist*, 209.
53. Pearce, *Savagism*, 24–5 and 90 and FitzGerald, *Schoolbooks*, 90. See also ch. 7, "Yellow, Red, and Black Men," in Dower, *War without Mercy*.

54. On the Samar pacification, see Linn, *Guardians*, 31. Peak diary, 15 July 1945, SC; Caldwell, *Secret*, 151–2; and Hunter, *Galahad*, 41.
55. Wyatt, "Super Breed," vol. I, 14–15, UT and Berry, *Semper Fi*, 84.
56. Lucas, *Letters*, 109–10.
57. Emory, *South Sea Lore*, 71 and *Getting about in New Guinea*, 14–20.
58. Dod, *Engineers*, 198.
59. Miller, *Guadalcanal*, 93. On the coastwatchers, see Lindstrom and White, *Encounters*, 47–51.
60. Riches, 4 Feb. 1944, SC and Toliver, *Artist*, 128.
61. *You and the Native*, 6; *Observer Report*, no. 46; and Dod, *Engineers*, 268–9.
62. On Lewis and Clark, see Stephen E. Ambrose, *Undaunted Courage: Meriwether Lewis, Thomas Jefferson, and the Opening of the American West* (New York: Touchstone, 1997), 423. On the Naga tribe, see Thompson and Harris, *Outcome*, 176–7; on the Lolos, *C.B.I. Pointie Talkie*, 169; and on the Kachin Rangers, Romanus and Sunderland, *Command*, 36–7 and Hunter, *Galahad*, 61.
63. Slotkin, *Environment*, 531.
64. Smith, *Virgin Land*, 19–22 and Thomson *et al.*, *Imperialists*, 6–9. Gibson, *Yankees*, 412. For an in-depth study of the Pacific Basin as a continuum of America's Western frontier, see also Gibson, *Yankees*.
65. Iriye, *Images*, 30, 46, and 50
66. The poem is quoted in Thomson *et al.*, *Imperialists*, 6. The letter is from Crout, 17 March 1945, UT.
67. On traps, see *Getting about in New Guinea*, 15–17. On Yunnan, see Scott, *God*, 261 and Frillmann and Peck, *China*, 154. On India, see Tramposch diary, 29 Dec. 1944 to 23 Jan. 1945, UT.
68. *Guide to Calcutta*, 9; *Islands of the Pacific*, 36–7; and *Guide to New Caledonia*, 6, 30, and 32.
69. *Guide to East Indies*, 2; *Islands of the Pacific*, 37; and Fahey, *Diary*, 340.
70. *Guide to India*, 28; Sterns letters, 3 Feb., 14 June, and 3 Aug. 1945, UT; Riegelman, *Biak*, 245; and Theobald diary, 22 and 31 July 1944, SC.
71. Mathias, *Jive*, 73–4; *Guide to Australia*, 7 and 9; *Guide to New Guinea*, 2, 18, and 21; Sharpe, *Brothers*, 239; and Hostetter, "Combat Doctor," 72, SC.
72. On China, see *Guide to Western Pacific*, 115. For New Guinea, Kaniarz, "Franz'l Kaney," 65, SC. For India, Elizabeth Gussak letter, 27 July 1945, SC.
73. On China, see *Magic Carpet*, 64 and *Guide to Shanghai*, 11–12. For Okinawa, *Guide to Okinawa*, 18; Giles, "Recollections," 178, UT; and Moore letter, 16 April 1945, SC.
74. The announcement is "The Orient, a New Frontier," in *To Do Today in Honolulu and Oahu: A Community 'Service to the Service' Magazine*, 12 May 1945, 13.

Chapter 2: Romantics

1. Slotkin, *Environment*, 11.
2. Gray, "I Remember," 443; Mathias, *Jive*, 56; and Kernan, *Line*, 9.
3. The soldier quotes are from Mathias, *Jive*, 96 and Hostetter, "Combat Doctor," 24, SC. The guides are *Guide to Hawaii*, 1 and *What You Should Know about China*, 1.
4. *What the Soldier Thinks*, April 1945, 7.
5. Fahey, *Diary*, 7; Gabard, 8 Aug. 1944, UT; and Snipes, 1 Aug. 1945, UT.
6. Mathias, *Jive*, 61; Frater diary, 19 Feb. 1944, SC; Morriss, *Diary*, 11; and Corkan letter, 2 July 1944, CP.

7. Wolfert, *Solomons*, 19 and Hynes, *Passage*, 159.
8. Seelig, *Marine*, 45. The booklets used by the 101st Quartermaster Regiment are in the Noonan file, ADP.
9. The War Department survey is in *What the Soldier Thinks*, Aug. 1943, 75. The quote is from Tramposch, 13 Nov. 1944, UT.
10. For a good survey of the European and American novels inspired by the Pacific, see Whitehead, "Writers as Pioneers," 379–407. The Pacific was more commonly known as the South Sea until the end of the eighteenth century. The term then became obsolescent, except when used for romantic purposes. See Edmond, *South Pacific*, 16.
11. Hutten, 9 Oct. 1944, SC and Morriss, *Diary*, 116. For the 1st Marine Division intelligence, see Weigley, *American Way*, 275.
12. Brion, *Lady*, 60.
13. For references to *Rain*, see Hostetter, "Combat Doctor," 27, SC and Trammell, untitled memoir, 67, UT. For allusions to *Tarzan* see, for example, Noonan diary, 12 Feb. 1943, ADP and Toliver, *Artist*, 198.
14. For *Tabu* as intelligence source, see Mason, *Pacific*, 43. For a sample of references to other movies and movie songs, see Mathias, *Jive*, 76 and 83; Brion, *Lady*, 78; and Baggerman letter, 23 May 1945, UT.
15. Warnings about Dorothy Lamour illusions can be found in, for instance, *Guide to New Guinea*, 2 and *Islands of the Pacific*, 1.
16. Boyington, *Black Sheep*, 37; Corkan, 4 March 1945, CP; and Gussak, 29 June 1944, SC.
17. Hutten, 4 Oct. 1944, SC.
18. Hunter, *Galahad*, 62; Lucas, *Letters*, 122; and Toliver, *Artist*, 228. The title of the famous 1963 war novel *The Thin Red Line*, written by Pacific veteran James Jones, was also an allusion to the poetry of Rudyard Kipling. See Nicholas J. Cull, review of *The Thin Red Line* (Twentieth Century Fox movie), *American Historical Review* 104 (June 1999): 1050.
19. Jespersen, *Images*, 25–6 and Gibson, *Yankees*, 414.
20. *Islands of the Pacific*, 1.
21. Kahn, *Tedium*, 4; Mathias, *Jive*, 96; and *Magic Carpet*, 62.
22. Hynes, *Passage*, 111; Hall, *Love*, 40–1; and Kahn, *Tedium*, 21. For the South Seas as the focus of Western man's quest for paradise and the setting for boys' adventure stories, see Gibson, *Yankees*, 18 and Edmond, *South Pacific*, 142–5.
23. Wu, "Surgery," 30 and Smith, *With Chennault*, 43.
24. On the mythology of the West as the Good Society and the Garden of the World, see Smith, *Virgin Land*, 12 and 123–4; Slotkin, *Regeneration*, 27–8; and Allen, *Garden*, xxv–xxvi.
25. McBride, *Good Night*, 32 and 58 and Toliver, *Artist*, 7.
26. Gabard letter, 24 Nov. 1944, UT and McBride, *Good Night*, 218.
27. On the porpoises see, for example, Lucas, *Letters*, 71.
28. Hynes, *Passage*, 161–2.
29. Frater diary, 12 March 1944, SC and Sterns letter, 3 July 1945, UT.
30. Powell, *Surgeon*, 68.
31. Jefferson is quoted in Allen, *Garden*, 114. For the Pacific as bounteous garden, see Edmond, *South Pacific*, 73–4.
32. The Cain quote is from Thorslev, "Revenge," 287. The description of Tami is from Toliver, *Artist*, 169. Hynes, *Passage*, 165–6.
33. Caldwell, *Secret*, 127–8 and *Guide to New Caledonia*, 22. The fishing is mentioned in, for example, Fahey, *Diary*, 25. The Lindbergh quotes are from his wartime *Journals*, 791–3.

34. Brion, *Lady*, 71–2; Kahn, *Tedium*, 181; and Toliver, *Artist*, 148.
35. Gerrish, "Army Days," 58, SC and Sabel letters, April 1943 and March 1944, UT.
36. Jungwirth, *Guardsman*, 105.
37. The New Guinea story is from Riegelman, *Biak*, 181–2. For Tibet and Ceylon as Shangri-las in the opinion of the GIs see, respectively, Corkan letter, 4 March 1945, CP and Sterns letter, 14 June 1945, UT.
38. *You and the Native*, 1 and Riegelman, *Biak*, 84.
39. On stretchers, see Hollenbeck diary, 6 Nov. 1942, SC. On home construction, see Hanson, "History," 26, SC and Sabel letter, May 1945, UT. On native vessels, see Milner, *Papua*, 108; Dod, *Engineers*, 596; and Winborn, *Wen Bon*, 66. The diary description of the New Guinea canoes is in Hall, *Love*, 102–3.
40. Toliver, *Artist*, 127, 129, 131, 215, 225, and 285 and Caldwell, *Secret*, 160.
41. Riegelman, *Biak*, 85 and Bradley, "World War Two," 6, UT.
42. Noonan diary, 7 May 1943, ADP; Kirk diary, 27 Nov. 1942, SC; and Moore letter, 11 Nov. 1944, SC.
43. Kaniarz, "Franz'l Kaney," 48, SC; Morriss, *Diary*, 34; and Vaughan diary, 25 July 1944, UT. On the mythology of Polynesian physical uninhibitedness see, for instance, Edmond, *South Pacific*.
44. Riegelman, *Biak*, 22 and 24 and Toliver, *Artist*, 125.
45. *Guide to Western Pacific*, 10 and 13 and *Guide to East Indies*, 16.
46. Bond and Anderson, *Flying Tiger*, 28–9 and Fahey, *Diary*, 179. In the nineteenth century the Pacific beach in particular had become the West's "imagined space of sexual freedom." See Edmond, *South Pacific*, 74.
47. On the *Essex* in 1813, see Heffer, *Pacifique*, 84. Gibson, *Yankees*, ix–x and 379. On otherness and sexual attractiveness, see Gilman, *Difference and Pathology*, 48, 53, 57, 79, and 99.
48. *Guide to Western Pacific*, 49 and 53. On the Orient and sexuality see, for instance, Said, *Orientalism*, 188.
49. Calvert, *Submarine*, 140.
50. Roeder, *Censored*, 115.
51. Soldier quotes are from Lucas, *Letters*, 66; Boyington, *Black Sheep*, 124; and Bond and Anderson, *Flying Tiger*, 193–4. On the whalers in Hawaii, and the Pacific as brothel for Americans, see Heffer, *Pacifique*, 108–10. On prostitution in Honolulu during the war, see Bailey and Farber, *Strange Place*, 95, 98–9, and 101.
52. *Guide to Japan*, 14–16.
53. Morison, *Naval Operations*, vol. VII, 177–8; Boyington, *Black Sheep*, 34–5; Caldwell, *Secret*, 157; and Wu, "Surgery," 32.
54. Toliver, *Artist*, 242 and Sabel letter, May 1945, UT.
55. Selee diary, 22 Feb. 1945, SP and Toliver, *Artist*, 254.
56. Frillmann and Peck, *China*, 151 and Lucas, *Letters*, 156–7.
57. Morriss, *Diary*, 68; Hynes, *Passage*, 164; and Sabel letters, Feb. and March 1943, UT.
58. Hynes, *Passage*, 178–9 and O'Sullivan, "Saga," 9. One soldier's memoir was titled *Robinson Crusoe, U.S.N.: The Adventures of George R. Tweed in Jap-Held Guam*. New York, 1945.
59. Guaranti diary, 6 Feb. 1942, ADP and Lucas, *Letters*, 104 and 133.
60. White, "Forms of Wildness," 26.
61. Lucas, *Letters*, 248–50.
62. Hall, *Love*, 182; *Guide to India*, 14 and 45; and Tapert, *Lines*, 212.
63. Gabard letter, 11 Aug. 1944, UT. Also, Maule, *Letters*, 209 and Sabel letter, May 1944, UT.
64. Kahn, *Tedium*, 169.

65. Kahn, *Tedium*, 229. On wilderness, primitivism, and regeneration, see Smith, *Virgin Land*, 253; Pearce, *Savagism*, 136; and Slotkin, *Regeneration*, 29–30.
66. Toliver, *Artist*, 132.

Chapter 3: Missionaries

1. *Guide to Okinawa*, 19 and *What You Should Know about China*, 12–13.
2. Bailey and Farber, *Strange Place*, 38–9 and 55.
3. *Guide to Western Pacific*, 113. For similar interpretations among American agricultural advisers in China between 1898 and 1937, for example, see Stross, *Stubborn Earth*, 8–9. On the deeply rooted American view of a backward China lacking dynamism, see Thomson *et al.*, *Imperialists*, 14 and 16–17 and Miller, *Immigrant*, 34.
4. *Magic Carpet*, 6.
5. Corkan letters, 13 Aug. and 22 Nov. 1944, CP and Powell, *Surgeon*, 156.
6. *Guide to China*, 11; *Guide to India*, 26; and *Guide to Japan*, 43–4.
7. Winborn, *Wen Bon*, 29; Owens, *Hell*, 37; and Bond and Anderson, *Flying Tiger*, 33. For the Chinese poverty figures, see Schaller, *Crusade*, 3.
8. Sterns letter, 4 Jan. 1945, UT and letter to Fox, 19 May 1944, UT.
9. Wallace letter, 6 June 1945, UT.
10. Pyle, *Chapter*, 107–8 and Sherrod, *Westward*, 70 and 281.
11. Boyington, *Black Sheep*, 124.
12. The quote is from Iriye, *Images*, 4. On primitivism and savagism, see Pearce, *Savagism*, 136. On the conflicting American images of the Pacific, India, and China, see Heffer, *Pacifique*, 112–13; Hess, *India*, 2–8 and Thomson *et al.*, *Imperialists*, 12–17 and 25.
13. *Guide to New Guinea*, 45–6. The excerpts from witnesses are respectively from Lindbergh, *Journals*, 855 and Maule, *Letters*, 234 and 239. For the concepts of *exotisme de la beauté* and *exotisme du ridicule*, see Tirefort, "Vision de l'Afrique," 181.
14. Boyington, *Black Sheep*, 124–5.
15. Frillmann and Peck, *China*, 71 and 126. *Guide to Burma*, 15.
16. Gabard letter, 2 April 1945, UT and Lucas, *Letters*, 286.
17. Romanus and Sunderland, *Mission*, 36.
18. Powell, *Surgeon*, 85–6.
19. Nickell letter, 21 Dec. 1944, UT. For examples of the soldiers' dismissal of native estimates, see Milner, *Papua*, 137; Crowl and Love, *Seizure*, 348; and Morison, *Naval Operations*, vol. V, 124.
20. Toliver, *Artist*, 136–7.
21. FitzGerald, *Schoolbooks*, 64–5. Montaigne is quoted in White, "Forms of Wildness," 31.
22. *Guide to New Guinea*, 45–6; *Guide to China*, 12–13; *Guide to Okinawa*, 14; and *Guide to East Indies*, 28–9.
23. Sharpe, *Brothers*, 32–3 and Stohrer letter, 5 May 1945, SC. On the handing out of clothing on New Guinea, see Augustin, "Angel," 25, SC and Schichler, untitled memoir, 2, SC.
24. Tramposch diary, 24–25 Nov. 1944, UT; Zimmer letter, 5 March 1945, SC; and Winborn, *Wen Bon*, 78. The Burma excerpt is from *Guide to Burma*, 23. Dennis Noble has shown that US troops stationed in China from 1900 to 1937 became convinced, too, that "the Orientals lacked moral standards." See Noble, *Eagle*, 147.

25. *Guide to East Indies*, 20.
26. *Guide to New Caledonia*, 10–11; Noonan diary, 24 July 1942, ADP; and *Observer Report*, no. 46, 1944.
27. Morison, *Naval Operations*, vol. VIII, 103. On Asian lethargy, see *What You Should Know about China*, 53; Powell, *Surgeon*, 48; Corkan letter, 17 Jan. 1945, CP; and Kernan, *Line*, 155.
28. *Memo Marianas*, 3 and *You and the Native*, 14.
29. Toliver, *Artist*, 137 and 140; Zimmer letter, 1 March 1943, SC; and Kirk diary, 12 Jan. 1943, SC.
30. Romanus and Sunderland, *Mission*, 294 and 299.
31. Hunter, *Galahad*, 45 and 50–1.
32. Boyington, *Black Sheep*, 95. Official explanations of 'squeeze' are in *Guide to China*, 22–3 and *Handbook China*, 32–3.
33. *Guide to Western Pacific*, 10 and *Guide to New Caledonia*, 30.
34. Sharpe, *Brothers*, 197.
35. Winborn, *Wen Bon*, 80 and 109–10 and Smith, *With Chennault*, 83.
36. O'Sullivan, "Saga," 13; Poynter, Q27, ADP; and Boyington, *Black Sheep*, 26–7.
37. The pilot is Boyington, *Black Sheep*, 40. For American images of the barbaric treatment of children in China and India, see Thomson *et al.*, *Imperialists*, 13–15 and 25 and Hess, *India*, 6. See also Miller, *Immigrant*.
38. Boyington, *Black Sheep*, 49 and Sharpe, *Brothers*, 208.
39. The pamphlet excerpts are from *Guide to New Guinea*, 47 and 49; *Guide to India*, 22; *Guide to Japan*, 54–5; and *Guide to Burma*, 10. Cary Grant is quoted in LaFeber, *Clash*, 222. For the Okinawa incident, see Donner, untitled memoir, 105, SC. For American images of the debasement of women in China and India, see Thomson *et al.*, *Imperialists*, 15 and Hess, *India*, 6. For the image of American Indian women, see Vibert, *Traders' Tales*, 127 and FitzGerald, *Schoolbooks*, 91.
40. On the Chinese theater, see *Handbook China*, 18. The soldier quotes are, respectively, from Sherrod, *Westward*, 76; Donner, untitled memoir, 4, SC; Winborn, *Wen Bon*, 105; and Sharpe, *Brothers*, 32. For the image of Chinese men as effeminate, see Thomson *et al.*, *Imperialists*, 25. On the crossing of sexual boundaries among Pacific islanders, see Edmond, *South Pacific*, 69.
41. On the small physical stature, see Fahey, *Diary*, 12 and *Guide to East Indies*, 9. The quote is from Maule, *Letters*, 319–20. On the New Guineans as children, see Lindbergh, *Journals*, 855. The quotes are from *You and the Native*, 10; Hall, *Love*, 109; and Sharpe, *Brothers*, 32. On the Chinese and Indians as childish, see Powell, *Surgeon*, 44 and Elizabeth Gussak letter, 25 Sept. 1944, SC. On the representation of less advanced cultures as feminine and child-like, see Edmond, *South Pacific*, 74, 110–11, and 157; Said, *Orientalism*, 207; and Herzog, *Women and Exotics*, xi–xii, xv, 60, and 62. On Native Americans as children, see FitzGerald, *Schoolbooks*, 91–2.
42. Sabel letter, March 1944, UT; *Guide to Western Pacific*, 39; and *You and the Native*, 16.
43. Maule, *Letters*, 309.
44. On European and American paternalism towards Asia and the Pacific, see Iriye, "Western Perceptions," 11–12; Edmond, *South Pacific*, 9; Jespersen, *Images*, xvii and 1–3; Heffer, *Pacifique*, 168; and Linn, *Guardians*, xii and 20–1. President McKinley is quoted in Drinnon, *Facing West*, 333.
45. *Guide to New Guinea*, 10–11.
46. The soldier quotes on the Philippines are from Sharpe, *Brothers*, 116 and 118; Lee, 6 April 1945, UT; and Hutten, 28 Feb. 1945, SC. The military pamphlet is

We Return to the Philippines, 13–14 and 19. See also Edward Harris letter, 10 May 1945, UT and Mayo, *Ordnance*, 412.

47. Corkan, 23 Jan. 1945, CP.
48. On American missionary activities in the Pacific Basin, China, India, and Burma, respectively, see Gibson, *Yankees*, 268–9, 292, and 414; Ninkovich, "China Policy," 472; Hess, *India*, 6; and Cady, *Burma*, 10. See also Heffer, *Pacifique*, 174–83.
49. *Guide to New Guinea*, 14; *You and the Native*, 10; and *Guide to East Indies*, 14. On the German Sisters, see Caldwell, *Secret*, 156.
50. On Eniwetok, see Crowl and Love, *Seizure*, 358. On Guadalcanal, see Miller, *Guadalcanal*, 319 and *Marine Corps Operations*, vol. I, 283 and 285. On New Guinea, see Dod, *Engineers*, 248 and Milner, *Papua*, 115–16. On New Georgia, see Miller, *CARTWHEEL*, 174.
51. Tapert, *Lines*, 281 and Sterns letter, March 1945, UT.
52. *Guide to Shanghai*, 21; Smith, *With Chennault*, 43; and Bond and Anderson, *Flying Tiger*, 188–9.
53. *Guide to New Guinea*, 12–13.
54. On sanitation, health, and education, see *Guide to New Guinea*, 12 and *What You Should Know about China*, 17. On the English language, see *Guide to Western Pacific*, 105.
55. *Guide to Western Pacific*, 19 and 33–4.
56. *Guide to Western Pacific*, 34; McGuire, "Fighter Pilot," 114; and *Islands of the Pacific*, 4. Theodore Roosevelt is quoted in May, *Philippines*, 179.
57. On the presence of bibles see, for instance, Riegelman, *Biak*, 208.
58. The warnings regarding non-Christians can be found in *Guide to East Indies*, 20; *Guide to India*, 14–15; and *Magic Carpet*, 6.
59. Sterns letter, 2 April 1945, UT and Toliver, *Artist*, 245.
60. On American religious activities on New Britain and Guadalcanal and in the Western Pacific in general, see Lindstrom and White, *Encounters*, 163–73. On those on Emirau Island, see Brennen, "Ten Yard," 79, SC.
61. Maroon, *South Pacific*, 49.
62. Hall, *Love*, 63–4.
63. On the Philippines, see Sharpe, *Brothers*, 117 and 187. On Okinawa, Feifer, *Tennozan*, 167. On India, see Sterns letter, 9 Jan. 1945, UT and Wellens letter, 19 April 1945, SC.
64. Wellens letter, 10 Aug. 1945, SC; Powell, *Surgeon*, 71; and Hunter, *Galahad*, 45, 49, and 51.
65. On betel chewing, see *Guide to India*, 23; *Guide to Burma*, 11; and Corkan letter, 17 Jan. 1945, CP.
66. For a general treatment of American germ consciousness and corresponding cleanliness, see Tomes, *Gospel of Germs*.
67. Herman, *Sick Bay*, 133; *Guide to New Guinea*, 51; *Guide to Calcutta*, 92; *C.B.I. Pointie Talkie*, 12 and 16; Riegelman, *Biak*, 114; "Comparative Study of Dispensary Dispositions Female versus Male Personnel," Folder "Women in SWPA," Box 27, CC; and *Observer Report*, no. 275, 23 April 1945.
68. Stohrer letter, 9 June 1945, SC.
69. Brion, *Lady*, 77 and *What You Should Know about China*, 32–3.
70. Saillant journal, Aug. 1943, SC.
71. King, *Vignettes*, 14–15.
72. Pyle, *Chapter*, 107–8.

73. On New Guinea, see Brion, *Lady*, 114 and Maule, *Letters*, 234. On the Philippines, see Wayman, 10 March 1945, WP.
74. For the Filipino toothbrush drills, see Friend, *Blue-Eyed Enemy*, illus. 3. For the soldiers' mission in dental hygiene, see Fessler, *No Time*, 35 and Sharpe, *Brothers*, 33–4.
75. *Guide to Western Pacific*, 120.
76. Romanus and Sunderland, *Mission*, 295 and *Time*, 242 and Condon-Rall and Cowdrey, *Medical Service*, 298–9.
77. *Guide to Western Pacific*, 35 and Sharpe, *Brothers*, 34.
78. On Burma, see Romanus and Sunderland, *Command*, 36–7. The story of the ambulance driver is from Bradley, "World War Two," 6–7, UT.
79. For the interpretation of American knowledge as magic by Pacific islanders, see Lindstrom, "Working Encounters," 408–9. On the New Hebrides and Dutch New Guinea, see King, *Vignettes*, 101 and Peak diary, 10 Dec. 1944, SC.
80. Romanus and Sunderland, *Mission*, 103 and *Time*, 92–3.
81. On the Chengtu hospital, see Fessler, *No Time*, 116 and Caldwell, *Secret*, 81–2. On the Chinese guerrillas at Shempa, see Herman, *Sick Bay*, 187.

Chapter 4: Imperialists

1. *Guide to Burma*, 2–3.
2. On Guadalcanal, see Miller, *CARTWHEEL*, 86 n. 22. On ANGAU and NICA see, for instance, Miller, *CARTWHEEL*, 323 and Smith, *Approach*, 391, 443, and 490.
3. On Milne Bay and New Britain, see Milner, *Papua*, 41 and Miller, *CARTWHEEL*, 282–3. On Assam, see Romanus and Sunderland, *Mission*, 204.
4. For the ambivalent American responses to European colonialism during the war, see Iriye, *Power and Culture*, 76; Bills, *Empire*, 5–8; and Hess, *India*, 45.
5. *Guide to New Caledonia*, 8–11 and 34 and *Guide to New Guinea*, 12–13.
6. *Guide to East Indies*, 14, 16–17, and 47.
7. *Guide to India*, 2, 20, 37–8, and 43.
8. On the Solomons, see Tapert, *Lines*, 91. On India, see John Gussak diary, 15 Aug. 1944, SC.
9. *Guide to Calcutta*, 77; and Wellens letter, 25 Nov. 1944, SC. On New Guinea, see *Guide to New Guinea*, 44–5; Sanders, untitled memoir, ch. 6, 3, UT; and Zimmer letter, 23 Oct. 1944, SC. In an opinion poll held in infantry divisions still stationed in the US in August 1943, 26 percent of the officers and 32 percent of the enlisted men thought Great Britain was more interested in dominating the world than in building a democratic world. See *What the Soldier Thinks*, Aug. 1943, 80–1. On the scorn for the status quo in India among American soldiers who saw the country's conditions, see also Thorne, *Allies*, 239.
10. FitzGerald, *Schoolbooks*, 63–4.
11. Fessler, *No Time*, 113 and 119; Berry, *Semper Fi*, 270; and *Guide to Hawaii*, 2.
12. Goolsby, 14 Nov. 1944, UT and Fahey, *Diary*, 300.
13. Demott, 21 Aug. 1944, UT.
14. *We Return to the Philippines*, 25 and *Guide to Hawaii*, 13, 16–17, and 19.
15. The Slotkin quotes are from the chapter "Recovering the Frontier: Regeneration through Imperialism" in *Gunfighter*, 51–62. See also Gibson, *Yankees*, 6–7 and Hodgson, "Immigrants and Frontiersmen," 525.
16. Hutten, 4 March 1945, SC.

17. On European plantations, see Toliver, *Artist*, 147 and Romanus and Sunderland, *Mission*, 342–4. On the friction with European colonial officials, see Henningham, "New Caledonia," 34; Riegelman, *Biak*, 123; and Toliver, *Artist*, 200–1.
18. On the American presence in British hill stations see, for instance, Hutten letter, 19 July 1945, SC and Smith, *With Chennault*, 33–5. See also Francis G. Hutchins, review of *The Magic Mountains: Hill Stations and the British Raj*, by Dane Kennedy, *American Historical Review* 102 (Oct. 1997): 1214–15.
19. Webb, "Odyssey," 103 and Whalen letter, 5 March 1945, WP. Also, Wallace letter, 20 May 1945, UT and Frillmann and Peck, *China*, 234. See also William K. Storey, "Big Cats and Imperialism: Lion and Tiger Hunting in Kenya and Northern India, 1898–1930," *Journal of World History* 2 (1991): 135–75.
20. Calvert, *Submarine*, 132.
21. Wolfert, *Solomons*, 61 and Hunter, *Galahad*, 6.
22. Zimmer, 16 Nov. 1943, SC.
23. Baggerman, 25 April 1945, UT.
24. For the *G.I. Roundtable* discussion, see *Islands of the Pacific*, 6–7, 13–15, and 39–43.
25. Hall, *Love*, 188.
26. For the importance of the region's raw materials see, for instance, *Guide to Calcutta*, 9; *Islands of the Pacific*, 6 and 36–7; *Guide to East Indies*, 2; and *Guide to New Caledonia*, 6.
27. Toliver, *Artist*, 229–30.
28. Fahey, *Diary*, 330.
29. Sabel letter, 21 Feb. 1943, UT.
30. Noonan letters, 22 July and 7 Aug. 1945, ADP.
31. Corkan, 29 Jan. 1945, CP.
32. Smith, *With Chennault*, 61 and 91; Bond and Anderson, *Flying Tiger*, 72; and Winborn, *Wen Bon*, 69.
33. *We Return to the Philippines*, 24; Sharpe, *Brothers*, 129; Fahey, *Diary*, 319; and Smith, *Triumph*, 278.
34. On New Caledonia, see *Guide to New Caledonia*, 21 and Morriss, *Diary*, 34. On the 350th Engineers and Los Negros, see Sabel letters, 148 and 185, UT and Kaniarz, "Franz'l Kaney," 64, SC.
35. Smith, *With Chennault*, 62 and 67.
36. Sherrod, *Tarawa*, 139 and *Westward*, 85 and 126; Fessler, *No Time*, 57; and Hynes, *Passage*, 190.
37. On wilderness and the American mind, see Nash, *Wilderness*, xi–xiii. For the nature of the US agrarian frontier in the Pacific Basin, see Gibson, *Yankees*, 6–7, 237–8, and 412. The GI pamphlets on white settlements and the Chinese way of dealing with nature are *Islands of the Pacific*, 45 and *Handbook China*, 39 and 41.
38. Sabel letter, 152, UT; Kirk, 1 Dec. 1942, SC; and Riches, 14 May 1943, SC.
39. Corkran letter, 13 Aug. 1944, CP; O'Callaghan, "Memoirs," 16–17, SC; and Sabel letter, 107, UT.
40. Sabel letter, 103, UT and Baggerman letter, 14 Jan. 1945, UT.
41. On planting see, for example, Elizabeth Gussak letter, 31 Jan. 1945, SC and Selee diary, 10 July 1944, SP. Quote is from Hutten, 9 Oct. 1944, SC.
42. For the concept of agriculture as colonization in the American experience, see Knobloch, *Culture of Wilderness*, 1–5. On the garden as a form of possession, see John MacKenzie, "Missionaries and the Environment in the 19th and Early 20th Century" (paper presented at the Institut Universitaire de Hautes Études Internationales, Geneva, Switzerland, May 1999). On bringing

culture to wilderness, see Zimmer letter, 18 Dec. 1944, SC and Young diary, 22 Oct. 1944, SC.

43. Sabel letters, 100, 105, and 111–12, UT and Wellens, 1 May 1945, SC.
44. *Islands of the Pacific*, 14–15, 39–40, and 42–3.
45. Wolfert, *Solomons*, 61; Augustin, "Angel," 24, SC; Sanders, untitled memoir, ch. 6, 1, UT; and Baghetti, "World War II," 10, UT. See also Toliver, *Artist*, 137.
46. Lindstrom and White, *Encounters*, 13–14, 18, and 21 and White and Lindstrom, *Representations*, 9, 10, and 220.
47. *You and the Native*, 4–5; Gabard letter, 15 Sept. 1944, UT; Sharpe, *Brothers*, 29–30; and Kahn, *Tedium*, 151. Quote is from Sharpe, *Brothers*, 18.
48. Kernan, *Line*, 85 and Kaniarz, "Franz'l Kaney," 64, SC.
49. Hutten letter, 4 March 1945, SC.
50. Lindstrom and White, *Encounters*, 57, 59–61, and 63–5; White and Lindstrom, *Representations*, 25; Condon-Rall and Cowdrey, *Medical Service*, 238; and Morison, *Naval Operations*, vol. XII, 49. The quote on Saipan is from Hynes, *Passage*, 190.
51. Quanchi and Adams, *Culture Contact*, 87–93 and Gibson, *Yankees*, 167–9.
52. On the shortage of US service troops in Australia and the South Pacific, see Drea, "Patience," 24; Bergerud, *Touched with Fire*, 106–7; and Bykofsky and Larson, *Transportation*, 490 and 495.
53. On New Georgia, see Miller, *CARTWHEEL*, 183. On New Guinea, see Lindstrom and White, *Encounters*, 71, 74, and 82 and White and Lindstrom, *Representations*, 25 and 398. Quotes on New Guinea are from Lindbergh, *Journals*, 867 and Hall, *Love*, 61 and 185. For the quartermaster recommendation, see *Observer Report*, no. 275, 23 April 1945.
54. Henningham, "New Caledonia," 27–30.
55. White and Lindstrom, *Representations*, 31–3; Lindstrom and White, *Encounters*, 71–93; and Stauffer, *Quartermaster*, 317. Photographs of New Guineans used as tractors and steamrollers are in Craven and Cate, *Guadalcanal*, 174–5. Quote is from Peak diary, 27 June 1944, SC.
56. Stauffer, *Quartermaster*, 279, 281–3, and 318; Dod, *Engineers*, 653; Cannon, *Leyte*, 150–1, 236, and 204; Smith, *Triumph*, 131; and *Observer Report*, no. 249, 30 March 1945. Quote is from *Guide to Western Pacific*, 82.
57. Romanus and Sunderland, *Mission*, 205, 247, and 307 and Dod, *Engineers*, 401 and 465. Quote is from Dod, *Engineers*, 401.
58. Winborn, *Wen Bon*, 65 and 101.
59. Dod, *Engineers*, 451; Craven and Cate, *Matterhorn*, 67–9; and Romanus and Sunderland, *Command*, 115. Quote is from Close, "B-29s," 11.
60. Gray, "I Remember," 448; Toliver, *Artist*, 20; Calvert, *Submarine*, 29 and 213; and Wayman letter, 23 Dec. 1944, WP.
61. Sterns, 27 April 1945, UT; Elizabeth Gussak letter, 8 June and 26 Sept. 1944, SC; Tramposch diary, 1–7 Dec. 1944, UT; Wellens letter, 30 Aug. 1944, SC; and Maule, *Letters*, 322–3.
62. Toliver, *Artist*, 127 and Wellens, 10 Aug. 1945, SC.
63. Smith, *With Chennault*, 74 and 91; Scott, *God*, 176–7; and *What You Should Know about China*, 69.
64. Crowl, *Marianas*, 332, 381–2, and 408; Morison, *Naval Operations*, vol. VIII, 373; and Condon-Rall and Cowdrey, *Medical Service*, 249.
65. Morison, *Naval Operations*, vol. XII, 143; Cannon, *Leyte*, 113 and 148; Mathias, *Jive*, 115–16 and 136–7; and Smith, *Triumph*, 230. Quotes are from *We Return to the Philippines*, 27–9; Sharpe, *Brothers*, 131; and Lee letter, 25 May 1945, UT.

66. Lindstrom and White, *Encounters*, 14–21; White and Lindstrom, *Representations*, vi, 9–13, 18, 173–5, 197, 220, 310, 364–5, and 410–11; and Henningham, "New Caledonia," 39. Quotes are from *Islands of the Pacific*, 4; Wolfert, *Solomons*, 27; and *You and the Native*, 2–4.

Chapter 5: Nature

1. *Getting about in New Guinea*, 1.
2. Hynes, *Passage*, 163.
3. On Lindbergh, see Wolfert, *Solomons*, 21–2. On Earhart, see Sharpe, *Brothers*, 28 and Wolfert, *Solomons*, 22–3.
4. Quote is from John Gussak diary, 29 June 1944, SC. On the disorientation in time see also, for example, Mathias, *Jive*, 157 and Demott letter, 1 Dec.1944, UT.
5. See, for instance, Mathias, *Jive*, 60; Fahey, *Diary*, 43; and Sledge, *Breed*, 180.
6. On Saint Elmo's fire, see Spencer, *Hump*, 8. On the jet stream, see Sherrod, *Westward*, 151–2 and Pyle, *Chapter*, 37. For the *Hornet* incident, see Kernan, *Line*, 65.
7. On the lost B-24s, see *Final Journey Home, 20/20*, American Broadcasting Company, 8 Aug. 1999.
8. Nash quote is from *Wilderness*, 3. *Guide to Western Pacific*, 5. *South Dakota* quote is from Miller, "Battleship X," 165.
9. Herman, *Sick Bay*, 161.
10. On the Marshalls, see Condon-Rall and Cowdrey, *Medical Service*, 227. Ulithi quote is from Hynes, *Passage*, 163.
11. On the 'Green Ray,' see O'Callahan, *Chaplain*, 25. On phosphorescence, see Lucas, *Letters*, 64 and Calvert, *Submarine*, 192. On Hawaii, see Lucas, *Letters*, 153.
12. McBride, *Good Night*, 66.
13. Morison, *Naval Operations*, vol. XIV, 319–30.
14. For New Guinea, see Hall, *Love*, 262; for Luzon, Morison, *Naval Operations*, vol. XIII, 59–84. Destroyer quote is from Welch, "Typhoon," 76.
15. Appleman *et al.*, *Okinawa*, 68 and Morison, *Naval Operations*, vol. XIV, 298–309.
16. Scott, *God*, 94–5.
17. Wolfert, *Solomons*, 24–5 and Fahey, *Diary*, 13.
18. On regulations regarding soldiers falling overboard, see Kirk diary, 8 Nov. 1942, SC. Officer quote is from Lucas, *Letters*, 4. Sea burial quote is from Bradley, "World War Two," 4, UT; see also O'Callahan, *Chaplain*, 121.
19. On censorship regulations see, for instance, Gabard letter, 2 April 1945, UT and Lucas, *Letters*, 281.
20. New Britain and Guam quotes are from Riches, 12 July 1944, SC and Baggerman, 14 Aug. 1945, UT.
21. On the First Lady's visit to the Pacific, see Maga, "Humanism," 36. Surgeon quote is from Sharpe, *Brothers*, 188.
22. Hynes, *Soldiers' Tale*, 160.
23. Bradley, "World War Two," 4, UT.
24. Norberg, "Pacific," 167 and Noonan diary, 6–8 April 1943, ADP.
25. Kahn, *Tedium*, 178 and Hutten, 2 Nov. 1944, SC.
26. WAC quote is from Brion, *Lady*, 121. On troops in Luzon and Palawan, see Mathias, *Jive*, 115 and Mayo, *Ordnance*, 431.
27. On the disappointment in the Philippines see, for example, Craven and Cate, *Matterhorn*, 388–9 and Toliver, *Artist*, 257. On Manila, see Brion, *Lady*, 125–6 and Zimmer, 11 March 1945, SC.

28. On the ruins of Naha, see Condon-Rall and Cowdrey, *Medical Service*, 395 and Hynes, *Soldiers' Tale*, 160.
29. Wolfert, *Solomons*, 26 and 199.
30. John Gussak, 26 June 1944, SC and Pyle, *Chapter*, 67.
31. Lucas, *Letters*, 25 and 218.
32. Morison, *Naval Operations*, vol. XII, 50 and Kernan, *Line*, 142–3. Quote is from Morison, *Naval Operations*, vol. XIV, 110.
33. On Pavuvu and Middleburg, see Sledge, *Breed*, 35 and Kirk, 11 Feb. 1945, SC. For the strain on pilots, see Craven and Cate, *Guadalcanal*, 274.
34. Romanus and Sunderland, *Mission*, 348–50 and *Magic Carpet*, 62.
35. The surgeon's memoir is Sharpe, *Brothers*.
36. On the *Tern* and evacuation hospital, see Lucas, *Letters*, 25 and Young, Nov. 1943, SC.
37. For the survey on leisure-time activities in New Guinea, see *What the Soldier Thinks*, Dec. 1943, 15.
38. Morriss, *Diary*, 158–9.
39. Smith, *With Chennault*, 74–5.
40. Verberg, "Reflections," 17, SC and McGuire, "Fighter Pilot," 117.
41. Sherrod, *Tarawa*, 38 and Hynes, *Passage*, 168.
42. Sterns, 26 March 1945, UT.
43. McClain, UT.
44. Thompson *et al.*, *Test*, 463 and Romanus and Sunderland, *Mission*, 306–7.
45. Bergerud, *Touched with Fire*, 76 and Miller, *Guadalcanal*, 241, 247–9, and 260.
46. Smith, *Approach*, 58.
47. Crowl, *Marianas*, 113, 129–30, and 134–5.
48. Stauffer, *Quartermaster*, 281–3.
49. Manchester, *Goodbye*, 159.
50. Military pamphlets on volcanoes are *Guide to Western Pacific*, 6–7; *Guide to Japan*, 5; and *Guide to East Indies*, 35.
51. On Bougainville, see Miller, *CARTWHEEL*, 245. On the volcanic storm, see Charles W. Hayes, SC.
52. Morison, *Naval Operations*, vol. XIV, 6; Winters, *Elements*, 228; Terkel, *Good War*, 181; Sherrod, *Westward*, 176; and LaPorte, untitled memoir, 45, SC. Quote is from Ira H. Hayes, untitled memoir, 2, SC.
53. On Bougainville, see Miller, *CARTWHEEL*, 267; *Marine Corps Operations*, vol. II, 275; and Trammell, untitled memoir, 123, UT. On Manila, see Smith, *Triumph*, 285 and 302–4. *Guide to Japan*, 5.
54. O'Sullivan, "Saga," 6 and Berry, *Semper Fi*, 67.
55. Sherrod, *Westward*, 45 and Lucas, *Letters*, 181.
56. For the effects of heat on equipment, see Craven and Cate, *Guadalcanal*, 101; Close, "B-29s," 8; and Sherrod, *Tarawa*, 121.
57. For figures on heat victims, see Reister, *Medical Statistics*, 204–5 and 208–9.
58. On the impact of the sun, see Winborn, *Wen Bon*, 150; Fahey, *Diary*, 275; Sledge, *Breed*, 80 and 142; and Noonan, 21 Dec. 1942, ADP. On the symptoms of heat victims, see Condon-Rall and Cowdrey, *Medical Service*, 125; Miller, *Guadalcanal*, 77; Hynes, *Passage*, 179; and Fahey, *Diary*, 47–8.
59. On the discussion surrounding the effects of torrid zones on whites, see Blaut, *Colonizer's Model*, 69–71; Drinnon, *Facing West*, 305–6 and 517; and Linn, *Guardians*, 119. See also Hutchins review of *The Magic Mountains*, 1214–15.
60. "Comparative Study," Folder "Women in SWPA," Box 27, CC.
61. *Observer Report*, no. 238, 29 March 1945.

62. Figures on precipitation are from Bergerud, *Touched with Fire*, 62 and Romanus and Sunderland, *Mission*, 82 and 202–3.
63. Aarons, 12 Jan. 1944, SC.
64. Morriss, *Diary*, 122.
65. On the paralyzing effects of rain, mud, swamps and paddies, see Miller, *CART-WHEEL*, 83, 86, and 90; Crowl and Love, *Seizure*, 103; Kleber and Birdsell, *Chemical Warfare*, 496–7 and 504; Romanus and Sunderland, *Mission*, 348–50; Smith, *Approach*, 62–3 and 67 and *Triumph*, 639 and 645; Thompson *et al.*, *Test*, 187–8 and 463; and Cannon, *Leyte*, 65–6 and 76. *Observer Report*, 16 May 1945.
66. Appleman *et al.*, *Okinawa*, 360, 365–6, 369–70, and 401 and Hynes, *Passage*, 234–6. Marine quote is from Hynes, *Passage*, 235.
67. On the *Gamble*, see Hansen, "Navy," 24, UT. For another example of fresh water provisions aboard ship, see Lucas, *Letters*, 206 and 222–3.
68. Miller, *Guadalcanal*, 204 and 354–5; Romanus and Sunderland, *Command*, 189–90; and Smith, *Approach*, 337 and 385.
69. Sledge, *Breed*, 67 and 75–6 and *Marine Corps Operations*, vol. IV, 128–9.
70. Dod, *Engineers*, 218 and 220 and Romanus and Sunderland, *Mission*, 201–3; *Command*, 280; and *Time*, 318.
71. Smith, SC.
72. For the effect on fabrics, see Stauffer, *Quartermaster*, 165 and 204–6; Folder "Women in SWPA," Box 27, CC; and *Magic Carpet*, 45. On Ceylon, see Sterns letter, 14 June 1945, UT. On the use of condoms, see Berry, *Semper Fi*, 264 and Kahn, *Tedium*, 157.
73. Miller, *Guadalcanal*, 317 and Thompson *et al.*, *Test*, 480; Mayo, *Ordnance*, 363; Romanus and Sunderland, *Command*, 281; and Riches letter, March 1944, SC.
74. Stauffer, *Quartermaster*, 204–5 and Kleber and Birdsell, *Chemical Warfare*, 497. On Leyte, see *Observer Report*, no. 201, 3 Feb. 1945.
75. On the symptoms and treatment of 'jungle rot,' see Condon-Rall and Cowdrey, *Medical Service*, 125 and 140; Winters, *Elements*, 240; King, "Medical Report," 4, ADP; Sharpe, *Brothers*, 79; and Moore letter, 24 June 1945, SC. On the removal of rings, see Shields letter, 28 July 1945, SC.
76. On the occurrence of skin infections in the various campaigns, see Condon-Rall and Cowdrey, *Medical Service*, 131–2, 208, 249, 351, and 405 and King, "Medical Report," 2, ADP.
77. Sledge, *Breed*, 32–3.
78. Tramposch, 23 Nov. 1944, UT and Hunter, *Galahad*, 17.
79. On Guadalcanal, see Morriss, *Diary*, 140 and Manchester, *Goodbye*, 160.
80. Smith, *Approach*, 55 and *Triumph*, 315; Miller, *CARTWHEEL*, 190 and 290–2; and Stauffer, *Quartermaster*, 87–8.
81. Riegelman, *Biak*, 28; Morriss, *Diary*, 47; and Kaniarz, "Franz'l Kaney," 46, SC. On fecundity's threatening quality, see also Cameron, *Samurai*, 71–2.
82. Zika, "War Dogs," 171, SC; Gerrish, "Army Days," 59, SC; and Boyington, *Black Sheep*, 37.
83. Sherrod, *Tarawa*, 72 and 122; Bergerud, *Touched with Fire*, 84–6; and Riegelman, *Biak*, 27.
84. Riegelman, *Biak*, 80 and Craven and Cate, *Guadalcanal*, 643.
85. Miller, *Guadalcanal*, 318 and Hostetter, "Combat Doctor," 58 and 60, SC.
86. Peak, 15 March 1944, SC; Riegelman, *Biak*, 126; Wolfe, *Testament*, 189; and O'Sullivan, "Saga," 7.

87. On soldiers overestimating distances covered, see Miller, *CARTWHEEL*, 154. On Guadalcanal, New Guinea, Guam, and Bougainville, see Miller, *Guadalcanal*, 313 and Wyatt, *Super Breed*, vol. I, 30, UT; Winters, *Elements*, 242; Crowl, *Marianas*, 409; and Kleber and Birdsell, *Chemical Warfare*, 495. For friendly fire on Guam, see *Marine Corps Operations*, vol. III, 560.

88. On air support over New Georgia, see Craven and Cate, *Guadalcanal*, 231–2. On air support problems, see also *Marine Corps Operations*, vol. I, 297; Miller, *CARTWHEEL*, 265; and *Observer Report*, no. 70, 7 June 1944. For friendly fire on New Guinea, see Riegelman, *Biak*, 64–5.

89. On the various military complications caused by dense vegetation, see Thompson and Harris, *Outcome*, 194–5; Smith, *Approach*, 128; Kleber and Birdsell, *Chemical Warfare*, 550; Bergerud, *Touched with Fire*, 280; Miller, *CARTWHEEL*, 246; Mayo, *Ordnance*, 82; and Miller, *Guadalcanal*, 309. On Burma, see Romanus and Sunderland, *Command*, 152.

90. Crowl, *Marianas*, 405–6.

91. Artist's quote is in Tarkov, "Sketchbook," 106. Dod, *Engineers*, 206 and Miller, *Guadalcanal*, 175.

92. Milner, *Papua*, 115 and Romanus and Sunderland, *Command*, 189 and 230.

93. On training in Hawaii, see Dod, *Engineers*, 491 and Crowl, *Marianas*, 45. On Guadalcanal, see *Naval Operations*, vol. V, 67–8.

94. Wolfe, *Testament*, 189.

95. Schroeder, "Military Service," 17, SC and Toliver, *Artist*, 122. For the perception of the "anthropomorphic aggression" of weeds in the American West, for instance, see Knobloch, *Culture of Wilderness*, 119.

96. Sledge, *Breed*, 31.

97. Brion, *Lady*, 138 and Pyle, *Chapter*, 17.

98. Lytle, "Environmental Approach," 292–4. On the ecological dimension of settlement in America, Australia, and New Zealand as opposed to that of colonization in Africa, the Middle East, and Asia see, for example, the work of historians Alfred Crosby, William Cronon, and William H. McNeill.

99. Sabel letters, March and April 1944, UT; Brennen, "Ten Yard," 126, SC; and Hutten letter, 16 July 1945, SC.

100. Baggerman letters, 5 Feb. and 28 May 1945, UT.

101. Morriss, *Diary*, 37 and Zimmer, 18 Feb. 1945, SC.

102. See, for example, Sharpe, *Brothers*, 121 and 185; Toliver, *Artist*, 296; and Mathias, *Jive*, 119.

103. Pyle, *Chapter*, 107 and 131 and, also, Moore letter, 6 May 1945, SC; Sledge, *Breed*, 194, 197, and 208; Appleman *et al.*, *Okinawa*, 72 and 74; and Cameron, *Samurai*, 189–91.

104. On wild animals and the experience of American pioneers, for example, see Nash, *Wilderness*, 24. Herman Melville, *Moby Dick* (Ware, England: Wordsworth Editions, 1993), 409.

105. Riegelman, *Biak*, 101.

106. For wound admissions resulting from animal attacks, see Reister, *Medical Statistics*, 204–5. On tigers, see Selee, 25 June 1945, SP and Fessler, *No Time*, 108.

107. John Gussak diary, 10 Aug. 1944, SC and Stohrer, 3 June 1945, SC. On rabies in India see, for instance, *Guide to Calcutta*, 93.

108. *Guide to Western Pacific*, 85 and Riegelman, *Biak*, 224.

109. Scott, *God*, 85; *Guide to Western Pacific*, 84–5; and *Guide to New Guinea*, 30–1.

110. *Guide to Western Pacific*, 15; *Memo Marianas*, 10; and Mason, *Pacific*, 241.
111. Matthias, *Jive*, 80–1 and Fessler, *No Time*, 120.
112. Fahey, *Diary*, 66 and Morison, *Naval Operations*, vol. V, 168 and 179–80.
113. *Guide to New Caledonia*, 22 and Wolfert, *Solomons*, 199.
114. Fahey, *Diary*, 239 and Sterns letter, 6 March 1945, UT.
115. *Guide to New Guinea*, 28.
116. Peak diary, 4 July 1944, SC.
117. For the meaning of the snake in American culture and the Genesis and Parkman quotes, see Stott, "Sacred Serpent," 638.
118. On hospital admissions for snake bites, see Reister, *Medical Statistics*, 204–5. On Burma and India, see Smith, *With Chennault*, 32 and Bartholomae, 14 Aug. 1943, BP.
119. *Guide to Okinawa*, 23–6; Pyle, *Chapter*, 96 and 131; and Manchester, *Goodbye*, 351–2.
120. Aarons letter, 17 Dec. 1943, SC.
121. Burns diary, 13–14, ADP; Maroon, *South Pacific*, 23; and Schroeder, "Military Service," 8–9, SC.
122. Sledge, *Breed*, 144.
123. Fahey, *Diary*, 48; Sterns letter, 2 April 1945, UT; and Riegelman, *Biak*, 113.
124. Dod, *Engineers*, 501 and Pyle, *Chapter*, 113.
125. Kernan, *Line*, 145–6 and Selee, 25 March 1945, SP.
126. Condon-Rall and Cowdrey, *Medical Service*, 138 and Milner, *Papua*, 324.
127. See, for example, Sharpe, *Brothers*, 38.
128. On the causes and effects of malaria, see Condon-Rall and Cowdrey, *Medical Service*, 46. On malaria in the Southwest Pacific, see Condon-Rall, "Malaria," 91, 103, and 106; Miller, *Guadalcanal*, 141, 318, and 225–7; Bergerud, *Touched with Fire*, 96; and *Marine Corps Operations*, vol. I, 359. On malaria in China–Burma–India, see Romanus and Sunderland, *Command*, 286–7. For the daily noneffective rates caused by malaria, see Reister, *Medical Statistics*, 38–9.
129. On scrub typhus, see Condon-Rall and Cowdrey, *Medical Service*, 140 and 265–6. On the incidence in Burma, see Romanus and Sunderland, *Command*, 226 and 237. On the outbreak on Owi and Biak Islands, see Smith, *Approach*, 392 and Fessler, *No Time*, 44.
130. On dysentery and other diarrheal diseases, see Reister, *Medical Statistics*, 40–3. On China–Burma–India, see Condon-Rall and Cowdrey, *Medical Service*, 294 and Romanus and Sunderland, *Command*, 230, 237, and 284–8. On Halsey's fleet, see Fahey, *Diary*, 161.
131. On the disease characteristics of the various theaters in the war against Japan, see Condon-Rall and Cowdrey, *Medical Service*, 45, 116, 218, 219, 226, 244, 249, 287, 292–4, 329, 351, and 405–6.
132. Reister, *Medical Statistics*, 42–5.
133. For the ratio between combat and disease victims, see Winters, *Elements*, 232. For the disease death rates, see Condon-Rall and Cowdrey, *Medical Service*, 441.
134. Quote is from Condon-Rall and Cowdrey, *Medical Service*, 443.
135. Condon-Rall and Cowdrey, *Medical Service*, 45, 109, 216, 265–6, 405, and 443. On the 608th Clearing Company and 77th Division, see Sharpe, *Brothers*, 19 and Schichler, untitled memoir, 10, SC.
136. Thorpe, *East Wind*, 143.
137. On Myitkyina and Chinese measures against dysentery, see Romanus and Sunderland, *Command*, 253–4 and Winborn, *Wen Bon*, 27.

Chapter 6: Masses

1. *Guide to Burma*, 14; *Guide to East Indies*, 1 and 35; *Guide to India*, 7; *What You Should Know about China*, 9; and *Guide to Okinawa*, 4–5.
2. Romanus and Sunderland, *Command*, 275.
3. On the concept of Yellow Peril, see Heffer, *Pacifique*, 185–9 and Jürgen Osterhammel, "Europe's Sense of Difference: Some Enlightenment Perspectives" (paper presented at the Institut Universitaire de Hautes Études Internationales, Geneva, Switzerland, 29 Jan. 1998).
4. *Guide to New Guinea*, 15.
5. Morriss, *Diary*, 186.
6. McBride, *Good Night*, 60. On Hawaiian population figures, see Bailey and Farber, *Strange Place*, 25–6 and Okihiro, *Cane Fires*, ix.
7. *Guide to New Guinea*, 1. On Indians and Chinese as insects, see Zika, "War Dogs," 163, SC and Powell, *Surgeon*, 148.
8. On the Chinese as ant-like creatures, see Winborn, *Wen Bon*, 24 and 102; Romanus and Sunderland, *Command*, 391–4; Corkan letter, 22 Nov. 1944, CP; Warnock, "Composite Wing," 30; and *Magic Carpet*, 63. On Indians, see Wellens letter, 30 Nov. 1944, SC and Craven and Cate, *Matterhorn*, 64. On Korean laborers, see Cameron, *Samurai*, 106–8.
9. On the issue of fertility and race competition, see Hofstadter, *Social Darwinism*, 176–7 and Drinnon, *Facing West*, 239–41.
10. On the association of the primitive with unbridled sexuality, see White, "Forms of Wildness," 29 and Gilman, *Difference and Pathology*, 79–83, 99, and 213. King, *Vignettes*, 97.
11. Thorpe, *East Wind*, 140 and Riegelman, *Biak*, 84.
12. On the prophesied extinction of Pacific islanders, see White and Lindstrom, *Representations*, v and Edmond, *South Pacific*, 14–15. On their regeneration, see *Islands of the Pacific*, 20–3.
13. *Islands of the Pacific*, 21–3.
14. On the Western image of the Orient as sexual and fecund, see Said, *Orientalism*, 188. For the GI in the Philippines, see Kahn, *Tedium*, 228. On the American image of China as sexually depraved, see Thomson *et al.*, *Imperialists*, 13–15 and 25 and Miller, *Immigrant*, 163 and 194. For the officer in India and China, see Corkan, 13 Aug. 1944 and 5 Feb. 1945, CP.
15. On Saipan and Okinawa, see Sherrod, *Westward*, 70 and Brennen, "Ten Yard," 174, SC.
16. On the Sikhs, see Morison, *Naval Operations*, vol. VIII, 84. On Tarawa and Makin, see Crowl and Love, *Seizure*, 73. On the Palaus and Noemfoor, see Smith, *Approach*, 421–2 and 578.
17. On Hawaii, see Bailey and Farber, *Strange Place*, 7. On Filipino and Chinese hatred of Japanese, see Hutten letter, 20 Jan. 1945, SC; Fahey, *Diary*, 318; and Winborn, *Wen Bon*, 180.
18. On Asian dislikes of Chinese, see Romanus and Sunderland, *Mission*, 74 and Owens, *Hell*, 88. On Burmese and Indians, see *Guide to Burma*, 39.
19. Cady, *Burma*, 7–12 and *Guide to East Indies*, 39.
20. Friend, *Philippines*, 232 and *Guide to India*, 15.
21. Gray, "I Remember," 472; Gerrish, "Army Days," 77, SC; and Owens, *Hell*, 30–2.
22. Roeder, *Censored*, 91 and *Guide to China*, 65–75.
23. Wu, "Surgery," 31 and Hutten letter, 20 Jan. 1944, SC.

24. Riches, 15 October 1942, SC.
25. On the Western fear of Pan-Asianism, see Thorne, "Racial Aspects," 354–7; Iriye, *Power and Culture*, 4–5, 49–50, and 74; and Heffer, *Pacifique*, 191.
26. Crowl and Love, *Seizure*, 217, 225, and 297–8.
27. Owens, *Hell*, 34 and Thorpe, *East Wind*, 171.
28. Appleman *et al.*, *Okinawa*, 52–4 and 103; *Guide to Okinawa*, 5; Demott letter, 1 April 1945, UT; and Tanaka, *Horrors*, 211.
29. Theobald diary, 22 June 1944, SC.
30. For the Filipino 'nigger' epithets, see Linn, *Guardians*, 125. On the Western fear of a pan-colored movement, see Thorne, "Racial Aspects," 354–5. On the Philippines, see Kahn, *Tedium*, 270.
31. Sharpe, *Brothers*, 199–200 and Dunbar, "Charles Dunbar," 5, SC.
32. Kalnasy, 31 Jan. 1943, SC.
33. For the relationship between white and black Americans, see *What the Soldier Thinks*, Aug. 1943, 59 and Maga, "Humanism," 42.
34. Smith, *Triumph*, 651 and 657–8.
35. Linn, *Guardians*, 123–4 and 162. For the OSS report, see Thorne, "Racial Aspects," 359.
36. Hess, *India*, 137; Romanus and Sunderland, *Command*, 264; and Thorne, "Racial Aspects," 359.
37. *What You Should Know about China*, 9 and Stouffer *et al.*, *American Soldier*, vol. 2, 628–9.
38. Bagby, *Eagle*, 130–1 and *What You Should Know about China*, 48.
39. *Guide to China*, 4–8; *Handbook China*, 43–4; and *What You Should Know about China*, 5, 57, and 63. See also Jespersen, *Images*.
40. On the Fourteenth Air Force, see Warnock, "Composite Wing," 26–7. On Assam, see Elizabeth Gussak, 20 Oct. 1944, SC.
41. Drinnon, *Facing West*, 464.
42. The Roosevelt comment is from LaFeber, *Clash*, 217. *Guide to East Indies*, 9.
43. The US minister is quoted in Thorne, "Racial Aspects," 357, n. 2. On US–Australian relations at the front, see Milner, *Papua*, 274 n. 29 and 334–5.
44. On relations with Australian civilians, see Heffer, *Pacifique*, 275 and Fahey, *Diary*, 58. On General Casey's speech, see Hall, *Love*, 79.
45. Winborn, *Wen Bon*, 62.
46. Riegelman, *Biak*, 119.
47. On the association of disease and the Other, see Gilman, *Difference and Pathology*, 130, 132, and 151. On contamination fears of the late nineteenth century, Chinese immigrants, and Filipino colonials, see Tomes, *Gospel of Germs*; Miller, *Immigrant*, 160; Heffer, *Pacifique*, 190–1; Karnow, *In Our Image*, 11–12; and Drinnon, *Facing West*, 349.
48. Hutten, 18 Dec. 1943, SC.
49. On plague, see Romanus and Sunderland, *Mission*, 308; Herman, *Sick Bay*, 187; and Elizabeth Gussak letter, 23 Jan. 1945, SC.
50. Toliver, *Artist*, 219–20. See also Edmond, *South Pacific*, 209 and Geslin, "Nouvelles-Hébrides," 276–7.
51. Edmond, *South Pacific*, 196–7 and Miller, *Immigrant*, 164, 186, and 198.
52. Owens, *Hell*, 34–5 and King, *Vignettes*, 62–3. See also, for instance, Bond and Anderson, *Flying Tiger*, 107; Jungwirth, *Guardsman*, 111–12; Maroon, *South Pacific*, 33; and Norberg, "Pacific," 168.
53. White and Lindstrom, *Representations*, 402. On the intersection of septic and racial fears and the legitimization of segregation around the turn of the century see, for example, Tomes, *Gospel of Germs* and Swanson, "Sanitation Syndrome."

54. Link and Coleman, *Medical Support*, 828–30.
55. Romanus and Sunderland, *Command*, 287 and *Time*, 301–3.
56. On Hawaii, see Bailey and Farber, *Strange Place*, 191–2. On Vella Lavella, see Bergerud, *Touched with Fire*, 492.
57. On Guadalcanal, New Caledonia, and Luzon, see Kalnasy diary, 29 Sept. 1943, SC; Vaughan diary, 17 March 1944, UT; and Riegelman, *Biak*, 211–12.
58. On the 1st Marine Division, see Cameron, *Samurai*, 79. On the *Tern*, see Lucas, *Letters*, 14 and 16.
59. Young diary, 25 June 1944, SC; Brion, *Lady*, 84; and Cameron, *Samurai*, 77–8.
60. Kahn, *Tedium*, 198–9.
61. On Atabrine, see Miller, *Guadalcanal*, 227. On elephantiasis, see Sharpe, *Brothers*, 30 and Boyington, *Black Sheep*, 37. On Saipan, see Sherrod, *Westward*, 77.
62. Gilman, *Difference and Pathology*, 24.
63. For a poignant illustration of the clash between romantic myth and Pacific realities, see Cameron, *Samurai*, 76–7.
64. Noonan, 7 May 1943, ADP; McBride, *Good Night*, 122; and Morriss, *Diary*, 43.
65. Vaughan diary, 10 March 1944, UT; Riegelman, *Biak*, 25; and song transcript in Stephens file, SC. See also, for example, Thorpe, *East Wind*, 141 and Young diary, Nov. 1943, SC.
66. Hynes, *Passage*, 245–6 and Maule, *Letters*, 323.
67. *Guide to New Guinea*, 49. Weeks, "Tonga," 407. *Guide to East Indies*, 25.
68. *Guide to India*, 22. On Kunming, see Frillmann and Peck, *China*, 154 and 196.
69. Kahn, *Tedium*, 254 and Sharpe, *Brothers*, 208.
70. On race in GIs' relations in Hawaii as "a fundamental fact" and "significant obstacle" with serious legal and social ramifications, see Bailey and Farber, *Strange Place*, 194 and 203.
71. On VD rates, see Condon-Rall and Cowdrey, *Medical Service*, 57–8, 101, 138, 140, 292, 294, 330, and 421. On the New Hebrides, see White and Lindstrom, *Representations*, 412.
72. On China, see Link and Coleman, *Medical Support*, 911 and *JAG: China–Burma–India*, vol. 3, 17. On Burma, see *JAG: China–Burma–India*, vol. 3, 39. On India, see *JAG: China–Burma–India*, vol. 3, 213. On VD rates in the Army Air Forces in CBI, see Link and Coleman, *Medical Support*, 901.
73. On Manila, see Mathias, *Jive*, 151.
74. For the 1940 US Army VD rate, see Condon-Rall and Cowdrey, *Medical Service*, 57–8. On the segregation of brothels, see Rose, "The 'Sex Question,'" 902 and Henningham, "New Caledonia," 25–6.
75. Kernan, *Line*, 18–19 and Miller, *Immigrant*, 162–4 and 194.
76. *Guide to Burma*, 32. *Guide to Western Pacific*, 82–3. *Guide to East Indies*, 48.
77. John Gussak, 6 Dec. 1944, SC and Bond and Anderson, *Flying Tiger*, 74.
78. LaMagna, Q16, SC and Theobald, 25 May 1944, SC.
79. Bond and Anderson, *Flying Tiger*, 192–5 and Mathias, *Jive*, 152–3.
80. On New Caledonia's lepers, see King, *Vignettes*, 62–3. Edmond, *South Pacific*, 194 and 196.
81. On the link between miscegenation and leprosy, see Edmond, *South Pacific*, 198. On interracial offspring as degenerate, see Gilman, *Difference and Pathology*, 107 and Choy *et al.*, *Coming Man*, 134–5. Quote is from L. P. Curtis, Jr., review of *Gothic Images of Race in Nineteenth Century Britain*, by H. L. Malchow, *American Historical Review* 103 (June 1998): 887–9.
82. The military booklets are *Guide to New Caledonia*, 14 and *Guide to East Indies*, 18. For the US posters, see Brcak and Pavia, "Racism," 683.
83. On Hawaii and Manila, see Lucas, *Letters*, 145 and Thorpe, *East Wind*, 169.

Chapter 7: Mind

1. *Handbook Japanese Forces: TM 30-480*, 168.
2. Coox, "Remarks," 248 and Kahn, "United States Views," 486.
3. Berry, *Semper Fi*, 267 and Thorne, "Racial Aspects," 367 n. 3.
4. The lieutenant from California is Durley, Q44, ADP. On China, see Caldwell, *Secret*, 211–12. On the preparations for Japan, see Owens, *Hell*, 222–3.
5. *Guide to India*, 1–2. Sherrod, *Westward*, 15. The *New York Times* quote is from Chappell, *Bomb*, 32–3.
6. *You and the Native*, 10–11. *Guide to New Guinea*, 28; *Guide to Calcutta*, 6; *Guide to East Indies*, 39; and *C.B.I. Pointie Talkie*, No. 4.
7. *Pocket Guide to China*, 1 and *Memo Marianas*, 11.
8. Frillmann and Peck, *China*, 152–3 and Sherrod, *Westward*, 96.
9. *Handbook China*, 20–1 and Lindsay, "South of Yontan," 2D, UT.
10. Romanus and Sunderland, *Command*, 190.
11. *Observer Report*, No. B-M-20, 12 Sept. 1944 and *Observer Report*, 1 May 1945.
12. Hall, *Love*, 112 and 94.
13. Sharpe, *Brothers*, 104–5.
14. Kaniarz, "Franz'l Kaney," 68, SC.
15. Tregaskis, *Diary*, 121 and Powell, *Surgeon*, 133–4.
16. *Guide to Western Pacific*, 80–1.
17. On the spirit worlds of Kanaks, New Guineans, and Igorots see, for example, *Guide to New Caledonia*, 11 and 16; Toliver, *Artist*, 179; Milner, *Papua*, 94; and Sharpe, *Brothers*, 241–2.
18. On Assam, see Clare, *Eastward*, 277. On Chinese superstitions, see Spencer, *Hump*, 39–40 and Fessler, *No Time*, 110.
19. On ancestor worship among Chinese and Okinawans, see Mathias, *Jive*, 155; *Guide to Okinawa*, 14; Mayo, *Ordnance*, 458; Manchester, *Goodbye*, 364–5; and Spencer, "Memories," 24, UT.
20. *C.B.I. Pointie Talkie*, no. 4, 52.
21. Owens, *Hell*, 125.
22. Baghetti, "World War II," 9, UT.
23. The Marshall quote is from Romanus and Sunderland, *Mission*, 250. Sherrod, *Westward*, 31.
24. Boyington, *Black Sheep*, 66.
25. Sun Tzu, *Art of War*, 96–7. Noonan diary, 27 Dec. 1942, ADP.
26. Sledge, *Breed*, 247–8. On the daytime invisibility of the Japanese see also, for example, Noonan diary, 9 Oct. 1942, ADP; Tregaskis, *Diary*, 112; and Hunter, *Galahad*, 43.
27. On Japanese training in night warfare, see Harries, *Soldiers of the Sun*, 328–31.
28. Morison, *Naval Operations*, vol. V, 114 and 153 n. 8.
29. Lindbergh, *Journals*, 846–7.
30. Wolfert, *Solomons*, 138. On Saipan, see *Observer Report*, 24 Oct. 1944.
31. On infantry preparations for the night see, for example, Miller, *Guadalcanal*, 307 and *CARTWHEEL*, 266 and 329; and Crowl, *Marianas*, 346. Pyle, *Chapter*, 97.
32. On night illumination see, for example, Miller, *CARTWHEEL*, 355 and Morison, *Naval Operations*, vol. XIV, 217 and 245. On Japanese night infiltration see, for example, Crowl and Love, *Seizure*, 108. On Buna and New Georgia, see Milner, *Papua*, 224; Miller, *CARTWHEEL*, 109; and Donner, untitled memoir, 25, SC.

33. For the destroyer sailors, see McBride, *Good Night*, 254. On the Okinawa landings, see Morison, *Naval Operations*, vol. XIV, 174 and the television documentary *Kamikaze*, in the BBC series *Timewatch*.
34. Kahn, *Tedium*, 59.
35. On the oddity of some Japanese articles, see Toliver, *Artist*, 164 and 241. On adopted Japanese equipment, see Mayo, *Ordnance*, 81; Smith, *Marine Corps*, 437; and Sherrod, *Westward*, 126.
36. On enemy cigarettes, see Muse diary, 23 Aug. 1942, UT. On Japanese food, see Tregaskis, *Diary*, 58; Crowl, *Marianas*, 382; and Sherrod, *Westward*, 71.
37. Pyle, *Chapter*, 121 and 136–7.
38. Kahn, *Tedium*, 147; Kaniarz, "Franz'l Kaney," 81, SC; and Lane, untitled memoir, 69, UT.
39. Sharpe, *Brothers*, 155.
40. Pyle, *Chapter*, 5 and 124.
41. Fessler, *No Time*, 78; and Morriss, *Diary*, 47. See also Gilmore, "Japanese Prisoners," 200–2.
42. For a warning about the Japanese knowledge of the English language and American slang, see *Guide to China*, 71. On passwords see, for example, Berry, *Semper Fi*, 83; Sledge, *Breed*, 82; and Owens, *Hell*, 42. On Tokyo Rose, see Leach, "Hear This," 82. On the American education of Japanese soldiers, see Tregaskis, *Diary*, 173. See also, for example, Fahey, *Diary*, 25; Morriss, *Diary*, 42; and Wolfert, *Solomons*, 50. On Okinawa's English schoolbooks, see Donner, untitled memoir, 67–8, SC.
43. On Japanese propaganda, see Brcak and Pavia, "Racism," 677. On Los Negros, see Miller, *CARTWHEEL*, 335 n. 37.
44. Cameron, *Samurai*, 110 and Terkel, *Good War*, 64.
45. Tregaskis, *Diary*, 54. For the opinion of Pacific veterans on Japanese POWs, see Stouffer *et al.*, *American Soldier*, vol. 2, 161.
46. Laurie, "Dilemma," 101. See also Gilmore, "Japanese Prisoners," 203–4, 210–12, and 214–15.
47. On the use of Nisei, see *Observer Report*, B-M-20, 12 Sept. 1944. On the use of 'bait-boys,' see Crowl and Love, *Seizure*, 288 and Appleman *et al.*, *Okinawa*, 467. On Okinawa, see *Marine Corps Operations*, vol. V, 357 n. 89
48. Sledge, *Breed*, 294.
49. Kahn, "United States Views," 476–7. On the soldiers' appreciation of enemy equipment, see Winborn, *Wen Bon*, 8 and, for example, McFadden, Stannard, and Webb answers to question 44 of USMHI survey, ADP.
50. On industrial weakness and its impact on Japanese forces, see Coox, "Japanese Military," 34–5 and 38.
51. For the GI views of Japanese equipment flaws, see Sledge, *Breed*, 70; McLaughlin, Q44, ADP; and Fahey, *Diary*, 143.
52. On Chinese economy and improvisation, see Winborn, *Wen Bon*, 48, 69, and 70–2 and Powell, *Surgeon*, 58.
53. Toliver, *Artist*, 296–7 and 315.
54. *Handbook Japanese Forces: TM-E 30-480*, 271; Appleman *et al.*, *Okinawa*, 152; Lindsay, "South of Yontan," K-1, UT; Dod, *Engineers*, 583 and 598; and Cannon, *Leyte*, 163.
55. On animists and Parsees, see *Guide to Burma*, 13 and Whalen, 29 Jan. 1945, WP. On Kweiyang, see Powell, *Surgeon*, 146–7.
56. Hall, *Love*, 64.

57. *Guide to East Indies*, 50.
58. Winborn, *Wen Bon*, 80 and 129.
59. On the sixth sense, see Toliver, *Artist*, 125 and *Observer Report*, 1 Aug. 1944. See also Manchester, *Goodbye*, 94.
60. *Handbook Japanese Forces: TM-E 30-480*, 85, 94, and 120.
61. Linderman, *World within War*, 170. For General Krueger's report, see Cannon, *Leyte*, 246.
62. On the zoomorphism of New Guineans, see O'Sullivan, "Saga," 15–16. On Japanese imitations of animal sounds, see Morison, *Naval Operations*, vol. VI, 199 and Hostetter, "Combat Doctor," 56, SC.
63. *Guide to East Indies*, 15 and 38. On simian imagery regarding Filipinos and New Guineans, see Mayo, *Ordnance*, 407 and Hall, *Love*, 99.
64. On Japanese tree snipers in Papua, see Milner, *Papua*, 339–40. On Tarawa and Makin, see Sherrod, *Tarawa*, 90–1 and Crowl and Love, *Seizure*, 90 and 95. On New Georgia, see Miller, *CARTWHEEL*, 112 and 133 and Clements, *Memories*, 21.
65. Sun Tzu, *Art of War*, 85. Linderman, *World within War*, 172 and Sherrod, *Westward*, 183. Appleman *et al.*, *Okinawa*, 280.
66. Sabel letter, Feb. 1944, UT and Schichler, untitled memoir, 1, SC.
67. Sherrod, *Westward*, 135 and Morison, *Naval Operations*, vol. XII, 42.
68. Bergerud, *Touched with Fire*, 424; Donner, untitled memoir, 102, SC; and Smith, *Triumph*, 579.
69. Appleman *et al.*, *Okinawa*, 56–7 and *Marine Corps Operations*, vol. IV, 265.
70. On Japanese hygienic measures see, for example, Appleman *et al.*, *Okinawa*, 189–90. On the smell of Japanese, see Miller, *CARTWHEEL*, 133 and Fahey, *Diary*, 45–6. On the Philippines, see Kirk, 6 March 1945, SC.
71. On Western interpretations of cannibalism, see Curtis review of Malchow's *Gothic Images of Race*, 888; "Cannibals and Christians: European vs. American Indian Culture," ch. 2 of Slotkin's *Regeneration*, 25–57; and Heffer, *Pacifique*, 28.
72. Miller, *Guadalcanal*, 229 and 238. Lindbergh, *Journals*, 902–3. On Burma, see Romanus and Sunderland, *Command*, 345. On Japanese cannibalism in general and its occurrence in New Guinea and the Philippines in particular, see Tanaka, *Horrors*, 112, 115–17, 122, 124–30, and 235 n. 9.
73. Tregaskis, *Diary*, 107; Kahn, *Tedium*, 69; and Toliver, *Artist*, 150.
74. Sledge, *Breed*, 282. The marine on Eniwetok is quoted in Morison, *Naval Operations*, vol. VII, 299.
75. *Guide to Japan*, 5 and 7.
76. Terkel, *Good War*, 64.
77. Tanaka, *Horrors*, 132. For the Jekyll and Hyde metaphor, see also *Guide to Japan*, 54 and Bischof and Dupont, *Pacific War*, 194.
78. On American Indians and torture, see Pearce, *Savagism*, 99–100. On the Japanese and hardship, see *Guide to Japan*, 54 and Fahey, *Diary*, 194.
79. On Asians as beasts of burden, see Hunter, *Galahad*, 42 and 109 and Sharpe, *Brothers*, 187 and 240. See also Sterns letter, 2 April 1945, UT and Sledge, *Breed*, 122–3.
80. OSS quote is from Bagby, *Eagle*, 13 and Bradley, "World War Two," 1, UT.
81. On the cruelty of American Indians and Chinese, see FitzGerald, *Schoolbooks*, 65 and 91 and Iriye, *Images*, 262.
82. Chappell, *Bomb*, 24.
83. On American soldiers and enemy cruelties, see Cameron, *Samurai*, 112–14; Bergerud, *Touched with Fire*, 408–11; Lindbergh, *Journals*, 818; Morison, *Naval Operations*, vol. V, 69 and vol. XII, 400; Miller, *CARTWHEEL*, 341–2; Smith,

Triumph, 299 and 344; and Cannon, *Leyte*, 164. On the disrespect for medical personnel, see Miller, *Guadalcanal*, 241; Hostnik and Rury, "Medics," 16; and Sharpe, *Brothers*, 26–7.

84. On the Subic Bay stories, see Fahey, *Diary*, 297. For the GI polls, see Stouffer *et al.*, *American Soldier*, vol. 2, 162.

85. The Americal veteran is McFadden, Q44, ADP. On the Chinese during the war, see *What You Should Know about China*, 56–7 and *Guide to Western Pacific*, 113.

86. *Guide to India*, 9 and 12; *Magic Carpet*, 44; and Sterns letter, 162, UT.

87. *Guide to Japan*, 7 and Romanus and Sunderland, *Command*, 346.

88. Noonan diary, 23 Sept. 1942, ADP; Crowl and Love, *Seizure*, 156; Condon-Rall and Cowdrey, *Medical Service*, 224; *Observer Report*, B-M-20, 12 Sept. 1944; and Appleman *et al.*, *Okinawa*, 384.

89. Sherrod, *Tarawa*, 84 and Tapert, *Lines*, 237. See also Hall, *Love*, 77 and Kernan, *Line*, 31–2.

90. Sherrod, *Westward*, 146–7.

91. Sherrod, *Tarawa*, 110–11. On *kamikazes*, see Fahey, *Diary*, 221 and Hynes, *Passage*, 223–4.

92. Crowl and Love, *Seizure*, 260; Pyle, *Chapter*, 7–8; Morison, *Naval Operations*, vol. V, 192–3; Crowl, *Marianas*, 249 and 365; *Marine Corps Operations*, vol. III, 489; Condon-Rall and Cowdrey, *Medical Service*, 346.

93. On the civilians of Saipan, see Hynes, *Passage*, 217; Sherrod, *Westward*, 146–7; and Crowl, *Marianas*, 264–5. On the Keramas, see Appleman *et al.*, *Okinawa*, 58; Feifer, *Tennozan*, 456–7; Morison, *Naval Operations*, vol. XIV, 123; and Searles, "Memories," 13–16, UT.

94. Sledge, *Breed*, 260; Gray, "I Remember," 473; and Toliver, *Artist*, 149.

95. Miller, "Battleship X," 155.

96. Lee diary, 14 Dec. 1944, UT.

97. Toliver, *Artist*, 276 and Pyle, *Chapter*, 24 and 26. See also Linderman, *World within War*, 161–3.

98. Cameron, *Samurai*, 125; Tregaskis, *Diary*, 210; and Kiesel, Q43, SC. See also Crowl and Love, *Seizure*, 123.

99. Appleman *et al.*, *Okinawa*, 462 and Reichman, 22 June 1945, SC.

100. Gilman, *Difference and Pathology*, 23, 228–30, and 132. *Guide to Hawaii*, 1. *Guide to Japan*, 44.

101. *Guide to Japan*, 44 and 46.

102. Scott, *God*, 255. See also Linderman, *World within War*, 163–7 and Dower, "Race," 180–3.

103. Bernheim, 2 April 1945, SC. *Handbook Japanese Forces: TM 30-480*, 98 and 166 and *TM-E 30-480*, 6. General Shepherd is quoted in Appleman *et al.*, *Okinawa*, 314. Sherrod, *Tarawa*, 105.

104. *Guide to Japan*, 42 and *Handbook Japanese Forces: TM-E 30-480*, 9.

105. Wolfert, *Solomons*, 128–31. Dickinson, Q43, SC. *Guide to Japan*, 47. LaPorte, untitled memoir, 22, SC.

106. For an explanation of the role of the Emperor, see *Guide to Japan*, 49–50. McBride, *Good Night*, 142.

107. *Handbook Japanese Forces: TM 30-480*, 101–2 and 169 and *TM-E 30-480*, 9 and *Guide to Japan*, 47 and 81.

108. *Guide to Japan*, 47; *Guide to Okinawa*, 6; and McBride, *Good Night*, 171–2.

109. Roeder, *Censored*, 126 and 144.

110. On Calcutta, see Zika, "War Dogs," 169, SC; Sterns letter, 162, UT; Wellens letter, 30 Aug. 1944, SC; and Winborn, *Wen Bon*, 21. On Bengal, see Romanus

and Sunderland, *Command*, 12 and Hess, *India*, 13. On China, see *What You Should Know about China*, 56–7; Spencer, *Hump*, 95; Caldwell, *Secret*, 111. See also *Guide to Western Pacific*, 120.

111. Sherrod, *Tarawa*, 99.
112. Sherrod, *Westward*, 98.
113. Winborn, *Wen Bon*, 107.
114. Pyle, *Chapter*, 128 and Toliver, *Artist*, 164. On Japanese POWs volunteering to work for the Americans, see Hunter, *Galahad*, 152–3.
115. Manchester, *Goodbye*, 6.
116. *Guide to Japan*, 33–4.
117. Owens, *Hell*, 56 and 57–8.
118. *Guide to New Guinea*, 42–3 and *Guide to Western Pacific*, 20, 39, and 54.
119. Riegelman, *Biak*, 25.
120. Riegelman, *Biak*, 130–1; King, *Vignettes*, 18; and Sabel, Feb. 1944, UT.
121. Winborn, *Wen Bon*, 52.
122. Thorpe, *East Wind*, 177–8. See also Owens, *Hell*, 208.
123. *Guide to East Indies*, 22–3.
124. Augustin, "Angel," 25, SC.
125. Ninkovich, "China Policy," 498.
126. Milner, *Papua*, 90, 112, and 200; Dod, *Engineers*, 198 and 531; Noonan diary, 3 Feb. 1943, ADP; and Hall, *Love*, 113 and 170. Also, Lindstrom and White, *Encounters*, 77 and 91–2.
127. Craven and Cate, *Guadalcanal*, 412; Dod, *Engineers*, 451; and Stauffer, *Quartermaster*, 318.
128. Pyle, *Chapter*, 129.
129. Pearce, *Savagism*, 99–100 and FitzGerald, *Schoolbooks*, 64–5 and 90.
130. Sun Tzu, *Art of War*, 66. Smith, *Approach*, 271; Morison, *Naval Operations*, vol. VII, 134; Cameron, *Samurai*, 124; and Smith, *Approach*, 509.
131. Sun Tzu, *Art of War*, 66. Milner, *Papua*, 175 and Hall, "532d Field Artillery," 12, SC.
132. Sun Tzu, *Art of War*, 108. Dod, *Engineers*, 628; Cannon, *Leyte*, 152; and Morison, *Naval Operations*, vol. VI, 251.
133. Tregaskis, *Diary*, 146; Lee letter, 27 Dec. 1944, UT; and Jackson, "War Stories," 24, SC.
134. Powell, *Surgeon*, 62 and Bagby, *Eagle*, 14–15.
135. Cannon, *Leyte*, 250 and Owens, *Hell*, 165.
136. Frillmann and Peck, *China*, 112 and 120.
137. *You and the Native*, 1 and 13 and O'Sullivan, "Saga," 14.
138. Toliver, *Artist*, 236.
139. Heffer, *Pacifique*, 275–6 and Munholland, "Yankee Farewell," 187–8. See also Lindstrom, "Working Encounters," 413.
140. Weeks, "Tonga," 409. Lindstrom, "Working Encounters," 396, 399, and 404–5.
141. *Islands of the Pacific*, 33–4. The State Department official is quoted in Melvyn P. Leffler, "The Cold War: What Do 'We Now Know'?" *American Historical Review* 104 (April 1999): 522. On India, see Craven and Cate, *Guadalcanal*, 416–17 and Dod, *Engineers*, 398 and 400. See also White, "Histories of Contact," 4, 22, and 28.
142. Smith, *With Chennault*, 75 and Tramposch diary, UT. See also Winborn, *Wen Bon*, 90 and 109–10.
143. Owens, *Hell*, 84–5, 128, 159, and 187.

144. On Del Monte's plantations, see Mayo, *Ordnance*, 440–1. On Luzon and Leyte, see Owens, *Hell*, 126, 175, and 58. See also, for example, Lindstrom and White, *Encounters*, 171.

Chapter 8: 'Going Asiatic'

1. Verberg, "Reflections," 17, SC.
2. Slotkin, *Regeneration*, 15 and 18 and *Gunfighter*, 11–13; John Canup, review of *The Name of War: King Philip's War and the Origins of American Identity*, by Jill Lepore, *American Historical Review* 104 (Dec. 1999): 1659; and Millett and Maslowski, *Common Defense*, 11.
3. Smith, *Virgin Land*, 176–7.
4. Edmond, *South Pacific*, 63–4.
5. Noble, *Eagle*, 171–4 and Linn, *Guardians*, 65 and 115.
6. Mayo, *Ordnance*, 358; Riegelman, *Biak*, 30; and *South Sea Lore*, 71. On New Georgia, see Saillant, 31 Aug. 1943, SC. On New Guinea, see Hutten, 16 Feb. 1944, SC.
7. Sledge, *Breed*, 31 and Sterns, 23 July 1945, UT.
8. Fahey, *Diary*, 107.
9. Maga, "Humanism," 38, 40, and 46.
10. Kernan, *Line*, 87.
11. The marine on Peleliu is quoted in Linderman, *World within War*, 183; Riegelman, *Biak*, 183; and Hall, *Love*, 116. See also White, "Forms of Wildness," 6–7.
12. Lane, untitled memoir, 76, UT.
13. Reister, *Medical Statistics*, 43–5 and Condon-Rall and Cowdrey, *Medical Service*, 109, 126–7, 264–5, 293, and 351.
14. Pyle, *Chapter*, 5 and Craven and Cate, *Guadalcanal*, 412.
15. On Leyte, see Owens, *Hell*, 59. On New Guinea, see Toliver, *Artist*, 161. On letter writing, see *What the Soldier Thinks*, April 1944, 15. On the Philippines, see Toliver, *Artist*, 265. A June 1945 report on "Medical and Social Conditions of Women in Military Service in the South-West Pacific Area" concluded that female personnel in this theater, assigned mostly to rear and staging areas, "have suffered more from inactivity than from overwork." Craighill, Box 6, CC.
16. Fahey, *Diary*, 41–2, 49, and 88.
17. For the soldiers' names for this particular mental condition see, for example, Pyle, *Chapter*, 5; Linn, *Guardians*, 74; Kahn, *Tedium*, 154; and Weeks, "Tonga," 414.
18. Craven and Cate, *Guadalcanal*, 275–7 and *What the Soldier Thinks*, April 1944, 16.
19. Tapert, *Lines*, 212.
20. Melville, *Moby Dick*, 341. McGuire, "Fighter Pilot," 116.
21. Zimmer, 4 Sept. 1944, SC.
22. Craighill, Box 5, "Medical and Social Conditions of Women in Military Service in Ceylon," 6 April 1945, CC and Sharpe, *Brothers*, 99.
23. Lindbergh, *Journals*, 852 and Toliver, *Artist*, 231. See also, Zimmer letter, 6 Nov. 1943, SC.
24. Mason, *Pacific*, 133; King, "Medical Report," 7, ADP; and Morriss, *Diary*, 57.
25. Miller, *CARTWHEEL*, 108–9, 120–2, and 187; Spector, *Eagle against the Sun*, 236; Condon-Rall and Cowdrey, *Medical Service*, 184–5; Donner, untitled memoir, 25, SC; and Saillant journal, 10 July 1943, SC.

26. Appleman *et al.*, *Okinawa*, 384–6 and 414 and Condon-Rall and Cowdrey, *Medical Service*, 403–4.
27. McFadden, Q17b, ADP.
28. Sharpe, *Brothers*, 112 and 170 and Joseph, Q17b, SC. Out of a total of 45 veterans of 6 different marine divisions surveyed by the US Army Military History Institute in its World War II questionnaire, only one marine said he remembered a drug problem, a case of morphine abuse. A similar survey of 24 veterans of the 24th Division again had only one soldier refer to drug abuse, also of morphine.
29. Press quote is from Choy *et al.*, *Coming Man*, 124–5. Bailey and Farber, *Strange Place*, 107; Hunter, *Galahad*, 60; and LaPorte, untitled memoir, 20, SC. On Calcutta, see Spector, *Eagle against the Sun*, 404.
30. Clayton, Q17b, SC. On China, see Winborn, *Wen Bon*, 126–7. On Okinawa, see Feifer, *Tennozan*, 493. On Assam, see *JAG, China–Burma–India*, vol. 2, 261–6. See also Fletcher, Q17b, SC and Dunbar, "Charles Dunbar," 8, SC.
31. Clayton, Q17b, SC.
32. On military alcohol allowances see, for example, Riches letter, 7 Dec. 1944, SC and John Gussak diary, 23 Dec. 1944, SC. On home-front support, see Bernheim, 16 March 1945, SC.
33. On New Caledonia and India, see Donner, untitled memoir, 6, SC and Bartholomae letter, 5 Aug. 1943, SC. On Biak, see Kahn, *Tedium*, 197. On India and Ceylon, see Sterns letter, 172, UT and Spencer, *Hump*, 97. On the Philippines and Guam, see Toliver, *Artist*, 298–9 and Berry, *Semper Fi*, 262. On China, see Smith, *With Chennault*, 45 and Caldwell, *Secret*, 67 and 71. On Manila, see Mathias, *Jive*, 146 and 160. See also Fahey, *Diary*, 305 and 319.
34. Riches letter, 26 Nov. 1944, SC; Condon-Rall and Cowdrey, *Medical Service*, 248; Brennen, "Ten Yard," 130, SC; and Young, 12 June 1944, SC.
35. Donner, untitled memoir, 45 and 50, SC.

Chapter 9: Human Rage

1. Peak, 19 June 1945, SC and Stouffer *et al.*, *American Soldier*, vol. 2, 174–5.
2. Kahn, *Tedium*, 217 and Bernheim, 21 Feb. 1945, SC.
3. Morriss, *Diary*, 65.
4. Toliver, *Artist*, 162 and 234.
5. Durley, McLaughlin, and Poynter, Q46, SC; Krammer, "Japanese Prisoners," 69 n. 6.
6. Durley, Q44d, SC and Bernheim letter, 12 April 1945, SC.
7. Laurie, "Dilemma," 113.
8. For the enemy dead on Guadalcanal, see Miller, *Guadalcanal*, 166. On the shortage of burial units, see Stauffer, *Quartermaster*, 252, 254, and 258 and Dod, *Engineers*, 177.
9. On Leyte, see Searles, "Memories," 10, UT. On Guadalcanal and Roi, see Stannard, Q46b, SC; Bergerud, *Touched with Fire*, 468–9; and Lindbergh, *Journals*, 919.
10. Peak, 16 June 1944, SC and Lindsay, "South of Yontan," E2, UT.
11. Kalnasy diary, vol. 8, SC. On the health hazards posed by poorly buried enemy dead, see Condon-Rall and Cowdrey, *Medical Service*, 215 and 226.
12. For GIs on Okinawa urinating on dead Japanese, see Sledge, *Breed*, 198–9 and Feifer, *Tennozan*, 488–9. On "rebutchery," see Wolfe, *Testament*, 173. Also, LaPorte, untitled memoir, 13, SC. On New Georgia, see Sabel letter, 124, UT. On the removal of gold teeth see, for example, Dunbar, "Charles Dunbar," 8, SC;

Lindbergh, *Journals*, 919; Morriss, *Diary*, 67 and 72; and Boyington, *Black Sheep*, 172–3.

13. Weingartner, "Trophies of War," 66. On Okinawa, see *Kamikaze*, in the BBC television series *Timewatch*; Searles, "Memories," 23, UT; and Brennen, "Ten Yard," 181, SC.

14. Terkel, *Good War*, 376 and Toliver, *Artist*, 152.

15. Lindstrom and White, *Encounters*, 62, 65, and 68. Also, Lindbergh, *Journals*, 821–2.

16. On the Philippines, see Smith, *Triumph*, 694. On the Marshalls and Marianas see, for example, Crowl and Love, *Seizure*, 298, 300, and 331 and Crowl, *Marianas*, 247–8.

17. *Marine Corps Operations*, vol. V, 175 and Donner, untitled memoir, 92, SC.

18. Feifer, *Tennozan*, 170; Hynes, *Passage*, 217; and Moore, notes, 10, SC.

19. Brennen, "Ten Yard," 173, SC.

20. For a general discussion of the phenomenon of wartime rape, see Tanaka, *Horrors*, 106–9. Also, Keen, *Faces of the Enemy*, 129. On control through (sexual) demeaning, see Gilman, *Difference and Pathology*, 239–42.

21. On Okinawa, see Tanaka, *Horrors*, 103 and 234 n. 80 and Feifer, *Tennozan*, 497. On rape in occupied Japan, see Tanaka, *Horrors*, 103.

22. Lee, 18 May 1945, UT; Lindbergh, *Journals*, 829; and *Guide to Burma*, 26. On sharks, see Lucas, *Letters*, 209. On snakes, see Fessler, *No Time*, 120; McGuire, "Fighter Pilot," 114; and Toliver, *Artist*, 49 and 122. On the American pioneers' "elimination of everything even remotely connected with the snake symbol," see Scott, "Sacred Serpent," 644–5.

23. Zimmer letter, 5 Jan. 1943, SC; Sledge, *Breed*, 32; and Lucas, *Letters*, 98.

24. For the war with Japan as an imperialist struggle see, for instance, Thorne, "Racial Aspects," 333. Kernan, *Line*, 26–7 and 55–6 and Morriss, *Diary*, 149.

25. Hall, *Love*, 92.

26. Hall, *Love*, 188. See also, for example, Calvert, *Submarine*, 133; McBride, *Good Night*, 116; and *What You Should Know about China*, 18

27. Cameron, *Samurai*, 94–8.

28. Sledge, *Breed*, 100.

29. Fahey, *Diary*, 173.

30. Schneider, 10 Feb. 1943, UT; Stouffer *et al.*, *American Soldier*, vol. 2, 75–6; and Kahn, *Tedium*, 183.

31. Stouffer *et al.*, *American Soldier*, vol. 2, 136, 174–5, and 612.

32. *We Return to the Philippines*, 13. On Japanese disrespect for churches, see Lindstrom and White, *Encounters*, 167 and Smith, *Marine Corps*, 367.

33. *Guide to Japan*, 49–51 and 57 and Blakefield, "Know Your Enemy," 131.

34. Fahey, *Diary*, 198 and 206. On Peleliu, see Sledge, *Breed*, 97.

35. The quote from *Yank* is in Mathias, *Jive*, 200.

36. Though John Dower's *War without Mercy* is undoubtedly the best-known study on the subject, the literature on the role of race in the war against Japan is much more extensive. The scholarship that I have found useful is mentioned in the bibliography at the end of this book. Stouffer *et al.*, *American Soldier*, vol. 2, 161. Tapert, *Lines*, 73.

37. Cameron, *Samurai*, 30–5. Miller, *Benevolent Assimilation*, 182–9 and *We Return to the Philippines*, 22.

38. Roeder, *Censored*, 175 n. 27.

39. On the Gilberts, see Lucas, *Letters*, 286. On India, see Bagby, *Eagle*, 93. Also, the GI guide *Calcutta Key*, 40 and 93. On China, see *Guide to China*, 41; Thorne,

Allies, 727; Bagby, *Eagle*, 102; Romanus and Sunderland, *Time*, 390 and *Command*, 34. Also, Caldwell, *Secret*, 180–1 and Walters, Q27, SC. For examples of violent racial incidents involving GIs and Filipinos, see Sharpe, *Brothers*, 161 and 206.

40. Turner is quoted in Smith, *Virgin Land*, 251. Morison, *Naval Operations*, vol. V, 187.
41. Slotkin, *Gunfighter*, 107 and 121.
42. Clare, *Eastward*, 128.
43. Wellens, 30 Aug. and 25 Nov. 1944, SC.
44. For the "mad dog" comparison, see Riches letter, 10 May 1945, SC. On the Japanese, see McFadden, Q44, SC; Fahey, *Diary*, 178; and Riches, 26 Jan. 1945, SC.
45. Kernan, *Line*, 82; Spector, *Eagle against the Sun*, 409–10; Sherrod, *Tarawa*, 43; and Sledge, *Breed*, 302.
46. Stouffer *et al.*, *American Soldier*, vol. 2, 34 and 157–9.
47. Spector, "Pacific War," 44 and 46 and Chappell, *Bomb*, 23–8.
48. Roeder, *Censored*, 86–7 and 109. Demott, 25 April 1945, UT.
49. Weingartner, "Subhumans," 563. Zinda, Q43, SC.
50. Cameron, *Samurai*, 106–9.
51. Herman, *Sick Bay*, 136.
52. Sears, untitled memoir, 2, UT and Manchester, *Goodbye*, 7. See also, for example, Kahn, *Tedium*, 41 and Owens, *Hell*, 91.
53. Sledge, *Breed*, 64.
54. Feifer, *Tennozan*, 486.
55. Feifer, *Tennozan*, 487; Stouffer *et al.*, *American Soldier*, vol. 2, 110; and Noonan, 14 Aug. 1942, ADP.
56. Tapert, *Lines*, 72; Stouffer *et al.*, *American Soldier*, vol. 2, 162; Noonan, 19 Dec. 1942 and 24 Jan. 1943, ADP; Bernheim, 27 Dec. 1944, SC.
57. Crowl, *Marianas*, 258.
58. Admiral Leahy is quoted in Laurie, "Dilemma," 119. Sherrod, *Westward*, 26.
59. Riches, 27 Feb. 1945, SC.
60. McBride, *Good Night*, 191, 252, and 271. On war of extermination and the logic of massacre applied to America's frontier and Filipino colony, see Slotkin, *Gunfighter*, 112.
61. Fahey, *Diary*, 68. Brennen, "Ten Yard," 93, SC. Admiral Halsey is quoted in Cameron, *Samurai*, 1.
62. Sledge, *Breed*, 117 and Sherrod, *Westward*, 97.
63. Milana, Q46, SC.
64. Sledge, *Breed*, 257–9.
65. On Biak, see Kahn, *Tedium*, 163. On Leyte, see Searles, "Memories," 10, UT and Hostetter, "Combat Doctor," 131, SC. Also, Owens, *Hell*, 66. On the Chinese, see Boyington, *Black Sheep*, 95 and Winborn, *Wen Bon*, 76 and 92. Also, Sparagana, "Psychological Warfare," 76; Hunter, *Galahad*, 165; and Eichelberger, Q46, SC.
66. Owens, *Hell*, 53.
67. Tapert, *Lines*, 198.
68. Noonan, 15 Dec. 1942, ADP.
69. Brennen, "Ten Yard," 76, SC and Tapert, *Lines*, 49.
70. Lindbergh, *Journals*, 875. See also, Cameron, *Samurai*, 126–7. For the concept of separation, regression and, ultimately, regeneration through violence, applied to the American frontier and the savage war of white settlers against Indians, see Slotkin, *Gunfighter*, 11–12.
71. Roeder, *Censored*, 154–5.

Chapter 10: Industrial Violence

1. *Handbook Japanese Forces: TM 30-480*, 169.
2. For the Japanese construction and understanding of 'Pure Self,' see ch. 8 in Dower, *War without Mercy*.
3. *Handbook Japanese Forces: TM 30-480*, 169.
4. John F. Kennedy is quoted in Tapert, *Lines*, 92.
5. For the overall constraints on supply to Asia and the Pacific, see Stauffer, *Quartermaster*, 224–5.
6. On the 32nd Division in New Guinea, see Drea, "Patience," 37 and Milner, *Papua*, 324. On India, see Fessler, *No Time*, 106 and Craven and Cate, *Matterhorn*, 64. On the typewriters, see Stauffer, *Quartermaster*, 211–12.
7. On the Gilberts and Leyte, see Crowl and Love, *Seizure*, 51 and Cannon, *Leyte*, 36. On China, see Romanus and Sunderland, *Time*, 340–1.
8. Toliver, *Artist*, 141.
9. *Marine Corps Operations*, vol. V, 390 and Condon-Rall and Cowdrey, *Medical Service*, 389.
10. Noonan, 13 July 1942, ADP and *Marine Corps Operations*, vol. IV, 610.
11. On Guadalcanal, see Weigley, *American Way*, 276; Miller, *Guadalcanal*, 73 and 83–4; and Wyatt, "Super Breed," vol. I, 38, UT. On supply problems in New Guinea, see Stauffer, *Quartermaster*, 191–200 and Fessler, *No Time*, 43.
12. Kahn, *Tedium*, 34 and Selee, 18 Feb. 1945, SP.
13. *Observer Report*, no. 275, 23 April 1945.
14. Sherrod, *Tarawa*, 69–70.
15. McBride, *Good Night*, 251.
16. Mayo, *Ordnance*, 87 and 372; Dod, *Engineers*, 212, 264, 267, and 533; Romanus and Sunderland, *Command*, 271–2 and *Time*, 313; Cannon, *Leyte*, 352; Smith, *Triumph*, 128; and Miller, *CARTWHEEL*, 344.
17. Toliver, *Artist*, 272–3. Also, Morriss, *Diary*, 156–7.
18. *Marine Corps Operations*, vol. IV, 610.
19. On Guadalcanal, see Morriss, *Diary*, 52. On Port Moresby, see Condon-Rall and Cowdrey, *Medical Service*, 128. On sea pollution, see Hitchcock, "Saga," 23, UT and McBride, *Good Night*, 156.
20. Toliver, *Artist*, 139 and *Observer Report*, no. 275, 23 April 1945.
21. Toliver, *Artist*, 139 and Sharpe, *Brothers*, 20–1. See also, Noonan diary, 8 and 9 Oct. 1942, ADP; Brion, *Lady*, 79; Kernan, *Line*, 139–40; and Sabel letter, 108–9, UT.
22. On the 'feast-and-famine' phenomenon and Oro Bay, see Stauffer, *Quartermaster*, 193 and 196. On New Britain, see Riches letter, 27 May 1944, SC. On the *Autauga*, see William Hayes, "Road to Tokyo," 22–3.
23. Stauffer, *Quartermaster*, 192–3.
24. Stauffer, *Quartermaster*, 243–8 and 268; Mayo, *Ordnance*, 415 n. 21; and *Observer Report*, 16 May 1945.
25. Geslin, "Nouvelles-Hébrides," 280–4.
26. Fahey, *Diary*, 113 and Geslin, "Nouvelles-Hébrides," 284.
27. Tramposch, 26–30 Nov. 1944, UT.
28. Morison, *Naval Operations*, vol. VII, 111; Romanus and Sunderland, *Time*, 97; Feifer, *Tennozan*, 166; and Stauffer, *Quartermaster*, 154.
29. Sharpe, *Brothers*, 223.
30. On Guadalcanal, see Gerrish, "Army Days," 60, SC. On Luzon, see Smith, *Triumph*, 91, 420–1, and 478. Sparagana, "Psychological Warfare," 143.

31. Sharpe, *Brothers*, 140 and 150 and Tregaskis, *Diary*, 91. On the weakness of Japanese tanks, see Smith, *Approach*, 310.

32. Lane, untitled memoir, 51, UT. See also, Crout letter, 21 May 1945, UT. On Japan's wartime industrial shortages, see Coox, "Japanese Military," 19–21.

33. On China, see Link and Coleman, *Medical Support*, 921; *Handbook China*, 7; Boyington, *Black Sheep*, 85; and Bykofsky and Larson, *Transportation*, 557–8. Also, Winborn, *Wen Bon*, 62–3 and 72 and Bond and Anderson, *Flying Tiger*, 148. On Saipan, see Bykofsky and Larson, *Transportation*, 521. On Leyte, see Cannon, *Leyte*, 184–5 and Dod, *Engineers*, 582. On Calcutta, see Wellens, 19 April 1945, SC.

34. Tregaskis, *Diary*, 57; Miller, *CARTWHEEL*, 42; Sharpe, *Brothers*, 48; and Smith, *Triumph*, 91.

35. Sherrod, *Westward*, 291, and also 26, 290, and 293. The Okinawa correspondent is quoted in Spector, *Eagle against the Sun*, 539. On the *kamikaze* attacks during the Philippine campaigns and battle for Okinawa, see Spector, *Eagle against the Sun*, 440–1, 518–20, and 535–9 and Appleman *et al.*, *Okinawa*, 362 and 364.

36. Milner, *Papua*, 320 and 364 and Sharpe, *Brothers*, 48. On Kolombangara, see Sabel, 142, UT. On Tarawa, see Sherrod, *Tarawa*, 125. On German technological assistance, see Manchester, *Goodbye*, 104. Also, Muse diary, 25 Oct. 1942, UT.

37. On Western views of women, nonwhites, and technology, see Herzog, *Women and Exotics*, xi–xii. On the example of China, see Blaut, *Colonizer's Model*, 115.

38. *Handbook China*, 7–8.

39. Romanus and Sunderland, *Command*, 346; Bykofsky and Larson, *Transportation*, 587–8; and Powell, *Surgeon*, 153.

40. Sun Tzu, *Art of War*, 122. Wolfert, *Solomons*, 60–1.

41. On 'buzzing,' see Hall, *Love*, 163 and Munholland, "Yankee Farewell," 187. Also, Hynes, *Passage*, 167.

42. *Guide to Hawaii*, 11. On Pacific islanders' perceptions of American military might, see Lindstrom and White, "War Stories," 11–15; Carucci, "Marshallese Cosmology," 85–6; Zelenietz and Saito, "Kilenge and the War," 173–8; Counts, "Shadows of War," 198–200; Lepowsky, "Soldiers and Spirits," 219 and 227; and Davenport, "Santa Cruz Islanders," 273 and 276.

43. Scott, *God*, 264. Compare this, for instance, with the findings on the work of American agricultural advisers in China before the war in Stross, *Stubborn Earth*, 4 and 7.

44. Sherrod, *Westward*, 30.

45. Milner, *Papua*, 323 n. 51 and Dod, *Engineers*, 500 and 621.

46. On Saipan, see *Observer Report*, 24 Oct. 1944 and Sherrod, *Westward*, 62. On Okinawa, see Appleman *et al.*, *Okinawa*, 253 and Donner, untitled memoir, 110, SC.

47. Toliver, *Artist*, 168; Sharpe, *Brothers*, 58; and Kirk diary, 17 July 1944, SC.

48. Hynes, *Passage*, 227–8.

49. Sharpe, *Brothers*, 29.

50. *Observer Report*, no. 156, 6 Sept. 1944 and no. 218, 19 Feb. 1945. See also, Mathias, *Jive*, 149. Winborn, *Wen Bon*, 132; Link and Coleman, *Medical Support*, 908; Brion, *Lady*, 133; Sledge, *Breed*, 134; and Sabel letter, 109, UT. On Burma, see Theobald diary, 20 June 1944, SC. On Hawaii, see Gerrish, "Army Days," 56, SC.

51. On Oro Bay, see Wolfe, *Testament*, 188–9.

52. On Peleliu, see *Marine Corps Operations*, vol. IV, 150–1. On the Marianas, see Baggerman, 19 Feb. 1945, UT.

53. On the Army Air Forces and the use of insecticides, see Link and Coleman, *Medical Support*, 807–10, 827, 830, and 901. The study concluded (827) that DDT "never became available in sufficient quantities to fill all needs."
54. Link and Coleman, *Medical Support*, 813; Smith, *Approach*, 392; and Kleber and Birdsell, *Chemical Warfare*, 304 and 308.
55. Cecil, *Herbicidal Warfare*, 9–11. See also, Knobloch, *Culture of Wilderness*, 138–40.
56. Lindbergh, *Journals*, 919. On the ecological damage caused by American forces during World War II, see also Coates and Morrison, "American Rampant," 215.
57. On brush, cane fields, and kunai grass, see Miller, *CARTWHEEL*, 333; *Marine Corps Operations*, vol. III, 351 and 426; and Dod, *Engineers*, 199 and 274. On the Russells, see Zimmer, 6 May 1943, SC. On Espíritu Santo, see Sabel, 96–7, UT. On New Georgia, see Miller, *CARTWHEEL*, 140. On Luzon, see Condon-Rall and Cowdrey, *Medical Service*, 345. On Bougainville, see Dod, *Engineers*, 544.
58. On the reduction of coral to construction material, see Dod, *Engineers*, 385–6. On Middleburg Island, see Kirk diary, 4 Sept. 1944, SC. On Tinian, see Gray, "I Remember," 471.
59. Toliver, *Artist*, 228; Pyle, *Chapter*, 19 and 142–3; Hynes, *Passage*, 200–1; and Appleman *et al.*, *Okinawa*, 81.
60. Baggerman, 2 March 1945, UT. Also, 10 March 1945. Nero, "Palau," 126–7. See also, Geslin, "Nouvelles-Hébrides," 254, 261, and 263. Discussing the construction of wharfs near the Sarakata River on Santo Island, Geslin concludes (261): "Ainsi la physionomie de la côte, surtout à l'Est de Sarakata fut complètement transformée et rendue méconnaissable, même pour ses familiers." (Thus the features of the coast, especially east of the Sarakata, were completely transformed and rendered unrecognizable even to those familiar with it.)

Chapter 11: Technological Destruction

1. In his study of the 1st Marine Division, for example, Craig Cameron has shown that it was especially "in the final months of the war where technology bridged the gap between the marines' exterminationist warrior ethos and the means to realize it." *Samurai*, 17. See also his chapter on Okinawa, entitled "Technology Empowers Ideology."
2. Morriss, *Diary*, 94. *Handbook Japanese Forces: TM 30–480*, 217. On Saipan, see Sherrod, *Westward*, 78. On Luzon, see Sharpe, *Brothers*, 179.
3. For the production levels of ammunition, see Coox, "Japanese Military," 21. For the shell wound rates, see Reister, *Medical Statistics*, 204–5 and 208–9.
4. On public opinion, see Chappell, *Bomb*, 45–6. For the *Chicago Tribune* cartoon, see Brcak and Pavia, "Racism," 676.
5. On the Solomons and Papua, see Miller, *CARTWHEEL*, 161; Milner, *Papua*, 374–5; and Mayo, *Ordnance*, 372. On Bougainville, see Miller, *CARTWHEEL*, 364.
6. On the *Montpelier*, see Fahey, *Diary*, 15–16. On New Georgia, see Miller, *CARTWHEEL*, 146 n. 6.
7. Crowl and Love, *Seizure*, 40, 131, and 159; Weigley, *American Way*, 286; and Spector, *Eagle against the Sun*, 268.
8. Crowl and Love, *Seizure*, 230–1 and Weigley, *American Way*, 286–7.
9. Morison, *Naval Operations*, vol. XIV, 12–13, 35 n. 4, and 48; Weigley, *American Way*, 307; and Sherrod, *Westward*, 186.

10. Appleman *et al.*, *Okinawa*, 69, 194, 253, and 255 and Morison, *Naval Operations*, vol. XIV, 34 and 35 n. 4, and 245–6. Pyle, *Chapter*, 98–9. Blome, "531st Field Artillery," 12 and 15, SC.
11. On artillery dependency, see Millett, "United States Armed Forces," 78. On New Georgia and the Philippines, see Miller, *CARTWHEEL*, 163 and Cannon, *Leyte*, 245–6.
12. On tree demolition, see Miller, *CARTWHEEL*, 114 and Peak diary, 4 Aug. 1944, SC. On cave warfare, see Riegelman, *Biak*, 151; Crowl and Love, *Seizure*, 270; Smith, *Approach*, 375; and Dod, *Engineers*, 648. On reef demolition, see Mason, *Pacific*, 244. Also, Crowl, *Marianas*, 127 and Smith, *Approach*, 58 and 423. On fishing, see Sabel letters, 109 and 119, UT and Counts, "Shadows of War," 189. On the Solomons, see Wyatt, "Super Breed," vol. I, 15, UT.
13. Crowl and Love, *Seizure*, 232; Brown, *Marine*, 65; and Fahey, *Diary*, 285.
14. Sherrod, *Tarawa*, 110; Toliver, *Artist*, 154 and 232; and Sabel letters, 124–6, UT.
15. Gray, "I Remember," 460; Smith, *Approach*, 244, note 24, 269, and 273; and *Guide to Okinawa*, 3.
16. The soldier is quoted in Cannon, *Leyte*, 130; Admiral Ota in *Marine Corps Operations*, vol. V, 321.
17. On the Marianas, see Gray, "I Remember," 472 and *Observer Report*, 24 Oct. 1944. On Manila, see Smith, *Triumph*, 264, 275, 291, 293–7, and 301. On Okinawa, see Appleman *et al.*, *Okinawa*, 389 and 400–2.
18. Cannon, *Leyte*, 195.
19. On Saipan, see Harries, *Soldiers of the Sun*, 433. On Manila, see Smith, *Triumph*, 307. For Okinawa's civilian casualty numbers, see Cameron, *Samurai*, 188. Also, Feifer, *Tennozan*, 532–3.
20. Webb, "Odyssey," 116.
21. Tapert, *Lines*, 246.
22. McBride, *Good Night*, 78 and 242.
23. Whalen, 29 Jan. 1945, WP; Kahn, *Tedium*, 56–7; and LaPorte, untitled memoir, 27, SC. On the horrors phosphorus caused in American ranks see also, for example, Fahey, *Diary*, 136 and Herman, *Sick Bay*, 110.
24. Gerrish, "Army Days," 56, SC; Hitchcock, "Saga," 23, UT; Giles, "Recollections," 109, UT; and Brennen, "Ten Yard," 118, SC. See also, Sledge, *Breed*, 32 and 165–6.
25. Smith, *Approach*, 445; Craven and Cate, *Guadalcanal*, 643; and Lindbergh, *Journals*, 877.
26. Miller, *Guadalcanal*, 118 and 126. Crowl, *Marianas*, 44–5; *Marine Corps Operations*, vol. III, 364 and 425; and Morison, *Naval Operations*, vol. VIII, 359. Sherrod, *Westward*, 42.
27. Kleber and Birdsell, *Chemical Warfare*, 534–7.
28. Riegelman, *Biak*, 69. On New Georgia, see Kleber and Birdsell, *Chemical Warfare*, 539. On Peleliu, see Kleber and Birdsell, *Chemical Warfare*, 567–8 and Sledge, *Breed*, 118 and 121.
29. Kleber and Birdsell, *Chemical Warfare*, 293, 553, 557, 579, and 586 and *Marine Corps Operations*, vol. III, 241. McBride, *Good Night*, 237.
30. On the use of fire against Native Americans and Filipinos see, for example, Millett and Maslowski, *Common Defense*, 15; Drinnon, *Facing West*, 214; and Linn, *Guardians*, 17. On New Britain, see Toliver, *Artist*, 152. On Burma, see Terkel, *Good War*, 376. Cannon, *Leyte*, 351. On Saipan, see Crowl, *Marianas*, 143.
31. Kleber and Birdsell, *Chemical Warfare*, 586; Cameron, *Samurai*, 178–80; *Marine Corps Operations*, vol. V, 333; Feifer, *Tennozan*, 446 and 488; and Giles, "Recollections," 196, UT.

32. Roeder, *Censored*, 108.
33. On Hawaii, see Riches, 15 Oct. 1942, SC. On Guadalcanal, see Berry, *Semper Fi*, 84 and Tregaskis, *Diary*, 227. For the soldier on Fiji, see Kirk, 24 July 1943, SC. Lindbergh, *Journals*, 906. On the problems with masks and impregnated clothing in tropical climates, see Kleber and Birdsell, *Chemical Warfare*, 249 and Stauffer, *Quartermaster*, 203.
34. Hall, *Love*, 187–8. For the polls, see *What the Soldier Thinks*, Jan. 1945, 1–2. On China, see Winborn, *Wen Bon*, 23. On Luzon, see Kahn, *Tedium*, diary entry for 24 Dec. 1944. On Okinawa, see Donner, untitled memoir, 42, SC; Sledge, *Breed*, 268; and Moore notes, 5, SC. For gas scares in Burma, see Selee diary, 4 Jan. 1945, SP. On accusations by both sides of the use of poison gas in the Pacific, see Chappell, *Bomb*, 182–3 n. 20.
35. For an explanation of the Japanese and American positions on gas warfare, see Kleber and Birdsell, *Chemical Warfare*, 652–6. It should be noted that, despite the apprehensions mentioned, American interwar defense plans concerning both Hawaii and the Philippines regarded poison gas as an acceptable tool. See Linn, *Guardians*, 197–8. On New Caledonia, see Noonan diary, 15 Oct. 1942, ADP.
36. *Observer Report*, no. 126 and Riegelman, *Biak*, 151. However, when General Eichelberger and other high-ranking officers asked Riegelman on Biak for his opinion on using captured Japanese "poison smoke candles" against the caves, Riegelman claims he advised against it. *Biak*, 153. So many people died from fumes released by phosphorus grenades thrown into caves that after the war some Okinawans charged that poison gas had been used in some cases and demanded an investigation. See Feifer, *Tennozan*, 496–7.
37. On the growing voices in favor of the use of poison gas in the press and among military leaders, see Chappell, *Bomb*, 86–92 and van Courtland Moon, "Project SPHINX," 303–6. On Iwo Jima, see *Marine Corps Operations*, vol. IV, 612–14. Shields letter, 4 May 1945, SC.
38. Niader, 28 May 1945, SC.
39. Sharpe, *Brothers*, 212; Gabard, 18 Sept. 1944, UT; and Harris, 27 June 1945, UT. See also Brown, *Marine*, 67.
40. Fahey, *Diary*, 201. Sterns letter, 16 May 1945, UT. On Stilwell, see Romanus and Sunderland, *Command*, 255. On the invasion of China, see Fahey, *Diary*, 320 and Kahn, *Tedium*, diary entry for 7 Aug. 1945 (see also entries for 6 Oct. and 7 Dec. 1944 as well as 27 Jan. and 7 Feb. 1945).
41. Sherrod, *Westward*, 202 and 196. On Biak, see Kahn, *Tedium*, 180. On the increased power of Japanese artillery, see *Marine Corps Operations*, vol. IV, 726–7 and Appleman *et al.*, *Okinawa*, 91–2, 110, 250, 384, 386, and 414. See also, for example, Walker, Q43, SC. Craig Cameron has noted that on Okinawa "the Japanese had begun to shift away from the purely intangible, spiritual aspects of soldiering and to move toward a more instrumental approach." *Samurai*, 185.
42. The sailor quotes are from Fahey, *Diary*, 191; Lee letter, 24 Nov. 1944, UT; and Kernan, *Line*, 154. For the American casualty figures, see Weigley, *American Way*, 307–8; Appleman *et al.*, *Okinawa*, 473; Chappell, *Bomb*, 41; and LaFeber, *Clash*, 241–2. For the GI slogans predicting the war's duration, see Bailey and Farber, *Strange Place*, 50.
43. Pyle, *Chapter*, 141.
44. Vaughan, 11 July 1944, UT; Gabard, 27 Jan. 1945, UT; and McBride, *Good Night*, 191.
45. *Marine Corps Operations*, vol. IV, 705.

46. Howes letter, 9 May 1945, UT; Wallace, 11 May 1945, UT; and Sterns letter, 12 May 1945, UT.
47. Tapert, *Lines*, 117.
48. On Tinian, see Crowl, *Marianas*, 288. On the tactical use of fire bombs, see Kleber and Birdsell, *Chemical Warfare*, 319–20 and 633–5.
49. On Luzon and Paoching, see Kleber and Birdsell, *Chemical Warfare*, 633–4. On the Solomons, see Lindstrom and White, *Encounters*, 62 and 65 and "War Stories," 24.
50. Craven and Cate, *Matterhorn*, 696–7 and Sherry, *American Air Power*, 311.
51. For the history of the B-29 raids against Japan, see Spector, *Eagle against the Sun*, 488–94; Schaffer, *Wings of Judgment*, 125–37; Daniels, "Before Hiroshima," 16–18; and Kleber and Birdsell, *Chemical Warfare*, 624–30. On the *Montpelier*, see Fahey, *Diary*, 169.
52. Hutten, 22 Feb. 1945, SC.
53. Selee, 12 March 1945, SP. *Time* is quoted in Hopkins, "Bombing," 470–1.
54. Baggerman, 26 March and 1 April 1945, UT.
55. Elizabeth Gussak letter, 21 June 1945, SC and Selee, 27 July 1945, SP.
56. Weaver, 15 Aug. 1945, UT and Childress, *Pacific Journal*, 26. The airplane mechanic is Kirk, SC.
57. Fahey, *Diary*, 371; Gabard, 6 Aug. 1945, UT; and Snipes, 7 Aug. 1945, UT. See also, Lindsay, "South of Yontan," 36, UT and Hostetter, "Combat Doctor," 222–3, SC.
58. Kahn, *Tedium*, 275; Tapert, *Lines*, 286 and 288; Mathias, *Jive*, 199; Lee diary, 7 Aug. 1945, UT; and Tramposch diary, 8 and 12 Aug. 1945, UT. See also Fink letter, 8 Aug. 1945, UT.
59. Long letter, 10 Aug. 1945, UT; Tapert, *Lines*, 288; Spaulding, 11 Aug. 1945, UT; and Kahn, *Tedium*, 278–9.
60. Sharpe, *Brothers*, 248–9; Spaulding letter, 15 Aug. 1945, UT; Owens, *Hell*, 229; and Hynes, *Passage*, 253–4.
61. For the polls, see Bernstein, "Politics of Surrender," 11 n. 43. Young, 15 Aug. 1945, SC.
62. Howes letter, 12 Aug. 1945, UT and Kahn, *Tedium*, 276. See also, Tapert, *Lines*, 287 and Fink letter, 8 Aug. 1945, UT.
63. Miller, "Battleship X," 163.

Bibliography

Primary sources

I Manuscripts

(A) *The United States Army Military History Institute,*
Carlisle Barracks, Pennsylvania

1. The World War II Survey Collection
11th Airborne Division
Augustin, James H. Questionnaire. Memoir: "Once an Angel."
Bernheim, Eli D. Questionnaire and letters to his mother.
6th Infantry Division
Peak, Earl W. Diary.
24th Infantry Division
Hostetter, Philip H. Memoir: "Combat Doctor in the South Pacific or Red Beach to
    Mandog Hill."
Reichman, Marvin O. Letters to his mother.
27th Infantry Division
O'Callaghan, Garry. "Memoirs of Garry O'Callaghan: My 1,462 Days in World War II."
31st Infantry Division
Stohrer, Clifford H. Letters to his wife.
33rd Infantry Division
Kaniarz, Frank A. Memoir: "Franz'l Kaney Goes Off to the Wars."
McNeil, William S. Memoir: "World War II 1941–1946: My Own Story."
37th Infantry Division
Hanson, Edwin E. Memoir: "My Military History."
Kalnasy, Louis. Diary.
38th Infantry Division
DeAugustinis, Elmer V. Questionnaire.
40th Infantry Division
Gerrish, Paul M. Memoir: "My Army Days."
Riches, Sidney A. Letters to his parents.
43rd Infantry Division
Dix, Harvey A. Untitled memoir.
Dunbar, Charles. Memoir: "Charles Dunbar Remembers World War II and Korea."
LaMagna, Salvatore N. Questionnaire. Memoir: "Silent Victory World War II."
Pichler, Peter. Letters.
Saillant, Richard. Diary.
Smith, Slade S. Diary and letters to his wife.
Zimmer, Joseph E. Letters to his family and fiancée.
77th Infantry Division
Schichler, Ernest A. Questionnaire and untitled memoir.
96th Infantry Division
Dazey, William B. Questionnaire.
Jackson, Robert A. Memoir: "War Stories."

Moore, Ellis O. Letters and notes.
Schroeder, Marvin F. Memoir: "My Military Service in World War II."
Americal Division
DePorto, Carlo. Questionnaire.
Durley, W. Mark, Jr. Questionnaire.
Lovett, Richard C. Questionnaire.
McFadden, Herchel N. Questionnaire.
McLaughlin, William J. Questionnaire.
Poynter, Ray E. Questionnaire.
Stannard, John E. Questionnaire.
1st Marine Division
Donner, Christopher S. Untitled memoir.
Joseph, John L. Questionnaire.
Kiesel, Leonard. Questionnaire.
Milana, Richard E. Questionnaire.
Niader, William. Letters to his parents.
Peto, George, Jr. Memoir: "Peleliu."
2nd Marine Division
Shields, Volney C. Letters to his parents.
3rd Marine Division
Walker, Reginald G. Questionnaire.
4th Marine Division
LaPorte, Arthur T. Untitled memoir.
Potucek, Eldridge G. Memoir: "The Molding and Shaping of a Marine."
Velotta, Vincent F. Questionnaire.
5th Marine Division
Clayton, Bert A. Questionnaire.
Hayes, Ira H. Untitled memoir.
Zinda, Stanley R. Questionnaire.
6th Marine Division
Asma, H. John. Questionnaire.
Brennen, George L. Memoir: "My Ten Yard."
Artillery
Blome, Gordon A. Memoir: "531st Field Artillery BN World War 2."
Busch, Vernal F. 8th Marine Defense and Anti-Aircraft Artillery Battalion. Memoir: "World War II."
Colvin, Randall. 612th Field Artillery Battalion. Diary.
Hall, Lloyd C. "532nd Field Artillery Battalion APO 235: Report of Operations Ryukyus Campaign, 31 March to 30 June 1945."
Whitesides, Joe E. 213th Field Artillery Battalion. Memoir: "The Personal History of Joe Edward Whitesides."
Medical
Aarons, Erma E. 360th Station Hospital. Letters to her parents.
Frater, Janibell. 41st Field Hospital. Diary.
Gamso, Robert R. 603rd Medical Clearance Company. Letters to his family.
Gussak, Elizabeth. 69th General Hospital. Letters to her family.
Hayes, Charles W. Letter to newspaper.
Heidbrink, Virgil E. 172nd General Hospital. Letters to his sister.
Hollenbeck, Stanley W. 14th Portable Surgical Hospital. Diary.
Hutten, Edwin C. 23rd Field Hospital. Letters to his family.
Theobald, Paul G. 45th Portable Surgical Hospital. Diary/memoir.

Verberg, Milton W. 204th General Hospital. Memoir: "Reflections of a Soldier Who Survived Pearl Harbor."

Vissex, Richard. 44th Portable Surgical Hospital. Diary.

Young, George G. 58th Evacuation Hospital. Diary.

Others

Dickinson, LeRoy E. Merrill's Marauders. Questionnaire.

Eichelberger, John F., Jr. Merrill's Marauders. Questionnaire.

Fletcher, James S. Kachin Rangers. Questionnaire.

Gussak, John. Provost marshal for Assam and north Burma. Diary.

Horst, Carl H. 127th Quartermaster Bakery Company. Letters to his sister.

Kirk, Buster. 38th Service Squadron. Diary.

Shupe, Joseph B. Questionnaire.

Stephens, Wilson P. 570th Quartermaster Battalion. Letters to his wife.

Wellens, Cecelia. WAC. Letters to her parents.

Zika, Richard J. War Dog Detachment. Memoirs: "War Dogs of CBI" and "War Dog Det. – CBI."

2. The Americal Division Papers

Burns, Robert D. Diary.

Guaranti, Arthur. Diary.

King, Arthur G. "Medical Intelligence Report on Guadalcanal."

Noonan, Ralph T. Diary and letters to his wife.

Vera, Fernando. Memoir: "Perils of Pauline: World War II."

3. The George Bartholomae Papers

22nd Field Hospital. Letters to his girlfriend.

4. The Lloyd A. Corkan Papers

843rd Anti-Aircraft Artillery Battalion. Letters to his wife.

5. The Margaret Craighill Collection

Box 5. Folder: "Medical and Social Conditions of Women in Military Service in Ceylon."

Box 6. Folder: "Pacific Ocean Area Notes."

Box 27. Folder: "Women in SWPA."

6. The Richard Selee Papers

45th Engineers. Diary.

7. The Martha A. Wayman Papers

WAC. Letters to her mother.

8. The Charles W. Whalen, Jr. Papers

628th Quartermaster Refrigeration Company/45th Quartermaster Battalion. Letters to his family.

(B) *James D. Hoskins Library, University of Tennessee, Knoxville*

The World War II Collection

Army

Giles, Kenneth R. 96th Infantry Division. Memoir: "Recollections or 'Come on Giles – The War's Over!'" MS-1881/Box 11, Folder 9.

Greene, Wayland H. 32nd Infantry Division. Memoir: "Why Are You So Yellow?: 38520190 32nd Division." MS-1881/Box 11, Folder 16.

McGill, Troy A. 5th Cavalry. Letters to his family. MS-1881/Box 18, Folder 12.

Sabel, William O. 350th Engineers. Letters to his parents. MS-1892/Box 8, Folder 6.

Searles, Glenn. 77th Infantry Division. "Memories of 'My War.'" MS-2012/Box 13, Folder 34.

Sears, Edward J. 164th Infantry. Untitled memoir. MS-1881/Box 24, Folder 4.

Spencer, Richard E. 77th Infantry Division. "Memories of My Army Experiences, 1941 to 1945." MS-1892/Box 11, Folder 6.

Army Air Forces

Ash, Omar L. Letters to his family. MS-1314/Box 1, Folder 4.

Baggerman, William F. XXI Bomber Command. Letters to his parents. MS-1764/Box 4, Folders 6, 7, 10, and 16.

Baghetti, Frank. Memoir: "As I Witnessed World War II, 1941–1945." MS-2012/Box 1, Folder 20.

Crout, George C. 42nd Bomb Group. Letters to his mother. MS-1881/Boxes 4 and 5.

Harris, Edward G. 63rd Bomb Squadron. Letters to his family. MS-1259/Box 5, Folder 1.

Hitchcock, Fred, Jr. Memoir: "Saga of the Seventy-Ninth or from Savannah to Chofu: A Personal Diary of My Life and Experiences in the 79th Airdrome Squadron WWII." MS-1608/Box 16, Folder 22.

Nickell, Charles. 342nd Fighter Squadron. Letters to his family. MS-2012/Box 11, Folder 19.

Poole, Edward P. 73rd Fighter Squadron. Untitled memoir. MS-1608/Box 14, Folder 25.

Sterns, George. 97th Army Air Force Emergency Rescue Boat Crew. Letters to his parents. MS-2012/Box 14, Folder 9.

Tinsley, Stanley. Letters. MS-1427/Box 8, Folder 1.

Trmposch, Albert F. 529th Fighter Squadron. Diary. MS-1881/Box 30, Folder 4.

Vaughan, Meeks B. 517th Photo Reconnaissance Squadron. Diary. MS-1298/Box 7, Folder 8.

Wallace, George B. 16th Combat Cargo Squadron. Letters to his family. MS-1764/Box 18, Folder 37.

Weaver, William C. XXI Bomber Command. Letters to his wife. MS-2012/Box 14, Folder 43.

Wiberley, Charles C. Letters home. MS-1764/Box 19, Folder 20.

Wotring, Maxon L. 5th Air Force. Memoir: "A Day that Was." MS-2012/Box 15, Folder 24.

Marine Corps

Lane, John E. 25th Marines. Untitled memoir. MS-1298/Box 3, Folder 29.

Schneider, Leslie C. 5th Marines. Letters to his mother. MS-1881/Box 20, Folder 29.

Trammell, Paul C. 3rd Marines. Untitled memoir. MS-2012/Box 14, Folder 28.

Wyatt, George W. Memoirs of various men from the 1st Marine Division: "Super Breed." MS-1764/Box 20, Folder 7.

Medical

Bradley, William J. 151st Medical Detachment. Memoir: "World War Two – My War." MS-1881/Box 2, Folder 8.

Demott, Robert J. Letters to his parents. MS-1230/Box 1, Folder 5.

Navy

Fink, Harold S. Letters to his wife. MS-1230/Box 1, Folder 15.

Gabard, William M. USS *Admiralty Islands*. Letters to his family. MS-1608/Box 2, Folder 1.

Goolsby, Walter. USS *McCoy Reynolds*. MS-1427/Box 1, Folder 15.

Hansen, Richard. Memoir: "United States Navy, 1941–1945." MS-2012/Box 7, Folder 1.

Harris, H.E., Jr. Letters to his family. MS-1881/Box 12, Folder 6.

Howes, Robert M. USS *Dayton*. Letters to his wife. MS-1892/Box 4, Folders 3–8.

Landers, Guy F. USS *Arkansas*. Diary. MS-1298/Box 3, Folder 28.

Lee, Walter A. USS *O'Bannon*. Diary and letters to his mother and aunt. MS-1764/Box 12, Folder 30.

Lindsay, Charles S. 1st Bomb Disposal Company. Memoir: "South of Yontan, Okinawa." MS-1881/Box 15, Folder 18.
Long, John R. USS *Wilkes-Barre*. Letters to his wife. MS-1298/Box 3, Folders 36 and 42.
Marin, Joseph. USS *Alabama*. Letter to his mother. MS-1764/Box 14, Folder 4.
McClain, William A. USS *Tabberer*. Letters to his wife. MS-1881/Box 18, Folder 4.
Muse, Robert P. Diary. MS-1608/Box 13, Folder 32.
Ramsey, James A. USS *Abercrombie*. Diary. MS-1298/Box 6, Folder 14.
Sanders, Charles N. Untitled memoir. MS-1892/Box 8, Folder 7.
Snipes, Robert J. USS *Bataan* and *Cowpens*. Diary. MS-2012/Box 14, Folder 1.
Spaulding, Leon F. Letters to his wife. MS-1881/Box 28, Folder 1.
Others
Cummings, Clarence. Letters home. MS-1881/Box 3, Folder 19.
Fox, Victor J. Letters from soldiers. MS-2012/Box 6, Folder 45.

II Published letters, diaries, and memoirs

Berry, Henry. *Semper Fi, Mac: Living Memories of the U.S. Marines in World War II*. New York: Arbor House, 1982.
Bond, Charles R., Jr. and Terry Anderson. *A Flying Tiger's* Diary. College Station: Texas A & M University Press, 1984.
Boyington, Gregory. *Baa Baa Black Sheep*. Blue Ridge Summit, Penn.: Tab Books, 1989.
Brion, Irene. *Lady GI: A Woman's War in the South Pacific: The Memoir of Irene Brion*. Novato, Calif.: Presidio Press, 1997.
Brown, David Tucker, Jr. *Marine from Virginia: Letters 1941–1945*. Chapel Hill: University of North Carolina Press, 1997.
Caldwell, Oliver J. *A Secret War: Americans in China, 1944–1945*. Carbondale: Southern Illinois University Press, 1972.
Calvert, James F. *Silent Running: My Years on a World War II Attack Submarine*. New York: John Wiley & Sons, 1995.
Childress, Jerrell P. *Pacific Journal: Journal Covering Service on the USS* Ingersoll *(DD 652), April–November 1945*. N.p.: privately published, 1989.
Clare, Thomas H. *Lookin' Eastward: A G.I. Salaam to India*. New York: Macmillan, 1945.
Clements, Charles O. *South Pacific Memories of World War II: Charles O. Clements, Survivor*. N.p.: privately published, 1994.
Close, Winton R. "B-29s in the CBI: A Pilot's Account." *Aerospace Historian* 30, no. 1 (1983): 6–14.
DeWitt, Gill. *The First Navy Flight Nurse on a Pacific Battlefield: A Picture Story of a Flight to Iwo Jima by Lieutenant Gill DeWitt, USN*. Fredericksburg, Tex.: Admiral Nimitz Foundation, 1983.
Fahey, James J. *Pacific War Diary, 1942–1945*. Westport, Conn.: Greenwood Press, 1974.
Fessler, Diane Burke. *No Time for Fear: Voices of American Military Nurses in World War II*. East Lansing: Michigan State University Press, 1996.
Frillmann, Paul and Graham Peck. *China: The Remembered Life*. Boston: Houghton Mifflin, 1968.
Frost, Edwin C. "China Convoy." *Aerospace Historian* 30, no. 1 (1983): 15–23.
Gray, Denver D. "I Remember Pearl Harbor: A Nebraska Army Air Force Officer in the Pacific Theatre during World War II." *Nebraska History* 62, no. 4 (1981): 437–80.
Hall, Gwendolyn Midlo, ed. *Love, War, and the 96th Engineers (Colored): The World War II New Guinea Diaries of Captain Hyman Samuelson*. Urbana and Chicago: University of Illinois Press, 1995.

Hayes, William E. "On the Road to Tokio: A Sailor's Recollection of the Pacific War." *Wisconsin Magazine of History* 75, no. 4 (1992): 284–305 and 76, no. 1 (1992): 21–50.

Herman, Jan K. *Battle Station Sick Bay: Navy Medicine in World War II*. Annapolis, Md.: Naval Institute Press, 1997.

Hostnik, Frank and John Rury. "Michigan Medics in Action: The 107th Medical Battalion in WWII." *Michigan History* 72, no. 1 (1988): 12–18.

Hunter, Charles N. *Galahad*. San Antonio, Texas: Naylor, 1963.

Hynes, Samuel. *Flights of Passage: Reflections of a World War II Aviator*. New York: Frederic C. Beil and Annapolis, Md.: Naval Institute Press, 1988.

Jungwirth, Clarence J. *Diary of a National Guardsman in World War II, 1940–1945*. Oshkosh, Wisconsin: privately published, 1991.

Kahn, Sy M. *Between Tedium and Terror: A Soldier's World War II Diary, 1943–45*. Urbana and Chicago: University of Illinois Press, 1993.

Kernan, Alvin. *Crossing the Line: A Bluejacket's World War II Odyssey*. Annapolis, Maryland: Naval Institute Press, 1994.

King, Arthur G. *Vignettes of the South Pacific: The Lighter Side of World War II*. Cincinnati, Ohio: privately published, 1991.

Leach, Douglas Edward. *Now Hear This: The Memoir of a Junior Naval Officer in the Great Pacific War*. Kent, Ohio: Kent State University Press, 1987.

Lindbergh, Charles A. *The Wartime Journals of Charles A. Lindbergh*. New York: Harcourt Brace Jovanovich, 1970.

Lucas, George B. *Every Other Day: Letters from the Pacific*. Annapolis, Md.: Naval Institute Press, 1995.

Manchester, William. *Goodbye, Darkness: A Memoir of the Pacific War*. Boston: Little, Brown, 1980.

Maroon, Thomas J. *War in the South Pacific: A Soldier's Journal*. N.p.: privately published, 1995.

Mason, John T., Jr., ed. *The Pacific War Remembered: An Oral History Collection*. Annapolis, Md.: Naval Institute Press, 1986.

Mathias, Frank F. *G.I. Jive: An Army Bandsman in World War II*. Lexington: University Press of Kentucky, 1982.

Maule, Harry E. *A Book of War Letters*. New York: Random House, 1943.

McBride, William M., ed. *Good Night Officially: The Pacific War Letters of a Destroyer Sailor: The Letters of Yeoman James Orvill Raines*. Boulder, Colo.: Westview Press, 1994.

McGuire, Sue Lynn. "'Things Are Tough All Over': An American Fighter Pilot in New Guinea." *Tennessee Historical Quarterly* 52, no. 2 (1993): 113–21.

Michel, John J. A. *Mr. Michel's War: From Manila to Mukden: An American Navy Officer's War with the Japanese, 1941–1945*. Novato, Calif.: Presidio Press, 1998.

Miller, David B. "Life Aboard 'Battleship X': The USS *South Dakota* in World War II." *South Dakota History* 23, no. 2 (1993): 142–65.

Mills, Robert B. "Reflections of a PBM Pilot." *Aerospace Historian* 33, no. 1 (1986): 19–20.

Morriss, Mack. *South Pacific Diary, 1942–1943*. Lexington: University Press of Kentucky, 1996.

Mund, Lester S. *Musings of a Soldier*. N.p.: privately published, 1981.

Norberg, Carl A. "In the Southwest Pacific with the Army's Navy." *Aerospace Historian* 27, no. 3 (1980): 163–8.

O'Callahan, Joseph T. *I Was Chaplain on the Franklin*. New York: Macmillan, 1956.

O'Sullivan, Charles P. "Sully's Sage: Braving the Jungles of Papua-New Guinea, 1943." *Air Power History* 41, no. 4 (1994): 4–17.

Owens, William A. *Eye-Deep in Hell: A Memoir of the Liberation of the Philippines, 1944–1945*. Dallas, Tex.: Southern Methodist University Press, 1989.

Peckham, Howard H. and Shirley A. Snyder, eds. *Letters from Fighting Hoosiers.* Vol. 2 of *Indiana in World War II.* Bloomington: Indiana War History Commission, 1948.

Powell, Lyle S. *A Surgeon in Wartime China.* Lawrence: University of Kansas Press, 1946.

Pyle, Ernest T. *Last Chapter.* New York: Henry Holt, 1946.

Riegelman, Harold. *Caves of Biak: An American Officer's Experiences in the Southwest Pacific.* New York: Dial Press, 1955.

Scott, Robert L., Jr. *God Is My Co-Pilot.* New York: Charles Scribner's Sons, 1943.

Seelig, Frederick A. *One Marine Mustang's Memoirs: Fifty Months with Defense Battalions in the Pacific, 1940–1945.* New York: Vantage Press, 1997.

Sharpe, George. *Brothers beyond Blood: A Battalion Surgeon in the South Pacific.* Austin, Tex.: Diamond Books, 1989.

Sherrod, Robert. *On to Westward: The Battles of Saipan and Iwo Jima.* Baltimore, Md.: The Nautical & Aviation Publishing Company of America, 1990.

Sherrod, Robert. *Tarawa: The Story of a Battle.* New York: Duell, Sloan and Pearce, 1944.

Sledge, Eugene B. *With the Old Breed at Peleliu and Okinawa.* Novato, Calif.: Presidio Press, 1990.

Smith, Robert M. *With Chennault in China: A Flying Tiger's Diary.* Blue Ridge Summit, Penn.: Tab Books, 1984.

Smith, Stanley E., ed. *The United States Marine Corps in World War II.* New York: Random House, 1969.

Spencer, Otha C. *Flying the Hump: Memories of an Air War.* College Station: Texas A & M University Press, 1992.

Tapert, Annette, ed. *Lines of Battle: Letters from American Servicemen, 1941–1945.* New York: Times Books, 1987.

Tarkov, John. "A Pacific Sketchbook." *MHQ: Quarterly Journal of Military History.* 3, no. 2 (1991): 102–11.

Terkel, Studs. *'The Good War': An Oral History of World War Two.* New York: Pantheon Books, 1984.

Thorpe, Elliott R. *East Wind, Rain: The Intimate Account of an Intelligence Officer in the Pacific, 1939–49.* Boston, Mass.: Gambit, 1969.

Toliver, Oleta Stewart, ed. *An Artist at War: The Journal of John Gaitha Browning.* Denton: University of North Texas Press, 1994.

Tregaskis, Richard. *Guadalcanal Diary.* New York: Random House, 1943.

Webb, Robert G. "The Pacific Odyssey of Capt. William H. Daly and the 147th Field Artillery Regiment, 1941–1946." *South Dakota History* 23, no. 2 (1993): 101–21.

Welch, Robert R. "Typhoon – 1944." *US Naval Institute Proceedings* 113, no. 1 (1987): 74–6.

Winborn, Byron R. *Wen Bon: A Naval Air Intelligence Officer behind Japanese Lines in China.* Denton: University of North Texas Press, 1994.

Wise, James W. *Very Truly Ours: Letters from America's Fighting Men.* New York: Dial Press, 1943.

Wolfe, Don M., ed. *The Purple Testament.* Garden City, New York: Doubleday, 1947.

Wolfert, Ira. *Battle for the Solomons.* Boston: Houghton Mifflin, 1943.

Wu, William F. "Surgery in the Field." *Military History* 8, no. 2 (1991): 26–32.

III Government publications

The Calcutta Key. United States Army Forces in India–Burma. Information and Education Branch. Services of Supply Base Section Two, 1945.

C.B.I. Pointie Talkie. No. 4. N.p., n.d.

Flying Tigers' Guide to Shanghai. Headquarters Fourteenth Air Force Shanghai. Information and Education Section. Special Services, 1945.

Getting about in New Guinea. Allied Geographical Section. Southwest Pacific Area, 1943.

Guide to Japan. CINCPAC-CINCPOA Bulletin. No. 209–45, 1945.

Guide to the Western Pacific: For the Use of the Army, Navy, and Marine Corps of the United States of America. CinCPac, 1944.

Handbook on Japanese Military Forces. TM 30-480. Washington, DC: War Department, 1941.

Handbook on Japanese Military Forces. TM-E 30-480. Washington, DC: War Department, 1944.

Here's How: A Handbook for American Troops in China. United States Army Forces. China–Burma–India, 1944.

Holdings and Opinions. Board of Review. Branch Office of the Judge Advocate General. China–Burma–India. India-Burma Theater. Vols. 2 and 3. Washington, DC: Office of the Judge Advocate General, 1946.

Holdings and Opinions. Board of Review. Branch Office of the Judge Advocate General. Pacific Ocean Areas. Vol. 1. Washington, DC: Office of the Judge Advocate General, 1946.

Holdings and Opinions. Board of Review. Branch Office of the Judge Advocate General. South West Pacific Area. Pacific. Vols. 2 and 3. Washington, DC: Office of the Judge Advocate General, 1946.

Memo on the Marianas. JICPOA, n.d.

Nansei Shoto: A Guide to the Garden Spot of Okinawa. Washington, DC: War Department, 1945.

A Pocket Guide to Australia. Washington, DC: War and Navy Departments, 1943.

A Pocket Guide to Burma. Washington, DC: War and Navy Departments, 1943.

A Pocket Guide to China. Washington, DC: War and Navy Departments, 1942.

A Pocket Guide to Hawaii. Washington, DC: Army Information Branch. Information and Education Division, 1942.

A Pocket Guide to India. Washington, DC: War and Navy Departments, 1943.

A Pocket Guide to Netherlands East Indies. Washington, DC: War and Navy Departments, 1944.

Pocket Guide to New Caledonia. Washington, DC: War and Navy Departments, 1944.

A Pocket Guide to New Guinea and the Solomons. Washington, DC: War and Navy Departments, 1943.

U.S. Army Field Forces. Reports of Observer Boards. Pacific Ocean Areas. United States Armed Forces Far East, 1942–5.

We Return to the Philippines. Headquarters USAFFE. Information and Education Section n.d.

What Future for the Islands of the Pacific? G.I. Roundtable Pamphlet. Washington, DC: US Government Printing Office, 1944.

What the Soldier Thinks: Digest, with Charts, of a Year's Research Studies Indicating the Attitudes, Prejudices, and Desires of American Troops. War Department. Services of Supply. Special Service Division. Information and Education Division. Research Branch. February 1943.

What the Soldier Thinks: Quarterly Report, with Charts, of Research Studies Indicating the Attitudes, Prejudices, and Desires of American Troops. War Department. Army Service Forces. Special Service Division. Information and Education Division. Research Branch. August 1943.

What the Soldier Thinks: A Monthly Digest of War Department Studies on the Attitudes of American Troops. War Department. Army Service Forces. Morale Services Division. Jan. 1944 to Sept. 1945.

What You Should Know about China: Information of Importance to Personnel of the United States Forces in the China Theater. N.p., 1945.

YANK's Magic Carpet: A Souvenir Booklet Specially Prepared for U.S. Army Personnel in China, Burma and India. Calcutta, India: Yank CBI Edition, 1945.

You and the Native: Notes for the Guidance of Members of the Forces in Their Relations with New Guinea Natives. Allied Geographical Section. Southwest Pacific Area, 1943.

IV Other publications

Emory, Kenneth P. *South Sea Lore*. Honolulu, Hawaii: Bernice P. Bishop Museum, 1943.

A Guide Book to Calcutta, Agra, Delhi, Karachi and Bombay. The American Red Cross of the China–Burma–India Command, 1943.

Secondary sources

I Official histories

Appleman, Roy E., et al. *Okinawa: The Last Battle*. United States Army in World War II: The War in the Pacific. Washington, DC: Historical Division, Department of the Army, 1948.

Bykofsky, Joseph and Harold Larson. *The Transportation Corps: Operations Overseas*. United States Army in World War II: The Technical Services. Washington, DC: Office of the Chief of Military History, Department of the Army, 1957.

Cannon, M. Hamlin. *Leyte: The Return to the Philippines*. United States Army in World War II: The War in the Pacific. Washington, DC: Office of the Chief of Military History, Department of the Army, 1954.

Condon-Rall, Mary Ellen and Albert E. Cowdrey. *The Medical Department: Medical Services in the War against Japan*. United States Army in World War II: The Technical Services. Washington, DC: Center of Military History, United States Army, 1998.

Craven, Wesley F. and James L. Cate, eds. *The Pacific: Guadalcanal to Saipan, August 1942 to July 1944*. Vol. IV of *The Army Air Forces in World War II*. Chicago: University of Chicago Press, 1950.

Craven, Wesley F. and James L. Cate, eds. *The Pacific: Matterhorn to Nagasaki, June 1944 to August 1945*. Vol. V of *The Army Air Forces in World War II*. Chicago: University of Chicago Press, 1953.

Crowl, Philip A. *Campaign in the Marianas*. United States Army in World War II: The War in the Pacific. Washington, DC: Office of the Chief of Military History, Department of the Army, 1960.

Crowl, Philip A. and Edmund G. Love. *Seizure of the Gilberts and Marshalls*. United States Army in World War II: The War in the Pacific. Washington, DC: Office of the Chief of Military History, Department of the Army, 1955.

Dod, Karl C. *The Corps of Engineers: The War against Japan*. United States Army in World War II: The Technical Services. Washington, DC: Office of the Chief of Military History, United States Army, 1966.

Frank, Benis M. and Henry I. Shaw, Jr. *Victory and Occupation*. Vol. V of *History of U.S. Marine Corps Operations in World War II*. Washington, DC: Historical Branch, US Marine Corps, 1968.

Garand, George W. and Truman R. Strobridge. *Western Pacific Operations*. Vol. IV of *History of U.S. Marine Corps Operations in World War II*. Washington, DC: Historical Branch, US Marine Corps, 1971.

Hough, Frank O., Verle E. Ludwig, and Henry I. Shaw. *Pearl Harbor to Guadalcanal*. Vol. I of *History of U.S. Marine Corps Operations in World War II*. Washington, DC: Historical Branch, US Marine Corps, 1958.

Kleber, Brooks E. and Dale Birdsell. *The Chemical Warfare Service: Chemicals in Combat*. United States Army in World War II: The Technical Services. Washington, DC: Office of the Chief of Military History, United States Army, 1966.

Link, Mae Mills and Hubert A. Coleman. *Medical Support of the Army Air Forces in World War II*. Washington, DC: Office of the Surgeon General, United States Air Force, 1955.

Mayo, Lida. *The Ordnance Department: On Beachhead and Battlefront*. United States Army in World War II: The Technical Services. Washington, DC: Office of the Chief of Military History, United States Army, 1968.

Miller, John, Jr. *CARTWHEEL: The Reduction of Rabaul*. United States Army in World War II: The War in the Pacific. Washington, DC: Office of the Chief of Military History, Department of the Army, 1959.

Miller, John, Jr. *Guadalcanal: The First Offensive*. United States Army in World War II: The War in the Pacific. Washington, DC: Historical Division, Department of the Army, 1949.

Milner, Samuel. *Victory in Papua*. United States Army in World War II: The War in the Pacific. Washington, DC: Office of the Chief of Military History, Department of the Army, 1957.

Morison, Samuel Eliot. *History of United States Naval Operations in World War II*. Boston: Little, Brown, 1947–62.

Reister, Frank A., ed. *Medical Statistics in World War II*. Washington, DC: Office of the Surgeon General, Department of the Army, 1975.

Romanus, Charles F. and Riley Sunderland. *Stilwell's Command Problems*. United States Army in World War II: China–Burma–India Theater. Washington, DC: Office of the Chief of Military History, Department of the Army, 1956.

Romanus, Charles F. and Riley Sunderland. *Stilwell's Mission to China*. United States Army in World War II: China–Burma–India Theater. Washington, DC: Office of the Chief of Military History, Department of the Army, 1953.

Romanus, Charles F. and Riley Sunderland. *Time Runs Out in CBI*. United States Army in World War II: China–Burma–India Theater. Washington, DC: Office of the Chief of Military History, Department of the Army, 1959.

Shaw, Henry I., Jr. and Douglas T. Kane. *Isolation of Rabaul*. Vol. II of *History of U.S. Marine Corps Operations in World War II*. Washington, DC: Historical Branch, US Marine Corps, 1963.

Shaw, Henry I., Jr., Bernard C. Nalty, and Edwin T. Turnbladh. *Central Pacific Drive*. Vol. III of *History of U.S. Marine Corps Operations in World War II*. Washington, DC: Historical Branch, US Marine Corps, 1966.

Smith, Robert Ross. *The Approach to the Philippines*. United States Army in World War II: The War in the Pacific. Washington, DC: Office of the Chief of Military History, Department of the Army, 1953.

Smith, Robert Ross. *Triumph in the Philippines*. United States Army in World War II: The War in the Pacific. Washington, DC: Office of the Chief of Military History, Department of the Army, 1963.

Stauffer, Alvin P. *The Quartermaster Corps: Operations in the War against Japan*. United States Army in World War II: The Technical Services. Washington, DC: Office of the Chief of Military History, Department of the Army, 1956.

Thompson, George Raynor and Dixie R. Harris. *The Signal Corps: The Outcome (Mid-1943 through 1945)*. United States Army in World War II: The Technical Services. Washington, DC: Office of the Chief of Military History, United States Army, 1966.
Thompson, George Raynor, et al. *The Signal Corps: The Test (December 1941 to July 1943)*. United States Army in World War II: The Technical Services. Washington, DC: Office of the Chief of Military History, Department of the Army, 1957.

II   Dissertations

Sparagana, Eleanor. "The Conduct and Consequences of Psychological Warfare: American Psychological Warfare Operations in the War against Japan, 1941–1945." Brandeis University, 1990.

III   Books and articles

Allen, John Logan. *Passage through the Garden: Lewis and Clark and the Image of the American Northwest*. Urbana: University of Illinois Press, 1975.
Ambrose, Stephen E. and Brian Loring Villa. "Racism, the Atomic Bomb, and the Transformation of Japanese–American Relations." In *The Pacific War Revisited*. Edited by Günter Bischof and Robert L. Dupont. Baton Rouge and London: Louisiana State University Press, 1997.
Bagby, Wesley M. *The Eagle–Dragon Alliance: America's Relations with China in World War II*. Cranbury, NJ: Associated University Press, 1992.
Bailey, Beth and David Farber. *The First Strange Place: Race and Sex in World War II Hawaii*. Baltimore, Md.: The Johns Hopkins University Press, 1994.
Bartov, Omer. *The Eastern Front, 1941–45: German Troops and the Barbarisation of Warfare*. Basingstoke, England: Macmillan, 1985.
Bates, Milton J. *The Wars We Took to Vietnam: Cultural Conflict and Storytelling*. Berkeley, Los Angeles, and London: University of California Press, 1996.
Bergerud, Eric. *Touched with Fire: The Land War in the South Pacific*. New York: Viking, 1996.
Bernstein, Barton J. "The Perils and Politics of Surrender: Ending the War with Japan and Avoiding the Third Atomic Bomb." *Pacific Historical Review* 46, no. 1 (1977): 1–27.
Bills, Scott L. *Empire and Cold War: The Roots of US–Third World Antagonism, 1945–47*. New York: St. Martin's Press, 1990.
Blakefield, William J. "A War Within: The Making of 'Know Your Enemy – Japan.'" *Sight & Sound: International Film Quarterly* 52, no. 2 (1983): 128–33.
Blaut, James M. *The Colonizer's Model of the World: Geographical Diffusionism and Eurocentric History*. New York: Guilford Press, 1993.
Bloom, William. *Personal Identity, National Identity and International Relations*. Cambridge: Cambridge University Press, 1990.
Braisted, William Reynolds. *The United States Navy in the Pacific, 1897–1909*. New York: Greenwood Press, 1969.
Braisted, William Reynolds. *The United States Navy in the Pacific, 1909–1922*. Austin and London: University of Texas Press, 1971
Brcak, Nancy and John R. Pavia. "Racism in Japanese and U.S. Wartime Propaganda." *The Historian* 56, no. 4 (1994): 671–84.
Cady, John F. *The United States and Burma*. Cambridge, Mass. and London, England: Harvard University Press, 1976.
Cameron, Craig M. *American Samurai: Myth, Imagination, and the Conduct of Battle in the First Marine Division, 1941–1951*. New York: Cambridge University Press, 1994.

Cantril, Hadley, ed. *Public Opinion, 1935–1946*. Princeton: Princeton University Press, 1951.

Carucci, Laurence Marshall. "The Source of the Force in Marshallese Cosmology." In *The Pacific Theater: Island Representations of World War II*. Edited by Geoffrey M. White and Lamont Lindstrom. Honolulu: University of Hawaii Press, 1989.

Cecil, Paul F. *Herbicidal Warfare: The RANCH HAND Project in Vietnam*. New York: Praeger, 1986.

Chappell, John D. *Before the Bomb: How America Approached the End of the Pacific War*. Lexington: University Press of Kentucky, 1997.

Choy, Philip P., Lorraine Dong, and Marlon K. Hom, eds. *The Coming Man: 19th Century American Perceptions of the Chinese*. Seattle: University of Washington Press, 1995.

Coates, Ken and W.R. Morrison. "The American Rampant: Reflections on the Impact of United States Troops in Allied Countries during World War II." *The Journal of World History* 2, no. 2 (1991): 201–21.

Condon-Rall, Mary Ellen. "The Role of the US Army in the Fight against Malaria, 1940–44." *War & Society* 13, no. 2 (1995): 91–111.

Coox, Alvin D. "Concluding Remarks." In *The American Military and the Far East*. Edited by Joe C. Dixon. S.l.: US Air Force Academy, 1980.

Coox, Alvin D. "The Effectiveness of the Japanese Military Establishment in the Second World War." In *The Second World War*. vol. 3 of *Military Effectiveness*. Edited by Allan R. Millett and Williamson Murray. Boston: Allen and Unwin, 1988.

Counts, David. "Shadows of War: Changing Remembrance through Twenty Years in New Britain." In *The Pacific Theater: Island Representations of World War II*. Edited by Geoffrey M. White and Lamont Lindstrom. Honolulu: University of Hawaii Press, 1989.

Culmsee, Carlton F. *Malign Nature and the Frontier*. Logan: Utah State University Press, 1959.

Daniels, Gordon. "Before Hiroshima: The Bombing of Japan, 1944–5." *History Today* 32 (Jan. 1982): 14–18.

Davenport, William H. "*Taemfaet*: Experiences and Reactions of Santa Cruz Islanders during the Battle for Guadalcanal." In *The Pacific Theater: Island Representations of World War II*. Edited by Geoffrey M. White and Lamont Lindstrom. Honolulu: University of Hawaii Press, 1989.

Dower, John W. "Race, Language, and War in Two Cultures: World War II in Asia." In *The War in American Culture: Society and Consciousness during World War II*. Edited by Lewis A. Erenberg and Susan E. Hirsch. Chicago: University of Chicago Press, 1996.

Dower, John W. *War without Mercy: Race and Power in the Pacific War*. New York: Pantheon Books, 1986.

Drea, Edward J. "'Great Patience is Needed': America Encounters Australia, 1942." *War & Society* 11, no. 1 (1993): 21–51.

Drea, Edward J. *In the Service of the Emperor: Essays on the Imperial Japanese Army*. Lincoln: University of Nebraska Press, 1998.

Drinnon, Richard. *Facing West: The Metaphysics of Indian-Hating and Empire-Building*. Minneapolis: University of Minnesota Press, 1980.

Duus, Peter. "Imperialism without Colonies: The Vision of a Greater East Asia Co-Prosperity Sphere." *Diplomacy & Statecraft* 7, no. 1 (1996): 54–72.

Edmond, Rod. *Representing the South Pacific: Colonial Discourse from Cook to Gauguin*. Cambridge: Cambridge University Press, 1997.

Farber, David and Beth Bailey. "The Fighting Man as Tourist: The Politics of Tourist Culture in Hawaii during World War II." *Pacific Historical Review* 65, no. 4 (1996): 641–60.

Feifer, George. *Tennozan: The Battle of Okinawa and the Atomic Bomb*. New York: Ticknor & Fields, 1992.

FitzGerald, Frances. *America Revised: History Schoolbooks in the Twentieth Century*. New York: Random House, 1980.

Flint, Roy K. "The United States Army on the Pacific Frontier, 1899–1939." In *The American Military and the Far East*. Edited by Joe C. Dixon. S.l.: US Air Force Academy, 1980.

Friend, Theodore. *Between Two Empires: The Ordeal of the Philippines, 1929–1946*. New Haven, Conn.: Yale University Press, 1965.

Friend, Theodore. *The Blue-Eyed Enemy: Japan against the West in Java and Luzon, 1942–1945*. Princeton: Princeton University Press, 1988.

Fujita, Fumiko. *American Pioneers and the Japanese Frontier: American Experts in Nineteenth-Century Japan*. Westport, Conn.: Greenwood Press, 1994.

Fussell, Paul. *Wartime: Understanding and Behavior in the Second World War*. New York: Oxford University Press, 1989.

Gallicchio, Marc. "Colouring the Nationalists: The African–American Construction of China in the Second World War." *The International History Review* 20, no. 3 (1998): 571–96.

Geslin, Yves. "Les Américains aux Nouvelles-Hébrides au cours de la Seconde Guerre Mondiale." *Journal de la Société des Océanistes* 12 (1956): 245–85.

Gibson, Arrell Morgan. *Yankees in Paradise: The Pacific Basin Frontier*. Albuquerque: University of New Mexico Press, 1993.

Gilman, Sander L. *Difference and Pathology: Stereotypes of Sexuality, Race, and Madness*. Ithaca, NY and London, England: Cornell University Press, 1985.

Gilmore, Allison B. "'We Have Been Reborn': Japanese Prisoners and the Allied Propaganda War in the Southwest Pacific." *Pacific Historical Review* 64, no. 2 (1995): 195–215.

Gleason, Philip. "Americans All: World War II and the Shaping of American Identity." *The Review of Politics* 43, no. 4 (1981): 483–518.

Harries, Meirion and Susie Harries. *Soldiers of the Sun: The Rise and Fall of the Imperial Japanese Army*. New York: Random House, 1991.

Heffer, Jean. *Les états-Unis et le Pacifique: Histoire d'une Frontière*. Paris: Albin Michel, 1995.

Henningham, Stephen. "The French Administration, the Local Population, and the American Presence in New Caledonia, 1943–44." *Journal de la Société des Océanistes* 1 (1994): 21–41.

Henrikson, Alan K. "Mental Maps." In *Explaining the History of American Foreign Relations*. Edited by Michael J. Hogan and Thomas G. Paterson. New York: Cambridge University Press, 1991.

Herzog, Kristin. *Women, Ethnics, and Exotics: Images of Power in Mid-Nineteenth-Century Fiction*. Knoxville: University of Tennessee Press, 1983.

Hess, Gary R. *America Encounters India, 1941–1947*. Baltimore, Md.: The Johns Hopkins Press, 1971.

Hodgson, Godfrey. "Immigrants and Frontiersmen: Two Traditions in American Foreign Policy." *Diplomatic History* 23, no. 3 (1999): 525–37.

Hofstadter, Richard. *Social Darwinism in American Thought*. Boston: Beacon Press, 1955.

Hopkins, George E. "Bombing and the American Conscience during World War II." *The Historian* 28, no. 3 (1966): 451–73.

Horsman, Reginald. *Race and Manifest Destiny: The Origins of American Racial Anglo-Saxonism*. Cambridge, Mass.: Harvard University Press, 1981.

Hunt, Michael H. *Ideology and U.S. Foreign Policy*. New Haven, Conn.: Yale University Press, 1987.

Huntington, Samuel P. *The Clash of Civilizations and the Remaking of World Order.* New York: Simon & Schuster, 1996.

Huston, John W. "The Impact of Strategic Bombing in the Pacific." *The Journal of American–East Asian Relations* 4, no. 2 (1995): 169–79.

Hynes, Samuel. *The Soldiers' Tale: Bearing Witness to Modern War.* New York: Allen Lane/Penguin Press, 1997.

Iriye, Akira. "Contemporary History as History: American Expansion into the Pacific since 1941." *Pacific Historical Review* 53 (May 1984): 191–212.

Iriye, Akira. *Mutual Images: Essays in American–Japanese Relations.* Cambridge, Mass. and London, England: Harvard University Press, 1975.

Iriye, Akira. *Power and Culture: The Japanese–American War, 1941–1945.* Cambridge, Mass. and London, England: Harvard University Press, 1981.

Iriye, Akira. "Western Perceptions and Asian Realities." In *The American Military and the Far East.* Edited by Joe C. Dixon. S.l.: US Air Force Academy, 1980.

James, D. Clayton. "Introduction: Rethinking the Pacific War." In *The Pacific War Revisited.* Edited by Günter Bischof and Robert L. Dupont. Baton Rouge and London: Louisiana State University Press, 1997.

Jespersen, T. Christopher. *American Images of China, 1931–1949.* Stanford, Calif.: Stanford University Press, 1996.

Johnson, Sheila K. *American Attitudes toward Japan, 1941–1945.* Washington, DC: American Enterprise for Public Policy Research, 1975.

Kahn, David. "United States Views of Germany and Japan in 1941." In *Knowing One's Enemies: Intelligence Assessment before the Two World Wars.* Edited by Ernest R. May. Princeton: Princeton University Press, 1984.

Karnow, Stanley. *In Our Image: America's Empire in the Philippines.* New York: Random House, 1989.

Keen, Sam. *Faces of the Enemy: Reflections of the Hostile Imagination.* San Francisco: Harper & Row, 1986.

Knobloch, Frieda. *The Culture of Wilderness: Agriculture and Colonization in the American West.* Chapel Hill: University of North Carolina Press, 1996.

Krammer, Arnold. "Japanese Prisoners of War in America." *Pacific Historical Review* 52 (1983): 67–91.

LaFeber, Walter. *The Clash: A History of U.S.–Japan Relations.* New York: W.W. Norton, 1997.

Laurie, Clayton D. "The Ultimate Dilemma of Psychological Warfare in the Pacific: Enemies Who Don't Surrender, and GIs Who Don't Take Prisoners." *War & Society* 14, no. 1 (1996): 99–120.

Lepowsky, Maria. "Soldiers and Spirits: The Impact of World War II on a Coral Sea Island." In *The Pacific Theater: Island Representations of World War II.* Edited by Geoffrey M. White and Lamont Lindstrom. Honolulu: University of Hawaii Press, 1989.

Linderman, Gerald F. *The World within War: America's Combat Experience in World War II.* New York: Free Press, 1997.

Lindstrom, Lamont. "Working Encounters: Oral Histories of World War II Labor Corps from Tanna, Vanuatu." In *The Pacific Theater: Island Representations of World War II.* Edited by Geoffrey M. White and Lamont Lindstrom. Honolulu: University of Hawaii Press, 1989.

Lindstrom, Lamont and Geoffrey M. White. *Island Encounters: Black and White Memories of the Pacific War.* Washington and London: Smithsonian Institution Press, 1990.

Lindstrom, Lamont and Geoffrey M. White. "War Stories." In *The Pacific Theater: Island Representations of World War II*. Edited by Geoffrey M. White and Lamont Lindstrom. Honolulu: University of Hawaii Press, 1989.

Linn, Brian McAllister. *Guardians of Empire: The U.S. Army and the Pacific, 1902–1940*. Chapel Hill and London: University of North Carolina Press, 1997.

Lytle, Mark H. "An Environmental Approach to American Diplomatic History." *Diplomatic History* 20, no. 2 (1996): 279–300.

Maga, Timothy P. "Humanism and Peace: Eleanor Roosevelt's Mission to the Pacific, August-September, 1943." *The Maryland Historian* 19, no. 2 (1988): 33–47.

Marx, Leo. *The Machine in the Garden: Technology and the Pastoral Ideal in America*. New York: Oxford University Press, 1964.

May, Glenn A. *Social Engineering in the Philippines: The Aims, Execution, and Impact of American Colonial Policy, 1900–1913*. Westport, Conn.: Greenwood Press, 1980.

Miller, Stuart Creighton. *'Benevolent Assimilation': The American Conquest of the Philippines, 1899–1903*. New Haven and London: Yale University Press, 1982.

Miller, Stuart Creighton. *The Unwelcome Immigrant: The American Image of the Chinese, 1785–1882*. Berkeley and Los Angeles: University of California Press, 1969.

Millett, Allan R. "The United States Armed Forces in the Second World War." In vol. 3 of *Military Effectiveness*. Edited by Allan R. Millett and Williamson Murray. Boston: Allen and Unwin, 1988.

Millett, Allan R. and Peter Maslowski. *For the Common Defense: A Military History of the United States of America*. New York: Free Press, 1984.

Munholland, Kim. "Yankee Farewell: The Americans Leave New Caledonia, 1945." In *Proceedings of the Sixteenth Meeting of the French Colonial Historical Society. Mackinac Island, May 1990*. Edited by Patricia Galloway. Lanham, Md.: University Press of America, 1992.

Murray, Williamson and Allan R. Millett. *A War To Be Won: Fighting the Second World War*. Cambridge, Mass. and London, England: The Belknap Press of Harvard University Press, 2000.

Nash, Roderick. *Wilderness and the American Mind*. New Haven and London: Yale University Press, 1982.

Nero, Karen L. "Time of Famine, Time of Transformation: Hell in the Pacific, Palau." In *The Pacific Theater: Island Representations of World War II*. Edited by Geoffrey M. White and Lamont Lindstrom. Honolulu: University of Hawaii Press, 1989.

Ness, Gayl D. and William Stahl. "Western Imperialist Armies in Asia." *Comparative Studies in Society and History* 19, no. 1 (1977): 2–29.

Ninkovich, Frank. "Cultural Relations and American China Policy, 1942–1945." *Pacific Historical Review* 49 (Aug. 1980): 471–98.

Noble, Dennis L. *The Eagle and the Dragon: The United States Military in China, 1901–1937*. Westport, Conn.: Greenwood Press, 1990.

Okihiro, Gary Y. *Cane Fires: The Anti-Japanese Movement in Hawaii, 1865–1945*. Philadelphia: Temple University Press, 1991.

Pearce, Roy Harvey. *Savagism and Civilization: A Study of the Indian and the American Mind*. Berkeley and Los Angeles: University of California Press, 1988.

Pyne, Stephen J. *Fire in America: A Cultural History of Wildland and Rural Fire*. Seattle and London: University of Washington Press, 1997.

Quanchi, Max and Ron Adams, eds. *Cultural Contact in the Pacific: Essays on Contact, Encounter and Response*. Cambridge: Cambridge University Press, 1993.

Rediker, Marcus. *Between the Devil and the Deep Blue Sea: Merchant Seamen, Pirates, and the Anglo-American Maritime World, 1700–1750.* Cambridge: Cambridge University Press, 1993.

Roeder, George H., Jr. *The Censored War: American Visual Experience during World War II.* New Haven and London: Yale University Press, 1993.

Rose, Sonya O. "The 'Sex Question' in Anglo-American Relations in the Second World War." *The International History Review* 20, no. 4 (1998): 884–904.

Rosenberg, Emily S. *Spreading the American Dream: American Economic and Cultural Expansion, 1890–1945.* New York: Hill and Wang, 1982.

Said, Edward W. *Orientalism: Western Conceptions of the Orient.* Harmondsworth, England: Penguin Books, 1995.

Sbrega, John J. *Anglo-American Relations and Colonialism in East Asia, 1941–1945.* New York: Garland, 1983.

Schaffer, Ronald. *Wings of Judgment: American Bombing in World War II.* New York: Oxford University Press, 1985.

Schaller, Michael. *The U.S. Crusade in China, 1938–1945.* New York: Columbia University Press, 1979.

Schrijvers, Peter. *The Crash of Ruin: American Combat Soldiers in Europe during World War II.* Basingstoke, England: Macmillan and New York: New York University Press, 1998.

Sherry, Michael S. *The Rise of American Air Power: The Creation of Armageddon.* New Haven and London: Yale University Press, 1987.

Slotkin, Richard. *The Fatal Environment: The Myth of the Frontier in the Age of Industrialization, 1800–1890.* New York: Atheneum, 1985.

Slotkin, Richard. *Gunfighter Nation: The Myth of the Frontier in Twentieth-Century America.* New York: Atheneum, 1992.

Slotkin, Richard. *Regeneration through Violence: The Mythology of the American Frontier, 1600–1860.* New York: HarperCollins, 1996.

Smith, Henry Nash. *Virgin Land: The American West as Symbol and Myth.* Cambridge, Mass.: Harvard University Press, 1950.

Spector, Ronald H. *Eagle against the Sun: The American War with Japan.* New York: Vintage Books, 1985.

Spector, Ronald H. "The Pacific War and the Fourth Dimension of Strategy." In *The Pacific War Revisited.* Edited by Günter Bischof and Robert L. Dupont. Baton Rouge and London: Louisiana State University Press, 1997.

Stanton, Shelby L. *Order of Battle: U.S. Army, World War II.* Novato, Calif.: Presidio Press, 1984.

Stevens, Richard L. *The Trail: A History of the Ho Chi Minh Trail and the Role of Nature in the War in Viet Nam.* New York and London: Garland Publishing, 1993.

Stott, R. Jeffrey. "The Sacred Serpent: Old Symbols and New Ideas." *Journal of American Culture* 1 (1978): 638–48.

Stouffer, Samuel A., et al. *The American Soldier: Adjustment during Army Life.* vol. 1 of *Studies in Social Psychology in World War II.* Princeton: Princeton University Press, 1949.

Stouffer, Samuel A., et al. *The American Soldier: Combat and Its Aftermath.* vol. 2 of *Studies in Social Psychology in World War II.* Princeton: Princeton University Press, 1949.

Stross, Randall E. *The Stubborn Earth: American Agriculturalists on Chinese Soil, 1898–1937.* Berkeley and Los Angeles: University of California Press, 1986.

Sun Tzu. *The Art of War.* Oxford: Oxford University Press, 1963.

Swanson, Maynard W. "The Sanitation Syndrome: Bubonic Plague and Urban Native Policy in the Cape Colony, 1900–1909." *The Journal of African History* 18, no. 3 (1977): 387–410.

Tanaka, Yuki. *Hidden Horrors: Japanese War Crimes in World War II*. Boulder, Colo.: Westview Press, 1996.

Thomson, James C., Jr. *While China Faced West: American Reformers in Nationalist China, 1928–1937*. Cambridge, Mass.: Harvard University Press, 1980.

Thomson, James C., Jr., Peter W. Stanley, and John Curtis Perry. *Sentimental Imperialists: The American Experience in East Asia*. New York: Harper Colophon Books, 1982.

Thorne, Christopher. *Allies of a Kind: The United States, Britain and the War against Japan, 1941–1945*. London: Hamish Hamilton, 1978.

Thorne, Christopher. "Racial Aspects of the Far Eastern War of 1941–1945." *Proceedings of the British Academy* 66 (1980): 329–77.

Thorslev, Peter L., Jr. "The Wild Man's Revenge." In *The Wild Man Within: An Image in Western Thought from the Renaissance to Romanticism*. Edited by Edward Dudley and Maximillian E. Novak. Pittsburgh, Penn.: University of Pittsburgh Press, 1973.

Tirefort, Alain. "'Faut-il interdire Jules Verne aux enfants?': La vision de l'Afrique dans les 'Voyages extraordinaires.'" In *Histoire d'Europe et d'Amérique: Le monde Atlantique contemporain. Mélanges offerts à Yves-Henri Nouailhat.* Nantes: Ouest Editions, 1999.

Tomes, Nancy. *The Gospel of Germs: Men, Women, and the Microbe in American Life*. Cambridge, Mass.: Harvard University Press, 1998.

Turner, Frederick. *Beyond Geography: The Western Spirit against the Wilderness*. New Brunswick, NJ: Rutgers University Press, 1992.

van Courtland Moon, John Ellis. "Project SPHINX: The Question of the Use of Gas in the Planned Invasion of Japan." *Journal of Strategic Studies* 12, no. 3 (1989): 303–23.

Vibert, Elizabeth. *Traders' Tales: Narratives of Cultural Encounters in the Columbia Plateau, 1807–1846*. Norman and London: University of Oklahoma Press, 1997.

Warnes, Kathleen. "Nurses under Fire: Healing and Heroism in the South Pacific." In *The Pacific War Revisited*. Edited by Günter Bischof and Robert L. Dupont. Baton Rouge and London: Louisiana State University Press, 1997.

Warnock, A. Timothy. "The Chinese American Composite Wing: A Case Study of the Versatility of the Composite Concept." *Air Power History* 39, no. 3 (1992): 21–30.

Weeks, Charles J., Jr. "The United States Occupation of Tonga, 1942–1945: The Social and Economic Impact." *Pacific Historical Review* 56, no. 3 (1987): 399–426.

Weigley, Russell F. *The American Way of War: A History of United States Military Strategy and Policy*. New York: Macmillan, 1973.

Weingartner, James J. "Trophies of War: U.S. Troops and the Mutilation of Japanese War Dead, 1941–1945." *Pacific Historical Review* 61 (Feb. 1992): 53–67.

Weingartner, James J. "War against Subhumans: Comparisons between the German War against the Soviet Union and the American War against Japan, 1941–1945." *The Historian* 58, no. 3 (1996): 557–73.

White, Geoffrey M. "Histories of Contact, Narratives of Self: Wartime Encounters in Santa Isabel." In *The Pacific Theater: Island Representations of World War II*. Edited by Geoffrey M. White and Lamont Lindstrom. Honolulu: University of Hawaii Press, 1989.

White, Hayden. "The Forms of Wildness: Archaeology of an Idea." In *The Wild Man Within: An Image in Western Thought from the Renaissance to Romanticism*. Edited by Edward Dudley and Maximillian E. Novak. Pittsburgh, Penn.: University of Pittsburgh, 1973.

Winters, Harold A. *Battling the Elements: Weather and Terrain in the Conduct of War.* Baltimore, Md.: The Johns Hopkins University Press, 1998.

Whitehead, John S. "Writers as Pioneers." In Arrell Morgan Gibson. *Yankees in Paradise: The Pacific Basin Frontier.* Albuquerque: University of New Mexico Press, 1993.

Wolpert, Stanley. *A New History of India.* New York: Oxford University Press, 1997.

Yavenditti, Michael J. "The American People and the Use of Atomic Bombs on Japan: The 1940s." *The Historian* 36, no. 2 (1974): 224–47.

Zelenietz, Marty and Hisafumi Saito. "The Kilenge and the War: An Observer Effect on Stories from the Past." In *The Pacific Theater: Island Representations of World War II.* Edited by Geoffrey M. White and Lamont Lindstrom. Honolulu: University of Hawaii Press, 1989.

Ziemke, Earl F. "Military Effectiveness in the Second World War." In vol. 3 of *Military Effectiveness.* Edited by Allan R. Millett and Williamson Murray. Boston: Allen and Unwin, 1988.

Index